Imbalance and Rebalance

Yang Li · Xiaojing Zhang

Imbalance and Rebalance

To Create a New Framework of Global Governance

中国社会科学出版社
CHINA SOCIAL SCIENCES PRESS

Springer

Yang Li
Chinese Academy of Social Sciences
Beijing
China

Xiaojing Zhang
Chinese Academy of Social Sciences
Beijing
China

Translated by Lichao He, College of Foreign Languages, Shanghai Maritime University, Shanghai, China

ISBN 978-981-10-6149-3 ISBN 978-981-10-6150-9 (eBook)
https://doi.org/10.1007/978-981-10-6150-9

Jointly published with Chinese Academy of Social Sciences

The print edition is not for sale in China Mainland. Customers from China Mainland please order the print book from: China Social Sciences Press.

Published with financial support of the Innovation Program of the Chinese Academy of Social Sciences.

Library of Congress Control Number: 2017951999

Printed on acid-free paper

This Springer imprint is published by Springer Nature
The registered company is Springer Nature Singapore Pte Ltd.
The registered company address is: 152 Beach Road, #21-01/04 Gateway East, Singapore 189721, Singapore

Preface[1]

How it Got Started

Since the outbreak of the global financial crisis in March, 2007, "global economic imbalances" has become one of the catchphrases frequently used by monetary authorizes around the world. Developed economies, among them the U.S. in particular, liked to use this term looking for the root cause of the crisis. By attributing the turmoil to imbalances, which was depicted as a "global phenomenon", they may shift the responsibility of the crisis easily to other countries, especially emerging economies like China. In fact, talks like "China is the responsible party" and the so-called "China threat" are theoretically backed by on other concept than the "global imbalances".

Relevant governmental departments in China remain highly alert in face of such allegations. They tried to avoid the use of "global imbalances" on public occasions, especially at international conventions. A friend told me that at the G20 summits over the years, one of the major tasks of the Chinese delegation was to keep the term and related expressions from appearing in the communiqués and declarations.

What those departments did is truly understandable. However, from an economist's point of view, using "euphemism" to get around the real issue seems to me the kind of behavior, as one Chinese proverb describes, of "mistaking the shadow of a bow in one's cup as a snake," which is as unreasonable as "burying one's head in the sand." Admittedly, on the one hand, it seems that so far people cannot find a better culprit that caused the economic crises other than global imbalances; on the other hand, though, China should not take the blame imposed by a few countries that tried to shake off their responsibility by falsely accusing the Asian economies for causing the crises. So, instead of circumventing the real issue, we need to

[1] Translator's Note: In translation of direct quotes, some of the quotes are retrieved from the original English texts with notes by the translator. The rest was translated from Chinese text since the original English text is not accessible. Some of the direct quotes in this book are without citations.

confront the imbalances so as to uncover the truth that global crises was caused by imbalances created by some developed countries; meanwhile, conduct serious research on imbalances will also help us become better aware of the deeply-rooted causes for China's domestic problems such as unreasonable ways to development and the imbalances in economic structure that remain incorrigible for years.

In early 2009, I attended the Forum for Global Economists co-hosted by the then Chinese Premier Wen Jiabao and British Prime Minister Blair at No.10, Downing Street in London. More than 20 world-renowned economists, including Joseph Stiglitz, attended the forum. As the only scholar from China and one of the five speakers, I shared my views on global imbalances at the consent of the Premier. My talk touched upon four main points: First, as problem that has not drawn much attention until recent years, global imbalances have existed as the symbiosis of globalization and with the introduction of the Bretton Woods system. Second, tracking the global economic evolution will reveal clearly that as the only super power, the U.S. has always been the deficit country; at the other end of the spectrum, countries have taken turns in the role surplus country, first Germany and Japan, and since the 1970s, the "four small dragons of Asia", followed by the "four small Asian tigers", who were joined not until recently by China and OPEC countries. If the current crisis was rooted in imbalances, then the ultimate cause lies with the US. Third, in the globalized world economy, global imbalances inherently mean domestic imbalances in different countries. Therefore, to solve the crisis and put the world economy back on track, countries need to join their efforts to adjust the path of development by economic restructuring; and since the developed economies take the lead in globalization, they are obliged to take up the responsibility in initiating the transformation. Fourthly, as early as the end of the twentieth century, the Chinese government had set the strategic goal of transforming pattern of economic development, restructuring domestic economy, and achieving scientific development, for the purpose of solving the economy's over dependency on external demands and domestic investment. Actions were taken as the concrete measures to re-balance the world economy.

Feedback at and after the forum showed that my view was received positively by most of the participants.

It is this forum that led me to focus my attention on the research of global imbalances, among a number of research subjects. The above-mentioned viewpoints also evolved into the main arguments of this book.

Equilibrium and Balance

Imbalances and Re-balancing are the catchwords of most Western political figures and dignitaries. However, few have elucidated what those words actually mean. To explore this issue of crucial importance both in theory and practice, one has to have a close look at the concept of "balance" in the first place.

The "balance" of dichotomy of imbalances and rebalancing has two connotations: equilibrium and balance.

"Balance" is an extensively used concept. The *Dictionary of Modern Chinese* defines "balance" as "quantitatively or qualitatively being equal or offsetting each other in opposing elements."

"Equilibrium" is a concept of physics, referring to static caused by a state of balance between opposing but equal forces. In economics, equilibrium refers to the state of the market when the two opposing market forces, i.e., demand and supply are in equal amount. To take a step further, there are two types of "equilibrium" in economics: one is the Walrasian equilibrium, achieved when supply equals demand, with market clearing; the other is non-Walrasian equilibrium, which posits that price mechanism alone cannot clear the market, and market balance in most cases is non-Walrasian, i.e., supply does not always equal demand, but the market remains stable regardless. Obviously, compared with Walrasian equilibrium, non-Walrasian equilibrium is a concept in a broader sense, proposing that after adjustment of variables in the system, there will be no tendency for further change. Such equilibrium, when extrapolated, presumes that when external forces cause the equilibrium to deviate beyond the balancing point, there will always be an internal movement that will bring the system back to balance. In this sense, non-Walrasian equilibrium is a stable equilibrium. On the other hand when external forces tip the balance, and the economy will not return to equilibrium, the equilibrium is unstable.

Notably, in economics, "equilibrium" and "imbalance" refer to two totally different things. Equilibrium is a typical economics terminology, and a concept has long been a subject of discussion among economists. As for "balance", the definition is relatively vague, and in many cases, it is used to describe surplus, referring to the equal match between supply and demand, asset and liability.

The "imbalance" discussed in this book is derived from the concept of equilibrium, since the authors are not particularly concerned about the surplus or deficit in international balance of payments. Actually, imbalances are normal for countries, often in the forms of trade surplus and deficit, imbalances on current account, and even reflected in imbalances of international balance of payments, in the form of international imbalances in savings and investment, i.e., the relative inadequate savings in developed economies, and the "excessive" savings in emerging economies. What we really care about is that whether such imbalance can be sustained.

"Good Imbalances" and "Bad Imbalances"

The differences (surplus or deficit) on a country's foreign trade or international balance sheet result from cross-border allocation of resources of the country. Economic implications of imbalances can be reviewed from the perspective of dynamic allocation of resources. With this approach, current account imbalances can be categorized into two types: "good imbalances" and "bad imbalances."

"Good imbalances" result from the optimal decision reached regarding allocation of consumption and investment within a relatively long period. For example, current account deficit comes from optimization of dynamic and forward-looking policies about savings and investment. Imbalances as such brings no harm to economy, instead, they contribute to the welfare of the society. "Good imbalance" is possible in at least one of the following three situations: First, the imbalances and alternating shifts between surplus and deficit happen synchronizing with the cyclic periods of domestic economy. Second, the imbalances occur when a country's economy is reasonably structured, its enterprises are developing soundly, and the macroeconomy foretells a bright prospect. In this case, imbalances are the outcome of making optimal decisions about domestic economy, which will definitely bring about favorable economic results. Third, the imbalances appear when the term and regional structure for foreign investment are sound. Long-term imbalances on current account will inevitably trigger corresponding responses on capital and financial items. Therefore, if the term and regional structure of capital and financial items are reasonable, domestic economy will become resilient under pressure from international capital and able to maintain overall balance in international payments, even when current account imbalances (either surplus or deficit) are deteriorating.

"Bad imbalances" refers to the situation where a country fails to achieve long-term optimal allocation of domestic and foreign resources, and has been sustaining one-way increase in either surplus or deficit, which eventually leads to distorted economic structure with aggravating risks. "Bad imbalances" often take the following forms: first, an imbalanced domestic economic structure, i.e. irrational industrial and sector structure; and failure to adjust the export-oriented strategy in a timely manner; second, imperfect financial structure, including irrational saving behavior, bad loans, lack of financial supervision and regulation, over-evaluation of local currency, etc.; third, excessively capital flows, which increase external risks and further distort the matching of currencies and terms in the existing, unreasonable foreign debts, which results in either shortage or excessive growth of foreign currency reserve.

It is worth noting that surplus does not necessarily mean "good imbalances" and deficit "bad imbalances," because either could imply a country's inability to effectively allocate domestic resources, which will compel the monetary authority to resort to the international market to achieve balance. Therefore, whether the imbalances are "good" or "bad" depends on a country's capability of allocating global resources. Meanwhile, imbalances also mean long-term, one-way movement of internal capital under capital and financial items, which has prolonged impact the domestic financial system. In an inefficient domestic financial market, such external impact will harm the real economy by way of foreign exchange rate, interest rate, international reserve, credit and loans, as well as securities market. If such situation continues, the country's domestic monetary policy will in effect be "hijacked," and only a well-versed monetary authority with a sound monetary policy structure can put an end to this tendency. Otherwise, the countries' monetary policy will gradually go out of effect.

Sustainability of Imbalances

Since our discussion of imbalances is built on the concept of equilibrium, sustainability of imbalances is the crux of the issue. In fact, the above-mentioned "good imbalances" are sustainable, because they help a country's real economy develop soundly, and bring dynamics to its microeconomic entities with a good prospect.

In essence, global imbalances mirror the situation of the real economy. In a "pure" real economy without currency as the intermediary, imbalances is nowhere to be found, since exchange through "barter" leaves no space for trade difference.

The international monetary system makes imbalances not only possible, but also highly complicated. If deficit countries can clear the account and pay the difference in its local currency, imbalances will be sustained to a great extent within long period of time. In this sense, the focus of the debate on global imbalances should be shifted from issues like the causes and magnitude of the imbalances to sustainability: if, in the world economic system, deficit countries are allowed to pay off the deficit by local currencies, imbalances can be sustained; otherwise, imbalances will trigger global economic crisis.

The evolution of the Bretton Woods system has testified to this argument and left a trajectory of the world economic development with sustainable imbalances to imbalances that is no longer sustainable.

The Bretton Woods system was founded in an unbalanced world economy, where the US remained the surplus country vis-à-vis other deficit countries, constituting a pattern that had lasted for a long time. The pattern begun to change in the 1960s, when the US's foreign debts exceeded its gold reserve, to one that featured the US being the debtor and other countries the creditors, as the gap between them kept on widening. Such imbalances had been maintained to the 1960s, because the Bretton Woods system was dominated by the US dollar, and the US enjoyed the privilege of issuing the dollar to cover the differences on its current account—while all other countries, debtor or creditor, had to use dollar to pay and settle. This trend was reserved after the "Nixon Shock" of 1971, when the domestic prices in the US begun to soar and the value of dollar in foreign markets plummeted unstoppably. What had happened made the US and other countries realize that it was no longer profitable to stick to the dollar standard, and subsequently triggered the outbreak of global financial crisis, which lasted for almost a decade and ended with the demise of the Bretton Woods system.

However, this is not the end of story for the dollar. After the collapse of the Bretton Woods system, although the dollar's dominant role as the international reserve currency has been greatly challenged by a number of reserve currencies that emerged as was represented by the euro, the rising of the Asian countries has actually eased the pressure. Most of those countries pegged their currencies to the dollar in one way or the other, and among them some even adopted fixed exchange rate pegged to the dollar. As those economies rose as the new "periphery" of the dollar, the dollar hegemony was enhanced, subsequently bring the dollar-centered international system back to life. The predominance of the US dollar in the international monetary system had been further consolidated with the "drastic transformation" in the former Soviet Union and Eastern European countries. Prior to the 1990s, the former Soviet bloc countries adopted a monetary system in parallel to the Bretton Woods system, with rubble as the major reserve currency. After the drastic changes, those Eastern European countries endorsed market economy with no exception, making the US dollar their reserve currency. The "defection" of economies of such a magnitude further consolidated the status of the dollar at the core of the world monetary system.

Following the trajectories of imbalances, some researchers gave the name of "Bretton Woods System II" to the international monetary system after the Jamaica Agreement. In our view, this term is not unjustified taking into consideration the fact that the US still has the privilege of issuing the major reserve currency. Nevertheless, in terms of the obligations assumed to the US, the two systems are widely different. Today, free from any constraints and pressure, the US takes no responsibility to address global imbalances and facilitate global economic development, let alone is willing to pay any cost for necessary adjustments. In our view, complete separation of rights and privileges is the major contradictions of the current international monetary system. With no external constraints, the US monetary policies are targeted at domestic goals, disregarding the financial "deluge" in other countries. Such contradiction makes reform of the international financial system an imperative task if the world needs to bring its economy back to balance.

Heading Towards New Balance

Global imbalances remains the biggest conundrum of today's world, hence rebalancing the world economy becomes our top priority. The reason being, global imbalances were the root cause of the 2007 global crisis, which is still running rampant.

If, by definition, crisis is the symptom of a "derailed" economy, then economic recovery can only be achieved in the following two ways: to steer the economy back onto the old track; or, as the alternative, to blaze a new path. Often, crises on small scale did not rattle the whole system, and therefore could be dealt with by patchwork measures that would bring the economy back onto the right track after chaos; however, if the crisis became so severe that it shook the whole system with global impact at much deeper level, and with new factors intervening the process, recovery will take on a totally new trajectory.

The current financial crisis obviously falls into the second category, since after the crisis, global economy has undergone two major transformations that most probably would usher in a new global system.

In the first place, the transformation is taking place in the real economy. Since the end of the 1980s, the emerging economies have contributed more to global output increase than their developed counterparts. The crisis has mired the latter in sluggish economy for long periods of time; meanwhile, the emerging economies have seen sustained high growth, a trend which is going to continue in the foreseeable future. Such economic power shift is historical, and will allow the emerging economies to take over the leading role in global development step by step, as new patterns of economic growth starting to replace this round of globalization under the leadership of the developed economies. In the similar vein, transformation is taking place in the financial sector. Capitalist global economic crisis are always accompanied by financial crisis, which mostly featured debt crisis of the developing countries or emerging markets. With no exception, no recoveries could be achieved without global debt restructuring, which in effect had consolidated and strengthened the hegemonic role of the developed economies in the international financial system. The current crisis, however, has a totally different picture. This time it is the developed countries, the rule markers of the system and issuers of the international reserve currencies that are deep in debt and not able to pull themselves out of the quagmire. Being tied up by the genie set free by themselves from the bottle, the developed countries created international coordination mechanisms like the G20 in the hope that the emerging markets may come to their rescue. As the result, the emerging economies have bigger voices and more influence in the international financial sector, in an effort to diversify the international reserve currencies; in the meantime, the decision-making power of the developed economies regarding rule-making has been gradually weakened. The trend suggests that a new pattern of global economy is taking shape.

The transformations towards a new balance also give China new opportunities to achieve development. First, as the world economy and industries started to restructure, China is in a favorable situation to foster the "new edges" and "seize the strategic commanding heights for future development amid the competitors." Second, as far as global development is concerned, with the "rising of the emerging markets," and the world economy enters the "stage of governance reform", China can build up its strength and participate more effectively in global governance.

It is true that every several decades would witness a new round of global industrial and economic restructuring, even governance reform, and such occurrences have become an normality of the economic cycle; but now it is the first time since the Industrial Revolution that the emerging economies have caught up with the developed economies in terms of economic aggregate, a transformation teamed with new opportunities. For China, it is the opportunity once in a thousand years. Whether China can seize this opportunity and find its new position in the rebalancing process depends on whether the country will be able to transform its development model and economic structure, making them more efficient and better in quality.

This is where the real challenge lies.

In the end, I would like to express my appreciation to Tang Duoduo, Li Cheng, Chang Xin, Wang Jia, and Kuang Keke, for their contribution to this book. My appreciation also goes to editors at the Chinese Social Sciences Press, especially the Director and Editor-in-Chief, Mr. Zhao Jianying, whose hard work made this book possible.

Beijing, China

Yang Li
Xiaojing Zhang

Contents

Part I
Global Imbalances: From the Monetary Perspective

Introduction

Global imbalances, in the final analysis, are phenomenon of the real economy. In one of his speeches in 2005, Mr. Rodrigo de Rato, the then Managing Director of the IMF, described the phenomenon in the following vernacular terms: "Global imbalance as such is the phenomenon where a nation has tremendous trade deficit, but the corresponding trade surplus is concentrated in some other nations.".

However, the real economy in the "purest" form that is not interfered by currency will never produce any type of imbalance, as transactions conducted through "barter" will leave no space for trade gap.

When gold emerged as currency and became the means of international payment and transactions, imbalances were made possible. The emergence of currency introduced time as a dimension, thus successfully solved the issue of inter-temporal allocation of savings and investment within a country; by the same token, the emergence of international currency has freed countries from the need to deliberately maintain the current period balance. Most importantly, as taking and giving loans become possible, countries are able to balance the trade through financial means. Debts have to be paid, needless to say, and flow of international capital does nothing more than making imbalances and re-balancing more complicated. When precious metals are used as the ultimate means to pay off trade deficit, balance of trade among countries only happen on small scale and cannot be sustained long. In other words, under gold standard, long-term "global imbalances," a term that would make people turn pale at the mentioning of it, did not exist.

What has turned global imbalances into normality is credit currency, the scourge that impedes the sound development of global economy.

The birth of modern nation-states made it possible for individual countries to create their own credit currencies within their borders and grant them the status of "legal tender." Worldwide, with the rising of the economic hegemony, the credit currency of a single country would become the international currency acknowledged by all other states. Up to now, only the pound sterling (GBP) and US dollar (USD) have been crowned with the honor of being the global credit currency.

The replacement of pound by dollar as the world's hegemonic currency is due to the latter's capacity to maintain on the whole the necessary conditions for the implementation of the gold standard. Backed by its overwhelming economic strength and a gold reserve accounting for two-thirds of the world's total, the US successfully overtook Britain, by replacing the old international monetary system with the Bretton Woods institutions.

The Bretton Woods system is an attempt by human society to mimic the gold standard systematically. Nevertheless, the "double peg" system carefully designed by the world's financial elite in the woods at New Hampshire in America was born with the Triffin Dilemma: To sustain adequate fluidity globally, the US needs to have long-term deficits on recurrent items; however, accumulation of tremendous amounts of dollar at overseas markets and long-term recurrent item deficits will inevitably undermine the stability of the dollar's value. Such "original sin" had predestined the eventual collapse of the Bretton Woods system.

It is worth noting that, in the nascent stage of the Bretton Woods system, the world economy was imbalanced. The basic pattern when the system was first introduced had been based on the long-term US trade surplus, corresponding to trade deficits of other countries. Since the end of the 1960s, such a pattern under the Bretton Woods system gradually transformed into one that was dominated by trade deficits of the US and corresponding trade surplus of the other countries. As the situation kept on deteriorating, turbulences in domestic prices in the US and plummet of the external value of the dollar made the US and other countries realize that the gains cannot make up for the losses if they held on to the dollar standard. As the result, after nearly a decade of global financial crisis, the Bretton Woods system came to its demise. Now looking back, we would especially like to point out that the global imbalances with the US at one end of the teeterboard and the other countries at the other, either in turns or all at the same time, had started as early as the 1970s.

Since the 1970s, the practice of the US issuing the dollar to make up for its recurrent item deficits has repeated time and again. Up to now, global economic fluctuations were accompanied by debates on the US's recurrent item deficits and monetary policy games among nations. In this context, we believe that the main cause of the current global crisis is the abuse of the privilege by countries issuing international reserve currencies and their disregard of the constantly enlarging imbalances with other countries. From this perspective, reform of the current international monetary system is undoubtedly the prerequisite to achieve the recovery of the current crisis.

Today, the international monetary system has for sure entered the "Warring States Period." As early as the time when the first dollar crisis occurred, reform of international monetary system had begun, moving toward reserve currency diversification. A number of events, including the creation of the SDR, the collapse of the Bretton Woods system, the global economic crisis in the 1980s, the Asian Financial Crisis in the 1990s, the emergence of the euro at the end of the 1990s, and the current global financial crisis in particular, have prompted the trend that is now irreversible.

While exploring the possible future trajectories of the new international monetary system, we have kept a close watch on the progress of the currency swap agreements reached among central banks of the major countries. On October 31, 2013, the world's six major central banks, i.e., the Federal Reserve, the European Central Bank, the Bank of England, the Swiss National Bank, Bank of Canada, and Bank of Japan, made the announcement concurrently that they were changing the existing, provisional, bilateral fluidity swap agreements into long-term agreements. Apart from that, any of the central banks can provide fluidity in one of the five other currencies under the central bank's jurisprudence. This marked the forging of a long-term, multilateral, multicurrency, and infinite super-reserve currency network among the major developed economies. This network has, in fact, integrated the currency supply mechanisms of the developed economies from within. It is particularly worth mentioning that currency swap not only involves the floating of currency among the member states, but also the exchange rates arrangements, which eventually promotes the in-depth coordination of the macroeconomic policies of the member states. In other words, a full-fledged international monetary system is composed of three key elements, namely, choice of reserve currency, systematic arrangements of exchange rates, and a coordination mechanism of international balance of payments. The three elements should be clearly defined and manifested in the currency swap network. The long-term, infinite, and multilateral nature of such arrangements has illustrated the propensities of the developed economies in future development of the international monetary system.

Part I has two chapters:

Chapter 1 analyzes the evolution of the international monetary system, from the gold standard to the system of pound sterling, and how the latter was replaced by the dollar standard. The highlight of the chapter is that it devotes much space to discussing the "forgotten" history of the Ruble district, a monetary system of the "socialist camp" dominated by the former USSR and Eastern European countries, one that runs in parallel with the Bretton Woods system. Analysis of the role and function of the Ruble district, especially how its disintegration has facilitated the resurrection of the centrality of the dollar, has contributed new materials and contexts to the research on the evolution of the international monetary system. At the end of the chapter, the authors analyzed the inevitability, drawbacks, and the moderate "positive role" of the rise of the monetary hegemony, which has broadened perspectives of the research in the field.

Chapter 2 is entitled "The Warring States Period", which illustrates its focus on the trends of diversification of international reserve currency. First, the authors looked at a number of historical conjunctures including the initiation of SDR, the breakdown of the Bretton Woods system, the global economic crisis in the 1980s, Asian countries' attempt to seek a common currency in the 1990s, the emergence of the Euro at the end of the 1990s, and the challenges to the dollar hegemony posed by the current global financial crisis. The analysis was followed by discussion about the ramifications of those occurrences, which led to two major conclusions. First, if we presume that it is nearly impossible to find a single international currency to replace the dollar in the forthcoming future of several generations, then, to reform the international monetary reform, it is imperative to reject the various, single currency proposals, and adopt a realistic attitude and deliberate a mechanism to adjust exchange rates and address imbalances of international payment among nations. Second, now currency swap among central banks is gaining momentum, as the central banks of the US, EU, UK, Japan, Canada, and Switzerland on October 31, 2013 announced that they would made the provisional currency swap long-term, infinite, and multilateral arrangements. These changes show clearly that the establishment of long-term and stable currency swap networks among central banks may evolve into the fundamental framework of the international monetary system in the future.

Chapter 1
The Rise and Fall of Monetary Hegemony

Exploring the world market, capitalists made the production and consumption of all nations international.

—Karl Marx and Friedrich Engels

If Britain's pound sterling is no longer the country's national currency, the commerce in the British Empire, and even the whole Europe, had to be done in dollars but not in pounds. To me that would be a big disaster.

—Winston Churchill

The earliest, recorded economic transactions among nations shows that cross-border trade and flow of capital can be traced back to the period of Mongol Empire and the Yuan Dynasty in China. However, globalization in the real sense cannot be achieved without distinctive international division of labor and continuous flow of goods (services) and capital across the national border. In this sense, the first wave of globalization took place in the 1970s.

Monetary hegemony came into existence only against the backdrop of globalization. Pound sterling rose as the hegemonic currency in the heyday of the first globalization. The era of pound sterling is in itself the times of the classical gold standard, which was later replaced by the dollar hegemony as globalization had deepened. It was the gold standard that ushered in the dollar hegemony, which in turn introduced the era of credit standard.

1.1 The Era of the Hegemony of Pound Sterling Ushered in by "The Empire on Which the Sun Never Sets"

In 1588, the mighty Spanish Armada met its defeat in the Atlantic. As the winner coming out of the naval battle that had shaken the world, in the ensuing two centuries, Britain concentrated on strengthening the nation and vigorously expanded its territories, and rose to become a great power with fast-growing national strength.

Y. Li and X. Zhang, *Imbalance and Rebalance*,
https://doi.org/10.1007/978-981-10-6150-9_1

Undergoing the capitalist revolution, the Anglo-Dutch Wars, four Anglo-French wars, the Industrial Revolution, and in 1815 after it vanquished Napoleon Bonaparte, the military genius with great ambition, Britain, striding across seven continents and four oceans, had risen to become "The Empire on Which the Sun Never Sets". In his renowned book, *The Rise and Fall of the Great Powers*, Paul Kennedy, the American historian, described the British Empire at its zenith in 1860: with 2% of the world's population, "It alone was responsible for one-fifth of the world's commerce, but for two-fifths of the trade in manufactured goods. Over one-third of the world's merchant marine flew under the British flag (Kennedy 1990)".[1] Unlike the gigantic Roman, Han, Mongol and Ottoman empires that rose to power, flourished and decayed, the British Empire rose in a completely new era: with the opening of new shipping routes and the roaring of the steam engines, the once isolated nations, states and civilizations on the globe went into touch with each other either actively or passively in unprecedented depth and breadth. It is fair to say that the British Empire had seen the first beam of the dawn of economic globalization, and became the first global hegemon in the real sense in human history, whereas the rest of the world had yet to be awakened to this new vision.

Even today, many would mention with awe how the first hegemon had flexed its military muscle, and some would still dwell upon the glory of the era of industrial achievement led by the Empire. However, few know about the Act for the Resumption of Cash Payments (1819) passed in 1819. As "obscure" as it might seem to be, in our view, the Act signifies the legal removal of the bimetallism and establishment of the Gold Standard that ushered in the "Era of Pound Sterling" across the globe that lasted for over one century.[2]

Backed by Britain's hegemonic power, the influence of pound sterling had spread far beyond the British Isles. Before the mid-19th century, few major powers except for Britain had their based monetary system on the gold standard. As an ascending power, the British Empire had accumulated tremendous amount of gold reserve through colonial expansion and overseas trade and investment. Domestically, the birth and growth of the Bank of England in 1694 became the hallmark of a modern financial system taking shape, with London gradually taking place of Amsterdam of the Netherlands as the financial center of Europe and the world as well. The pound sterling, making headway in the vast colonial territories, had become the most important international instrument of payment and reserve currency—it was the most trusted equivalent of gold and could be exchanged freely in the world's capitalist economies. The Britain—dominated world economic order had compelled western industrialized countries like Germany, France and the US to follow suit and made them earnestly copy the British experience and adopt the gold standard in the 1870s one after another. According to Chernyshoff et al. (2009),

---

[1]Translator's note Kennedy (1987).

[2]It is worth noting that as early as 1717, the prestigious Sir Isaac Newton, who then was the Master of The Royal Mint, linked Pound Sterling to gold, which led to the gradual retreat of silver from circulation. For this reason, some believe that ever since then, Britain had instituted the de facto single Gold Standard. See detailed comments by Friedman and Kindleberger.

etc., by 1913, 48% of the world's countries had adopted the Gold Standard, who took up 67% of the world's total GDP and 70% of the global trade.[3]

1.2 Gold as the Standard

Between 1870 and the outbreak of World War I, the gold standard in its purest form—Gold Specie Standard—was adopted by the world's major countries.[4] Currencies issued by those countries were backed by gold, and gold coins could be exchanged, exported and imported freely.

Such a system enjoys three advantages, three of which are relevant to international economic relations, and one to domestic economic activities.

Firstly, it was a de facto fixed exchange rates system, because face value of currencies was directly tied to gold. In other words, nations with the gold standard joined a "common currency area" like today's Euro Zone, because the unit of any specific currency, be it pound sterling or French franc was the token of a fixed amount of gold denominated in par value. Though discrepancies might exist due to the cost of transportation of gold, fluctuations were anchored within narrow limits due since the distance of transportation was short. In this case, there was not much difference between international and domestic trade.

Secondly, according to classic quantity theory of money, flow of gold can automatically adjust international imbalances. The theory posits that the optimum balance of trade is zero. A simplified version may illustrate the point: in a world where only gold standard is practiced, when a country has trade deficit as the result of import minus export, gold will flow out of the country and subsequently reduce the quantity of currency in circulation. As the result, the rise of exchange rate and decline in price of goods will enhance the competitiveness of goods produced in the country, thus stimulating import and dampening export, and eventually re-balancing the payments. In contrast, when a nation enjoys surplus in international payments, it will adjust in reverse manner, until the balance is reached again. In short, with the movement of gold and price fluctuation, international payments balance is adjusted automatically. This is the well-known "price-specie-flow" mechanism named by David Hume, the British thinker.

Thirdly, under the gold standard, central banks can operate by the so-called "rules of the game" proposed by John Maynard Keynes. In face of trade deficit and outflow of gold, the central bank may raise interest rates by selling national assets to attract flow of gold; when trade surplus appears, the central bank could make reverse adjustments. This is how imbalances in international payments can be dealt with.

---

[3]Please see Meissner (2002) for history of major powers' transition to the gold standard in the second half of the 19th century.

[4]The other two types of Gold Standard are the Gold Bullion Standard and Gold Exchange Standard. They will be described in detail later.

Lastly, in terms of domestic economy, since the amount of currency that can be issued is limited by a nation's gold reserve, the risk of inflation arising from over-issuance of currency is greatly reduced. In fact, before WWI, a number of countries under gold standard had been hit by inflation, although none of the inflations was serious. Friedman observed that between 1891 and 1940, the average inflation rates of Britain and the US only reached one fourths of those in the second half of the 20th century.

There is no denying that gold standard has its drawbacks, which mainly comes from its core mechanism, namely, the restrictions on the issuance of currency imposed by a country's gold reserve. When the economy prospers, gold production often falls short of the demand for currency due to the increasingly active flow of goods. Such situation most probably will lead to currency deflation.[5]

When the economy is not performing well, as the anchor of currency, gold reserve will keep a country from adopting expansionary monetary policy when it tries to deal with problems like unemployment and production recession. Moreover, due to its property, gold as a precious metal is unevenly distributed geographically across the world and its production output is unstable. Uneven distribution and unstable output means that a country's gold reserve often does not match in proportion its economic strength and growth rate. Paucity of gold puts restraints on the development of a nation. Besides, under the gold standard, mechanism maintaining international balance of payments has huge deficit in practice. On the one hand, the aforementioned "price-specie-flow mechanism" is based on the presumption that the price of goods and wage can be automatically adjusted within a short period of time. However, as many economists are well aware of, in the real world, the variables are in most case "sticky," and therefore it will hard make such adjustment in a timely manner. This means that the mechanism proposed by Hume is not quite relevant to the *laisser-faire*, classical gold standard system. On the other hand, in reality, when central banks play by the "rules of the game" and apply the mechanism to adjusting the unbalanced international payments, it seldom works. As Krugman and Obstfeld have observed, the surplus nation is far less motivated than deficit nation to make adjustments. Actually, it is the latter that one-sidedly shoulders the burden of balancing. Such inequitable sharing of responsibility makes it more difficult for arranging monetary coordination among nations, and compels the deficit nation to adopt tight monetary policies and even be trapped in grave unemployment. Besides, before the WWI, central banks often resorted to sterilization policies to offset the impact of the "rules", i.e., they bought national assets when gold flew out, and sold national assets when gold flew into the country. In effect, such behavior detached the flow of gold from currency supply and further

[5]For example, the severe deflation suffered by the U.S. at the end of the 19th century.

debilitated the self-adjustment mechanism of international payment under the Gold Standard.[6] Therefore it is reasonable to say that those inherent deficiencies of the Gold Standard are endogenous and directly led to the collapse of the system.

In one word, the period between the 1970s and the outbreak of the WWI can be characterized as the Classical Gold Standard Era or the Golden Era of the Gold Standard. It saw a relatively stable international monetary system clothed by "laisser-faire," and the gold standard had greatly facilitated international trade and created the investment boom, giving rise to the "first wave of globalization".[7]

1.3 Trade, Investment and Imbalances Under Classical Golden Standard

Table 1.1 shows the rapid increase in global trade during the Classical Golden Era. Among the nations listed, Europe's trade growth reached 294%, and those of the other regions reached 379%. In terms of trade dependence rate (see Table 1.2), trade dependence rate of the UK had risen from 43% in 1870 to 51.2% in 1913; for Europe, the figure had risen from 29.9% in 1870 to 36.9% in 1913. At the meantime, foreign investment had also increased very fast (Table 1.3). As a result, the UK became the global creditor in the real sense.

1.4 The Global Creditor

Being the world's primary beneficiary of the classical gold standard, the UK enjoyed great advantages in economic expansion and imperial exploration, and its capital export increased drastically as its investment scale had far exceed other major western nations (see Chart 1.3).[8] Between 1870 and 1914, British overseas investment accounted for 41.8% of the total global overseas investment, far

---

[6]Giovannini (1986) in his quantitative analysis shows that the Bank of England did not abide by the "Rule of the Game" under the Classical Gold Standard.

[7]Quantitative analysis by López-Córdova and Meissner (2003) shows that between 1880 and 1910, 20% of global trade increase can be attributed to the adoption of the Gold Standard. This conclusion is basically consistent with the findings by Estevadeordal, etc., (2003). Taylor (1996) also found after studying the relations between "investment" and "consumption" that during the Gold Standard Era, international capital had been in constant flux and the markets were increasingly integrated. Similarly, Meissner (2002) also analyzed the globalization of trade and capital market and its relations with the adoption of the Gold Standard.

[8]Among all of the UK's overseas investments, British investment in Argentina is especially spectacular. Between 1857 and 1910, the investment has risen from 26.1 million pounds to nearly 300 million pounds. For details, see *Man's Past and Present: A Global History of World since 1500 (Chinese Translation)* by L.S. Stavrianos.

Table 1.1 Real trade growth in Europe (1870–1913) (Unit: %)

Country	Growth rate	Country	Growth rate
Austria	333	Norway	283
Belgium	492	Spain	335
Denmark	376	Sweden	274
Finland	415	Switzerland	418
France	222	The United Kingdom	222
Germany	465	Weighted mean	294
Italy	158	Weighted mean of other regions in the world	379
The Netherlands	151		

Source Madison (2001)

Table 1.2 Share of trade in GDP of the United Kingdom and Europe (Unit: %)

Country	1870	1880	1890	1900	1913
The United Kingdom	43.6	46.0	46.6	42.4	51.2
Europe	29.9	33.4	32.6	31.9	36.9

Source Daudin, Morys and O' Rourke (2008)

exceeding those of France (19.8%) and Germany (12.8%)—the second and third biggest investor. It is especially noteworthy that the capital sources of the top three investors were domestic savings. For example, between 1905 and 1914, nearly half of Britain's domestic savings were used for overseas investment. By 1914, Britain's net overseas national wealth had taken up 32.1% of the nation's total national wealth (see Table 1.4). Britain's situation at the time differed fundamentally from that of the contemporary US. Nowadays, despite its spectacular overseas investment, the US is also burdened with tremendous amount of overseas debts, and with the latter offsetting the former, the country's monetary supply has been restricted by its liabilities.

Huge volume of trade and capital influx inevitably resulted in imbalances among nations. As is illustrated by Charts 1.1 and 1.2, Britain, France and Germany had

Table 1.3 Foreign investment of major powers by years (Unit: Million Dollars)

Country	1825	1840	1855	1870	1885	1900	1913
United Kingdom	500	750	2300	4900	7800	12100	19500
France	100	(300)	1000	2500	3300	5200	8600
Germany	*	*	*	*	1900	4800	6700
The Netherlands	300	200	300	500	1000	1100	1250
The United States	N	N	N	N	N	500	2500

Note * No data; N: negligible
Source Chapter 12 of *A Financial History of Western Europe* by Charles P. Kindleberger

Table 1.4 Overseas investment by UK, France and Germany (1870–1914) (Unit: %)

	The United Kingdom			France	Germany
	Percentage of savings to GDP	Percentage of overseas investment to GDP	Percentage of overseas investment to savings	Percentage of overseas investment to savings	Percentage of overseas investment to savings
1870–1979	12.3	4.0	32.5	23.9	10.2
1880–1989	12.2	4.7	38.5	5.1	18.8
1890–1999	11.0	3.4	30.9	16.5	12.1
1900–1909	12.6	3.7	29.4	19.1	8.3
1905–1914	13.1	6.5	49.6	17.3	7.5
Net wealth of overseas nationals in 1914	32.1			–	–
Percentage of global investment	41.8			19.8	12.8

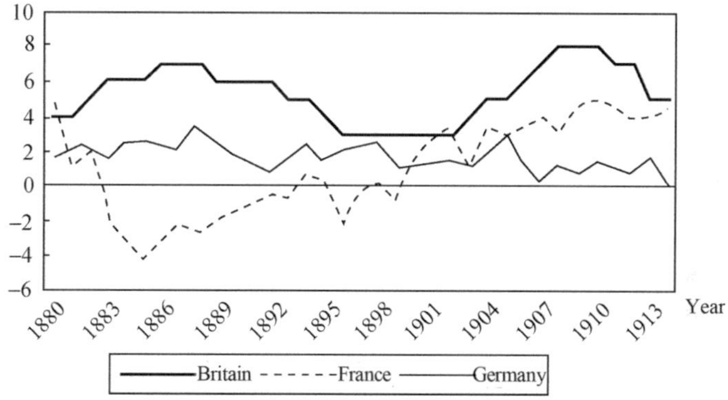

Chart 1.1 Surplus countries in the gold standard era. *Source* Obstfeld and Taylor (2004)

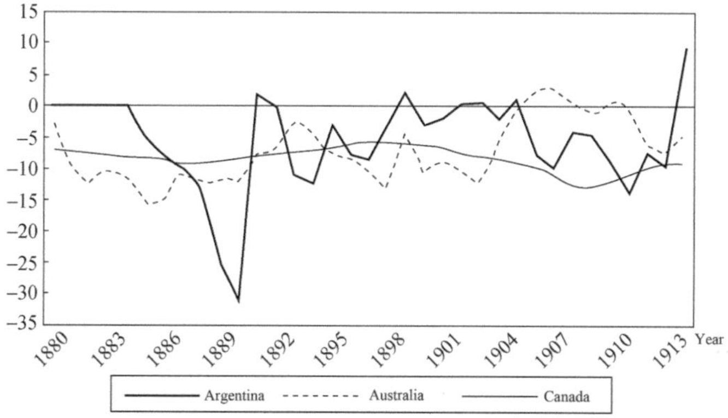

Chart 1.2 Deficit countries under gold standard. *Source* Obstfeld and Taylor (2004)

risen out of the classical gold standard system as the surplus economies, whereas Argentina, Australia and Canada had become deficit countries. The British surplus had once reached 8% of the country's GDP, and Argentina's trade deficit amounted to as high as 30% of its GDP. For most countries, the deficit/GDP percentage was around 5–10% of the GDP. Looking back, one has to say that the world at the time was experiencing tremendous payment imbalances.

Worldwide investment brought about gigantic profits to the UK. Matthews has mentioned that the percentage of capital income to GDP in the UK has risen progressively from merely 2.8% between 1855 and 1873 to 5.5% between 1874 and 1890, and eventually reached 6.8% between 1891 and 1913. During the half century, despite of the small trade deficit, the UK had been able to maintain surplus on recurrent items that is spectacular even by today's standard.

These figures could make the British feel proud, yet from a different point of view, maintaining such amazing trade surpluses for as long as half a century has nonetheless testified the failure of the adjustment mechanism under the gold standard system. Obviously, when the Bank of England was unable to provide stimulus to correct international imbalances, it was hard to maintain long-term trade surplus, only when and how the surplus went to the end.

1.5 Early Version of "The End of History"

It is worth noting that the earliest version of "The End of History" made its appearance during the heyday the UK's economic and financial conquest all over the world. Arnold J. Toynbee, the renowned British historian described the British people's illusion about the history: "In their eyes, history has already ended. In foreign affairs, it ended with the War at Waterloo in 1815; in domestic affairs, it ended with the birth of the "Reformation Act" in 1832; as for the Empire, history has ended with the Mutiny in 1959, and they have all the reasons to celebrate the permanent bliss with the end of history". (Indirect quote from *Man's Past and Present: A Global History of World since 1500 (Chinese Translation)* by L.S. Stavrianos). Both proponents and opponents of "the end of history" could but smile knowingly at each other. In 1897, Britain held the Diamond Jubilee to celebrate the 60-year reign of Queen Victoria. While the tune of God Bless the Queen was still resounding among the Queen's subjects, the glory of the Queen and her British Empire started to fade gradually in its due course.

Britain, the world's super power at the end of the 19th century was faced with tremendous challenges in the era of transformation. Not far across the Strait, Germany had risen as an emerging power after Prussia was unified under the leadership of the "iron chancellor" Bismarck. Across the vast Pacific, a young nation—the United States had just survived its biggest domestic challenge after its birth, and the industrial, capitalist north rose triumphantly out of the American Civil

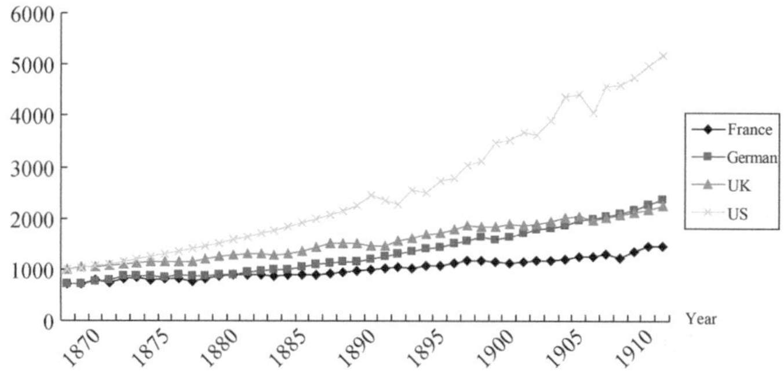

Chart 1.3 Comparison of GDP of major powers (1990 International US Dollar: $ billions). *Source* Maddison (2006)

War. The two emerging nation-states rose quickly after unification and in political stability. Dipping their fingers in the pie of the first globalization with Britain the super power, the two new powers had overtaking the hegemon with economic might. According to Maddison's statistics (see Chart 1.3), in 1872, Britain was overtaken by the United States and by Germany in 1908 in GDP with comparable price.

As the British-dominated international economic system was in gradual transition, the international monetary system dominated by pound sterling/gold also teemed with undercurrents and hidden crisis.

First of all, since pound sterling was the currency for international settlement and reserve, Britain needed to keep the gold standard "untarnished" to ensure free exchange of pound for gold and free, cross-border movement of gold. Nevertheless, after decades of capital coming into and going out of the country, the ubiquitous presence of pound around the globe had subjected Britain's gold reserve to grave, potential threat. In 1913, for example, half of the world's foreign currency reserve was deposited in pound sterling, while the British central bank—Bank of England held only 3% of the world's total gold reserve (Officer 2008).

Meanwhile, cloaked by the shining glamour of the gold standard, cumulative imbalances of the recurrent international items were not remedied as people had wished. Such imbalances put pressing demands for structural adjustment on creditors like the UK, France, and Germany as well as the debtors like Argentina, Australia, Canada and the US. As the beneficiary of the gold standard system, Britain borrowed from other countries without paying interests, thus having neither motive nor mechanism for structural adjustment; the imbalances of payment, nearly impossible to be sustained, was covered up by the fact that international capital could move with relative freedom (Meissner 2010).

As contradictions rising from uneven economic development and international payment imbalances became acute, a bloody total war was eventually staged in the so-called "civilized world". The merciless reality busted the British's illusion of the

"End of History," as people came to realize that "history", instead of being far from its end, had yet to blaze new trajectories, and with no mistake, the Golden Age of the British Empire was approaching its finale.

1.6 The "Lame Duck" Gold Standard and Its Disintegration

Historians who view the WWI from the military angle alone tend to agree that it was a long and dull military event. However, as far as international monetary system is concerned, WWI is a landmark event that mercilessly crushed the foundation of the Classical Gold Standard and tore down its façade. The colossal military expenditures drove the warring parties to issue paper money[9] that could not be exchanged for gold, thus abandoning gold as the anchor. At the same time, they took out domestic and foreign loans to fuel military spending. Everyone believed that "the enemies would be forced to pay indemnities once they lose the war" (Kennedy 1990). As the result, free exchange between paper money and gold was put to an end; coinage of gold was ceased, so were the import and export of gold. Hence the basis of the gold standard system had been completely demolished.[10]

Great changes took place in global economic system after WWI. European countries, either the victor or the defeated were weakened severely in economy. Across the Atlantic, the US came out of the war as the real winner. In comparable prices, the Britain's GDP in 1920 was 93% of that in 1913, for France and Germany, the figures were 87 and 71% respectively. In sharp contrast, the GDP of the US had reached 115% of that in 1913 (Maddison 2006). The international investment reshuffle was probably more thorough. In the old continent, European creditors were gravely hurt. The Great War had caused Britain to lose one fourths of its foreign investment, France one thirds and Germany nearly all its foreign investment (Stavrianos 1991). Across the globe, huge amounts of war loans to European countries quickly transformed the US from a debtor to the world's Number One creditor in no more than five to six years.[11]

The postwar power shift between Europe and America was accompanied by reconstruction of the international monetary system. In 1919, the US took the lead to reinstate the pure gold coin standard with a gold reserve taking up 40% of the

[9]For example, between 1913 and 1919, paper currency of pound sterling in circulation increased by 2.7 times, French Franc 6.1 times, and Deutsche Mark 14.5 times. Please see Kindleberger (2006).

[10]It is worth noting that, between 1914 and 1925, Britain's existing gold standard was not legally suspended; yet, requests to redeem gold with paper currency from the Bank of England were often turned down under pretexts of "moral persuasions" like patriotism. Export of gold was prohibited as it was regarded as "trade with the enemies". For further information, please see Officer (2008).

[11]Keynes estimated that in 1919, the Entente Powers owed the US 1.9 billion pounds. Please see Kindleberger (2006).

world's total. Backed by the strong gold coin, New York replaced London as the new world financial center. European countries also intended to go back to the gold standard. In 1922, major industrial countries except the isolationist US met at Genoa, where they reinstate the gold standard through the Program of Action, and expressed their willingness to enhance central bank coordination in dealing with the unbalanced economy. As the old time hegemon, Britain ardently supported the proposal, in the hope of reinvigorating the once powerful status of pound sterling. In 1925, the UK reinstated the gold standard, followed by France in 1926. Nevertheless, the countries except the US did not have enough gold reserved for international settlement, because gold coinage and fluidity were no longer in existence as they had been in the prewar years, which means the basis of the gold standard system was gone. What was Britain and France actually adopted then, was a limited gold standard—Gold Bullion Standard, a system that allowed only paper currencies to circulate, guaranteeing that people could use them to redeem gold at a floor rate (for example, Britain fixed the convertible rate at 400 ounces of gold for approximately 1700 pounds). At the same time, other "periphery" countries started to adopt the Gold Exchange Standard: they deposited in reserves only the currencies of the countries with the gold standard, namely, plus the US dollars and pound sterling; meanwhile, they pegged their own currencies to gold, and to currencies gold standard countries through fixed exchanges rates.

As was mentioned above, WWI not only took a heavy toll on the economy of major European powers including Britain, France and Germany and caused them, incurring huge loss of their gold reserves, as well as problems caused by military loans and war indemnities. European banks were bogged down by debts and insolvencies. However, major western countries still had faith in gold standard, which was by no means shaken by changes in the economic fundamentals, as it remained the dominant ideology among politicians and bankers at the time and its legitimacy was deemed unquestionable (Eichengreen 1992). Nevertheless, an unprecedented crisis was brewing and could be triggered at any moment. Realty soon showed that the reinstated gold standard could no longer maintain its legendary magic of its classical time, and its shining glow was merely an ominous sign for its demise.

The truth is, as the Great Depression had tremendously shattered people's faith in the gold standard, countries had to give up the institution. It is particular worth mentioning that the crisis of pound sterling compelled Britain to abandon the gold standard fairly quickly. Between 1929 and 1930, the loss on the British current account became worse, resulting in huge loss of the country's gold reserve. To fend off the outflow of gold, Bank of England raised discount rates, only leading to economic contractions and further destroying people's confidence in pound sterling. The currency crisis broke out shortly after. Under such circumstances, Britain had to temporarily suspend the convertibility of the pound sterling on September 19th, 1931, an action that marked the disintegration of the wartime gold standard system. Other countries followed suit by ditching the gold standard and pegging their currencies to the pound sterling. In early 1932, twenty four countries put an end to the convertibility of their local currencies, and deflated the local currencies to resist external pressure. In 1933, despite of its huge gold reserve, the US was also driven to give up the gold standard under international pressure, thus putting an end to the gold standard, which was made history in no time.

1.7 The Hegemony of the US Dollars Born in the "Woods"

In July 1944, when Europe and Asia were still shrouded by the smoke of the battlefield, representatives from forty four nations gathered at Bretton Woods in New Hampshire, the U.S., to discuss the plan for postwar international monetary order that would hopefully facilitate balanced international trade and achieve full employment and growth at home. There were two alternatives on the negotiation table: the White Proposal put forward by the US, and the Keynes Proposal by Britain. After make comparisons, scholars made the following comments in succinct and insightful words: "The White Proposal intended to establish international fund as a stabilizer. Member states were expected to deposit local currencies in the fund, and the latter would provide them with currencies for international settlement. Keynes proposed an international clearing union, which needed no deposit. Instead, international balance of payment would be realized through debiting and crediting on the country's account".[12] In short, White saw an international monetary system whereby every country, while attaining its currency sovereignty, acknowledged the central role of the US dollar in the global monetary system. His plan reflected the reality that the dollar was reigning as the world's reserve currency. In contrast, Keynes proposed to establish a supranational, intangible settlement account to balance international payments by weakening the monetary sovereignty of the countries. To the proponents, the plan seemed to be the only alternative in face of the decline of the hegemony of the pound sterling. The debate went along and did not end until White's Proposal eventually prevailed,[13] which was the prototype of the Bretton Woods institutions that dominated the international monetary system in more than three decades after the negotiation, and the world had seen the beginning of the Hegemony of the US dollar. Yet what had happened was alarming and full of irony: when the Bretton Woods System was founded, the US was at its heyday in terms of economic strength and financial power, apart from the huge gold reserve it held. In this context, the US never tried to conceal its intention to set up the dollar hegemony and therefore it openly rejected any suggestion that would weaken the role of the local currency. However, later in the 1960s, when the US had longtime deficit on its current account and was in the similar upsetting situation as Britain used to be, it did not hesitate to facilitate the IMF reformation and initiate the use of

[12]Williams (1944).

[13]Generally that was what happened then. However, the US also made concessions as to the British proposal, in respects like introducing adjustable fixed exchange rates and regulating international capital flow.

the Special Drawing Rights (SDR). Ironically, the principles of the SDR best reflected the spirit of Keynes' proposal.

1.8 The "Original Sin" of the Bretton Woods System

The Bretton Woods system worked through the so-called "double peg". Backed by its huge gold reserves, the US promised that foreign governments may redeem gold at the rate of 35 dollars per ounce; meanwhile, local currencies of the member states were pegged to the US dollar, and their currency exchange rates were decided by the ratio of the local currency to the US dollars, in accordance with their relative values measured by gold. Since the fixed exchange rates were adopted, the system allowed for fluctuations on small scale, and the governments were obliged to keep the exchange rates stable. For the system to run smoothly, the US had to provide countries with dollars as their reserve currencies and ensure their solvency in gold; it also needed to stabilize the value of the dollar by keeping the prices of fungible commodities stable.

Full of contradictions, the fine design of the Bretton Woods system had its inherent "original sin". When the global and American gold reserves were not able to keep up with the expansion of the world economy and trade, the "double peg" would mire the US in a predicament: the U.S. had to constantly increase the international payments deficit in order to keep dollar flowing to the growing world economy and trade; yet, constant increase of deficit and supply of dollar made it harder for the U.S. to maintain the "fixed" rate between the dollar and gold, which consequently undermined the "golden pillar" of the Bretton Woods system. Pressures for deflation of the dollar mounted as the deficit went up; it also made it difficult for the US to maintain the gold/dollar value ratio stable and when the ratio was no longer under control, the foundation of the system was severely eroded. The system's inherent contradictions as such could not be solved, hence the so-called "Triffin Dilemma". The contradictions had another problem: the impact of short-term capital movement. When international capital became aware of the "Triffin Dilemma," it would exploit the profit margin resulting from the contradictions to make profits. That explains why international hot money never missed a chance in almost every international financial crisis since the 1960s.

The Bretton Woods system constantly went under severe blows since the 1960s due to its endogenous, "original sin".

The first crisis took place in 1960. The international short-term debt of the US exceeded the country's gold reserve for the first time, which led to the under-selling of the dollar and panic-buying of gold from the US and other hard currencies.

The second crisis broke out in 1968. Due to the escalation of the Vietnam War, the financial situation of the US kept on deteriorating and inflation became worse. The foreign exchange market was engulfed by dollar dumping and panic-buying of gold. To deal with the crisis, the IMF tried to pacify the market by instituting "double-track prices" for gold (the market price was different from the official price); on the other hand, it invented the Special Drawing Rights (SDR) nicknamed "paper gold", in the hope that it could substitute some of the functions of the US dollar.

In 1970 the third crisis came along when the ratio of the US short-term international debt to the gold reserve reached postwar historical high. To make things worse, the first oil crisis plunged the US economy and the international monetary system into deep chaos unlike anything else in the past. In order to solve the crisis, on August 15th, 1971, US president Richard Nixon announced the "New Economic Policy" that forestalled redeeming of gold by the dollar and severed the official exchange of the dollar for gold. Further measures were taken to compel Germany and Japan to appreciate their currencies and freeze the salary standard in the US. In response to those policies, one by one major developed countries abandoned the fixed foreign exchange rate pegged to the dollar and started to adopt the floating exchange rate. In December 1971, the Smithsonian Agreement was reached to keep the Bretton Woods system running as usual, with the efforts of coordination among the developed countries. However, as the trade deficit of the US grew, the Agreement was unable to dampen the frenzy of dollar-dumping at the foreign exchange market.

In February, 1973, the Bretton Woods system officially failed after the fourth dollar crisis erupted at the foreign exchange market.

1.9 The Ruble Zone: A "Parallel" International Monetary System not to be Forgotten

People tend to focus their attention on the Bretton Woods system when it comes to the post WWII global financial system. Such a perspective is not without bias, because in the post WWII "Cold War" era that lasted forty decades, a "parallel" monetary system co-existed with the Bretton Woods system, namely: the Ruble Zone. It was the monetary system dependent on the economic and trade ties between the USSR and other socialist countries, in particular the member states of the Council for Mutual Economic Assistance (COMECON). The Ruble Zone was dominated by the Soviet Union and used transferable ruble as the tool of settlement. It also established international financial institutions like the International Bank for Economic Cooperation (IBEC) (1963–1991) and the International Investment Bank (1971–1991).

The Ruble Zone was founded against the backdrop of the international situation at the time. When the smoke of the battle field of the WWII had yet to dissipate, the US took the lead in reconstructing the postwar international economic and financial order. It was part of the country's international strategy to seek global predominance, one that would not allow for challenge from any potential rivals. It is out of this consideration that the US wanted to isolate countries that did not join the "mutually complemented" global order dominated by the US and who therefore posed threat to the economic network that served as the foothold of the US global economic strategy. At the time, the only challenger of the hegemon was no other than the Soviet Union. Naturally the Soviet Union and its allies were excluded from the Bretton Woods system. As the USSR representative to the United Nation General Assembly in 1947 had pointed out: "The Bretton Woods system was merely a 'franchise store of the Wall Street", and World Bank the tool of some big power to realize its political purposes. And this big power is the US".[14]

Discussion of the Ruble Zone will go nowhere without talking about the COMECON, whose emergence, development and dissolution could be traced to the global political order that took shape after the WWII.

With the end of the war, the US initiated the "European Recovery Program" (generally referred to as the Marshall Plan), for the purpose of restoring the economic order in the allied nations that was on the verge of breakdown and curbing the infiltration and expansion of the Soviet Union and its communist influence. Joseph Stalin, the leader of the Soviet Union, viewed the Marshall Plan as a severe threat to his grip over Eastern Europe, and responded by adopting the well known "Molotov Plan". The Plan focused on providing economic assistance to socialist countries in Eastern Europe, and promoting trade between those countries and the Soviet Union. In the similar way as the Marshall Plan had given birth to the European Economic Community, the Molotov Plan drew the blueprint for the COMECON.

On January 5th–8th, 1949, after consultations in Moscow, representatives for six countries, namely, the USSR, Bulgaria, Hungary, Poland, Romania and Czechoslovakia proclaimed the founding of the Council for Mutual Economic Assistance (COMECON). They were joined later by Cuba, the Republic of Mongolia, the Socialist Republic of Vietnam, and the German Democratic Republic (the GDR). Before its dissolution, member states of the COMECON distributed in major continents including Europe, Asia and the Americas, with a total population of 450 million people.

In the initial stage after its establishment, activities of the COMECON were limited within currency circulation, but gradually expanded to production and the nature from bilateral to multilateral with further efforts to coordinate national economic plans among its members. In 1969, the strategic plan to "integrate the socialist economies" was made, an embodiment of Stalin's theory about "two parallel world markets".

Being isolated, members of the COMECON traded among themselves and tried to channel their trade from with the traditional markets in the west to within the East Bloc. Admittedly the transformation was tremendously successful. In 1983, the total trade volume among member states was 285.3 billion rubles, an increase of 32 times over that of 1950, when the COMEON was founded. Besides, over 58% of foreign trade for all the members was realized among the member states.

[14]Mason and Asher (1973).

For the Soviet Union, trade with socialist countries including the COMECON member states accounted for 80 and 55% of its total trade volume respectively. Member states of the COMECON, especially the European members were major trading partners of the Soviet Union. Over the many years since the 1950s, trade with those countries had taken up over 50% of its total trade volume. The Soviet Union export to the COMECON countries products mainly included fuel, energy, raw materials and machinery products. The Soviet Union supplied 100% of the natural gas, 80% of oil, 75% of hard coal, 68% of electricity, 75% of iron ore and 100% of cotton imported by countries including Bulgaria, Hungary, the GDR, Poland, and Czechoslovakia. In other words, over half of the energy of East Europe had to depend on imports from the Soviet Union. Meanwhile, the latter imported from the former bulk commodities including machineries, foods, and daily consumer goods, and 60% of its technological products came for the COMECON partners.

The Soviet Union as such had been the No.1 trading partner of the East European countries. With the founding of the COMECON, the proportion of trade with the Soviet Union in the total trade volume of East Europe had been on the increase yearly, from 32.3% in 1975, to 41.6% in 1983. During the same period, the percentage of export to the Soviet Union had risen from 34.8 to 36.9% of the aggregated trade of East Europe (see Table 1.5).

1.10 Operation of the Ruble Zone

For a long time, the Soviet-East European trade had been carried out through “barter” with noncash settlements. The key element of noncash settlement is the settlement currency. In the market within COMECON, the settlement currency initially adopted was settlement ruble.

During the early days, trade and settlement among COMECON members was strictly bilateral, abiding by the principle of maintaining strict balance between commodities and payments between the trading partners. At the end of the settlement period, the deficit country had to pay off its debts by supplying the surplus country with commodities in the following year. It turned out that strict observation

Table 1.5 The proportion of trade with the Soviet Union to the total trade volume of six Eastern European countries (Unit: %)

Item	1975	1980	1981	1982	1983
Imports from the Soviet Union	32.3	33.4	37.8	40.7	41.6
Exports to the Soviet Union	34.8	32.6	33.9	35.9	36.9

Note The “six Eastern European countries” refers to: Bulgaria, the GDR, Poland, Romania and Czechoslovakia

Source Xiuying Chen, *Relations and Features of Trade between Eastern European Countries and the Soviet Union*

of bilateral balance of payments greatly curbed the growing circulation of commodities, because countries with strong potentials in export could not achieve their full potential unless their bilateral trading partners would be able to meet the terms with matching export capabilities. To deal with this deficiency, in the 1950s COMECON member states began to adopt a new system of settlement—the tri-lateral settlement system. Under this system, member countries did not have to maintain exact balance between import and export, as they were allowed to settle with the third party when there was a surplus. Compared with the bilateral agreement, the new system was obvious more elastic; however, as time went by, it could not keep up with the rapid increase in the commodity circulation. Therefore in 1957, the Multilateral Settlement Agreement was reached among the COMECON members, and it stipulated that trade imbalances could be settled multilaterally. This means that countries could import commodities and labor from other members of the agreement without exporting commodities or labor. In the same year, the Soviet Union established a settlement bureau at the central government level to conduct multilateral settlement through the settlement Ruble. In retrospect, however, during the nearly four decades of the COMECON history, bilateral settlement remained predominant despite of the multilateral settlements arrangement.

Adopting of the tri-lateral and even multilateral settlements required the use of a transaction media and reserve capital accepted by all parties within the COMECON, hence the transferable ruble was created. The transfer Ruble was an accounting unit for the members to complete multilateral settlement that was based on Ruble with almost equivalent value. Within the COMECON, buyers could use the transfer Ruble to settle with the sellers without delivering equivalents of the goods they had purchased. It is estimated that trade volume realized through the transfer Ruble amounted to 80% of the total within the COMECON.

Once the transfer Ruble was created for settlements, it automatically became the value measurement, purchase intermediary, as well as instrument of payment. In the inner trade circle of the COMECON, transfer Ruble was widely used to determine the prices of commodities, pay for energy, machinery, equipment, food, industrial products and other commodities, as well as labor expenses. It was also used to evaluate the expenditure for joint projects and economic, scientific and technological cooperation among the members. Apart from those functions, as a unit of account, the transfer Ruble was also used to convert the balance resulting from non-trade payments in local currencies of member countries into collective currencies (calculated with special conversion coefficient). Transfer Ruble was also widely used to pay for commodities and labor, pay off credits and loans among COMECON members and those borrowed from the International Bank of Economic Cooperation and International Investment Banks, as well as non-trade expenses. The transfer Ruble, as the result, had turned into instrument of payment and the local currency of the COMECON. Holders of transfer Rubles may deposit it into the International Bank of Economic Cooperation for interests. Member countries might engage in loan business and even jointly took part in the construction of projects or establishing international, economic organizations.

Admittedly, the transfer Ruble, becoming increasingly effective as a currency, had facilitated multilateral settlements among the members of the COMECON by enabling the countries to use capital with great flexibility and efficiency, especially in transferring capitals for settlement among the countries. By doing so, the transfer Ruble had played an important role in promoting economic integration of and cooperation in economy, science and technology among the COMECON countries.

When transfer Ruble took the stage as the de facto currency, it called for the establishment of international financial organizations.

The first such organization that came into existence was the International Bank of Economic Cooperation (IBEC) established in 1963, which served as the international financial center conducting settlement and making loans. It was founded by eight countries including Bulgaria, Hungary, the GDR, Mongolia, Poland, Romania, the Soviet Union and Czechoslovakia. Cuba became a member in 1974. With the joining of Vietnam in 1977, the bank became an international bank that served all COMECON countries, with authorized capital of 300 million transfer Rubles. After the joining of Cuba and Vietnam, the capital increased with another 53 million transfer Rubles. The authorized capital contributed by member countries was divided into two parts: one in the form of transfer Rubles and the other, free exchange currencies.

The contribution ratio of an individual country was decided by the proportion of their export to the countries' total trade volume. Apart from the authorized capital, the bank also had reserve, which came from the bank's annual interest earnings. The earmark was made once a year based the annual performance evaluation of the bank by the board of governors. The authorized capital collected and the reserve capital constituted the bank's equity capital. Other than the equity capital, the bank also derived its capital from the current and fixed deposits, saving them temporarily on the account.

The IBEC adopted a voting rights system different than that of the IMF. Upholding the principle of cooperation, it gives each country one vote, regardless of its contribution to the bank's capital. All decisions went into effect only with the unanimous vote.

The IBEC basically performed two functions: it acted as the settlement center of payment for trade; and it issued loans to the members. These loans were intended to make production more specialized and coordinated, stimulate trade, balance international payments and solve seasonal issues in member countries. It also engaged in free exchange of foreign currencies and gold. By attracting foreign savings from international financial market, it redistributed the money to the banks designated by its members. In 1964, there were only 900 million transfer Rubles on its free currencies account, but it increased to 99.1 billion in 1982. In early 1983, in terms of transfer Ruble, the IBEC held a total of 1.7 billion in foreign currency deposits.

Another COMECON bank is the International Investment Bank (IIB) founded in 1971 with a legal capital of 1.0526 billion transfer Rubbles. The ratio of contribution was arranged in the same way as the IBEC. Seventy percent of its legal capital was in transfer Rubble and the rest was in free foreign currencies and gold. The Soviet Union was the biggest stake holder with a contribution of 399.3 million

Rubles, accounting for 37.93% of the capital. The individual share by the GDR, Czechoslovakia and Poland was over 10%, while other member countries each held less than 10% and Mongolia a merely 0.43% of the legal capital. The IIB was mainly involved in providing medium and long-term loans to projects of industrial specialization so as to advance the economic integration of the COMECON.

1.11 Disintegration of the Ruble Zone

Since January 1st, 1991, the Soviet Union and other COMECON member states started to conduct bilateral economic transactions in cash and international hard currencies based on world market prices, thus giving up the old accounting system of the transfer Ruble. Actually, inner COMECOM trade ended on January 5th the same year, and with the dissolution of the COMECON on June 28th, 1991, the Ruble Zone entirely collapsed.

The disintegration of the COMECON and the symbiosis Ruble Zone was caused by the political transformation known to all, as well as deep-seated economic factors. The most crucial factors were the planned economic mechanism and the Soviet-dominated division of labor of the COMECON.

The COMECON ran its economy with a highly centralized plan, which is the immanent feature of the system. The campaign for common planning started in 1955, initiated at first to coordinate the five-year plans of the member states. However, since 1966, member states had to first went through policy coordination before they could make their individual five-year plan. The inverted procedure not only gave the COMECON, especially the Soviet Union the decision-making power in all economic policies, but also finalized the division of labor within the COMECON and the economic structure of its member countries. Individual country's economic planning had to serve the bloc's goal, in other words, the economic programs of the Soviet Union, thus subordinating the country's economic policies and structure to the inner-bloc trade and division of labor.

In the planned trading system, trade among COMECON members was not independently conducted by countries out of their domestic demands, but was planned jointly by the countries. Within the organization, as the market price was no longer the indicator for supply and demand, it could have done even less in distributing the resources. Within such a framework, representative enterprises were supposed to assume responsibilities to export certain brands of products in certain quantity before they went to the market, what they needed to do was to produce according to the order sheet issued by the government, who was also in charge of the "sales". Mechanism as such had replaced the enterprise-market relations with inter-governmental agreements.

The comprehensive, high-level planning had isolated the COMECON and its members from the global market; meanwhile, it created the horizontal division of labor system dominated by the Soviet Union. The political predominance and abundant resources of the Soviet Union compelled the other member countries to conduct bilateral trade negotiation with the Soviet Union before they negotiated bilateral trade agreements with other members; economic ties among member states other than the Soviet Union remained weak since the countries did have few vertical economic exchanges among themselves. Such mechanism gave the Soviet Union the predominance and hence tremendous edge in bilateral trade negotiations, and made Eastern European countries even more dependent on the Soviet Union. In one word, the "multilateral" economic relations were merely a façade for the economic relations with the Soviet Union at the center and the other countries at the periphery. Within the COMECON, trade between the Soviet Union and East European countries were 1.5–2 times of than among East European countries.

For the Soviet Union, the hegemon, the Eastern European countries should be suppliers of the communities for its needs: machineries, spare parts and other manufactured goods. So those countries had to "change" their economic policy and distribution of resources to fit into the model. Eastern European countries with poor natural resources and weak industrial foundations were forced to "exert to build comparative advantages" and transform into economies featuring heavy industries by setting up heavy machinery manufacturing, processing and fuel and energy complexes. Such "comparative advantages" were obviously distorted and the specialized production system had further aggravated East Europe's economic dependency on the Soviet Union.

Nothing illustrates the dependency better than the structure of the Soviet-East European trade. Eastern European countries imported the so-called "hard commodities"—fuels and raw materials and exported "soft-commodities"—machineries and industrial commodities. Imports of fuels and exports of machineries and equipment took up over 50% of its total import and export trade volume. As for "barter" transactions, the price in the Soviet-East European trade had for long years been fixed for a five-year period after it was first adopted: the Soviet Union import export fuels and raw materials at the price lower than that of the international market while Eastern European countries exported machinery and equipment and industrial commodities at cheaper prices. Admittedly, although the Soviet Union had dominated the division of labor with the COMECN and therefore the pricing-power, it seemed that it did not exploit the privilege in excess. In fact, before 1975, the Soviet Union had been in deficit in its trade with the East Europe. After 1975, however, with the rocketing of the energy prices in the global market and the deterioration of the conditions in oil mining in the country, the Soviet Union unilaterally made the decision to later the principle of pricing that had long been used. In the past, the price was set based on averaging the oil prices in the international market in the previous five years; and the Soviet Union changed the calculation period of three years, without adjusting the prices of machineries it imported from East European countries. In consequence, Eastern European countries no longer had surplus as they used prior to 1975 but became deficit countries. The sharp reverse in international energy prices in the 1980s caused the trade conditions of the Soviet Union to deteriorate further, making the country bear the growing burden of export subsidies for Eastern European countries. For example, the Soviet Union had to export oil at the price nearly half of the international market price, which means that one thirds of each export unit was subsidized. In 1987, the Soviet Union held a surplus of 60 million transferable rubles, but the surplus was replaced by a deficit of 2.4 billion transferable rubles in 1988, and the deficit kept on increasing from 4.08 billion in 1989 to 13 billion transferable ruble in 1990.

In a sense, the causes for the disintegration of the COMECON lied in real world economic factors including non-market nature of the economy of the COMECON and the ossification of the division of labor dominated by the Soviet Union.

The underlying weakness of transferable ruble also contributed to the collapse of the COMECON. As a unit of value, transferable ruble could only be used for settlement, credit and payment with the COMECON. Although it could be transferred freely from the accounts of one member to that of the other, it existed only on the account and could by no means enter circulation as a real currency. Moreover, the use of transferable ruble and even its mere existence meant potential loss for surplus countries. This is because, although it would make it easier for deficit countries to get short-term loans from the IBEC, surplus countries were only allowed to accumulate the earnings in transferable ruble on the book, and use them for payment of trade within the COMECON; in other words the surplus could be redeemed for currencies, let alone be put into circulation. No doubt it caused quite considerable loss in opportunity cost. Besides, just like the local currency of the Soviet Union, the ruble, transferable ruble could not be converted freely into gold or local currencies of the COMECON member states, let alone currencies of the western countries. The inconvertibility of transferable ruble was the tumbling block that prevented it from transforming into international currency.

Further, due to the lack of an exchange rate mechanism determined by the market, COMECON members frequently went into disputes over the issue unifying exchange rates to achieve the convertibility of their local currencies. By the end of the 1950s, the members proposed the "Berlin Solution", with the purpose of converting expenses calculated in local currencies into rubles and other currencies. In 1973, the Marx City Agreement was reached to determine the exchange and convertibility rates among the local currencies as well as between the local currencies and the ruble. Nevertheless, neither agreements were able to address the issue of coordination in determining exchange rates among COMECON member states and between COMECON and other countries in the world (in particular the US), because neither had touched upon the fundamental issues of free convertibility among currencies and exchange rate determination mechanism.

1.12 Legacies of the Ruble Zone

Prevalent Inner-Bloc contradictions made the members of COMECON to realize that they were prejudiced by the Soviet-dominated system. Before the breakdown of the Soviet Block, a number of Ruble Zone countries jointed the western monetary system in succession. Among them, Romania, Hungary and Poland joined the IMF in 1972, 1982, and 1986 respectively. In two to three years following the collapse of the Soviet Block, other member countries joined the IMF. On June 28, 1991, the international monetary system that had run parallel to the Bretton Woods System for over forty decade eventually dissolved in Hungary.

Today, the Soviet Bloc, COMECON, as well as the Ruble Zone had faded into obscurity and became objects of historical studies and were, in most cases, viewed negatively by people. Yet, as the world is again swept by a global financial crisis originated from the capitalist world and people are having a hard time to find the way out, they begin to review this part of history and tried to explore the deep causes for the crisis at the moment.

In our view the COMECON and the Ruble Zone as the institution of the past that affected lives of hundreds of million people had left considerable legacy as they had impacted, since the 1990s, not only the political configuration and trends of ideology in the world, but also the global economic and financial structure.

In terms of the real economy, the disintegration of the COMECON released hundreds of millions cheap and well-trained labor. With the rising of Asian economies like China and India and their integration into the global economy, the global labor market underwent transformations that greatly changed the relations of strength between capital and labor. In this way, global division of labor had been restructured (we will discuss in detail in Sect. 9 of Chap. 3), and developed into a situation of severe global economic imbalance of today.

When it comes to the areas of monetary and financial system, the collapse of the Ruble Zone and the defection of the member states to the Bretton Woods system had undoubtedly instilled new vitality into the US dollar that popped it up under the multiple attacks from the local currency of developed economies including Deutsch mark, pound sterling and Japanese Yen. At the same time, the rapid growth of the emerging economies like China and India in Asia and their "dollarization" to various extend had created great demands on the dollar and therefore helped strengthen the hegemonic status of the latter. While their economies started to take off with new momentum, former COMECON members and emerging economies like China and India with no exception had made the US dollar the "anchor" for their currencies, thus reinvigorating the Bretton Woods system that would otherwise have declined with faded glory. In other words, without those changes, the so-called "Bretton Woods II" would not be spoken of, and the US would not have abused its privileges as the currency issuing country which led to serious global economic imbalances and the global financial crisis.

1.13 Monetary Hegemony from the Perspective of International Public Goods

World currency, may it be pound sterling or the US dollar, is manifestation of the imbalances and inequality of the world economy (and even transferable ruble represented the similar token of inequality to some extent). To review the rise and fall of monetary hegemony, one has to render a fair argument. Monetary hegemony is not without merits. For example, with regard to providing public goods, it plays positive roles to an certain extent during different periods.

Kindleberger talked about the important role of international hegemony in providing public goods in the earlier times when he raised the well-known theory of "hegemonic stability". In his view (Kindleberger 1986), international public goods fall into three categories: World peace, how to restore and maintain it; international public goods in economic areas, including an open trade system, global currency and fixed exchange rate, etc., and the third kind of public goods refers to the maintenance of an open market.[15] He has pointed out that to maintain stability of the world economy requires some sort of "stabilizer," i.e. one certain country needs to take the responsibility to provide market for distress merchandise, and ensure smooth circulation of capital (instead of reverse circulation), and when the currency system was stagnant and inactive, this country would be able to introduce some kind of discount mechanism to guarantee solvency; the hegemon also has to supervise the structure of exchange rates and somehow coordinate countries' national monetary policies. Without the hegemon, international economic system will be subject to constant instability and chaos.[16]

Robert Gilpin developed Kindleberger's concept into the comprehensive hegemonic stability theory.[17] Gilpin believes that the hegemon that enjoys absolute advantage in politics, economy, military power and science and technology will make other countries acknowledge the international order it has established and thus achieve stability and prosperity of the international system through providing public goods to the international community, i.e., stable international monetary system, an open trade system, a reliable security system and efficient international aid system, etc.

From the perspective of international public goods, we can see that (monetary) hegemony may play a positive role in the era of globalization, because on the one hand, globalization is rapidly widening and deepening and on the other hand, mechanism of global governance and the related international public goods was in short supply. The following are major causes of such insufficiencies:

(1) Economic globalization has seen tremendous increase in population migration across the world that has created unprecedented demand on international public security and safety, and services in public health.
(2) Cross-border migration thus made the prevention and treatment of epidemic disease and even education and services new types of international public goods.
(3) With economic globalization, the scope of trans-boundary economic activities (international investment, international trade of commodities and services) have been expanding in scope and scale, exerting new demands for international

[15]Kindleberger (1986).
[16]Kindleberger (1986).
[17]Gilpin (1989).

public security and safety, economic security, international legal system, economic order, public facilities, prevention and treatment of animal and plant diseases and export control of animals and plants, global cooperation in environmental protection and solving issues related to climate change.

(4) As economic globalization has made domestic markets international and vice versa, an international economic order with fair trading and competition is in earnest demand.

(5) With economic globalization leading to growing cross-border migration, technological advancement, rapid proliferation of information, there have been higher demands for control of cross -border criminal activities, production and proliferation of cutting-edge military weapons, trans-boundary environmental pollution, international speculation, as well as the disseminating of the real information.[18]

In view of the society in general, there has always been an insufficient private supply of positive externalities and excessive supply of negative externalities, which is attributable to the shortage of supply of governance, or public goods as a result of the dilemma of collective action (Olson 1996).[19]

Olson proposed ways of solving this dilemma. One way is to reduce the members of the group or to allow them to form the "federation group". The less the members, the more the members are inclined to form interest groups. Less members also means bigger shares of the interest and the same time, the less the members of common interest become, the lower the cost of mutual supervision and coordination is, therefore it would be easier for members to act collectively other than "free riding". Out of certain shared interests, smaller groups may go into a bigger group, i.e. the "federation group". Another way is to provide "selective incentives", in other words, by punishing the members that do not shoulder the cost of collective action, or by providing incentives of the nature of "private goods": go those contribute to the collective interests, to coerce or induce the people to join the interest groups. The third major method is to allow the political entrepreneurs or leaders to organize the collective action of the potential members and greatly increase the possibility of the forming interest groups. When members had vastly different interests resulting from collection action, with one entity may gain over half of the collective interests, the collection action is more likely to happen since the latter will still profit from the action even it takes up the total cost. An example for this is the "hegemonic stability" theory. The hegemon, with superiority in politics, military affairs and economy is able to achieve absolute gain by providing international public goods without the participation of the other nations. Often acting as the "leader" or "the leading party", the hegemon has the propensity of playing the role of the leader in making international rules or system in politics, military affairs and economy due to its special advantage concerning its gains.

---

[18]Zeng and Wu (2006).

[19]Mancur Olson (1996).

We mentioned the "positive role" of the currency hegemony and acknowledged its appropriate status does not necessarily mean that we want to justify the dominance of the hegemonic power or even condone its imposing behavior. Actually we hope to emphasize an often neglected point if we approach the monetary hegemony from different angles: the long-existence of monetary hegemony and the acknowledgement of its power by those who are subject to its influence are attributable to a complex of reasons; and to a certain extent, it benefited the countries by the provision of international public goods. We also tend to note, based on the discussion of those factors, that when people try to pursue the "freedom" by getting rid of the monetary hegemony of a certain currency, they need to first find the substitute of such an international public good. To go one step further, anyone who wants to acquire the distribution power in the international monetary system has to first think about its own capability of providing such an international public good. There is no free lunch in this world.

The international monetary system after the collapse of the Bretton Woods system is generally called the "Era of the Jamaica Agreement", with the floating exchange rate mechanism as the main feature.

References

Chernyshoff N, Jacks DS, Taylor AM (2009) Stuck on gold: real exchange rate volatility and the rise and fall of the gold standard, 1875–1939. J Int Econ 77(2):195–205

Daudin G, Morys M, O'Rourke KH (2008) Globalization, 1870-1914. IIIS Discussion Paper No. 250

Eichengreen B (1992) Golder fetters: the gold standard and the great depression: 1919–1939, Oxford University Press

Estevadeordal A, Brian F, Alan MT (2003) The rise and fall of world trade: 1870–1913. Quart J Econ 118(2):359–407

Gilpin Robert (1989) The political economy of international relations (Translated). Economic Science Press, Beijing

Giovannini A (1986) Rules of the game during the international gold standard: England and Germany. J Int Money and Finance 5:4467–483

Kennedy P (1987) The rise and fall of the great powers: economic change and military conflict from 1500 to 2000. Random House, New York, p 151

Kennedy P (1990) The rise and fall of the great powers: economic change and military conflict from 1500 to 2000. Random House, 1987, New York, P 151

Kindleberger C (1986) International public goods without international government. Am Econ Rev 76(1):1–13

Maddison A (2001) The world economy: a millennial perspective. OECD, Paris

Maddison A (2006) The world economy: volume 1: a millennial perspective; volume 2: historical statistics, OECD

Mason ES, Asher RE (1973) The world bank since the bretton woods, Washing D.C, p 29

Meissner CM (2002) A new world order: explaining the emergence of the gold standard. NBER Working Paper 9233

Meissner CM (2010) Surplus reversals in large nations: the cases of france and great britain in the interwar period. In: Claessens S, Evenett S, Hoekman B (eds) Rebalancing the global economy: a primer for policymaking, Centre for Economic Policy Research, pp 61–70

Obstfeld M, Taylor A (2004) Global capital markets: integration, crisis and growth. Cambridge University Press, Cambridge

Officer L (2008) Gold Standard, EH. Net Encyclopedia. In: Whaples R, http://eh.net/encyclopedia/article/officer.gold.standard

Olson M (1996) The logic of collective action (chinese translation). Shanghai SDX Joint Publishing Company & Shanghai People's Publishing House, Shanghai

Taylor AM (1996) International capital mobility in history: the saving-investment relationship. NBER Working Paper, No.5743

Williams J (1944) Theses on postwar monetary plan, New York

Zeng G, Wu Q (2006) Several questions regarding provision of international public goods. Econ Rev vol 1

Chapter 2
The Warring States

Develop alternatives to US Treasuries as the dominant reserve asset, thereby accelerating the inevitable transition to a multipolar system. In particular, we recommend the issuance of mutually guaranteed European bonds. Also necessary (though in the more distant future) are opening of the Chinese capital account, convertibility of the yuan, and development of a yuan bond market.

—Farhi, Gourinchas and Rey[1]

People usually mention the international monetary system after the collapse of the Bretton Woods system by the term of "the Era of the Jamaica Agreement" and describe its major feature as the floating exchange rate mechanism. Though not incorrect, those terms fail to capture the reality properly when trying to trace the evolution of the international monetary system by following the transition of the exchange rate system only. In our view, the situation and transformation of the reserve currencies that reflects the essential properties of the monetary system should be regarded as the major clue of the trends of the system; in this case, the main feature of the Era of the Jamaica Agreement is the diversification of currency reserve.

Any type of international monetary system comprises of three key elements: the choice of the reserve currency (either one or multitude kind); the exchange rate arrangements among the reserve currencies and between the reserve currency and the non-reserve currencies (fixed, pegged, floating, or other); the adjustment mechanism worked out by countries to deal with the international imbalances (automatic adjustment, or adjustment through specific regulations and channels). The structure of the monetary system was built on the choice of the reserve currency and the exchange rate arrangement and adjustment for international balance of payment are subject to the different reserve currencies. In this sense, the reserve currency is the crux of the international monetary system and its situation and transformation is more closely tied to the nature of the monetary system.

---

[1]Translator's note: Farhi (2011).

Y. Li and X. Zhang, *Imbalance and Rebalance*,
https://doi.org/10.1007/978-981-10-6150-9_2

Accordingly, if we approach the evolution of the international monetary system from the perspective of the composite of the international reserve currency and its transformation, we will find that the reform of the monetary system that moving towards the diversification of the reserve currency dated back to as early as the first dollar crisis. This process, going through the breakdown of the Bretton Woods system, the global economic crisis in the 1980s, the Asia financial crisis in the 1990s and the emergence of the Euro at the end of the 1990s, and till the turbulent global financial crisis of today, has become an irreversible trend. In other words, the proposal of diversifying the reserve currency, deemed as a major part of the international monetary system reform after the current financial crisis, was actually in existence as early as the 1970s, and it has been acknowledged widely as a de facto consensus within the international community.

Today, the international community has entered the "period of the warring states" in the real sense. When the multipolar reserve currency system has become the reality, and it will be further consolidated in the foreseeable future, the reform of the international system will undoubtedly be shifted towards searching for a coordinating mechanism within the multi-currency reserve system and the creation of new international governance.

2.1 Diversification of the Reserve: Creation of SDR

As is mentioned before, one of the fundamental contradictions of the dollar dominance of international reserve is that the dollar could not be provided to the international community steadily without hurting its status (the dollar has to be depreciated at home and abroad). Being aware of the contradiction, the international community had have in an earlier time made efforts to search for a more reasonable and efficient monetary system, which were marked by the creation of the Special Drawing Right and the establishment of the Euro Zone.

People started to realize that the volume and growth of the reserve asset should play an active role in reflecting the need of the growth of global trade and economy, rather than being a passive dependent of the cumulative surplus from the international balance. To put it in another way, the international community should proactively and predicatively increase the international reserve with elasticity in response to the needs brought about by the increase in the global economy, international trade and investment. The IMF is expected to facilitate this transition and become the major provider of international fluidity that will be provided in the form of conditional financial assistance or by creating new fluidity. After as long as five-year's repeated consultation, the IMF officially declared its plan for introduction SDR, and completed the first distribution in 1970.

With its well-thought design produced by the great efforts of a group of the world's top experts, and despite of the promotional efforts by the IMF, the SDR, designed to be the world reserve asset that will replace gold and the dollar (as well as other sovereign or regional currency), has been far from fulfilling its original goal when it was contrived. Moreover, with the deepening of globalization, the goal appears to become far more distant as the world advances towards the other direction.

This is because the SDR is lacking in some essential elements as international reserve currency. Today, any currency in circulation is credit currency. In reality, any credit currency, in order to be widely accepted, has to meet both the necessary and sufficient conditions, namely, it has to be backed by the credit of a state, and therefore is conferred legal authority to enforce its circulation, and it requires the currency authorities that are specially established to deal with the affairs related to circulation and maintain the stability of its value by effective macro-regulation. If we take a look at the SDR, there is no doubt that it neither possesses the credit nor has a pricing mechanism. Although the SDR's value is determined by a basket of four sovereign currencies, it is still subject to the economic and financial situations of the "central" states, whose macro regulatory and control policies might exert unfavorable impact on other countries out of their own national interests. In this sense, the SDR standard is no other than the dollar standard with a few adjustments.

This deficiency was clearly manifested in the distribution mechanism of the SDR. Due to the lack of the elements to become credit currency, it can only be distributed within the framework of common drawing right. The draft on the distribution of the 250 billion SDR in US dollar promulgated by the IMF on July, 2009 is another manifestation of the fact that the SDR can only comply with the basic mechanism of the common drawing right. The paradoxical issue reveals the fact that if SDR is the extension or expansion of the common drawing right, then it contravenes the original purpose of creating the SDR; but if the SDR is distributed on the basis or other mechanism, i.e., the demands of the countries for reserves, then it would obviously be irrational terms of economy, and therefore is not feasible.

In essence, to give the full play to the SDR, some supranational central bank has to be established, preceded by a world that was "harmonized into one unity". No doubt there is still a long way to go and persistent efforts are needed to meet this condition.

2.2 Diversification of Reserve Currency: The Emergence of the Euro

European nations had for a long time taken the lead in human civilization since the Industrial Revolution. However, the scourges the two world wars in the first half of the twentieth century had ravaged the once rich and prosperous continent. The old capitalist powers like the UK, France, Germany and Italy had to step down into the "Second World," and not without distress they witnessed the emerging of the United States, a young nation, in the center stage with triumph and vitality.

Yet, with the end of the WWII, the Europeans who were good at drawing lessons from the past had risen from the grievances and started to take active measures to carry forward the mission of unification—a dream pursued by several generations of the Europeans. This time however, the unifying attempts were not in the form of military conquests like those achieved by Charlemagne and Napoleon but instead, were carried out over the past half century through the making of a series of landmark multilateral treaties, a process coming to fruition with the creation of the Euro.

Unlike what happened in the invention of the SDR, efforts to unify European currencies had been regional all along and focused on creating a single regional currency to protect the interests of nations of the region. Back in the 1950s, the process of European unification began after political consensus had been reached on broad basis. In 1950, the European Payment Union was established. In March, 1957, six western European nations signed the Treaty establishing the European Economic Community (EC) and the Treaty establishing the European Atomic Energy Community (commonly referred to as the Treaties of Rome), which gave birth to the European Community. At the end of the 1960s, the EC, after establishing the tariff union and adopting the common agricultural policies, took steps to promote the liberalization of labor and movement of capital. This is at this moment when the issue of unifying the currency made to the agenda. In 1972, the six EC member states initiated a series of arrangements of currencies exchange rates including the Snake Floating system to deal with the drastic fluctuations of the exchanges rates of the European currencies against the US dollar. In 1979, the EC nations established the "European Monetary System" (EMS), and eventually achieved the unification of the market in 1993 with the creating of the "European Monetary Unit" (EU). In January, 1999, the Euro was born. The significance of the creation of the Euro may be put in various ways; as for the author of the book, no comment is more insightful than one made by Jacques Chirac, the former French president: "Adoption of the Europe is a great transformation achieved without guns and barrels, and it has freed us from the manipulation of the others".

Admittedly, despite of the setbacks, hardships in the past, the unfulfilled goals have yet to accomplish, and no matter what difficulties and obstacles will appear in the future, the unification of Europe and emergence of the Euro will be recognized as mankind's great and so far successful trial to achieve regional unification through peaceful and multilateral means. After all, one cannot fail to see that one of the paramount initial goals set by the architects of the project has been accomplished: wars among European nations have become "not only unimaginable, but also impossible".[2]

Unlike the SDR, the Euro is an international currency that can pose real challenge to the US dollar.

First of all, the credit of the Euro is built on the truly enormous strength of the real economy in the region of the European Union. By 2012, the twenty eight

[2]Remarks made by Robert Shumann, the French Foreign Minister (1948–1953).

member states (EU 28) remains the world's No.1 economy with a total population of 510 million and GDP of $16.6 trillion. At the same time, the EU28 remains the world's top destination for import and export of goods and services excluding inner-regional trade, and it has maintained trade surplus for a long time. It is especially worth emphasizing that although Europe is still undergoing debt crisis, according to statistics from the Global Economic Outlook by the IMF, the structural deficit rate and total government debt rate are 2.3 and 93.0%, better than those of the US (6.3 and 102.7%) and Japan (9.2 and 238.0%) during the same period. Apparently, as an economic entity, the EU is doing much better than the US in terms of external balance and fiscal situation. Besides, Europe is also the world's leader in areas such as space industry, communications, environmental protection, machinery manufacturing, on par with the United States.

Secondly, from the very beginning, the European Central Bank (ECB) has maintained independence and adopted unique concepts relating to monetary operating policies, a practice that makes the EU distinctively different from the United States. The ECB, thanks to its close ties with the German Federal Bank, ranks the top in the world when it comes to maintaining independence in human resources and the fiscal and policy matters. There is no denying that due to the unique mechanism of organizing and the complex political, economic and social ramifications, the ECB's fiscal foundation is comparatively weak, rendering it incapable of dealing with external asymmetrical shocks. Nevertheless, it is this incapacity itself that has, to the greatest extent, prevented the member states from "being tempted" to utilize the ECB to finance the government's fiscal deficits, therefore reducing the "moral hazard" in operation of the monetary policies to the minimum. According to Article 105 of the Treaty on European Union (or the Maastricht Treaty), "The primary objective of the European System of Central Banks ESCB shall be to maintain price stability," and only in compliance with this objective shall the ECB support the general economic goals of the Community in aspects like creating jobs and promoting economic growth. The stipulation has restrained the Bank from making outstanding performances in dealing with crisis, like the case in the current financial crisis. On the other hand, however, the primacy of price stability over everything else is what makes the euro remain immensely popular among other countries even when the euro zone was impacted severely by sovereign debt crisis in many EU countries. To put it in another way, it may be difficult for the euro, a regional currency, and the ECB with its operation mechanism to fully play the role of regulating and supervising the regional economy, but since the euro, as an international currency, can better meet the demand for independence, stability, responsibility and transparency than other currencies, it came out of the crisis as strong as it used to be. For example, as was estimated by the Bank for International Settlements (BIS), proportion of the euro in the global reserve currencies rose from 26.4 to 26.5% between 2008 and 2010, whereas during the same period, that of the US dollar decreased from 64.1 to 62.1%. The rise and fall demonstrates clearly the degrees preferences towards the two currencies.

Other than the aforementioned factors, one has to note that the European sovereign debt crisis that broke out in 2010 and gradually swept across the whole region not only has exposed a myriad of contradictions and problems resulting from the imbalanced development in politics, economy and finance among the European nations, but also prompted those countries to take further steps in policy coordination and regional cooperation. Here is an example: during the initial stage of the crisis, in May 2010, the Community established the European Financial Stability Facility (EFSF) and the European Financial Stability Mechanism, who helped to raise the funds totaling 440 billion and 60 billion Euro respectively and supplied fluidity to countries including Greece, Ireland and Portugal, making remarkable contributions to lifting them out of their fiscal difficulties. Later on, after ratifying the revision of the Treaty of Lisbon, the two contingency organizations was replaced by a standing relief mechanism—the European Stability Mechanism (ESM), with the start-up fund of 80 billion Euros and lending scale as much as 500 billion Euros. As an inter-governmental organization founded on international treaties, the primary function of the ESM is to maintain the stability of the financial system of Europe (mostly the Euro Zone) by providing fluidity and other supports. From a certain perspective, the ESM seems to evolve into the "IMF" of Europe.

The above analysis shows that during more than one decade since its emergence, the Euro has demonstrated tremendous vitality as it has been widely used in many areas such as international foreign currency reserve, trade, investment, and is becoming the arch rival of the dollar thanks to the economic and political strength and regional integration of Europe. However, despite of the vigor it has shown so far, it is now still unable to shake the hegemon of the dollar for quite a long time in future, due to the disparities in the comprehensive national strength and potentials for economic growth, Europe's internal unbalanced development, low-level integration and other factors like the "inertia" of the international currency when it is use.

2.3 Diversification of Reserve Currency: The Demand of Asia

The evolution of the international monetary system tells us that the alternation of the international reserve has always been preceded by the waning and waxing of the economic strength of the issuing country. The pound sterling lost its hegemonic status like falling flowers because the UK has been overtaken by the US as early as 1872. The Euro has become the international currency second to the US dollar due to the fact that the aggregate economic volume of the Euro Zone ranked the top by the end of the twentieth century. Given this tendency, when the aggregate economic volume of Asia surpasses that of the Europe and the US as the top one, it is just natural for Asia to seek the appropriate status in the international monetary system.

Between 2004 and 2007, the proportion of the GDP of Asia to the global GDP had risen to 35%, whereas during the same period that of the US and the Euro Zone was below 50%. Nevertheless, as Table 2.1 illustrates the shares of the major

Table 2.1 The share of the major currencies in the currency zones (Unit: %)

Time (Year)	The dollar zone		The euro zone		The yen zone		The pound zone		Other	Total (1 billion US dollars)
	The US	Total	The euro zone	Total	Japan	Total	The UK	Total		
1970–1974	33.8	54.5	14.1	27.3	8.7	8.7	4.4	7.2	2.2	3675
1975–1979	29.0	50.5	15.2	30.9	10.5	11.9	4.1	5.3	1.3	7074
1980–1984	30.8	51.8	12.7	25.4	10.7	12.7	4.5	6.4	3.6	10,729
1985–1989	30.2	48.9	12.6	22.0	14.8	15.3	4.3	5.8	8.0	15,753
1990–1994	26.2	45.9	13.5	28.0	16.0	16.3	4.2	5.7	4.1	24,101
1995–1999	27.6	50.3	14.8	26.2	14.9	16.7	4.4	4.9	2.0	29,946
2000–2004	30.2	48.6	21.5	30.1	12.3	14.4	4.8	5.1	1.7	34,929
2005–2007	26.8	48.4	22.2	33.4	9.0	9.6	5.0	6.7	1.9	49,046

Note Calculated in terms of GDP (market foreign exchange rate, denominated in dollars)
Source Masahiro Kawai, International Monetary System and East Asia Monetary Cooperation, Jilin University Press, 2009

currencies in monetary zone, and it suggests that in terms of the areas covered by reserve currency, the dollar still assumed the predominant role, tailed by the Euro. The aggregate GDP of the two areas accounted for 81.8% of the global GDP by the end of 2007; in comparison, the currencies in Asia (mainly the Japanese Yen) accounted for only 9.6% of the global GDP. In this view, Asia is "marginalized" by the current international monetary system.

The severe mismatch between the ratios of GDP and the regional currency coverage, especially the lack of predominant regional currency has put the Asia currencies in the periphery, therefore making the regional economy and financial system prone to the concurrency and impact of the international economy and financial fluctuation. Looking back on economic and financial chaos experienced by Asian countries as the result of the Asian Financial Crisis in 1997 and the financial crisis this time, people will see clearly the various issues cause by the peripherization. Asian countries come to realize painfully that if such kind of peripherization remains unchanged, the regional economy and finance will inevitably be disturbed and harmed by the macro—policies of the US and European countries at the center. For this reason, for Asian countries, and East Asian countries in particular, it is a rational choice in their common interests to seek closer monetary and financial cooperation.

And the trend is moving towards a reasonable direction.

At the ASEAN Summit in 1997, reflecting on the lessons drawn from the Southeast Asian financial crisis by countries in the region, especially the ASEAN nations, Prime Minister of Malaysia, Mahatir Mohamad was the first to propose the idea of the "Zone of Asian Yuan". During the APEC meeting in 2001 in Shanghai, Robert Mundell, known as the Father of euro, presented his views on the future evolution of the international monetary system: "The world will see the emergence of three major currency zones—the Euro Zone, the Dollar Zone and the Asia Currency Zone (the Zone of Asian Yuan)". His remarks drew positive reactions from many East Asian countries. In early 2006, the Asian Development Bank (ADB) introduced a conceptualized currency token called "Asia Currency Unit (ACU)". Similar to the predecessor of the euro, the "Europe Currency Unit," it is not the real currency that can be circulated, but rather a virtual currency weighted by factors including the currency values of some Asian countries, their GDP and scale of trade, etc. It was planned that the ADB would determine its exchange rates with the dollar and euro, which will be publicized on the web to measure the fluctuation of the exchange rates and the controllability of the fluctuation; related countries can adjust the financial and monetary policies to move the monetary mechanism towards the ACU, therefore laying the foundation for the official adaptation of the Asian Yuan. However, due to political and technological controversies centering on issues like the choice of financial and the weights assigned to them, the plan has been prolonged indefinitely.

Despite of the abortion of the proposal of introducing the Asian Yuan, countries in Asia, especially in East Asia never stop taking further steps in cooperation in monetary and financial areas.

In September 1997, Japan proposed the idea of establishing the "Asian Monetary Fund" at the IMF and ABD meeting. The attempt failed due to the opposition from the US and IMF and the doubts raised by some East Asian countries, but the idea of introduction multi-layer monetary and financial cooperation in the region was put on the agenda of various countries.

In August, 1997, five ASEAN countries (Indonesia, Malaysia, the Philippines, Singapore and Thailand) initiated the ASEAN Swap Arrangement (ASA). In November, 1999, the ASEAN Plus Three Summit (ten ASEAN countries plus China, Japan and Korea) issued the Joint Statement on East Asia Cooperation at the 3rd ASEAN Plus Three Summit, promising to further strengthen dialogue, coordination and cooperation in financial, monetary and fiscal policies. In the spirit of the agreement, in May, 2000, at the ASEAN Plus Three Finance Minister's Meeting at Chiang Mai, Thailand issued the Chiang Mai Initiative, which mapped out plans for future cooperation including facilitating exchanges of statistics and information of capital movement, setting up networks for bilateral currency swap and securities trade, with an effort to improve the market for direct foreign exchange trading of local currencies and establish a financial settlement system to further expand trade among Asian countries using local currencies. In May, 2008, the ASEAN Plus Three decided to establish the common foreign exchange reserves fund worth $ 80 billion. In February, 2009, the ASEAN Plus Three Finance Ministers special meeting issued the Action Plan to Restore Economic and Financial Stability of the

Asian Region, which increased the fund to $120 billion. The meeting also proposed to establish an independent regional supervision entity and allow countries to use part of the foreign exchange reserve for special purposes. The Action Plan became the platform for conducting monetary and financial cooperation among Asian countries at a higher level.

Asian financial cooperation is also making progress. In June, 2002, Thailand initiated the idea of "Asian Bond Market" at the first Asian Cooperation and Dialogue (ACD). In August the same year, at the Executives' Meeting of East Asia Pacific Central Banks (EMEAP), Thailand made a further proposal to set up the Asian Bond Market Fund, which received positive response from East Asian countries and the whole region as well. In September the same year, China's Hong Kong raised the Asian Bond Market Initiative (ABMI) at the 9th meeting of ASEAN finance ministers, which was aimed at developing the regional market for the securitization of capital and credit guarantee. The ABMI was later endorsed by the meeting of ASEAN Plus Three Finance Ministers held in August, 2003. The blueprint outlined by the ABMI for the development of Asian bond market is to be completed in three steps during the three time periods of 2003–2005, 2005–2008 and 2008 to present. According to the plan, the third step, which is in process now, should facilitate issuance of bonds and securities denominated in local currencies and creation of demands for bonds of such kind, as well as build fundamental framework for the development, monitoring and management of the bond market. The 16th meeting of ASEAN plus Three Finance Ministers and Central Bank Governors held in May, 2013 reviewed and evaluated the ABMI's work under progress and approved the new initiative made by China on promoting the development of financing bonds for infrastructures.

Meanwhile, Asian countries also started to look for mechanisms of policy coordination and surveillance. Up to now, three mechanisms in this regard have been introduced, namely: the Manila Framework Group (November, 1997), the ASEAN Surveillance Process (October, 1998) and the ASEAN + 3 Surveillance Process (November, 1999). Besides, in April, 2011, as one of the institutional arrangements introduced by the multilateral Ching Mai Initiative, the independent ASEAN + 3 Macroeconomic Research Office was established to monitor the economic operation and risk of the financial market within the region, and assess, evaluate and maintain surveillance over the application, operation and usage of funds under the multilateral currency swap initiative. These mechanisms have made remarkable achievements. In May, 2013, the ASEAN Plus Three Meeting of Financial Ministers and Central Bank Governors reviewed and approved the initiative to upgrade the Office to become an international organization, and advised to continue enhancing its role in economic surveillance and assessment, so as to provide consistent support to the effective and multilateral cooperation under the Ching Mai Initiative.

It is true that due to the diversified economic structures and different level of economic development in Asia, the region is still not able to reach the level of currency uniformity within the region as was required by the optimum currency zone, and therefore it still has a long way to go to meet the ideal financial development level and unity. Since the movement of the fundamental elements within the region is still very much under various regulations and interferences, and due to the lack of consensus with regard to moving towards the economic and monetary integration, persistent and huge efforts have to be made before a unified Asian currency will be materialized. However, if the global real economy will still develop along the existing path under the pattern of the declining West and rising East, it is not totally unimaginable to see the emergency of a single regional currency in Asia in the end.

2.4 The Global Imbalances Under the Center-Periphery Structure

Dooley et al. (2003, 2009)[3] believed that the post WWII international monetary system can be characterized as the Bretton Woods System, which is divided into two periods by the Jamaica Agreement of 1974 and named the "Bretton Woods system I" and "Bretton Woods System II".

In their view, under the Bretton System I, the center-periphery structure existed: at the center of world economy was the US that predominated the whole system; other countries constituted the periphery. Being the "center," the US was over-privileged as it was able to provide the world with reserve currencies and convenience of settlement by creating deficit in its current account; on the other hand, it also financed the reconstruction of Europe and Japan as the international credit intermediary, backed by its highly-developed capital market. Meanwhile, as the emerging periphery region and country, Europe (Germany in particular) and Japan both turned to adopt the export-oriented development strategy. To enhance competitiveness, both tried hard to suppress the value of their currencies, and exercised strict capital regulation to prevent over speculation. The result is that the periphery countries had not only accumulated considerable amount of dollar reserve, but also absorbed tremendous US investment.

It is quite conceivable that the necessary condition for maintaining long-term stability of the "center-periphery" structure is the imbalance characterized by the state of having "deficit at the center and surplus at the periphery". As to the imbalance and its sustainability, the economists are divided by diametrically opposite views. One perception tends to believe that such imbalance is unsustainable. For example, the Director of the IMF Research Institute, Roger once remarked, "Although foreign governmental agencies are increasingly buying the American assets, but major entities that hold dollar assets are still private citizens—

[3]The readers need to be reminded that against the backdrop of the 2008 world financial crisis, political leaders including French president Sarkozy and British Prime Minister Brown made a proposal to reconstruct the international monetary system under the framework of G20. This conceptualized new system is also called the "Bretton Woods System II".

not central banks…and once private investors realize that the issue of US trade deficits are difficult to be solved, then the dollar is faced with the possibility of breaking down".[4] However, many people hold opposite views. For example, McKinnon and Schnabl (McKinnon and Schnabl 2004) have pointed out that due to the asymmetrical structure of the dollar system, the US can unilaterally lend to the world's countries unlimitedly, and therefore the system can be maintained. His view was echoed by Dooley et al., who believe that within certain degree, since this imbalance is in the interest of both the center and periphery and may become a win-win situation, the system can remain stable for considerably long time. It is fair to say that the global universal prosperity during the periods of 1950–1970 and the 1990s to the first decade of the 21st century has confirmed the view of the latter.

In our view, the two different opinions seem to be diametrically opposite but are fundamentally the same: they do not, in general worry about the imbalance, even less do they worry about the global imbalance built on the "center country," what they really care about is whether this system can be sustained; and their assessments about the sustainability are made on the linchpin of the universal acceptance of the dollar as a key currency around the world. Those who support the view that the system is sustainable think that the payment capability of the dollar is unlimited, whereas those who hold the opposite view believe that long-term deficit on the current account will damage the payment capability of the US and eventually lead to the collapse of the state of imbalance. And history has shown that the centrality of the US in the structure is what has granted the US the privilege to issue its currency to make up for the gap in the current account for the long term and to a great extent, which makes it possible to maintain the imbalance; nevertheless, if the US keep on abusing its privilege of currency issuance and eventually has to seriously reassess the value of the dollar, the imbalance will not be sustained any longer and will need a total crisis to bring it back to the old trajectory.

The history of the Bretton Woods illustrates the system's trajectory moving from the state of being able to maintain its sustainability to losing its sustainability. Since the time of its establishment, the economic world under the system was a imbalanced world. Its initial pattern featured the match between the trade surplus of the US and the trade deficits of the other countries, and this situation remained for quite a long time. In 1960, the US's foreign debts exceeded the gold reserve, and the imbalanced economic world structure under the Bretton Woods system moved into the situation where the trade deficit of the US has to be matched by the trade surplus of the other countries, and the situation had become increasingly severe. Even in this case, the imbalance was still sustainable until the end of the 1960s. The "Nixon Impact" of 1971 was the turning point in the real sense. In that year, the skyrocketing domestic prices within the US and the plummet of the value of the dollar led the US and other countries to come to realize that it is not worth it to maintain

[4]Speech made by Roger at a meeting sponsored by Crédit Suisse First Boston on March, 15, 2005 in Hong Kong, China.

the dollar standard. It was followed by the global financial crisis that lasted nearly one decade, which eventually led to the collapse of the Bretton Woods system.

The post Jamaica Agreement international monetary system, seen from our analytical perspective that differentiate the international monetary system based on reserve currency, can be called the "multi-reserve monetary system," as against the "Bretton Woods System II" named by Dooley et al., as the appropriateness of the term is still debatable. After the collapse of the Bretton Woods system, in terms of reserve currency, the dollar still plays a dominant role, but its status has been eroded by euro, pound, yen, and other "emerging" currencies; in terms of the arrangement of exchange rate, the fixed exchange rates that was maintained with much efforts under the Bretton Woods system has been replaced by the universal floating exchange rate; as to the mechanism of adjustment of international payments, countries pursue their own policies independently without much coordination. In this view, the post-Bretton Woods system is vastly different from its predecessor; and it is at most a transitory system before a new international monetary system takes shape. The transition, on the other hand, will last for pretty long time when the system will remain a mixture of legacies of the past and elements of the nascent system.

2.5 The Warring States

After the Jamaica Agreement was concluded, the international monetary system has seen variegated factors competing with each other. In view of international reserve currencies, the currencies of developed economies, including Deutschmark, French franc, Japanese yen, and pound sterling begin to play positive roles, prompting the diversification of the international reserve currencies (see Table 2.2). Though the diversification has begun, the predominance of the dollar has not be shaken fundamentally.

Europe has a well-developed and strong real economy and had materialized the common currency, the euro, which is competing with the dollar on a par. Yet, its role in the international monetary system still fall short of those of the UK at the end of the 19th century and the US under the Bretton Woods System. Frankly speaking, in the foreseeable future, either the EU or the euro is still teemed with hidden

Table 2.2 The percentage of major currencies in the international reserve (2000–2012) (Unit: %)

Item	2000	2002	2004	2006	2008	2010	2012
US dollar	71.1	67.1	65.9	65.5	64.1	62.1	62.2
Euro	18.3	23.8	24.8	25.1	26.4	26.5	23.7
Pound sterling	2.8	2.8	3.4	4.4	4	4.2	3.9
Japanese yen	6.1	4.4	3.8	3.1	3.1	3.3	3.9

Source Annual Statistics by BIS

contractions that may threaten its very existence and is full of various uncertainties; in particular, the trend of unification will not remain unchanged and irreversible. On the one hand, the "Sympathetic State" economic model touted by the Europeans has entailed enormous social costs and become the "Eurosclerosis", showing symptoms of high social welfare, high unemployment, and lack of innovation that people are familiar with. "Eurosclerosis" has made Europe's economic growth rate long lagged behind the US and world's average, and subjected the European countries to burden of debts. Unlike the UK and the US in their heyday, today's Europe is declining before ascending to the status of hegemony. Another factor is that the EU is not a unified country with a central government like the US. It is still hard for the EU to make breakthroughs along the path of unification in a number of areas including fiscal policy and taxation, administration, foreign policy, immigration and defense, etc. Admittedly, member states at different phases of economic development and with different historical and cultural background have salient disagreements and contradictions. In this sovereign debt crisis that swept across Europe, the disputes about the obligations and conflicts of interest between the European "central states" like Germany and France, and the "periphery states" like Greece and Ireland has vividly mirrored the inconsonance and system deficiencies in the EU. Such situation would remind us of the advice by made by Kennedy (1990) twenty years ago on the Europe's dim prospect: "If the European Community can really act together, it may well improve its position in the world, both militarily and economically. If it does not—which, given human nature, is the more plausible outcome—its relative decline seems destined to continue".[5]

Compared with the euro, internationalization of the currencies of other countries seems even slower. The pound sterling, Swiss franc, Canadian dollar, Australian dollar, Swedish kroner, New Zealand yuan, Hong Kong dollar and RMB yuan have all steadily improved their status in the international monetary reserve system, nonetheless, as the scale of economy of most of them are too small and their economies are tied to the US and (or) the Europe in various ways, it is even more difficult for the currencies of these countries (regions) to exert much impact on the US dollar.

Notable, also, is that since the 1990s, the reform of the international monetary system has gained new incentives. The new incentives come from the real economy. On the one hand, the old center country like the US and emerging "center countries" such as Europe and Japan have witnessed the slowing down of their economic growth rates; on the other hand, the economies of the emerging markets represented mainly by Asian countries are experiencing rapid economic growth. The transformation in the relative strength of their economies has again drawn the attention of the international society to the "center-periphery" system. Different from the past model, the current "center-periphery" system is dominated by the US, who is the major deficit state; and on the list of the periphery countries, Europe and Japan have been replaced by emerging economies in Asia, including China. It is

[5]Translator's note: Kennedy (1987).

true that the path to resurrection taken by the emerging economies in Asia since the 1990s is quite similar to that was taken by Europe and Japan after the WWII, and similarly it has also led to impressive economic achievements: In nearly two decades, the countries accumulated enormous amounts of trade surplus and foreign reserves, and realized high-speed economic growth. In a similar vein to what had happened in the 1950s, imbalance in international payment, especially the imbalance between China and the US that has always being in the spotlight, had been voluntary policy alternatives by the center and periphery countries out of the consideration of national interests. Likewise, this system is now also under the severe impact, as is seen in the global financial crisis. The US and other countries have been increasingly aware that it is no longer worthwhile to maintain this international monetary system in which the dollar is the primary reserve currency and all countries adopt the floating exchange rates mechanism, and adjust the imbalances of international payments individually in their own ways. It is in this sense that a new round reform of the global monetary and financial system has started.

2.6 Never Forget John Keynes

Talking about further reforming the international monetary system, people have to mention Keynes again. The Bretton Woods System was instituted by rejecting the plan by Keynes, and it was more caused by the power shift between the declining power—the UK, and the rising hegemon—the US, than being a choice based on merits. As Professor Triffin has pointed out, the failure of Keynes' plan was due to political factors, and "in narrower economic view, Keynes was absolutely correct". Triffin (1997) more importantly, as time passes and more problems resulting from the dollar hegemony have been exposed, to reform the international monetary system is becoming an imminent task, more and more people have again turned Keynes' plan and even started to look at it carefully. The reason is, the crux of the plan is to decline the direct fixation of the international reserve currency to the sovereign currency of one single country, and at the same time to avoid the asymmetrical adjustment cost between the creditor (surplus country) and debtor (deficit country). It pinpoints the major deficiencies of the current international monetary system, the problems whose answer have been much sought by the people.

In fact, the ideas embodied in the Keynesian plan appeared as early as the time during the making of the Versailles Treaty after WWI. Payment of war reparation was the top agenda of the Paris Convention, and was the major subject discussed by the famous thesis of Keynes: the *Economic Consequences of the Peace*. With detailed and accurate statistics, Keynes argued that Germany was able to pay about \$10 billion of war indemnity; but in 1921, the allied reparations committee set the amount of indemnity as high as \$33 billion, twice as much as the national income of Germany at the time. Keynes held that such an astronomical amount was unrealistic and as Germany did not have much means of payment, it could only pay the debt by expanding export. Consequently, Germany was overburdened, and moreover, since it was unable to fulfill its obligations of paying war reparations, the economic interests of Britain and France were also harmed. Keynes' presumption was proved by the reality: by the end of 1922, due to the insolvency of Germany, the war reparations had been deferred indefinitely. Under tremendous pressure of the war reparations, the deutschmark was depreciated, which brought about hyperinflation that plunged the Germans into deep agony and sufferings. Keynes in his paper remarked: "I dare to predict that such situation will not be pacified".[6] Unfortunately, it turned out that his prediction became reality, and the unwise reparations arrangement had directly led to Hitler's coming to power and sowed the seeds of disaster of the Second World War.

The painful lessons taught by the grave consequences of the Treaty of Versailles, and the wisdom of Keynes in his analysis of the economic consequences of the Treaty provided guidance for people's dealing with war reparations afterwards. At the end of the WWII, the US did not demand war reparations from Germany; on the contrary, it single-handedly made efforts to establish an international organization (the monetary fund, etc.) to provide loans for defeated countries, and immediately started to implement the Marshall Plan to help the latter to achieve economic recovery. Besides the international political concerns, the plan is also contrived out of the economic considerations. After the end of the war, the great productivity formed in the wartime has to be sustained by tremendous demand. So, if depleted the losers of the war and eventually bankrupt those countries, the domestic production of the US would shrink due to the inadequacy in consumption, which would lead to the slump of economic growth rate and in turn long-term recession; if, the defeated countries would be exempted from war indemnities and instead be provided with loans, European countries would afford the products that they needed and formed the market for the tremendous amount of products exported from the US. By doing so, the US would become the first beneficiary since it would be able to achieve long-term high speed economic growth when it was possible to maintain the balance between supply and demand within the country thanks to the huge and sustainable demand from foreign markets; and moreover, the US would be the only country to enjoy the mint profit for a long time. The indirect benefit lies in the fact that as the primary creditor in Europe and the world on the whole, countries around the world had to be submissive to the US and follow its lead. What happened during the decades after the WWII has proven that the advantages reaped by the US could in no way be overestimated.

The wisdom of Keynes not only provided guidance in solving the issue of settlements, but also the basic ways of thinking in adjusting the asymmetry between the debtors and creditors. These elements constituted the major part of the Keynesian Plan proposed when the Bretton Woods System was initiated.

---

[6]Maynard J. Keynes (2008).

In his very first proposal, Keynes suggested that a global bank (International Clearance Union, ICU) be set up and it would issue its own currency (Bancor), whose value is calculated based on the thirty representative commodities (including gold) and exchanged with other national currencies at fixed rate. All trade accounts should be noted in Bancor, and each country should open a Bancor account with the ICU (the account should be in balance, i.e., with minimum and even zero balance), and at the same has a certain amount of overdraft quota. When a country has large trade deficit (which exceeds half of its overdraft quota in Bancor), it has to pay interests on the account, adjust its national economy, exercise capital control and devaluate its national currency. Conversely, countries that have large trade surplus also need to pay expense of the similar nature, and would be asked to lift restrictions on foreign investment and appreciate the exchange rate of their national currencies. The Keynesian Plan was aimed at exerting concurrent pressure on the surplus and deficit nations to compel them to "clear" the balance on the accounts. This mechanism would be able to facilitate smooth and symmetrical adjustment among the countries and therefore best avoid the global imbalance.

Besides, the Plan would not ask the US or any other country to propose the currency they would like to choose. The essence of the Plan, therefore, was to enable the ICU to use the amount of surplus on the account of the surplus country if that country did not intend to make purchase of commodities or services or overseas investment. The right to use the surplus, though, would be temporary, but so long as a country did not designate the surplus to be used in any way, the ICU would be entitled to use it. As Bancor was not a national currency, the system would not grant any country the privilege to coin the currency. Neither would it allow the global currency to become the hostage of the domestic right of priority that belongs to any country.

2.7 The Ubiquity of the Triffin Dilemma

More than half a century has passed since Professor Triffin made his observation on the dilemma of the "clearance ability" of and "confidence" in the Bretton Woods System, and it has been over four decades since the collapse of the System, nonetheless, we are still living in the world defined by the Triffin Dilemma as the international monetary system is still dominated by the credit currency of some sovereign states (like the US). The only difference, however, is that the dilemma is manifested in a different form. Under the Bretton Woods System, the dilemma had been embodied in the inadequate support to the US dollar by gold (the contradiction between the over issuance of the dollar and the minimum increase of gold currency). Today, the dilemma was shown in inadequacy of fiscal capability to boost the issuance of the dollar securities. In fact, other countries and regions, among them the Euro Zone, that issue reserve currencies, are now faced with the same problem.

The root cause of this problem is, despite of the massive wealth accumulated with the economic growth of a group of countries (mainly the emerging economies and OPEC countries that have trade surplus), those countries are extremely lacking in means of investment with matching scale and both safe and fluid due to the underdevelopment of their domestic financial markets. Globally as far as financial markets are concerned, it seems that only the treasure bonds of the US is able to perform the function of currency pool as it takes the lead in terms of scale of economy, development level, the depth and width of the financial market. Although Europe and Japan may also provide channels of investment for surplus countries (such as the market for government bonds in these countries), they are a far cry from the US in terms of the scale and openness of the market. As the result, the US treasury bonds remains the primary investment alternative of the capital reserves of the surplus countries. Meanwhile and obviously, the value of this type of asset is guaranteed by the income capability (i.e., clearance capability), the stability of the internal and external values of the dollar, and even the potentials of economic growth of the US, and the cumulative effects of such investment will in the long run make the US being bogged down in the quagmire of debts. Research has shown that if a nation's debt goes too high (for example, the debt exceeds 90% of the GDP), it will not only endanger the government's solvency capacity, but also drag slow the economic growth of the country, a fact that is unavoidable when the global liquidity (or reserve capital) depends on a certain type of sovereign currency (Reinhart and Rogoff 2010). It should be acknowledged that the current major countries issuing reserve currencies are not able to sustain the value of their treasury bonds and thus have difficulty to maintain the stability of the value of their currencies. Apparently, the problem described here is merely a new version of the "Triffin Dilemma".

Realty shows that worries arising from the above-mentioned problem are not unjustified. In the recent years, the reserve assets of emerging economies and resource export-oriented countries have not only increased rapidly, but also become increasingly dependent on the US treasury bonds.[7] Such tendencies became even more noticeable against the backdrop of the rampage of the global financial crisis between 2008 and 2009, when there was a sharp surge in demand for hedge-type assets, and even after the Standard & Poor's down-graded the credit-rating of the US treasuries. In fact, whether the acknowledged high-quality bonds of the private sectors (like AAA bonds of enterprises), or sovereign bonds of some European countries are conspicuously weaker than the US treasuries in resisting the systematic risk of the market, and its "safety" will also be severely ruined as the crisis persisted. In the context of the worldwide, rapid shrinkage of the scale of safe assets, the US treasuries was once more sought after by countries across the globe,

---

[7]Farhi et al. (2011) have pointed out that investors' faith in the US treasuries has given the latter the liquidity-premiums enjoyed by the bonds of enterprises (AAA) with the same credit-rating, which means that the US government will pay relatively low interests for the bonds.

and its status as the primary type of international reserve assets was further solidified[8].

China's experience is another example. In the two years between 2008 and 2009, China had doubled its holdings of US treasury bonds, thus replacing Japan as the biggest foreign investor in US's national debt. By the end of September, 2011, of its total $3201.7 billion foreign reserve, nearly 36%, or $1148.3 billion dollars are US treasury bonds, which accounts for ¼ of the national debt of the US held by foreign countries. Actually, internal and external factors including the underdevelopment of China's domestic financial market, low level of internationalization of the RMB and the lack of international investment substitution all contributed to the uniformity of the composite of asset.

At the same time, the overall debt scale of the US government keeps on burgeoning, and its proportion to the country's GDP had climbed from 51% in 1988 to almost 100% in 2010. Since domestic savings from non-public sectors have seen considerable growth, the US became increasingly relied on selling its national debts by issuing treasury bonds and selling them to foreign investors. In terms of absolute volume, between 2002 and 2010, US debts held by foreign investors had increased nearly three times and in the same period, with the biggest increase taking place during the Subprime Mortgage Crisis since 2007 (see Chart 2.1). In relative terms, in 1988, US debts held by foreign investors accounted for only 13% of the national debts, whereas by 2011, the percentage rose to over 30%. Such situation truly posed unprecedented challenges to the sustainability of the US financial revenue and expenditure, as well the prospective economic growth.

It is worth noting that Triffin himself not only revealed the inherent inadequacies of the Bretton Woods System, but also, on the basis of the Keynesian Plan, put forward his own proposal to reform the international monetary system by transforming the IMF into the global central bank in the real sense (Triffin 1997). He perceived that contributions from the member states would be turned into savings of the nature of reserve capital, which would be the foundation of the loan reserves of the IMF, and further "replace the national currencies in the currency reserves of the member states". Meanwhile, to avoid global inflation resulting from lending wantonly, Triffin proposed that the right to loans within the IMF should be decided by the majority vote of the members. These proposals, although not being adopted for political reasons, have provided the theoretical basis for the later creation of the Special Drawing Rights (SDRs) and the so-called "collective currency" like the euro, etc.

---

[8]See "The Decline of Safe Assets," published online by the British *Financial Times* at: http://ftalphaville.ft.com/blog/2011/12/05/778301/the-decline-of-safe-assets/.

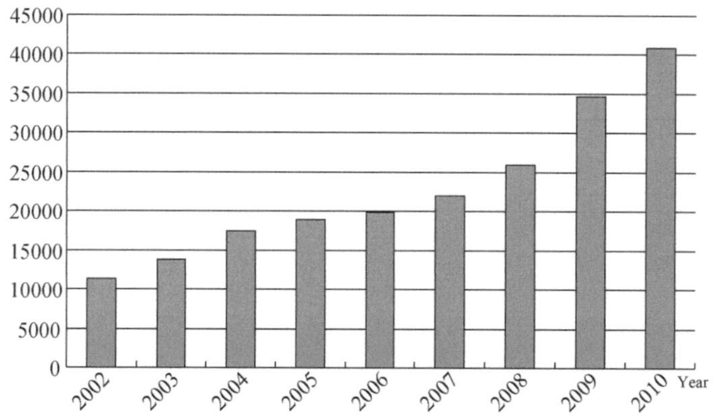

Chart 2.1 US debts held by foreign countries (Unit: billion US$) Year. *Note* the combined sum of long-term securities and short-term securities. *Source* The US Treasury Department

2.8 Break Free from the Myth of Single Currency

As people are counting the deficiencies of the dollar hegemon and talking about to reform the international monetary system, the first thing comes to their minds is to look for another single global currency to replace the dollar. As a matter of fact, among the different reform plans, to create a global, supra-sovereign currency has always been an alternative. Zhou Xiaochuan, the governor of the People's Bank of China remarked in 2009 that the financial crisis was the inevitable outcome of the deficiencies of the international monetary system, and only by introducing a supra-sovereign currency with stable denomination value and issued rationally in adjustable aggregate volume will be able to overcome "the inherent risks of the sovereign credit currency and make it possible to adjust the fluidity across the world".

On unifying the currency, Milton Friedman once incisively observed: "Currency union will persist only with deepened economic and political union". He had intended to say that in an open economy, the free movement of goods, labor and capital has to be guaranteed by a self-disciplined central financial institution and a powerful central bank, and the two institutions, serving as the two pillars to strengthen the currency, should be inseparable and none of them should be missing. If we look at the Euro Zone, as there is only a common central bank and no unified fiscal and monetary institution and not to mention a unified government, the euro as a supra-national currency is destined to be fundamentally inadequate.

What happened with the euro exerts negative impact on the effort to seek a new type of supra-sovereign international currency. In one word, in the current international political and economic situation, reform of the international monetary system is faced with difficulties in at least two aspects: firstly, the current multipolar or even conflicting international political system is not conducive to forging concerted efforts to propel the adoption of a supra-sovereign global currency.

In other words, the current international political, economic environment does not allow for the historical breaking through at the time when the euro was conceived. Secondly, the degree of global economic integration is still a far cry from that at the planning stage of the Euro Zone. When the scale and depth of political and economic integration still fall short of those at the time when the Euro Zone was initiated, it is obviously impossible to establish a unified, global monetary union (Lane 2006).[9]

For any currency to circulate internationally, it has to be backed firmly by credit. For metal currencies, the credit is decided by and guaranteed by the value of the metals; for credit currencies, the value of the currency is decided by the credit of the entity that issues it. Nowadays the dollar and euro are shunned by people mainly due to the undesirable fiscal situation in the US and the Euro Zone, the issuers that determine the value of the currencies—the US and the Euro Zone. Similarly, it is now hard to materialize the conception of a supra-sovereign currency because the credit basis is still missing until the necessary conditions are met by setting up a supranational, "universal" government with the monetary union and independent central bank system to go with it. It is notable, though, that there is still a long way to go before institutions like a supranational government, monetary union and an independent central bank, etc. are established.

Coming all the way to this part of the book, one cannot but think of the vicissitudes through which "Esperanto" has gone. It is well-known that as a "world language" with a history of more than a hundred years, Esperanto is easy to learn, but since it is not indigenously formed and therefore sponsored by any specific national or ethnic culture, few people are using it now. In a similar vein, being "supra-sovereign" is what makes the "so-called" supra-sovereign currency either a success or failure. If no individual country or country bloc tend to actively promote the idea, and countries lack the sincerity to cooperate with each other out of their national interest, what had happened to Esperanto will most probably be repeated in the case of the supra-sovereign currency.

If, as we may assume with certainty, that within the period of several generations, it would be close to impossible to find a single international currency go substitute the dollar, then talking about reforming the international monetary system we should decisively reject the plan of adopting a singular currency and turn to focus on the establishing and improvement of the international monetary system built on a realistic scenario of diversifying the reserve currencies. A report by the World Bank in 2011 projected boldly that by 2025, the six emerging economies will contribute over half of the world's economic growth, thus facilitating the creation of a multi-polar international currency reserve system whereby three major reserve currencies, i.e. the US dollar, euro and RMB in place of the old monetary system dominated by the dollar. Market competition among the major reserve currencies would put restraints on the issuing countries and meanwhile, currencies issuance will have to be supervised, managed and coordinated by international

[9]Lane and Philip (2006).

organizations on a new platform of governance. Former Chinese president Hu Jintao talked about reforming the international monetary system as early as at the G20 Summit in London: "The IMF should enhance and improve its oversight on the macroeconomic policies of various economies, major reserve currency issuing economies in particular, with a special focus on their currency issuing policies; … improve the international monetary system and regulation of reserve currency issuing mechanism, stabilize exchange rates of major reserve currencies, diversify and rationalize the international monetary system". Though some major stakeholders and the once pace-setters of the summit chose to "overlook" this proposal and refuse to put it in the Doha Declaration, such observation has been proved to be insightful and perspicacious by the course of events afterwards.

2.9 Explore New Paths While Salvaging the Crisis

Like blood to life, monetary and financial system is inseparable from running of the economy and therefore revamping of the system is usually carried out gradually and progressively. For any country, the monetary system has always been passed down on as deeply embedded legacy of the past sans earthshaking event takes places like regime change; even in the case of currency reform, proper arrangements will be made to smooth the transition from old to new systems, and even more so in the case of international monetary reform. Even for the Bretton Woods System which looked like a true innovation, the fundamental elements constituting the system had been in place and operation unnoticeably in the half century prior to its establishment; the official introduction of the System was merely the reformation of a long-existing reality making public by multilateral agreements.

Being well aware of the trajectory of the evolution of the financial and monetary system, people need to reject the way of thinking that tends to start everything from scratch at any moment, and set about analyzing the possibilities of solving the current crisis. We need to look at, with insights the measures taken in addressing a number of crises that differ in their manifestation, impacts and duration, and differentiate the policies that failed in practice from the successful ones, so that we will be able to tell what should be discarded and that what be adopted as they have been proved to be feasible and viable. Only after repeated and meticulous analyses, will we be able to identify the crucial factors that suggest patterns of commonality and general tendencies, and explore feasible plans of reform going in the direction pointed out by past experiences.

As the world enters the 21st century, it has witnessed two major global financial crises that have sweeping impact: the first crisis is the "9.11" incident that happened in 2002, and the other one is the ongoing crisis that began in March, 2001. As both broke out in the US, which is also the epicenter of the crises, it will be illuminating if we take a look at the measures taken by the monetary authorities of the US to tackle the challenges.

2.10 Dealing with the "9.11" Incident: The System of Payment and Clearance Is the Key

On the day of "9.11", Alan Greenspan, the then Chairman of the US Federal Reserve was flying back to Washington DC on a Swissair flight. In his memoir, Greenspan recalled his thoughts at the moment: "The possible economic crises were all too evident. The worst, which I thought highly unlikely, would be a collapse of the financial system. The Federal Reserve is in charge of the electronic payment systems that transfer more than $4 trillion a day in money and securities between banks all over the country and much of the rest of the world. We'd always thought that if you wanted to cripple the U.S. economy, you'd take out the payment systems. Banks would be forced to fall back on inefficient physical transfers of money. Businesses would resort to barter and IOUs; the level of economic activity across the country could drop like a rock. During the cold war, as a precaution against nuclear attack, the Federal Reserve had built a larger number of redundancies into the communication and computer facilities on which the money system relies. We have all sorts of safeguards so that, for example, the data of one Federal Reserve Bank are backed up at another Federal Reserve Bank hundreds of miles away or in some remote location. In the event of a nuclear attack, we'd be back up and running in all nonirradiated areas very quickly. This system was the one Roger Ferguson, the vice chairman of the Fed, would be taking the necessary steps to keep the world dollar system flowing".[10]

(Introduction, *Alan Greenspan's Memoir: The Age of Turbulence: Adventures in a New World*, 2007).

Greenspan, out of his long time experience working as the governor of the world's largest central bank, emphasizes that it is extremely importance of the safe running of the system of payment, clearing and settlement to maintain the normal and operation of the world monetary system and even the global economic system. In response to the crisis, Greenspan's ranking of priority not only echoed the insights of Keynes in his analysis of the Treaty of Versailles and wisdom on his part while helping to design the post WWII international monetary system, but also put down a footnote by such an international monetary event on the financial functional theory that started to gain popularity in the 1980s.[11]

The system of payment, clearing and settlement refers to the system composed of a number of elements including rules of monetary transfer, institutions providing

---

[10]Translator's Note: Greenspan (2007).

[11]Merton has defined six essential functions of finance: (1) Clearing and settling payments; (2) Pooling resources and subdividing shares; (3) Transferring resources across time and space; (4) Managing risk; (5) Providing information; (6) Providing incentive mechanism; however, most of these functions can be removed or replaced, and the only one that is irreplaceable is the function of clearing and settling payments, which is, in Merton's view, constitutes the most essential and irreplaceable function of financial system. Please see *Finance*, published by the People's University Press, 2004.

services in payment, clearing and settlement, methods that ensure the delivery of order of payment and money settlements, and it is the basic vehicle that carrying out trade in commodities and labor, clearing and settling debs and transferring money. If finance is the blood for the economic body, the system of payment, clearing and settlement is the "plumbing" through which the blood is transmitted, and without saying is of vital importance to economy.

In the economic system, if a party does not have adequate fund to settle the debt from another party within the system and in due time as expected (although at some point after the payment should be due, the party might have adequate fund to pay the debt within the system), there will the risk of liquidity. Risk of liquidity can be regarded as the most crucial risk in the system of payment, clearing and settlement. Risk of liquidity is contagious and lead to default and credit risk; and if the liquidity and credit risk of some players spread in the system, it will result in systematic risk. Liquidity risk will lead to the failure of the system of payment, clearing and settlement, which will in turn directly impact the supply of liquidity. In short, to keep a close watch on and ensure the normal functioning of the system of payment and settlement is just as important as to pay close attention to containment of liquidity risk.

2.11 Dealing with the Current Financial Crisis: Currency Swap Gaining Popularity

If, to say that during the "9.11" Incident period, Greenspan's major concern is whether the cornerstone of the financial infrastructure, the system of payment and settlement would be destroyed, after the breakout of the current financial crisis, what worried Bernanke was the catastrophic consequence under the impact of liquidity problems. Whereas Greenspan generated the standby system, Bernanke turned to the Currency Swap mechanism among central banks.

Currency Swap refers to transaction of trading the principals of two currencies and paying the interest generated from the process within a fixed period of time of according to the agreement reached between two contracting trading parties. As a genre of financial derivative trade created in the financial market in the 1980s, Currency Swap was firstly employed to deal with exchange rate fluctuations, and later is widely applied to a variety of financial trade. Currency Sway can be regarded as a kind of portfolio trading composite of a spot exchange transaction and a reserve, forward exchange transaction. Since the exchange rate of the forward exchange transaction is fixed, both parties of the transaction are no longer subject to the risk brought by changes in the exchange rate. Currency Swap enables the trading entities to use the comparative advantage in different currency markets and fulfill the business goals of reducing financing cost, containing exchange risks and optimizing the structure of assets and liabilities.

At its birth, currency swap has demonstrated its universal applicability. Monetary authorities soon came to realize that like repurchase, currency sway may be used extensively as a tool for publicizing market operation and to adjust and manipulate monetary supply, interest and exchange rate with different maturities. Besides, since it involves a variety of different currencies, currency swap is more suitable to help realize the multitude of goals of the central bank in globalization. In this way, currency sway is endowed with the regulatory role of monetary policy. In the present crisis, the Federal Reserve and the European Central Bank have put in use a large number of new policy tools to push ahead Quantity Easing (QE); most of those measures contain the elements of currency swap.

What is more, through currency swap, central banks are able to instill liquidity denominated in the local currencies of other countries directly into the market. Such practice will in effect allow the member of a currency swap agreement to obtain support from the overall system to their local base currency, or liquidity support, thus improving the liquidity of the global financial system and greatly strengthening the interfering capacity of the central banks.

The US dollar can be used as an example to illustrate the operation of currency swap among central banks and the exchange of national interest involved in the process. Once the central bank of a foreign country begins to implement the swap agreement with the Federal Reserve, it will sell a certain amount of its national currency to the latter at the market exchange rate in exchange for dollar asset. At the same time, the Federal Reserve will deposit the local currency on a special account. Correspondingly, the dollar asset is deposited in a special account opened by the central bank with the Federal Reserve in New York. An agreement will be signed between the Federal Reserve and the central bank regarding the second transaction, and stipulates that the foreign central bank will buy back the same amount of the dollar asset at the same exchange rate on a fixed date in future. In the final analysis the second transaction offsets the first one. When the second transaction is concluded, the central bank will pay market rate interest to the Federal Reserve. One can see that since the exchange rate is fixed in the swap, the real outcome of the transaction is that the Federal Reserve has issued a loan to the other swapper. Once the foreign central bank loans the dollar money obtained from the swap agreement to organizations and agencies outside its jurisdiction, the money will be transferred from the account opened by the central bank with the Federal Reserve at New York to the borrowing bank so that the latter will be able to pay in dollar. The foreign central bank should still fulfill its obligation and pay back the debts to the Federal Reserve. The Federal Reserve does not undertake joint liability, and the foreign central bank will be responsible for the credit risk of the loan.

The foreign currency acquired by the Federal Reserve becomes asset on its balance sheet. Since the swap is done at one fixed exchange rate, the asset's value in dollar will not be affected by the fluctuation of the market exchange rate. The asset in dollar deposited by the foreign central bank with the Federal Reserve in New York is liability on the balance sheet of the Federal Reserve.

2.12 International Monetary System to Be Transformed by Central Banks' Currency Swap

Experience in fighting against the financial crisis over the years has revealed that currency swap not only plays the irreplaceable role in coordinating the actions taken by monetary authorities of various countries, but also plays a unique role in reforming the international monetary system.

The global financial crisis that broke out in the first half of the year 2007 put tremendous stress on the liquidity at the international market. While the unprecedented, extraordinary interfering measures taken by central banks of countries did not yield noticeable results, the Federal Reserve was the first to initiate the currency swap. In November, 2007, the Federal Open Market Commission announced that it had already reached the currency swap agreement with the European Central Bank and the Swiss National Bank, and made the promise of supplying dollar liquidity to overseas dollar market. The agreement was afterwards applied to the central banks of some other countries when the commission announced that it would conduct currency swap with the following central banks: the Australia Reserve Bank, Brazil Central Bank, Bank of Canada, Danish National Bank, Bank of England, European Central Bank, Bank of Japan, Bank of Korea, Central Bank of Mexico, New Zealand Reserve Bank, Norges Bank, Monetary Authority of Singapore, Sweden Central Bank, and Swiss National Bank. The practices tells that the financial monetary systems of the world's major countries have been more closely connected with currency swap spread rapidly among central banks, a dynamic force that further solidify the status of the US dollar by helping it to expand much beyond its traditional dominion.

Honestly speaking, before April the 6th, 2009, the primary purpose of all currency swaps among central banks had been to satisfy the world's financial institutions' demand for US dollar. It is for this reason that major provisions of currency swap agreements have all stated that the Federal Reserve would provide the other central banks with liquidity in large amounts of dollar. The reality is that, under the international monetary system, the US dollar had maintained predominance and it could not be replaced by any other currencies (Zhihao Hu 2011).[12]

Nevertheless, with the deepening of the crisis and the inherent contradictions of international monetary system dominated by dollar were seen more clearly, currency swap no long has to repeat the old story of the dollar taking the opportunity of the "dollar shortage panic" to take over its once lost territories in the monetary system. On April 6th, 2009, the Federal Reserve announced a new currency swap agreement jointly with the central banks of the UK, EU, Japan and Switzerland. The agreement stated that the four central banks would, respectively, provide the Federal Reserve with liquidity in as high as €30 billion, €80 billion, 10,000 billion

[12]Hu Zhihao: "Salvage Europe's Agreement on the Currency Swap with Dollar", *Analytical Reports on Statistics—Current Review*, No.20111202, published by the Chinese Academy of Social Sciences.

Japanese yen, and 40 billion Swiss francs. The agreement marked that starting from that moment, the Federal Reserve was no longer the only central bank that can instill the US dollar into the financial systems of other countries through the local central banks, the central banks of the above-mentioned four countries could also, vice versa, instill pound sterling, euro, Japanese yen and Swiss franc into the financial system of the US through the Federal Reserve. The agreement has changed the old practice of one-way currency transfer in pursuit of dollar, and for the first time in history made the monetary transaction live up to its name. Moreover, it has integrated the money supply mechanism of the major developed economies from within.

Besides, while currency swap centered on the dollar has been carried out between the Federal Reserve and other central banks, bilateral swap between central banks also rules supreme. The most ostensible feature of such swaps is that in the transactions of goods and money among the signature parties, with dollar going out of view, local currencies become the leading player; meanwhile interest rates are determined on real-term trade between the parties. No doubt this pattern of multi-currency reserve will, as the trend moves along, be institutionalized in the end.

The mechanism of currency swap among central banks proves to be the fundamental approach to successfully resolve the "Triffin Dilemma", and it also curb the demand for reserve currencies. Currency swap like this has in fact guaranteed the monetary authorities of the signature countries the access to liquidity in crisis or other emergencies, therefore those authorizes are not as eager to accumulate reserve currencies, which lowers the demand. On the one hand, it has greatly cut the "rent" generated from the coinage tax obtained by countries that issue the reserve currencies; on the other hand, it has tremendously reduced the opportunity cost of holding the reserve currencies, by enabling the countries that do not issue reserve currencies to let their local currencies to partially play the role of reserve currencies. The popularization of the currency swap network has restored the true function of the international monetary system of providing convenience for payment, clearing and settlement. As the result, globally, net costs of circulation will be markedly reduced while the level of well-being will be tremendously lifted.

Of course, bilateral currency swap has its shortcomings and the following are the two major ones: First, while the bilateral agreement creates mutual benefits based on reciprocity, it also has risks, in particular the risk of sovereign default by the debtor. Once such default occurs, even though the creditor holds the collateral (the local currency of the debtor), loss in the value of the collateral may still incur once the local currency of the debtor is depreciated. Also if the collateral is big in scale, it is actually hard to be cleared. Such risks prevent many emerging economies from signing the currency swap agreement with the central banks of the major countries. Secondly, although currency swap is bilateral, once in operation, its innate asymmetrical effect will be apparent. For example, in order to boost its financial system or fight against speculation attack, country B needs liquidity support from country A, but the central bank of country A merely writes the corresponding amount in local currency of country B onto its own balance sheet as the collateral. Obviously, currency swap agreement is, in essence, to boost the global liquidity by means of foreign currency reserve. Since all local currencies are not the reserve currency, the asymmetry will demand a certain amount of reimbursement (i.e., insurance premium) for the reserve currency when it fulfills the goal.

2.13 Central Bank Currency Swap with China at the Center

It should be noted that since the crisis broke out, currency swap between China and other economies has been growing rapidly. Between November, 2008 and the end of October, 2013, the People's Bank of China has signed bilateral currency swap agreements involving over 2000 billion RMB Yuan with monetary authorities of 29 economies including the Republic of Korea, the Hong Kong SAR of China, Malaysia, Belarus, Indonesia, Argentina, Iceland, Singapore, New Zealand, Uzbekistan, Mongolia, Kazakhstan, Thailand, Pakistan, the United Arab Emirates, Turkey, Australia, and Ukraine (see Table 2.3). Afterwards, some of the agreements were extended and the scale of some of the currency swap transactions was enlarged. The central banks' currency swap centering on the RMB has expanded day by day, ushering in the RMB onto the stage of international monetary system in steady steps; at the same time, as China's monetary supplies has been connected more closely with the supply mechanism of other counties, China's monetary policy is bound to meet fresh challenges.

2.14 A New Model of Global Governance Model Is Emerging?

On October 31st, 2013, the world's six major central banks—the Federal Reserve, the European Central Bank, the Swiss National Bank, the Bank of England, the Bank of Canada (previous), and the Bank of Japan issued the press release to announce that they had reached an agreement on long-term multilateral currency swap.[13]

The banks, in their press releases, remarked that they would convert the current, temporary bilateral liquidity swap agreements into long-term agreements, and the current agreements remain effective before further notice. The latest swap arrangement allows any signature bank to provide liquidity in the form of any of the other five major currencies within its jurisdiction, and the two central banks involved should assess the relevant market conditions to guarantee the swap under their own monetary environment.

[13]See the online press release by the six central banks on October 31st, 2013.

Table 2.3 Local currency swap agreements between China and some countries (Regions)

Contractual party	Date	Quota
Republic of Korea	December 12, 2008	180 billion RMB Yuan/38,000 billion Korea Won
Hong Kong Monetary Authority	January 20, 2009	200 billion RMB Yuan/227 billion Hong Kong Dollar
National Bank of Malaysia	February 8, 2009	80 billion RMB Yuan/40 billion Malaysia Ringgit
Belarus	March 11, 2009	20 billion RMB Yuan/8000 billion Belarus Ruble
Indonesia	March 24, 2009	100 billion RMB Yuan/175,000 billion Indonesia Rupiah
Argentina	April 2, 2009	70 billion RMB Yuan/38 billion Argentine Peso
Iceland	June 9, 2010	3.5 billion RMB Yuan/66 billion Iceland Krona
Singapore	July 23, 2010	150 billion RMB Yuan/30 billion Singapore Yuan
New Zealand	April 18, 2011	25 billion RMB Yuan/5 billion New Zealand Yuan
Uzbekistan	April 19, 2011	700 million RMB Yuan
Mongolia	May 6, 2011	5 billion RMB Yuan/1000 billion Tögrög
Kazakhstan	June 13, 2011	7 billion RMB Yuan
Thailand	December 12, 2011	70 billion RMB Yuan/320 billion Thai Baht
Pakistan	December 23, 2011	10 billion RMB Yuan/140 billion Rupee
United Arab Emirates	January 17, 2012	35 billion RMB Yuan/20 billion Emirati Dirham
Turkey	February, 21, 2012	10 billion RMB Yuan/3 billion Turkish Lira
Australia	March 22, 2012	200 billion RMB Yuan/30 billion Australian Dollar
Ukraine	June 26, 2012	15 billion RMB Yuan/19 billion Ukrainian Hryvnia
Brazil	March 26, 2013	190 billion RMB Yuan/60 billion Brazilian Real
The UK	June 22, 2013	200 billion RMB Yuan/20 billion Pound Sterling
Hungary	September 9, 2013	10 billion RMB Yuan/375 billion Hungarian Forint
Albania	September 12, 2013	2 billion RMB Yuan/35.8 billion Albanian Lek
European Central Bank	October 9, 2013	350 billion RMB Yuan/45 billion Euro

Source The People's Bank of China

The press release by the Federal Reserve stated that: the existing provincial agreements have helped to ease the tension caused by currency shortage in the financial market and mitigated the impact of the shortage on the economy; long-term agreement will continue to stabilize liquidity. At the same time, the European Central Bank pointed out that the decision made by the Board of the European Central Bank to conduct currency swap with the other five major banks will ensure that the former will continue, upon request, to supply euro to the other central banks, and when necessary, supply Japanese yen, pound sterling, Swiss franc and Canadian dollar to the other parties of the transaction while continuing to provide dollar liquidity. The European Central Bank also made it clear that in case of any changes in the market, it will adjust the frequency and maturity time of dollar liquidity. It is worth noting that prior to that, the European Central Bank had concluded with the central bank of China a currency swap agreement of US $57.1 billion for a term of three years.

In a press release posted on its official website, the central bank of Canada also said that the currency swap arrangements with other central banks including the Federal Reserve would expire on February 1st, 2014, but with the new agreement in place, the currency swap would be conducted on a much wider scope: the Bank of Canada would not only provide Canadian dollar to the other five central banks, but also supply the five local currencies of the later to financial institutions of Canada; besides, both the Bank of Canada and the Federal Reserve would lift the US$ 30 million quota on the mutually beneficial swap. The Bank of Canada believed that through the currency swap, the central banks concerned would be able to provide funds in special currencies denominated in the five major reserve currencies to banks, enterprises and other institutions within its jurisdiction. It would be wise to put the relevant policies in use before putting the monetary tools in practice. The Bank of Canada would keep a close watch on the development of the global financial market and after setting out the specifics necessary for implementing those tools, enact the currency swap immediately.

The Swiss National Bank indicated that it had decided to conduct cooperation in currency swap with the other five major banks. In line with the multilateral currency swap agreement, the Swiss National Bank would provide Swiss franc to the other major central banks as required and at the same time, would be allowed to provide the Swiss banking system with other currencies other than US dollar on the basis of the existing swap with the US dollar. Of course, in view of the current situation, it is not necessary yet for Switzerland to activate the operations related to currency swap.

The Bank of England pointed out that the current provisional currency swap arrangement had effectively relaxed the tension in the financial market, and relieved the pressure it passed on to real economy. The long-term swap among the major central banks would continue to play the role as the last precaution of the liquidity.

The Bank of Japan held the view that the existing provisional agreement that centered on the Federal Reserve had played a conducive role in helping alleviating the pressure on the financial market and offsetting its impact on the health of the economy. In order to improve the running of Japan's currency market and ensure the stability of the financial market, the Bank of Japan had decided to rectify the current swap agreement and broaden the scope of transaction to the other five central banks, turning the provisional arrangement to the long-term agreement. The long-term agreement just concluded would continue to play its role as the means of providing liquidity with caution. The Bank of Japan also proclaimed that the swap agreement, after the revision, would maintain the interest rate of the loans supplied by funds in dollar.

As the global financial crisis enters the seventh year, the six major central banks jointed upgraded the currency swap, a fact that illustrated the following four tendencies that of paramount importance:

First, since currency swap among the central banks is the last resort in dealing with enormous external impact, upgrading the arrangement of currency swap among the six major central banks portend but two possibilities: either the crisis might further deteriorate in the near future, therefore preemptive methods need to be adopted; or, the major central banks are ready to retreat by adopting "quantitative ease," and in order to face with the possible protracted, seismic impact of undefined nature, it would also be necessary to make preparatory plans.

Secondly, an exclusive, international, supply-demand network of currency reserve that connects the major developed economies with the Federal Reserve at the center has taken shape. The network in fact has integrated the currency supply mechanism of the developed economies from within. An especially noteworthy facto is that currency swap not only involves the movement of currencies among the swappers, but also the exchange rates of those currencies, thus further concerns high-level coordination of the macro-economic policies of the parties of the agreement. In other words, the three essential pillars of a full-fledged international monetary system, namely: selection of reserve currency, exchange rate arrangement and mechanism of international balance of payments, have all been clearly laid out in the network.

Thirdly, since 2011, a series of negotiations among major developed economies has begun one after another, including the negotiations on the Trans-Pacific Partnership (TPP), Transatlantic Trade and Investment Partnership (TTIP), Plurilateral Services Agreement (PSA) and the Strategic Partnership Agreement between the EU and Japan, etc., formulating a network linking the developed economies that transcends the real economy. Together with the aforementioned monetary network, these two virtual and real networks come to form the new, exclusive "Holly Alliance" participated only by the developed economies, and the emerging economies, including China, and the developing countries have again been marginalized.

Fourthly, from the view point of the global governance and as far as real economy and trade are concerned, the existing mechanism of governance, represented by the World Trade Organization would probably be ostracized with the Doha Round negotiation being prolonged infinitely and coming to an eventual end; and in its place the new super free-trade zones such as the TPP would thrive. As far as monetary and currency are concerned, the current institutions of the governance, represented by the IMF, will also be cold shouldered and the various reforms under discussion will at best be carried out equivocally with no substantial results; and eventually these institutions will be replaced by the synchronized and well-coordinated policies and actions taken by the central banks of the developed countries. In this way, the economic "Holly Alliance" built on a super free-trade zones plus a super reserve currency network of supply and demand will dominate the future trajectories of the development of the global governance.

References

Dooley MP, Folkerts-Landau D, Garber P (2003) An Essay on the Revived Bretton Woods System? NBER Working Paper, No.9971

Dooley MP, Folkerts-Landau D, Garber P (2009) Bretton Woods II Still Defines the International Monetary System. NBER Working Paper, No. 14731

Farhi E, Gourinchas PO, Rey H (2011) Reforming the international monetary system. Centre for Economic Policy Research, Washington D.C, p 4. Accessed online at http://scholar.harvard.edu/farhi/books

Greenspan A (2007) The age of turbulence: adventures in a new world. The Penguin Press, New York, pp 2–3

Kennedy P (1987) The rise and fall of the great powers: economic change and military conflict from 1500 to 2000. Random House, New York, p 488

Kennedy P (1990) The rise and fall of the great powers. World Affairs Publishing House, Beijing

Keynes (2008) The Economic Consequences of the Peace, Beijing: HUAXIA Publishing House

Lane R, Philip R (2006) The real effects of European monetary union. J Econ Perspect 4:44–66

Mckinnon R, Schnabl G (2004) The East Asian Dollar Standard, Fear of Floating and Original Sin. Review of Development Economics, 8 August, 2004

Reinhart CM, Rogoff KS (2010) This Time is Different: Eight Centuries of Financial Folly (Chinese Translation). Beijing: China Machine Press

Triffin R (1997) Gold and the Dollar Crisis: The Future of Convertibility, Beijing: The Commercial Press

Zhihao Hu (2011): Salvage Europe's Agreement on the Currency Swap with Dollar. Analytical Reports on Statistics-Current Review, No. 20111202, Published by the Chinese Academy of Social Sciences

Part II
Global Imbalances: From the Perspective of Real Economy

Introduction

The primary approach to studying global economic imbalances is the global pattern of division of labor and its transformation. What works here is the fundamental logic of economic development: with no division of labor, there will be no transaction, and without transaction, there will be no imbalance to speak of.

The division of labor can be traced back to the fifteenth century, which is the starting point from where the global trade division pattern, economic imbalance, and rebalance have basically gone through three stages.

Before the eighteenth century, division and trade were still at extremely primitive stage, whereby complex production and value chain had yet to take shape, and the income and technological levels among different countries were not vastly different from each other, the division of labor was in a state of satisfying people's needs by mutual exchange of products. Equally important is that credit currency was not in widely used, and with unfledged international financial market, trade deficit had to be paid directly by precious metals. The stiff restraint exerted by the use of "hard currency" to strike the trade balance made it impossible for the global imbalance to grow into a very large scale or last for a long time.

In the "a hundred years of peace," with the Industrial Revolution taking place first in Britain, then in other western nations, the gap in technological development and income among different countries had widened rapidly, resulting in the amazing economic growth of a small group of western nations while the majority of the rest of the world were in stalemate. The division of labor, then, was manifested by the watershed difference between industrial and agricultural nations; and trade was mainly limited by the transaction of industrial products with grains and raw materials. During the period, international finance and service developed quickly. Being the "centre" of the system, Britain experienced long-term trade deficit. Nevertheless, the "empire on which the sun never sets" was able to maintain the imbalance in effect through the development of the service industry, the status of pound sterling as the international reserve currency and large-scale overseas investment. But once the predominance of pound sterling was challenged, the imbalance became no longer sustainable and was forced to be brought back to balance by the "earthshaking evolutionary change" that substituted pound sterling with US dollar. The rise and fall of pound sterling in the global economic arena reveals that when a country becomes predominant in the global monetary system, it is able to gradually release the pressure of, and even prolong the global imbalance by maintaining its deficit by exercising its prerogative of financing; inevitably, therefore, once the hegemonic role in the monetary system is challenged, the imbalance will lapse into crisis in no time.

Since the mid-twentieth century, international division of labor evolved into more complicated patterns with global production being integrated greatly. Meanwhile, countries at different stages of development had, respectively, found their posts in the international hierarchy of division of labor. Thanks to its strength in technology and finance, the US was positioned at the top of the system and could exploit its privilege to finance for the deficit on its current account by issuing loans in dollar, thus making the US the world's biggest creditor. The new global imbalance with the longest duration has emerged.

The predominance of dollar has been increasingly weakened after the collapse of the Bretton Woods System in the mid-1970s. However, since the 1990s, as the emerging economies and developing countries including China began to be integrated into the international system of division of labor, this trend was reversed. East and Southeast Asian countries were the first to become a major source of the world's labor force, followed by the Eastern European countries and the countries that used to be former Soviet Union Republics, and countries in Latin America. The expansion of the global economy dominated by the western countries created new momentum for globalization of labor and has further facilitated the old pattern of international division of labor. The traditional propensity for US dollar of the countries in those regions has enabled the US to redeem its hegemonic role in the monetary system.

Richard B. Freeman (2005), the renowned Harvard labor economist, once estimated that if China, Indian, and the former Soviet bloc were still excluded from the global economic system (dominated by the West), the world's labor force of 2000 would reach 146 million people in total. However, now that those countries have been integrated into the world economic system, the number has actually doubled from the presumed 146 million people to 292 people.

The IMF, in its "World Economic Outlook: Spillovers and Cycles in the Global Economy" published in April 2004, devoted a chapter to analyzing the globalization of the labor force and its profound impact on the world's economic growth and the balances among different countries. By introducing a weighted index of export dependency (export /GDP) and after weighing it against the work force population of different countries, the IMF reached the conclusion that the global effective supply of labor increased three times from 1980 to 2005.

It is no other than this change in the labor force that salvaged dollar from its declining and enabled dollar to resume global predominance. However, the US's misinterpretation of the latest trend has prevented it from recognizing the severe distortion in its way of development and economic structure, allowing the US to exercise its prerogative on a larger scale. Such practice of quenching a thirst with poison persisted and as the effects piled up it led to the breakout of a global economic crisis that would not occur even in a hundred years.

This part has two chapters.

Chapter 3 follows the traces of historical development that is divided into three stages, and discusses what had happened when global imbalance occurred and how the balance was restored. The authors of the book hold that global imbalance can be traced along to parallel clues: one is the process of the global division of labor. It is the division of labor and its transformation that gave rise to long-term imbalances; another clue is the evolution of the global reserve currency, which reveals that for any country that acted as the primary suppliers of major reserve, currency would be able to maintain the global imbalance in its own interest for a considerable long time; once the reserve currency is challenged, the imbalance would immediately result in the eruption of a global crisis.

Chapter 4 continues to discuss the real economy as the foundation of the global imbalance and focuses on the advancement of technology, which would change the relative position of economic development in the international system, followed by changes in a country's export and import. The chapter studies the four typical stages from technological innovation to the proliferation of the technology, i.e., incubation, introduction, the expansion, and maturity. Proceeding from that, the authors pointed out that during the different stages of technological progress, with the shrinking and increasing of entrepreneur opportunities within a country, the supply for consumption and investment would experience cyclical changes. The changing pattern of consumption and investment following the trends of technological innovation would cause the country's foreign trade balance in scale and tendency. In other words, imbalance caused by technological progress, another real economy factor, is not as daunting and even contains elements that will lead to cyclical balance.

Chapter 3
Transformation of International Division of Labor and Global Imbalances

Germany was quickly urbanized and industrialized. Gradually it begun to have trade "deficit" like the Great Britain. The public was in panic, which was not relieved until the country's economists explained that it was both normal and healthy for a well-to-do commercial and manufacturing country that invested overseas to import more than export.

—John Clapham

The emergence of China, India, and the former communist-bloc countries implies that the greater part of the earth's population is now engaged, at least potentially, in the global economy. There are no historical antecedents for this development.[1]

—Ben S. Bernanke

(August 25th, 2006)

If the rise and fall of monetary hegemony is a manifestation of the evolution of the global financial infrastructure, the transformation of the international division of labor has marked the essential changes of the world's real economy. With the deepening of today's globalization, it is increasingly important to provide a full and precise picture of the general trajectories of the world economy by looking at the relations with regard to the internal and external balances.

3.1 The Modern World System

International division of labor is no doubt the basis of global economic and financial integration; yet most of the mainstream textbooks of international economics scantly present detailed discussion on international division of labor and its evolution. The fact that the world economy is an organic whole has been "overlooked" by mainstream economists in the west, whose theoretical paradigm merely

[1]Translator's Note: Speech by Ben S. Bernanke at the At the Federal Reserve Bank of Kansas City's Thirtieth Annual Economic Symposium, Jackson Hole, Wyoming, August 25, 2006. (Accessed online at: http://www.federalreserve.gov/newsevents/speech/bernanke20060825a.htm.).

Y. Li and X. Zhang, *Imbalance and Rebalance*,
https://doi.org/10.1007/978-981-10-6150-9_3

regards different countries as individual entities with comparative advantages. The complicated network of international division of labor is simply generalized in the form of complementary activities like transaction of commodities and movement of factors of production. For anyone who has a full knowledge of the history of international division of labor, such is a narrow perspective as it merely describes the international division of labor at its nascent stage.

History tells people that our modern world grows out of past transformations. Schwartz (2008) has outlined how the transformation took place by comparing the indices of income changes over the time. He pointed out that as recent as 1800, Eurasia and North America basically had the same income level, and the per capita income of the richest country was at most two times of that of the poorest country; by the end of the 19th century, however, the per capita income of the economies like the UK and the US, the upstarts who snatched tremendous wealth from their colonies, had reached ten times that of Asia or India; by the mid-20th century, the per capita income of the developed countries was thirty times as high as that of the third world countries.

What is the driving force behind this transformation? What has caused such inequality? There are two diametrically different theoretical ways of thinking that try to address those questions.

The first explanation was given by the mainstream economists. Using individual country as the unit of analysis, they conclude that whether a country is poor or rich is decided by its culture, institution, factors of production, and natural endowment. In comparison, factors like international trade and economic relations are of secondary importance, and at best play the role of "complementarily supplying each other's needs", acting as links that tie up economic entities that operates independently from each other.

The second explanation is proposed by the theory of world systems. The proponents take the global economic system as the unit of analysis and emphasize the integral function of the world system composed by different parts that play different roles. Schools of this theory depict the structure of the world system based on the dichotomy of "center" as opposed to "periphery" and their mutual conversion.

In the view of the mainstream economics, poverty and wealth are the products of individual countries, and thus can be changed by, and only by reforming its own development strategy. In the eyes of the proponents of the world system theory, poverty and wealth mirror the overall situation of the global economic system, and countries, either poor or rich, are constituents of the system and playing different roles and performing various functions. More importantly, within the world system, the relations between the "center" and "periphery" have been constantly under dynamic, complicated adjustment.

Both way of thinking can be argued reasonably, but in the authors' view, the world systems is obviously a better depiction of the reality: it is a more insightful illumination of the division, imbalance and interactive dynamism among economies at different level of development, and thus is irreplaceable as the most apt analytical perspective to look at the current world economic crisis.

The world systems theory was proposed by the American scholar, Wallerstein (1998, 2000) in the 1970s. The unit of analysis is the "world system", an innovative perspective developed outside the so-called "mainstream" school of economy. According to Wallerstein although human history is composed of the histories of different tribes, ethnicities, nationalities and states, their experiences developed and evolved not in isolation but in connection with each other; and the "world system" emerged from such connections and interactions. Prior to the 16th century, the system is marked by the "world empire" with a unitary political center. After the 16th century, though, it was replaced by the "capitalist world system" with the Western Europe at the center, which has a self-contained economic network but no unified political center.

The world systems theory explores the international division of labor at the level of nation-state and serves a good basis for further economic analysis. The concept of division of labor no doubt plays an extremely important role, nevertheless, the mainstream schools of economy failed to carry out in-depth discussion in this regard. The world political system fills the gap. For the proponents of the world system theory, capitalist world economic system did not occur in any individual country only since its inception, instead, it emerged and grew as a integral world system. The system is structured in three layers: the center, the semi-periphery and the periphery, each layer has its own feature and plays different economic roles. Most importantly, the roles in the global economy also keep on changing.

Most proponents of the world system theory are well-established historians who try to explore the rules and dynamics of history through the analysis of history over long temporal spans. Their elaborated and substantial analyses are lacking in many of the study of the economics. After Wallerstein published his four-volume work, the Modern World System, many excellent works and scholars emerged in the field, such as *Unequal Development* by Amin (2000), *Reorient: Global Economy in the Asian Age* by Frank (2008). Recently, the issues hotly debated by economic historians are: was Europe the center of the world system before the 18th century? And how long has the world system lasted? Is it five hundred years, or even longer, say, five thousand years? Despite the divergences in their views, the majority of the scholars have reached consensus on the two following points: firstly, in its constant expansion, the world system keeps on integrating the areas and regions in periphery into the system, making these areas and regions the "periphery" in terms of the international division of labor. Secondly, the world system is not static or unchangeable, since within the system different parts have evolved in two opposite directions either ascending or descending in view of their vicinity to the system center: the periphery can ascend to semi-periphery, and at the same time, the center may also descend into semi-periphery, likewise, semi-periphery can also evolve into periphery.

The biggest divergence between the world systems theory and the mainstream economics is that the former stresses inequality in its comprehensive portrayal of the global production network and patterns of international division of labor. Mainstream economists believing in the theory of free trade hold that as free trade will benefits both parties, therefore it is fair. However, since international trade is preceded by international division of labor, which was likely teemed with inequalities in its inception. Wallerstein (1998) has pointed out that international division of labor is a hierarchical system built on different functional layers and the function that requires higher-level techniques and technology and larger capital will be the responsibility of the players at higher rank of the hierarchy. Moreover, the unbalanced distributions of the functional technical capabilities are self-fulfilled, being enhanced, rather than weakened by the market force. Therefore, the development trend of the world system further strengthened the economic and social gap among different areas and regions. As one of the proponents of the "dependency theory", Amin (2000) keenly observed that "underdevelopment" is the product of capitalist expansion.

In our view, the theory of world system and the highly relevant "dependency theory" direct people's attention to the international division of labor and its inherent irrationality, issues overlooked either intentionally or unintentionally by the mainstream economic theories. As the theory of world systems more comprehensively and truthfully reveals how the world actually operates, and turns out to be a framework enabling people to analyze the reality in a more profound and precise manner.

3.2 Six Hundred Years in Retrospect—A Bird's Eye

In theory, international trade and division of labor are two sides of the same coin. From this perspective, the history of international division of labor can be traced to the 15th century. Across a time span as long as this, the pattern of international division of labor has undergone three major phases of transformation: the phase of "the silver capital", the "a hundred years of peace" dominated by capitalism, and the phase of the two world wars and multinationals.

The first phase is called "The era of 'silver capital'" (1400–1800) (Frank 2008). The concept behind the delineating of the phases rejects the traditional "Eurocentrism" and traces the history of globalization to the Middle Ages; on the other hand, it highlights the important role of Asia (mainly China and India) in global development prior to the rise of the West. A perspective as broad as this has definitely enriched people's knowledge about the global trade and division of labor during the pre-industrialization age. In the darkness of the Middle Ages when the Industrial Revolution was still in its cradle, global division of labor was primarily the division of labor within agriculture following the rules of mutual complementarity. Division of labor and trade during this period of time had the following features: first, international trade was in its nascent stage and the industrial chain had not taken shape, countries had similar income levels and technological gap among them remained moderate. The international division of labor, for this reason, was vertical rather than horizontal. Secondly, credit currency was not circulated; therefore precious metals were the ultimate means of paying off trade deficit. At the time, because the trade gap was small and did not persist long, such a thing like the terrible "global economic imbalance" was unheard of, Thirdly, for many countries, like China, the primary goal of being engaged in international trade and division of labor was not to trade for clothes and food for life subsistence, but to acquire silver and gold to coin the currency. From the economic rules point of view and talk about the fairness of international division of labor, then the division in this period of time can be called the most equal one. The injustice, so to speak, was the outright plunder of some countries by the others by non-economic means like war and violence.

The Industrial Revolution and the subsequent institutionalization of capitalism ushered in the second phase of international division of labor, a period stretching over the "Hundred Years of Peace (1815–1914)"[2] followed by the two world wars. The international division of labor had seen the differentiation of industry from agriculture, and sub-divisions within different industries. Trade conducted on the basis of such divisions was actually exchanges of industrial products and the agricultural products and raw materials between the industrialized countries at the center and the agricultural, periphery countries. It is fair to say that the nascent capitalism had given birth to the world economic system. The system was composed of three layers: the center, semi-periphery and periphery and with its unique features, each layer assumed different roles in the economy. Countries at the industrialized center was equipped with powerful state machine became the rule marker of the system who controlled the operation of the market. Exploiting the raw materials and cheap labor from agricultural countries at the vast "periphery," the center countries made products and sold them to the periphery for profits. As for countries at the "periphery", the pattern of "self-reliance in production and supply" helped to maintain the basic subsistence of the huge population, and at the meantime they participated in the international division of labor by supplying raw materials, primary products and cheap labor, in exchange for the benefits of industrialization through its enormous market of commodities. Semi-periphery, on the other hand, refers to some emerging communities at the periphery, or some declining communities; with characteristics both of the "center" and "periphery", they were the indispensable, structural factor of the world economic system that serves as the transitional territory that connects the center and periphery, stabilizing the world system.

With the end of the WWII, global economic division of labor has entered its third phase, a historical transition driven by multinationals. The booming of multinationals—the "international citizens" in the real sense, was a real revolution to global development, because by transcending the boundaries of nation-state and ethnicity, and overriding the rigid shell of products, it had pushed the structure and scope of division of labor into individual procedures of production. The prospering of the multinational further acknowledged that both market and enterprise are

---

[2]Between the end of the Napoleonic War in 1815 to the outbreak of the WWI in 1914, apart from colonial wars, European powers including England, France, Prussia, Austria, Italy and Russia were not engaged in lengthy war among each other. Polanyi (2007) called the period "the Hundred Years of Peace."

institutions for exchange, and enterprises merely helped to internalize the market. Naturally, enterprise and market are in a substitution relationship. An enterprise chooses to make overseas investment instead of conduction international trade is because transaction within the enterprise is more efficient than exchanges on the market. The more uncertainties the market has, the more efficient is for the enterprise to internalize trade through performing the role of the market. One telling example is horizontal merger, in the case of which the enterprise, by controlling every independently operated productive element from supply of raw materials to production and sale, is able to distribute those elements in countries with comparatively advantages, so as to earn maximum profits. Multinationals have introduced production systems built on inner-product division of labor, which in turn has positioned economic entities at different areas and phases of the production of one product, and allows those entities to participate in cooperation and interest distribution under the global framework of production and value chains. The emergence of the inner-product division of labor is the crystallization of the advances in science and technology, as well as institutional reforms and revolutions: advances in production technology make it possible to dissect the value chain into smaller and transferrable parts; innovations in communications and transportation have greatly shrunk the temporal and spatial distances between countries, apparently raised the speed and efficiency, and tremendously reduced the cost of coordination; trade liberalization policies also lowered barriers for trade and investment. The inner-product labor division in the international labor division system can be found most evidently in the practices of East Asia. In general, East Asian production network is set up on cooperation among the following countries or groups of countries: Japan as the producer of the core parts, South Korea and the five ASEAN countries as the producer of the regular parts, and China that puts the separate parts together and turns out the final product. The balances of trade among the countries are ramifications of this kind of division of labor. For example, China's trade surplus with Europe and the US is the miniature reflection of the trade surplus of the whole East Asia region with Europe and the US, just because China is at the lower end of the long production chain, it has to shoulder the trade imbalance between Europe and the US for the entire region.

3.3 Silver as Capital (Prior to 1800)

Though Wallerstein's world systems theory pays attention to the less-developed regions outside the West Europe, his theory is still Eurocentric. Frank (2008) has went beyond such limit by extending his research to Asia, and by defying conventional wisdom, he pointed out that in the as long as four hundred years prior to the 19th century, as far as the global economic system is concerned, Asia, particularly China and India, had been the center of the world economic system. His theory not only rejected the conventional Eurocentrism, but also pointed out that the center/periphery relations was dynamic rather than static, and had been undergoing changes. In fact, such transformation keeps on going till today.

Frank (2008) gives a panoramic description of the global economy between 1400 and 1800, and through the lucent lens of his kaleidoscope that looks into global trade in different phases, we are able to take a glimpse of the system of the international division of labor and trade imbalances in evolution. Frank reveals two indisputable facts: first, "global trade and division of labor system that encompassed the entire world did exist. It connected the agricultural inland and border areas to their respective regional commercial centers, seaports or inland commercial towns." Secondly, imbalances were found in the system of international division of labor and trade. Specifically, "Four major regions have long maintained imbalances in commodity trades, namely, the Americas, Japan, Africa and Europe." Meanwhile, "In the world economic system then, the two most important 'core' areas are India and China. Their crucial status was based on the incomparable productivity in manufacturing both in absolute or comparable terms."

Here comes the question, under the international division of labor system with China and India at the center, did trade have imbalance? If it had, then how were the imbalances resolved? The answer is simple, it is trade imbalance among countries was inevitable; the debtor would pay the deficit with gold or silver, which would flow into the creditor country in large quantity. For example, China and India had long had trade surplus thanks to their highly developed economy and rich national resources, and naturally became the recipients of huge influx of gold and silver. Historical records shows that India was the second largest "secret vault" of silver and China the ultimate "secret vault" of silver in the world. It is worth noting that during this period, especially in the countries in the Orient, with its property of the currency, silver played a much bigger role than gold, a phenomenon that attracted the attention of the scholars at the time. Among them, Smith (1974) the founder of modern economics devoted huge space in the Wealth of Nations to "discuss in passing the fluctuations of the price of silver over the past four centuries," which reveals the significance of silver then.

3.4 "The Hundred Years of Peace (1800–1913)"

The Napoleonic War had brought about successive events that marked historical turning points and changes with tremendously outstanding characteristics.

First of all, the 19th century was when the gap among nations (regions) had been markedly enlarged, the so called "divergence" period by Kenneth Pomeranz. It is at this point where Europe and China started to go separate ways in terms of economic development, the divergence that later initiated the discussion of convergence among growth theorists in the 20th century. Table 3.1 presents the per capita GDP of then representative nations in the important years, which illustrates that in 1820, the per capita GDP of the UK, the then richest country was 3.3 times of that of the Australia, the poorest country at the time. By the year of 1913, the US became the

Table 3.1 Per capita GDP (1700–1913) (Unit: 1990 international dollar)

Year	UK	Germany	Portugal	US	Australia	Brazil	Argentina	China	India	Japan
1700	1250	910	819	527	400	459	–	–	–	–
1820	1706	1077	923	1257	518	646	–	600	533	669
1830	1749	1328	–	1376	848	–	–	–	–	–
1840	1990	–	–	1588	1374	–	–	–	–	–
1850	2330	1428	923	1806	1975	686	–	600	–	–
1860	2830	1639	883	2178	2894	–	–	–	–	–
1870	3190	1839	975	2445	3273	713	1311	530	533	737
1880	3477	1991	947	2880	4285	752	–	–	–	863
1890	4009	2428	1128	3392	4458	794	2152	540	584	1012
1900	4492	2985	1302	4091	4013	678	2756	545	599	1180
1913	4921	3648	1250	5301	5157	811	3797	552	673	1387

Source Angus Maddison (2009)

richest country, whose per capita GDP was 9.6 times that of the then poorest country, China. Table 3.1 is rich in information and thought-provoking for the study of the rise and fall of major nations within the century, an everlasting theme of research.

Secondly, along the drastic divergence in national incomes, the world had undergone amazing economic integration. It was an era that witnessed "…the spectacular growth of an integrated global economy, which drew ever more regions into a transoceanic and transcontinental trading and financial network centered upon Western Europe, and in particular upon Great Britain. These decades of British economic hegemony were accompanied by large-scale improvements in transport and communications, by the increasingly rapid transfer of industrial technology from one region to another, and by an immense spurt in manufacturing output, which in turn stimulated the opening of new areas of agricultural land and raw-material sources. The erosion of tariff barriers and other mercantilist devices, together with the widespread propagation of ideas about free trade and international harmony, suggested that a new international order had risen."[3] (Kennedy 2006).

Table 3.2 shows the changes in values of import and export between Britain and different regions in the two centuries. Notably, Britain's trade was no longer confined within the Europe but carried out throughout the world. The global trade prospered and grew noticeably particularly after 1870. Maddison (2003) has pointed out that between 1870 and 1913, global export increased by 4.3% annually. It is particularly worth noting that for almost all countries, trade grew at the faster rate than national income. In our view, the fact that the growth of trade overtook the economic growth is the primary manifestation of the deepening of globalization and the strengthening of ties among the nations.

Thirdly, another major feature of the 19th century is the so-called "Hundred Years of Peace", which has been highlighted by Polanyi (2007). Since the end of

[3]Translator's Note: Kennedy (1987), p. 143.

Table 3.2 Composite of import and export commodities of the UK by regions (1710–1913) (Unit: %)

Year	Europe	Asia	Africa	North America	British West Indies	Other countries in America	Australia and New Zealand
Import							
1710[a]	63.6	6.9	0.4	7.3	21.7	0.1	0.0
1774	46.1	11.4	0.4	12.5	29.3	0.3	0.0
1820	26.8	24.6	0.5	14.6	26.0	7.5	0.0
1913	40.7[b]	15.7	3.0	22.6	0.8[c]	9.6	7.6
Export and transfer							
1710[a]	87.6	2.1	1.2	5.1	3.4	0.6	0.0
1774	58.5	3.9	6.0	21.5	10.0	0.1	0.0
1820	61.8	7.1	1.1	11.7	9.0	9.3	0.0
1913	37.4[b]	22.7	6.4	13.5	1.0[c]	8.7	10.3

Source Angus Maddison (2003), p. 85, Table 2.23
[a]Including England and Wales
[b]Including North Africa
[c]Including all Caribbean Islands

the Napoleonic War in 1815 to the breaking out of the First World War in 1914, apart from colonial wars, no long-term, total war took place among major European powers including Britain, France, Prussia, Austria, Italy and Russia. Polanyi attributed it to the "factor of anonymity" of international finance, namely the banking families that resided in the European capitals. When international trade could only be realized on the basis of an international monetary system, which would be disrupted once a total war broke out, and cause damage to the interest of the European powers, the bankers who had close ties and often worked with the European powers acted as agents to glue the European powers together and lubricate their relations when the latter were willing to maintain peace and enjoy the benefits of peace. In this way the bankers contributed to the formation of the balance of power system in the 19th century, and made the "Hundred Years of Peace" a reality.

Put together, the three characteristics mentioned above reveals the irony of the period: in a whole century when the European and American powers co-existed peacefully and the global trade boomed, the income gap of those countries and the rest of the world kept on enlarging. In other words, countries in the world did not have the chance to share the windfall of peace and prosperity. What is more, to some extent the peace and prosperity for some were the causes of war and poverty for the other. Kennedy (2006) has elucidated two things: first, the so-called "Hundred Years of Peace" is peace among the major powers, not global peace. In fact, during the period, wars aimed to conquer the under-developed ethnic group in Europe and North America were intensified, often the military actions were results of overseas economic infiltration by the major powers and the decrease of the production quotas by the under-developed nations. Secondly, global trade and

Table 3.3 Per capita level of industrialization (1750–1913)

Year	Great Britain	France	Germany	Italy	Russia	United States	Japan	China	India
1750	10	9	8	8	6	4	7	8	7
1800	16	9	8	8	6	9	7	6	6
1830	25	12	9	8	7	14	7	6	6
1860	64	20	15	15	8	21	7	4	3
1880	87	28	25	25	10	38	9	4	2
1900	100	39	52	52	15	69	12	3	1

Note All entries are based on an index value of 100, equal to the per capita level of industrialization in Great Britain in 1900
Source Kennedy (2006), p. 186, Table 7

international division of labor resulting from industrialization in Europe and North America caused economic stagnation and even recession in the rest of the world, where nations there were ossified in at the lower end in the global production chain. For example, "When cheap and quality goods produced by textile factory in Lancashire entered the traditional market of China and India, those countries underwent the deindustrialization." Table 3.3 listed the changes of per capita levels of industrialization between 1750 and 1900, which shows clearly that during the period when the per capita level of income of the Great Britain jumped from 10 to 100, that of China slumped from 8 to 3, and India 7 to 1. The contrast is shocking. Indices of such inevitably lead to the conclusion that the rising of the West had incurred "double damage in both relative and absolute sense" for China, India and other non-European countries".

Another noteworthy fact is that, during the Hundred Years of Peace, as the hegemon challenged by the competition from newly industrialized countries like the United States and Germany, and Britain's economic strength also experienced wax and wane and kept on declining. The situation was such that in a letter to General Von Stein, a German industrialist wrote: "Give us another a hundred years' peace, and we will vanquish the Britain." (Clapham 2009).

3.5 The Victorian Era

The Hundred Years of Peace occurred in the Victoria Era of the British Empire (1837–1901), whose prosperity has been described in great details by British economists, Stanley Jervons: "The plains of North America and Russia are our cornfields; Chicago and Odessa our granaries; Canada and the Baltic are our timber forests; Australasia contains our sheep farms, and in Argentina and on the western prairies of North America are our herds of oxen; Peru sends her silver, and the gold of South Africa and Australia flows to London; the Hindus and the Chinese grow tea for us, and our coffee, sugar and spice plantations are in all the Indies. Spain and

France are our vineyards and the Mediterranean our fruit garden; and our cotton grounds, which for long have occupied Southern United States, are now being extended everywhere in the warm regions of the earth."[4] (Kennedy 2006).

Keynes gave a more vivid description, which went deeper into the feelings of the royal subjects of the British Empire: "The inhabitant of London could order by telephone, sipping his morning tea in bed, the various products of the whole earth, in such quantity as he might see fit, and reasonably expect their early delivery on his doorstep; he could at the same moment and by the same means adventure his wealth in the natural resources and new enterprise of any quarter of the world. He could secure forthwith, if he wished it, cheap and comfortable means of transport to any country or climate without passport or other formality, could dispatch his servant to the neighboring office of a bank for such supply of the precious metals as might seem convenient, and then proceed abroad to foreign quarters, without knowledge of their religion, language, or customs, bearing coined wealth upon his person, and would consider himself greatly aggrieved and much surprised at the least interference – He regarded this state of affairs as normal, certain, and permanent."[5] (Maddison 2003).

The per capita income of the British increased rapidly, thanks to three major factors: first, advancement in technology, manifested mainly in the rapid growth of the real capital stock, as well as improvement of the educational level of the labor force and their productive skills; secondly, amelioration of the international division of labor, which in turn raised the efficiency of the allocation of resources; and thirdly, the balance of power among the major powers and the ensuing peace among them. Kennedy (2006) compared the British economy to a big wind box that absorbs huge amount of raw materials and grains, and releases huge amount of textile, iron and other products. At the meantime, such tangible trade was complemented by a network that that runs alongside the trade, which included shipping, insurance and banking. In one word, during the period Britain had been on the forefront of the global production and technology development, occupying advantageous position in terms of trade of commodities and services.

The free trade policies by the Great Britain not only caused trade to thrive but also facilitated rapid spread of technologies with the expansion of British immigration across the world and foreign investment. Late comers like Germany and the United States gradually became powerful competitors in production by using advanced British technologies. Statistics by Matthews et al. (1982) shows that in the period of Hundred Years of Peace, British export had been constantly on the decrease: the average growth rate between 1873 and 1857 was 5.7%, and decreased to 3.1% between 1857 and 1873, and further to 2% between 1873 and 1913. At the same time, however, British import did not fall concurrently, which led to

---

[4]Translator's note: Kennedy (1987), pp. 151–152.

[5]Translator's note: Maddison, Angus. The World Economy: A Millennial Perspective [Development Center Studies: http://theunbrokenwindow.com/Development/MADDISON%20The%Economy—A%20Millennial.pdf, p. 100.

Table 3.4 Percentage of current account in the GDP of the Great Britain (1855–1913) (Unit: %)

Time (year)	Export of products (1)	Import of products (2)	Net value of services (3)	Surplus of products and services (1) − (2) + (3)(4)	Net income from abroad (5)	Net investment and gift (4) + (5) + (6)
1855–1873	17.9	20.9	4.7	1.7	2.8	4.5
1874–1890	18.4	23.9	5.1	−0.4	5.4	5.0
1891–1913	17.7	23.8	4.3	−1.8	6.8	5.0

Source Matthews et al. (1982), Table 14.7

deterioration of its trade balance and persistent trade deficit [as item (1) and (2) of Table 3.4 shows]. In contrast, Britain had considerable trade surplus in services, due to its long-standing strength in shipping, commerce, insurance and banking, etc. Thus, its trade deficit was offset by surplus in services, which kept its account in balance [as is shown in item (4) of Table 3.4]. When it comes to the third major item: “net income from abroad” [listed as item (5) of Table 3.4] on Britain’s current account, Britain reaped huge interest income and profits from its overseas investment, and with the rising of the investment, the account had seen considerable surplus [as is shown by item (6) of Table 3.4].

If there was any difference in terms of international division of labor between the Victoria era and the past, then it is the fact that the Victoria era saw the increasing international financial activities, including making international loans and foreign investment. Kindleberger (2003) noticed that after the Napoleonic War, the Barings Bank made a loan worth 700 million francs to the French government, as war reparations paid to the Central Powers. The loan turned out to be a great success, and marked the beginning for many financial achievements later. The study by Cuenca Esteban (2001) also pointed out that between 1816 and 1820, the average surplus of the current account of the UK was 4.875 million pounds, out of which 1.60 million became international reserve and 3.275 million pounds became net capital outflow on capital account. Meanwhile, as far as real economy was concerned, Britain was like a “big wind box” that drew in raw materials and turned out products, while taking lead in services industries such as shipping, insurance, banking, etc. In the field of finance, Britain made investments and loans in large quantity, which yielded great interest income and profits. Although Britain suffered substantial deficit in products trade by 1855 and the situation was becoming worse, the incomes from trade of services and overseas investment had far exceeded its loss on trade of products. As the result, the country’s current account had been showing considerable surplus. From another perspective, the increase in deficit in products trade was caused by the competitions from the newly industrialized countries. The British foreign invest had, as a matter of fact, fueled the industrial development in those nations. By the end of the 19th century, the products from Germany and the United States were no less competitive as the British products on the world market.

How to account for the deficit in products trade of a country? Clapham (2009), the famous British economic historian, once remarked that “Germany was quickly urbanized and industrialized. Gradually it begun to have trade "deficit" like the Great Britain. The public was in panic, which was not relieved until the country's economists explained that it was both normal and healthy for a well-to-do commercial and manufacturing country that invested overseas to import more than export." From the perspective of modern economics, this interpretation is valid. Robust import is an indicator of a nation's high domestic demand, and wealth and strong buying power of its citizens. So long as the deficit can be offset by services trade and overseas investments, such a phenomenon is truly normal and healthy.

The complexity of international balance of payment in the Victoria era proves to be an excellent example that tells about the conditions under which a powerful country at the center of the international system can avoid disrupting the international economic order, as to some extent, the nation itself constitute one of the necessary conditions for the normal running of the world economy; the example also illustrates that such a balance is not stable because it depends a complex of factors that interact among them and once any of them changes the balance will be tipped and cause earth shaking transformation in the global economic structure. This logical analysis clearly foretells the decline of the British Empire shortly after, and helps to set the stage for the transformation from balance to imbalance of the global system dominated by the United States since the second half of the twentieth century. Moreover, such a perspective gives people prescience when they examine the working conditions, internal contradictions, turning points and critical factors for change of the international monetary system formed on the basis of one sovereign currency of a single country.

3.6 Now It's the Turn of the United States

The "Hundred Years of Peace" was no more than a façade as behind the scene of prosperity of the British Empire, were the stagnation, recession and widespread poverty in countries "at the periphery" like China and India, as well as the race among the "later comers" like the United States and Germany to strengthen the national power driven by the hidden ambition for hegemony. The underlying contradictions surged and raged against each other, and eventually engulfed the humanity with the two catastrophic World Wars that not only lasted for three decades with painful memories that are unbearable for people to recall.

In fact, as early as the extravaganza of the 60th Jubilee for Queen Victoria in 1897, the dominance of the Great Britain over the world economy had faded like falling flowers, which was replaced by its former colonies—the United States. Prior to the WWII, the United States had become the new hegemon of the world economic system; and no sooner than the dust of the War was settled, US dollar had replaced pound sterling to become the new nexus of the international monetary system.

However, the law of history could not be altered even a bit by the power shift in the arena of international economy. After the United States gained economic

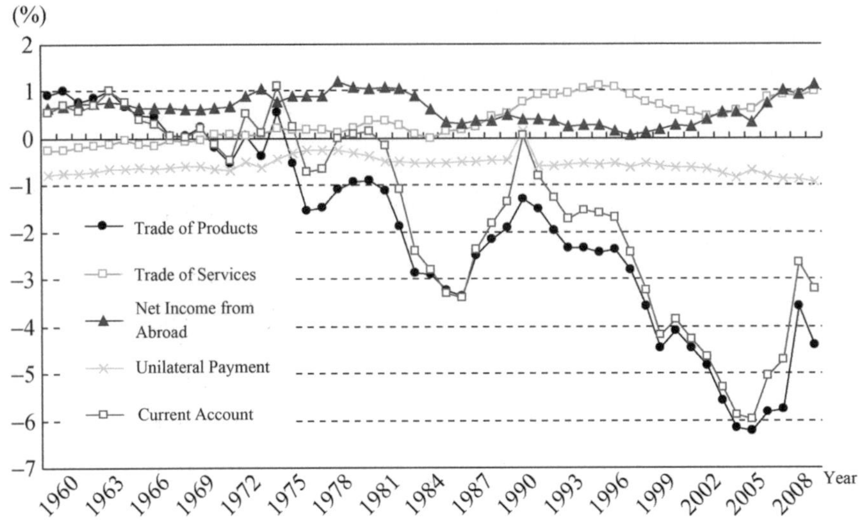

Chart 3.1 United States current account/GDP (1960–2010). *Source* Bureau of economic analysis of the United States (www.bea.gov)

predominance, its international balance of payment has also undergone the transformation from having surplus to deficit, correspondingly, the world has seen the "shortage of dollar" moving towards the "oversupply of dollar", with the international monetary system moving from one predominated by US dollar to the new pattern of "warring states" where many reserve currencies coexist in the system.

Such transformations can be traced along the changes of the items in the international balance sheet. Chart 3.1 depicts the US current account and its four items since 1960: surplus of products trade, surplus of services trade, net income from abroad and unilateral payment.

Between the end of the WWII and the 1970s, the United States had maintained surplus in products trade, which helped the nation to accumulate overseas assets in large quantity. Since the 1970s, its products trade begun to see deficit, and the situation kept on deteriorating; between 2005 and 2006, the surplus even exceeded 6% of its GDP (it reached 6.5% of the GDP in 2006). Chart 3.1 shows that the United States is able to maintain surplus in trade of services and net income from abroad, which has been, in most cases, within 1% of the country's GDP and therefore not big enough to balance its deficit from trade of products. In consequence, once the deficit of trade of products begun to deteriorate, so does the country's current account. The causes of the deficit and worsening situation lie in two aspects. From the perspective of production, the United States have been challenged by Japan and Germany prior to the 1980s, the Asia's "four small dragons" and "four little tigers" in the 1990s, and later by China. Products made by those countries or regions have made headway to the international market, hence shaking the role of the United States as the world's manufacturing power and causing the United States to lose its comparative advantage. Temporally, the rise of Japan, Germany, and later Asia's "four small dragons" and "four little tigers", followed by China, happened in succession, a tendency advancing with stronger momentum and on larger scale, which rendered the United States unable to recover once it lost the surplus in trade. On the other hand, from the consumption angle, as the United States has always encouraged the citizens to consume, the household savings rate has been lingering around 7%, never going up higher than 10%. The rapid development of the service industry, in particular the financial industry, has made high consumption feasible in reality. In the long run, the savings rate keeps on sliding and people have formed the undesirable habit of borrowing to consume.

Like the British Empire in the old days, the United States also utilizes its advantageous position in service industry and overseas investment in exchange for resources and products across the globe, and uses the surplus on the above-mentioned items to offset the deficit in trade of products. Nevertheless, since the 1970s and after the deficit became constant on the account, such a game could no longer go on. On the other hand, the United States adopts a mindset regarding the outside world different that of the British Empire. During the similar stage and under similar circumstances, Britain was open to the world and therefore facilitated its citizens to emigrate, exporting labor and capital. To a certain extent, this policy had relaxed the tension in domestic employment and economic expansion, enabling the capital to reap higher profits and interests outside the mother country, further balancing the trade deficit. Different from the British with the opening outlook, the Americans are essentially inward-looking, probably due to its past role as the long-time colonies of the old British Empire and its endowment of vast territories and rich and abundant natural resources. When tensions arising from domestic employment go up, the United States would quickly turn to trade protectionism, which will lead to restrictions on cross-border capital movement and sharp decline in the income from overseas foreign investment on the capital account. Therefore, if the then British Empire was able to use overseas investment through its capital account to balance the trade surplus in the early stages of the empire, and later when the cumulative profits from the large-scale investment flowed back to balance the trade deficit after the country stepped down from its dominant position, the United States, in comparison, could not do the same due to the lack of such mechanism. On the contrary, when the United States is at its heyday in terms of national strength, it tended to curb the outflow of capital, as is illustrated by its action in the 1950s which forced the emergence of the market of the "European dollar." Afterwards, when its trade started to have deficit, the United States tended to attract foreign investment by its advantage of currency and advanced domestic financial market. The result is the huge amount of debts and the situation has become severe day after day. Chart 3.2 shows the evolving trend of its current account and net cash position of international investment. As the current account was deficit and as the situation became worse, foreign debt quickly exceeded its credit, the United States was turned from a creditor to debtor. Its deficit keeps on enlarging. The imbalance of trade was a hidden risk and became the root cause of the global imbalances.

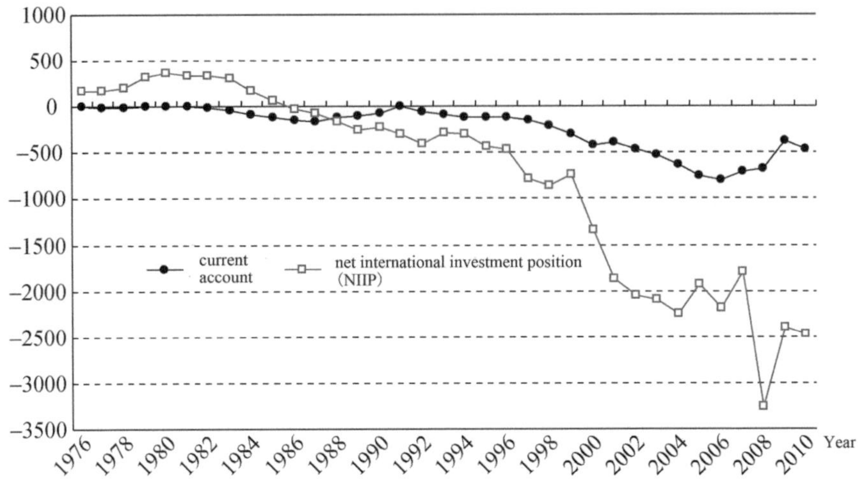

Chart 3.2 United States current account and net international investment position (1960–2010) (Unit: 1 billion US dollars). *Source* Bureau of economic analysis of the United States (www.bea.gov)

3.7 Oscillating Between Balance and Imbalance

The analysis above has briefly depicted the pattern of the three progressive stages from international division of labor, economic imbalances to solving the imbalances since the 15th century.

Prior to the 18th century, international division of labor was basically in the form of mutually exchange of needed goods, because division of labor and trade were still at the very primitive stage, production and value chains had yet to grow into their full-fledged pattern, income and technology of different countries were still at the similar level. Equally important is the fact that credit currency was still a rarity, and the international financial market was underdeveloped, trade deficit had to be settled in precious metals. When foreign debts could only be balanced by "hard currency", countries were compelled by such an ironclad restraint to deal with trade imbalances, especially trade deficit with caution and therefore global imbalances were limited within a certain scale and did not last for long periods time.

During the "Hundred Years of Peace", countries begun to diverge rapidly in terms of technology development and income, as the western nations led by Britain had achieved commendable economic growth, many other countries had seen their economies plunged into stagnation. The general pattern of international division of labor is delineated by the division between agricultural and industrial nations, while trade had been the exchange of industrial products for food and raw materials. During the period, international finance and service industry developed rapidly, Britain was able to tackle the long-existing deficit in commodity trading through its edge in the development of service industry, backed by pound sterling as the international reserve currency and overseas investment. However, when pound sterling had been challenged and the subsequent global imbalances were no longer sustainable, the imbalances had to be rectified with semiotic changes after US dollar forced out pound sterling to become the international reserve currency.

After the mid-20th century, international division of labor becomes more complex, as the global production has been greatly integrated. Meanwhile, as countries have been moving forward at their own pace and thus are at different stage of development, international division of labor assumes a hierarchical structure. On top of the system is the United States, backed by its strength in technology and finance, who rose to become the world's Number One creditor by exploiting the advantage of issuing dollar, the international reserve currency, to raise money for deficit on current account. Another, and the longest global economic imbalance begun. During a considerable time and to considerable extent, this imbalance will sustain, so long as there is the international monetary system with US dollar as the major currency. The privilege of the dollar as the primary international reserve currency has enabled the United States (as the cause of the global imbalances) to print paper dollars that circulate globally to make up for its imbalance, and compels other countries (who are also willing to do so, to some extent) to reserve a certain amount of dollar as means of adjusting international balance of payment and running their domestic economies. To sustain such imbalance, several conditions have to be met. If the imbalance goes on for a long time and its scale goes beyond a certain threshold, it will lead to over-issuing of currencies that can no longer be contained within the limit of the fiscal capability of the United States, the imbalances will immediately slide to its breaking point. At this time, any structural changes in the international economic system that may cause shift in economic power and thus weakening the predominant role of the United States, i.e., the decline of proportion of the US economy in the global GDP, or the development of the diversification of international reserve currency, the imbalances will turn into crisis. We believe that this round of international financial crisis manifests this consequence, because currently the trade deficit of the United States can no longer be sustained, as the diversification of international reserve currency can be seen ostensibly.

3.8 Globalization and International Division of Labor

Since the end of the 1990s, as developing countries begun to take part in the international division of labor, globalization of labor force has become the latest trend, leading to the rapid increase in supply of labor. East Asia and South Asia became the major suppliers of labor, and the Soviet Union, East Europe, as well as Latin America have also become major sources of labor. The globalization of labor no doubt has brought about profound changes to the old pattern of international division of labor.

The famous labor economist of Harvard University has estimated that if China, India and the former Soviet bloc countries were excluded from the global economic system, the world's total number of people in the labor force by 2000 would be around 1.46 billion. Since these countries have become part of the world economic system, the number of people in the global labor force doubled by 2000, from 1.46 billion to 2.92 billion. Freeman called this phenomenon "The Great Doubling", and holds that this doubling has transformed the balance of power between the capital and labor in world economy. The consequence is, as he points out, multinationals can hire lower-paid labor from China, India and the former Soviet bloc countries or outsourcing jobs to those countries. Freeman also stresses that while supplying labor in large number to the world, countries like China and India did not see corresponding increase in capital supply domestically, because both China and India were low-income countries that did not have sufficient capital; as for the Soviet Empire, despite of its higher level of economic development and investment rates as compared to China and India, the investment were mainly in military supplies and heavy industry, instead of civilian goods or new technologies. Against this background, in 2000, the capital to labor ratio decreased to 61% of its original value level.

In April, 2007, the IMF issued the "World Economic Outlook: The Spillovers and Cycles in the Global Economy" and devoted a whole chapter to analyzing the globalization of labor. It believes that in the past two decades, labor has become increasingly globalized. With the approach of weighing each country's labor force by its export-to GDP ratio, the report found that "the effective global labor supply quadrupled between 1980 and 2005, with most of the increase taking place after 1990."[6] And it is projected that "the effective global labor supply could more than double again by 2050."[7] The regional breakdown suggests that "East Asia contributed about half of the increase of the effective global labor supply, due to a marked rise in working-age population and rising trade openness,"[8] while South Asia and the former Eastern bloc countries also contributed positively to the increases. In the process, through import of end products, advanced economies offshore intermediates manufacturing and attract immigration to fully exploit the labor force. The globalization of labor force had lowered the cost of labor, raised production efficiency of the advanced economies, and with the prices remaining at lower levels for a long time, the cost of labor went up due to a number of intertwined factors. Calculations shows that over the twenty-five years before 2007, decline in the prices of tradable goods have raised the production output and real labor compensation by 6%. Despite of the advantages, labor globalization had negative impact on labor income ratio. Since the 1980s, the average ratio of labor

[6]IMF "World Economic Outlook: The Spillovers and Cycles in the Global Economy" Chap. 5 (April, 2007), p. 162.

[7]Ibid. p. 180.

[8]Ibid. p. 162.

had declined by 7%, and European countries and unskilled economic sectors had seen the sharpest decrease.

3.9 The Disintegration of the Soviet-Eastern Bloc and the New Pattern of International Division of Labor

During the Cold War, the former Eastern bloc countries adopted inward-looking strategies of development in isolation. Not only had they erected higher trade and investment barriers, but also imposed a multitude of restrictions on immigration. All the measures isolated the countries labor markets from the outside. With the disintegration of the Eastern bloc and the countries moving from planned economic to market and adopting the opening strategy, a large labor force with some degree of training in professional skills gradually emerged in the global labor force and transformed the pattern of the global division of labor profoundly.

According to the analysis and projections made by the United Population Division of the Department of Economic and Social Affairs, the ratio of working-age population to the total population in Eastern European countries kept on rising before 2000, from 62.5% in 1950 and 1975 to 63.3% in 2000, and the ratio was projected to drop after 2000. In the global context, Eastern European countries is in more advantageous position in terms of demographic structure, in comparison with the globe, developed economies, developing economies including regions of East Asia and Central and South Asia (it is in the year of 2000 only when the ratio was lower than that of East Asia).

In view of the trend of dependency ratio, since the 1950s, in Eastern European countries had seen drastic drop in child dependency ratio, and steady rise of elderly dependency ratio and constant decline of the total dependency ratio. It means that Eastern European countries can fully exploit its demographic bonus and enhance their competitiveness globally by paying lower cost for elements of production. Of course, this trend will somehow change, when the dependency ratio will no longer continue to fall but instead shall go up quickly, suggesting their edge in labor supply is gone and the population bonus would eventually be spent.

In further analysis, the comparatively rich supply of labor in the region, apart from the factor of natural growth of the population, is also attributable to the relocation of labor force and economic restructuring.

When the Eastern bloc collapsed, labor in agriculture took up a certain percentage, around 15–30% of the total working population, and in some countries, the percentage reached above 40%. The fact indicates that with the modernization of agriculture and increased productivity, a large number of people will be released from labor in agriculture and relocated to non-agriculture sectors.

Meanwhile, economic restructuring in Eastern European countries not only led to "frictional unemployment" produced by the upgrading of the economic structure, but also downsizing of the work force in enterprise reforms aimed at achieving higher efficiency. Such changes greatly impacted the labor market. As the restructuring started, unemployment rate in some of the countries immediately went up to over 10%, some even reached 15–20%. This created abundant reserves of labor and ensured a steady flow of labor supply.

Besides the advantage in the number of labor, Eastern European countries also had labor forces that are better educated than those in developing economies, thanks to the fact that after the 1980s to 1990s, they began to adopt the western educational model and push forward universal education at the high school and college level, and improve the quality of education in this regard. Such endeavor greatly improved the quality of the labor force. Among the developing economies and in terms of the ratio of skilled labor to the total labor force, regions like the Middle East, North Africa, Latin American and the Caribbean, Europe (Eastern Europe) and Mid-Asia are at higher levels than other regions in the world.

Supply of the strong labor in the former Eastern bloc countries helped them to keep the labor cost at lower level. The statistics of hourly labor cost issued by the EU Statistics Bureau serves as the basis for systemic comparative analysis of the costs of labor in the EU countries. The Bureau defined in 1999 that hourly labor cost is made up of two parts: direct costs and indirect costs. The former includes wages and salaries, overtime pay, shift premium, bonus paid on regular basis, remunerations for work on holidays and vacations, special bonuses, such as Christmas bonus, other compensations in cash and in kind. Extra costs include other costs in the annual income of employees, including social security contributions by the employer, wages and salaries for employees on sick leave, other social contributions and vocational training costs, etc. Table 3.5 shows that the average hourly cost of countries in the former Eastern bloc are less than four euros, 4% lower than Portugal, which is at the bottom among the major industrialized countries.

While being aware of the strength of the former Eastern European countries for having high abundant high quality and low cost labor resources, one should also note the latest trend of offshoring industrial production beginning in the 1990s.

With economic globalization and technological progress, the trend towards global allocation of production elements and division of labor in the industries are gaining momentum, while more and more multinationals began to earnestly looking for the different locations that serve best the sections of production of a single product along the value chain. Against this background, industrial relocations are carried out on much larger scope and at higher speed.

Privileged with the low-cost elements of production, former Eastern bloc countries successfully attracted the attention of international capital and became appealing destinations of direct foreign investment (FDI). In view of the statistics provided by the UN Conference on Trade and Development with regard to FDI attracted by countries in transition (mainly the former Soviet bloc countries), the inflow of FDI before 1980 was close to zero; between 1980 and 1990, it was meager; nevertheless, since 1991, the FDI inflow increased substantially and constantly, from $75 million in 1990 to $10.3 billion by 1997. After that, since the

Table 3.5 Comparison of hourly labor costs among major EU Countries (Unit: Euro)

Country	1997	1998	1999	2000	2001	2002	2003	2004	2005	2006	2007	2008
Belgium				26.61	27.89	29.17	29.58	30.3	30.62	31.43	32.56	33.66
Bulgaria		1.1	1.22	1.23	1.29	1.32	1.39	1.47	1.55	1.65	1.89	
Czechoslovakia	2.97	3.26	3.41	3.86	4.64	5.39	5.47	5.85	6.63	7.14	7.88	
Denmark	23.4	24.63	25.92	26.53	28.54	29.06	30.3	30.7	31.98	33.09	34.74	
Germany	23.3	23.6	24	25	25.6	26.2	26.8	26.9	27.1	27.6	27.8	
Estonia	2.13	2.42	2.6	2.85	3.22	3.67	4.01	4.24	4.67	5.5	6.6	7.51
Greece	9.77	9.77	10.61	10.98	11.62	12.46	13.37					
Spain	14.23	14.06	14.22	14.22	13.07	13.63	14.21	14.76	15.22	15.77	16.39	
France	22.52	22.94	23.57	24.84	26	27.04	27.68	28.46	29.13	30.08	31.06	31.78
Italy	18.92	18.3	18.68	18.99	19.27	19.99	20.64	21.39				
Cyprus	7.83	8.16	8.41	8.95	9.31	9.76	10.37	11.1	11.65	11.98	12.46	13.31
Latvia	1.59	1.71	1.85	2.22	2.29	2.39	2.37	2.52	2.77	3.41	4.41	5.42
Lithuania	1.7	1.98	2.31	2.63	2.78	3	3.1	3.16	3.56	4.21	5.09	
Luxemburg	21.26	21.56	22.52	22.31	25.39	26.21	27.02	29.97	31.1	31.98	33	33.63
Hungary	3.15	3.02	3.14	23.05	4.04	4.91	5.08	5.49	6.06	6.34	7.13	
Netherlands	19.13	20.18	21.14	4.48	23.88	25.19	26.45	27.23	27.41			
Austria	21.93	22.02	22.71	23.05	23.65	24.13	24.98	25.32	25.72	26.01	26.33	26.5
Poland	3.38	3.73	4.05	4.48	5.3	5.27	4.7	7.74	5.55	5.55	6.03	6.78
Portugal	7.4	7.6	7.99	8.13	8.6	9.1	9.6	10.2	10.6	10.97	11.32	11.73
Romania				1.41	1.57	1.67	1.6	1.76	2.33	2.68	3.4	
Slovenia	7.9	8.51	8.94	8.98	9.51	10.09	10.54	10.41	10.76	11.37	12.09	
Slovakia	2.61	2.91	2.76	3.07	3.26	3.59	4.02	4.41	4.8	5.33	6.41	
Finland	20.3	20.4	21.37	22.1	23.59	23.82	24.78	25.34	26.7	27.2	27.87	29.38
Sweden	23.79	24.17	25.34	28.56	27.33	28.57	30.03	31.08	31.55	32.16	33.3	
Britain	17.69	19.16	20.84	23.71	24.51	25.24	23.56	24.71	21.8	22.9	23.54	

Source Statistic bureau of the European Union (Eurostat)

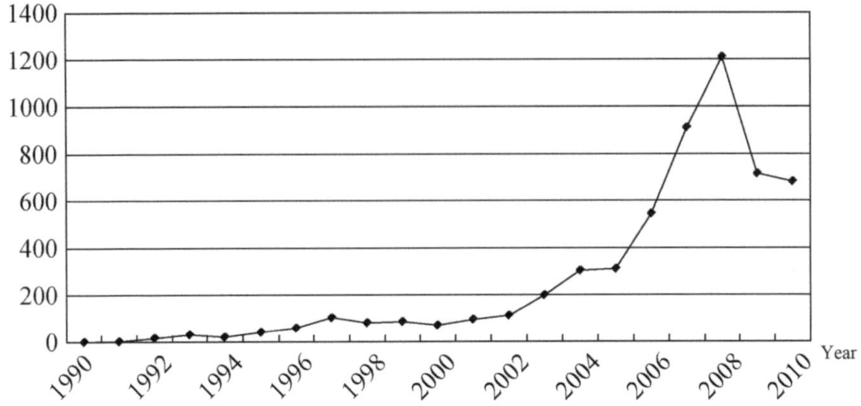

Chart 3.3 Changes in inflow of FDI in transitional countries (Unit: US dollar). *Source* Statistics United Nations conference on trade and development (UNCAD)

flow of capital was impacted by the Asian financial crisis, the inflow of capital decreased; but after 2001, it started to rise again, from $11.3 billion in 2002 to $121 billion US dollar in 2008. In recent years, the drastic increase was dampened by the global financial crisis (see Chart 3.3)

As the former Soviet bloc countries had facilitated shift and relocation of processing and assembly lines of the production chain across the globe, production and export of the manufacturing industrials in the countries had accelerated. The Competitive Industrial Performance (CIP) Index issued by the United Nations Industrial Development Organization (UNIDO) reveals that since the 1990s, those countries have registered rapid growth in terms of average gross value added by manufacturing per capita and the ratio of value added to the GDP.

It should also be noted that, when manufacturing operation have been relocated across the world, apart from labor-intensive products, even the labor-intensive part in the production of capital and technology—intensive products have been increasingly offshored to developing countries where the production cost are low, and serve as the processing and export bases of processing and assembling capital and technology-intensive products. Against this background, the cross-board proportion of the export of hi-tech products to the export of manufactured goods keeps on increasing rapidly.

Moreover, the industrial relocation is not limited to the processing and assembling of the manufacturing industry but also involves the service industry. The recent trend is that cross-border investment is concentrated on the service sector. With regard to the volume of flow of FDI, compared with the period of 1989 to 1991, the period of 2005 to 2007 saw an increase of FDI in services from 50 to 59%. In terms of volume of FDI stock, the proportion of FDI in services has been raised from 47.7% in 1990 to 64.9% in 2007. In the global relocation of services, the fields that saw the most rapid growth are the globalization of research and design, offshoring of non-crucial sections of the service chain. The UNCAD has estimated that over the past few years, the market of offshoring has registered annual growth rates of 20–30%.

Many former Soviet bloc countries are becoming offshore destinations for many enterprises in Europe, due to the relatively high educational level, low wage costs, geographical proximity, as well as proximity in language and culture. The near-shoring model in services has come to the fore. While getting actively involved in off-shoring, those countries also facilitate development in export of services, whose percentage in the GDP being maintained at comparatively high level.

In the end, it is worth pointing out that internationalization of the labor force in the former Eastern bloc countries has been achieved not only in trade related to industrial relocation, but also through trans–boundary movement of people. Due to the gap in average income and levels in wages and salaries, as well as geographical proximity, the number of people emigrating to neighboring countries from the former Eastern bloc countries has been constantly on the rise. Statistics from the EU shows that by the end of 2000, the original EU member states had taken a total of nearly 850 thousands immigrations from Middle and East European countries, accounting for 0.2% of the total population of the EU at the time. About 80% of the immigrants settled in countries that share border with Middle and East Europe, like Austria or Germany. Out of the 850 thousands immigrants, about 300 million are skilled labor, taking up 0.3% of the EU labor force. As for the number of immigrants who settled in Germany, during the three decades between 1950 and 1979 it was 102 thousand; 101 thousands in the decade between 1980 and 1989, 377 thousands within one year of 1989, and 397 thousands in the year of 1990 alone. It means that the former Eastern bloc countries participate in the international division of labor not only by absorbing capital elements in movement and integrating it with the local labor, but also by integrating the elements of labor and international capital. Labor and capital have been integrated on the two frontiers.

3.10 Production Network of East Asia and Restructuring of Global Value Chain

It has been mentioned before that the current account deficits of the United States came from deficits in commodity trade. A study of the country's commodity trade structure yield more surprising findings. According to statistics by the US Department of Commerce of the structure of Sino-US deficit in commodity trade, the deficits of the United States mainly came from manufactured goods exported from China. In 2007, deficit on this particular item reached 270 billion dollars. Meanwhile, the United States had surplus in trade of primary goods with China, which was 12.5 billion dollars in 2007. The figures show that the United States mainly exported raw materials to and imported manufactured industrial goods from China. Such a trade pattern is a déjà vu of the past relationship between the economic hegemon and the country at the periphery, whereby the former exported industrial products to the latter in exchange for cheap raw materials. Have the economic statuses of the two countries been reversed? Regrettably this is not the case. The formation of a pattern like this was in fact driven by the evolution of the model of international division of labor and the emergence of the latest model.

The model of international division of labor has evolved from division among industrials to inner-industrial division, and further to division of labor within the production of a single product. Corresponding, international trade is also moving from cross-industrial trade to eventually trade within the product. Multinationals have played revolutionary role in leading the transformation of the pattern of trade.

Multinational companies emerged in developed countries in Europe and the United States by the end of the 19th century, after the overseas colonization and expansion of the countries and developed with the export of capital and commodities. With capital accumulated in the first wave of colonization enabled many big companies in developed nations to invest oversea by setting up factories and subsidiaries. The Germany chemical company Friedrich Bayer established a subsidiary at Cologne in 1863, and bought an American aniline factory at Albany the in 1865, making it the first modern multinational company in real sense. After the WWII, multinationals expanded across the world by way of investment in construction and merger and acquisition. The rapid growth FDI gave birth to the global production system. Since the 1990s, economic globalization and revolution in information technology have greatly reduced the costs of production, which enables multinationals to further breakdown the value chain of production into sections where production and service are conducted following different specific procedures. The multinationals then relocate the operation of the production to countries and regions that have comparative advantages or competitiveness in corresponding notches along the production chain that specialize in production that are capital-intensive, labor-intensive or technology-intensive. At the same time, by tying up the separated links of manufacturing and service of one single product with trade, multinationals can fully exploit the advantages enjoyed by the regions and countries in elements of production, and through concerted commands and coordination within the company, they can further reduce the cost of trade. As the division of labor across the world is moving towards inner-product labor division, the value chain of the production is undergoing restricting across the globe. Take the production of cellular phone as one example. In early 2001, Ericsson made a statement that it would only be in charge of the technological design and marketing of the products, and would set up manufacturing plants in Brazil, Malaysia, Sweden and Britain, and the management of some of the plants in America would be transferred to Flextronics in Singapore. In general, making a cellular phone is completed in seven steps: research and development (R&D), designing, production, supply, marketing, sales and customer service. Ericsson had outsourced the production and supply chains while still controlling the major links of the value chain.

The major factors that have made the inner-product labor division possible are: advancement in science and technology makes it possible to separate the value chain into small and transferrable parts; innovations in communications and transportation shorten the temporal and spatial distance among countries, at higher speed and with obviously improved efficiency, and lower coordination cost; besides, the free trade policies adopted by government of the countries have also greatly lowered trade and investment barriers.

Inner-product labor division has played a significant role in building the production network in East Asia. The Sino-US trade and trade between East Asian countries and the United States is a case in point. Since the 1980s, with the rapid growth of FDI in the mainland of China by the United States and some East Asian economies, a network of inner-product labor division was created that connects the United States, China and the rest of the East Asia. In the network, the United States, Japan, South Korea are engaged in capital and technology intensive activities including R&D, design, and they produce and export the key parts of the product; the ASEAN countries and China's Taiwan produce and export component systems or modules; the mainland of China is in charge of labor-intensive processing and assembling work, providing parts and components in small quantity; Hong Kong of China takes care of sales and marketing in overseas markets like the United States, which in this case is the target market of the finished product (Chen and Liu 2008). Table 3.6 provides the statistics of trade of parts and components, which illustrates the patter of the inner-product division of labor. It shows that China has deficits in trade of parts and components with Japan, South Korea and the five ASEAN countries, and the deficits was climbing up on large scale. In the same period, South Korea and the five ASEAN countries also had trade deficits with Japan, though on a steady level.

From trade statistics about end products (see Table 3.7) shows that within East Asia and in 2010, China had deficits to Japan, South Korea and the five ASEAN countries; Japan had surplus with South Korea but deficit with ASEAN countries. To an extent, in East Asia, China, South Korea and Japan constitute the markets for end products. All East Asian economies, at the same time, had surplus to the United States. China, for one, has seen its surplus vastly increasing in the recent years, while Japan, South Korea and the five ASEAN countries have kept their surpluses relative stable; China's surplus to the United States was much higher than the total surpluses held by Japan, South Korea and the ASEAN countries to the United States. In 2010, China's surplus to the United States in trade of the end products was 18 times what was in 1995, whereas in the same year, China's deficits in trade of components with Japan, South Korea and ASEAN countries was 18 times what was in 1995. Obviously, China's trade pattern fits into the model of processing trade, which features the so-called "import and export at both ends of the channel while goods flowing in huge amount" (imports large quantities components and semi-manufactured products, and exports processed end products). China's trade surplus to the United States was merely the combination of the surpluses of the whole region of East Asia.

Chart 3.4 offers a candid observation of the trade pattern between East Asia and the United States, and it clearly reveals that China is the regional hub of the production network and shoulders the trade imbalances in entirety of in the economic relations between the region and the United States.

Table 3.6 Net export of parts and components among different economies (Unit: billion US dollars)

Year	China–Japan	China–South Korea	China–five ASEAN countries	Japan–South Korea	Japan–five ASEAN countries	Korea–five ASEAN countries	China–United States	Japan–United States	South Korea–United States	United States–five ASEAN countries
1995	−56.70	–6.30	0.17	42.94	268.36	45.21	−3.63	303.99	26.55	−6.83
1998	−56.55	−14.26	−14.05	27.32	140.91	45.28	−6.02	192.44	−10.97	−33.06
1999	−76.15	−22.51	−12.67	45.13	151.32	42.53	−7.11	225.12	−15.41	−38.14
2000	−92.95	−34.65	−28.02	47.67	185.93	28.87	2.80	251.38	5.58	−34.20
2001	−93.34	−33.49	−34.82	34.9	135.17	6.75	0.53	198.27	−8.99	6.46
2002	−119.36	−47.25	−54.27	40.65	140.35	10.28	19.28	176.97	−10.95	11.28
2003	−183.69	−91.69	−104.95	46.45	140.43	13.25	46.25	187.49	−15.24	47.17
2004	−227.71	−145.55	−139.91	50.34	155.31	20.68	60.53	226.16	−4.4	34.79
2005	−233.23	−223.96	−187.21	44.05	161.64	9.66	94.49	237.71	−3.51	17.92
2006	−269.08	−263.65	−224.2	39.22	146.6	26.73	127.48	214.41	6.16	17.26
2007	−296.75	−280.81	−278.82	29.47	163.48	15.59	155.8	215.54	13.37	58.38
2008	−300.38	−254.87	−233.38	33.73	180.65	−0.69	161.18	213.82	10.24	86.44
2009	−309.27	−265.27	−191.69	40.94	157.10	−4.47	118.61	153.15	16.32	4.95
2010	−393.12	−401.66	−334.21	43.86	250.95	–	189.15	215.13	–	8.62

Note The statistics refers to the combination of the parts and components of capital products and components and parts of transportation equipment (BEC–3) in the Broad Economic Categories (BEC); the net export involves two countries is based on government statistics provided by the country placed before the "–" (i.e. the China–Japan trade statistics is based on the statistics from China). Statistics by South Korea of trade between South Korea and all other countries in 2010 are not available

Source http://comtrade.un.org

Table 3.7 Net export of end products among different economies (Unit: 100 million US dollars)

Year	China–Japan	China–South Korea	China–five ASEAN countries	Japan–South Korea	Japan–five ASEAN countries	Korea–five ASEAN countries	China–United States	Japan–United States	South Korea–United States	United States–five ASEAN countries
1995	51.23	−29.75	−4.22	96.50	45.18	24.43	89.73	157.25	243.44	−241.8
1998	70.40	−73.36	−14.13	5.55	−59.05	5.66	217.02	331.21	227.83	−322.58
1999	62.62	−71.68	−23.69	23.43	−59.51	0.38	232.28	397.55	296.01	−356.09
2000	94.40	−84.50	−31.03	54.85	−75.01	−21.79	295.02	463.30	378.06	−387.83
2001	114.87	−75.09	−25.94	46.10	−112.18	−13.23	280.84	389.63	313.57	−339.96
2002	69.04	−83.08	−38.57	90.19	−83.97	−9.23	408.61	438.79	329.43	−371.75
2003	36.29	−138.64	−84.49	122.58	−91.40	−13.74	540.57	387.96	343.69	−394.18
2004	19.53	−198.68	−88.94	171.77	−74.86	−26.06	743.48	423.75	430.27	−414.30
2005	69.02	−193.16	−50.89	178.10	−99.14	−18.24	1049.90	467.72	414.99	−472.62
2006	28.58	−188.37	−23.94	190.20	−147.75	−24.02	1317.39	563.72	433.20	−493.98
2007	−22.13	−192.39	33.09	240.80	−133.39	1.43	1480.41	516.61	458.84	−486.89
2008	−44.30	−127.19	73.04	266.43	−159.18	39.13	1551.40	383.85	465.01	−417.32
2009	−20.99	−223.45	48.45	211.95	−94.81	28.84	1316.79	193.98	378.03	−303.37
2010	−163.8	−294.07	−25.63	294.01	−89.36	–	1621.31	298.83	–	−281.26

Note Statistics is calculated by the summed total of net export under the breakdown of the Broad Economic Categories (BEC) minus the net export of parts and components. Rest please refer to the notes of Table 2.1
Source http://comtrade.un.org

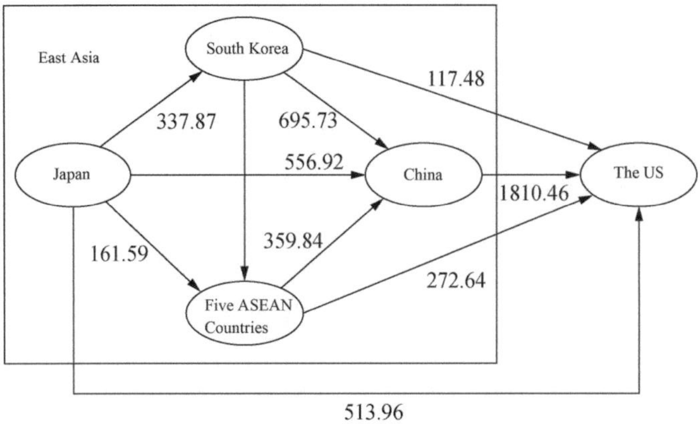

Chart 3.4 Trade structure of production network in East Asia (2010). *Note* Statistics are based on total net export under all items of the BEC, the total equals to the sum of the amount listed in Tables 3.6 and 3.7. *Source* http://contrade.un.org

With the framework of this model, analyze the trade deficit between China and the United States just from the perspective of the bilateral economic relations and jump to conclusion will oversimplify and misinterpret the situation. The only way to a good understanding is to put the Sino-US trade relations in context of the development and evolution of the global value chain.

Under the global value chain is the inequality in the division of labor and value among different regions. The most lucrative two ends of the value chain, i.e., the sales and marketing in the lower reach and the key components and parts in the upper reach of the value chain is often the turf of the enterprises or regions at the center, and the production at the middle of the chain is often located with the enterprises or regions at the periphery, where the profits have also been subject to extraction. According to the statistics published by iSuppli, a market research company, a 16G ipad with wifi is sold at 499 US dollars, but Apple pays the Chinese enterprises about 11.2 dollars for processing, which takes up merely 2.2% of the market price, a little bit higher than the price of the aluminum cover of the ipad, which is 10.5 US dollars. The cost of an ipad is about 259.6 US dollars, 239.4 dollar less than its market price, and the difference is paid to the creative ideas and design generated by Apple itself. The case of iPad, more than just revealing the distribution of the profits, shows that the deficits in the Sino-US trade have been overvalued. The last stop of an iPad before it hits the market is at the assembly line in Shen Zhen, China, where the last part of production is completed. However, all the deficits are put on China's balance sheet. If, hypothetically, the iPad was assembled in the United States, which would requires the producer to buy chips from Japan, the dominator from Taiwan, China, and other parts from different economies. With a industrial chain like this, the total trade surplus to the United States that are registered on China's account would be dispersed into various surplus held by the economies that take part in the production process respectively.

Notably, statistical calculations based on the current model of labor division have over-valued China's surplus, and even worse, it obscured the nature of the problem, which will easily to lead people astray and make it harder to solve the global issue of imbalances.

References

Cuenca Esteban J (2001) The British Balance of Payments, 1772–1820: India Transfers and War Finance. The Economic History Review, New Series, 54(1), pp.58–86

Kennedy P (1987) The rise and fall of the great powers: economic change and military conflict from 1500 to 2000. Random House, New York

Kennedy P (2006) The rise and fall of the great powers:economic change and military conflict from 1500 to 2000 (Chinese translation). International Culture Publishing House, Beijing

Matthews RCO, Feinstein CH, Odling-Smee IC (1982) British Economic Growth: 1856–1973, Oxford University Press

Chapter 4
Innovation of Technology, Changes in Productivity, and Global Imbalances

The single most significance of a country's competitiveness is the national productivity. Productivity refers to a country's (or an industry and enterprise's) capability to produce more wealth evenly in the world market. Upgrading national economy requires sustained growth of its productivity.

Michael E. Porter

Last chapter reveals the relations between international division of labor and the global imbalances. It can be seen that two factors determines how a country is positioned in international division of labor: the factor of real economy, i.e., the country's capability in technological innovation and industrialization; the monetary and financial factor, i.e., its strength in finance and status in the global financial system. This chapter focuses on the relations between technological innovation, changes of productivity and global imbalances, and the next chapter will discuss the role played by currency and finance in global economic imbalances.

4.1 Innovation and Finance: The Macro Model of Technological Transformation

In his book, Comparative Advantage, Creating and Sustaining Superior Performance, Porter points out that "the single most significance of a country's competitiveness is the national productivity. Productivity refers to a country's (or industry, enterprise) capability to produce more wealth evenly in the world market. Upgrading national economy requires sustained growth of its productivity." It means that a country's position in international division of labor is decided to a large extent by its technological strength and the corresponding level of productivity.

The importance of force of production or productivity can never be overestimated. The new growth theory that emerged in the 1980s regards productivity or innovation as the fountainhead of economic growth. Paul Krugman, the winner of

Y. Li and X. Zhang, *Imbalance and Rebalance*,
https://doi.org/10.1007/978-981-10-6150-9_4

Noble Prize in economizes once observed with a sense of humor that from the long-term perspective, all the driving force of economic growth is not the increase in productivity, but the increase in productivity is almost all of the driving force.

The conclusion is also valid if it is reversed, which is, the root cause of any economic recession or crisis that happened in any economy or the world is the decline in productivity. The crisis of stagnation in the 1970s is directly caused by the sliding productivity. The Asian financial crisis is believed to be caused by the distortion of economic structure and lack of innovation dynamics in the victim countries. The current round of financial crisis is also related to the slowdown of productivity since the beginning of the new century, when the Nasdaq Index plummeted and foreboded the incoming crisis. At the time as most people were confident in innovation and the following rise in productivity, they accepted with tolerance the prosperity of the virtual economy and the deteriorating of trade deficits of the United States. However, instead of seeing the fulfillment of their expectations for a good future, the productivity in the manufacturing sector began to slide after the IT bubble, and the overlapping effect of the bust of the real estate bubble, a large scale crisis eventually descended.

In the real economic process, technological innovation and financial innovation are like twins that are intimately connected, mutually stimulating, and develop in tandem. Innovation can only be realized with the strong financial support, and new narratives of venture capital investment needs fresh stories about innovation. Had there not been the expectations of big advancement in technology, people would not have looked forward to the new round of prosperity and gone crazy about venture capital investment. This is normal in the history of technological development.

Let us conduct an analysis of the interaction between innovation and finance by tracing back in the history of economic and finance. Perez's research renders great help in this regard by the rich resources it provides, which will help us to develop a macro model of transformation of technology.

Perez thinks that from innovation to popularization, technological development generally goes through four periods, namely, incubation period, installation period, deployment period and maturing period. Financial capital and production capital play different roles during the different periods; and the technological transformation itself also encounters different social economic paradigms that are either in harmony or conflict with it (see Chart 4.1).

From Chart 4.1, one can see that every major wave of technology has gone through two diametrically different periods: the installation period and deployment period, each of which had lasted two to three decades. In fact, the ups and downs of the waves constitutes the cycle of technological innovation, which had profound influence on, or even took the lead in the cycles of economic and social transformation.

First, let us take a look at the installation period. During the period, technological innovation started to gain momentum, which attracted great amount of investment into the new fields of technology. Quite often the investment came from venture capitals, drawn by the stories of wealth that would be generated by the new

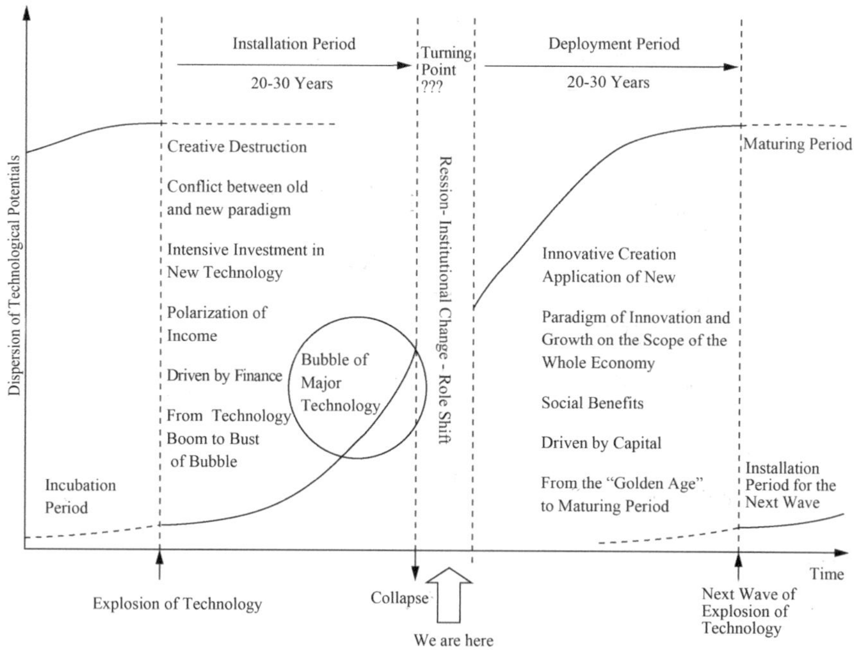

Chart 4.1 Periods of technological innovation

technology, which led the people to overinvest in the new technology, thus creating the big "bubble of technology." The railway bubble in the earlier days and the internet bubble in the new century are telling examples of the kind.

During the installation period, financial capital took control. It is because that during the maturing period of every technology, production capital was locked in the economic path of the technology in which the production capital had tremendous input by investing in the marketing net and management experiences under the old paradigm of the economic and technology which used to be revolutions. While the production capital would obstinately resisted paradigmatic innovation, the financial capital, free from such lockdown, is by nature flexible, wile and free, with a penchant for speculation and short-term profits. The emerging entrepreneurs rising with the new technology had technological skills and were ambitious, but were lacking in capital and political power, usually possessed by financial capital. This explains why financial capital gradually took over the leadership of the economy during the installation period and taking side with the entrepreneurs who had new technologies, financial capital challenged the obsolete system or paradigm that obstructed the progress. Meanwhile, during the past two hundred years, every wave of technological innovation was accompanied by over investment in new type of the infrastructure, which inevitably created investment bubbles after tremendous amount of capital flooded into the fields.

Besides, the emergence of new technology also led to and aggravated polarization in distribution of income. As great amount of wealth flows to the field of new technology (investor, people worked in the fields, including skilled workers who have commanded the new technology and financial professionals related to venture capital investment). This is the period of "creative destruction", which saw the conflicts between the old and new paradigm grow increasingly intense: the old paradigm served the traditional technology, and did not fit in the new technology, and should be replaced by the new paradigm to apply and develop the new technology.

Now let us take a look at the deployment period. As the bubble of technology broke, people came to realize that the speculation and pursuit of short-term profits driven by financial capital to reform the system had become the obstacle on the way to economic growth. Through the "creative destruction," although the bubble was broken, new infrastructures stayed and new paradigms had been gradually accepted by people, and the pillar industry was also established. After the transformation, there arises the demand for expansion of production and market, before the economy moves into the deployment period. To realize the goal, three conditions have to be met: first, decisions on long-term investment has to be made sans the pressure from the stock market, which means the financial capital has to yield it economic leadership to production capital; second, expansion of production requires expansion in demand, which in turn depends on redistribution of income, guaranteed by policies of the welfare state; third, the system of ethics and values needs to shift the emphasis on individual competition for survival to cooperation and collective social welfare.

In the view of Perez, such are the three conditions for the transition of technological innovation from installation to deployment. Once those conditions are met, the innovation enters the deployment stage. During the period, with exploitation of the wealth-generating potentials embedded in the new paradigm, economic growth is achieved that benefits the society cross the board. However, transition from the old to new paradigm often entails intense conflict and readjustment of relations of interests, such as changes in the power balance between the government and market. The income polarization resulting from the laisser-faire economic model of the installation period needs to be dealt with by government's efforts in coordination and balancing. Only by lessening the polarization of income can meet the needs of all social sectors and promote the new technology to spread widely.

Paradigm shift is going on in response to development of technologies, and to some extent the cycle of technology advancement precedes the transformation of cycle of social economic development. Looking back on history, one can see that since the Industrialization of Britain, the world economy swung between laisser-faire market economy and government intervention like a pendulum every twenty to thirty years driven by the internal dynamics of technology revolution.

At the beginning of the installation and bond by the old paradigm, economic growth often slowed down and even became trapped by stagnation. To evoke the internal dynamics of the economy, the ideology of free market would surge.

For example, in the 1970s when developed economies in Europe and North America were plunged into stagnation, the trend of the so-called "the end of Keynesianism" led to the rise of the new free economics. However, as soon as the deployment period begun, the trend was reversed as the over emphasis on laisser-faire had resulted in severe social, economic and political confrontations. At this time, only fierce financial crisis would be able to weaken the power of the financial capital, restore and enhance the government's power of supervision and control, as well as redirect the attention to public welfare. For example, the Great Depression of the 1930s had led to the rising of Keynesianism, and the current round of financial crisis had greatly shaken confidence of the market fundamentalists, and government intervention gained tremendous momentum across the world.

What can also be seen from Chart 4.1 is that we are now currently at the critical point in transition from the installation to deployment period. The successful transition depends on the three conditions mentioned above. At present, the conditions are interpreted as: firstly, financial capital needs to yield economic leadership to production capital. In developed economies, especially the United States where finance had overly developed, the finance sector needs to be "streamlined" by deleveraging finance. In emerging economies, finance needs to serve the real economy. Secondly, the issue of income redistribution needs to be solved. The movement of "Occupy Wall Street" demonstrated the confrontations between a few rich people and the majority of the regular people (the so-called 1% vs. 99%). The rapid spread of the movement in the United States and its repercussion in many other countries suggest that income polarization has already become a universal global issue. The problem has become aggravated since the 1980s. Under these circumstances, it is imperative for the government to use the "visible hand" to strike a balance again between the government and market. Moreover, in the installation period, much emphasis was on the interests of individual, and now more emphasis needs to put on the welfare of the community. In other words, it is necessary to put the relations between individual interests and community welfare back to balance.

The interaction between innovation and finance shows that, on the one hand, finance boosts innovation and it is the finance capital that pushes technological innovation into the deployment stage; on the other hand, financial expansion is not possible without the support form technological innovation. Although the expansion of the financial sector and the development in the financial innovation in the United States is attributable to the lessening of financial supervision, but if it were not for the bright prospect revealed by technological innovation, expansion and technological innovation would not have and driving force; the lessening of supervision, on the other hand, also reflected governmental supervisors' acknowledgement of the narratives of technological innovation.

4.2 Innovation and Changes in Productivity: "Condoning" the External Imbalance

Technological innovation not only fuels the sweeping development of the financial sector of the United States, but also holds up the system by preventing the imbalance from growing at a speed that will lead to the breakdown of the system. In the following chapters we will illustrate that the expansion and advantageous position of the finance sector happened to have "condoned" the external imbalance of the country. However, from the perspective of the real economy, the fundamental influential factors are technological innovation or changes in productivity.

With technological innovation emerging one after another and in great number, economy began to boom. In this period, investment is in great demand, economy develops healthily, expected income keeps growing, and people tend to consume more. In response, the government will cut down on savings, encourage investment and consumption, and borrow externally to increase the resources if the domestic savings can not satisfy the demand for investment and consumption; in this case, the earnings on the country's current account will drop and deficit will increase. When innovation slows down and the spillover eventually ends and exhausted, economic recession begins. People's expected income will slide, leading to reduction in consumption and increase in savings, in preparation for the smooth consumption if the income goes down. Plants and factories will also lower investment, which will lead increase in surplus on the current account and decrease in deficit.

In accordance with the theory of national economic accounting, surplus of international payment can be represented by the difference between domestic savings and investment. If the surplus is positive (surplus), it means that the country provide loans to other countries. If the surplus is negative, it shows that the country borrows loans for other countries. Following this way of thinking, external imbalances, be it positive or negative, is the result of the decisions made on savings and consumption by economic entities (residents, enterprises and government) based on the expected income in the future. Therefore, in the long run, expected income (measured in terms of GDP) growth is the fundamental force to rectify external imbalances. In this sense, deficit in a certain period is not necessarily a bad thing for the country, on the contrary, it might well suggest that people are optimistic about the income of the country in the future (Engel and Rogers 2006). And what is bolstering income growth is nothing other than technological innovation or changes in productivity. From this perspective, these two things are key factors that initiate external imbalances.

What happened in the United States since the end of the 20th century testifies to the theory. Since the 1990s, the United States has been in lead among the developed countries as far as economic growth rate is concerned. Statistics provided by Madison (Madison) shows that between 1991 and 2008, the average annual growth rate of real GDP the United States was as high as 2.73%, higher than those of the United Kingdom (2.37%), France(1.82%), of Germany (1.69%), and Japan

(1.24%). When it comes to the core dynamics of growth—advancement in technology, the United States also performed impressively. As is shown in Chart 4.2, over the past two decades, the productivity of the manufacturing industry of the United States grew faster than that of Japan and other developed economies in Europe, constituting the major driving force of the country's rapid economic growth. Similarly, as is shown in Chart 4.3, in information and communication technology (ICT) that led the "new economic wave", the United States enjoys prominent comparative advantage (especially during the middle and second half period of the 1990s). In one word, during the period, also the United States had gone through the busting of the IT bubble (also see Chart 4.3), the United States had achieved outstanding performances in economic growth with high quality and great potentials as were revealed by the advancement in technology. Quite reasonably, people felt confident in the long-term prosperity of the United States, and the Americans, therefore, had enough reasons to let themselves, by easily exploiting the cheap money flowing from the rest of the world, maintain the life style that "spend the future money on consumption of today."

Rigorous theoretical analysis also confirms the close ties between change in productivity and external imbalances of the United States. For example, an earlier study by Glick and Rogoff (1995) shows that 1% increase in the overall economic productivity of a nation (for example, measured in Total Factor Productivity, TFP), will leads to 0.15% decrease in the proportion of the surplus on the current account to GDP. Bussiere et al. (2005)[1] tried to look for the causes of deficits on the current account by tracing the improvement of productivity in the United States, and they believed that the rise in productivity had improved the expected Return on Assets

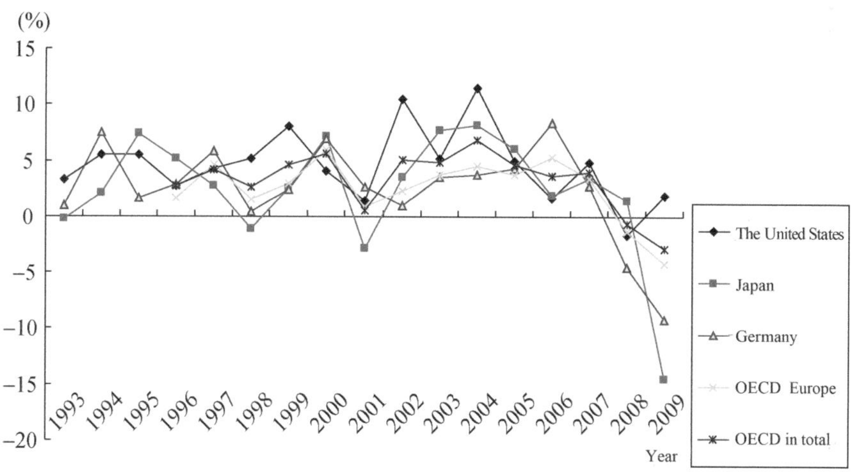

Chart 4.2 Annual change rate of manufacturing output. *Source* OECD

[1]Bussiere et al. (2005).

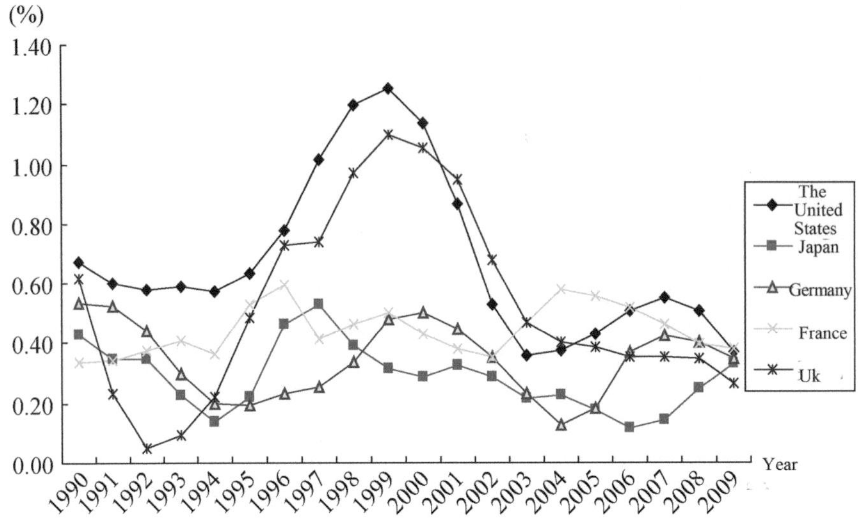

Chart 4.3 Rate of contribution to the GDP by investment in information and communications industry. *Source* The Conference Board Total Economy Database

ratio and helped to draw capital, leading to the appreciation of the dollar and persistent current account deficits. Cove et al. (2009) made a distinction the impacts of on external productivity changes between trade sector and non-trade sector. According to the Balassa-Samuelson effect, which depends on inter-country differences in the relative productivity of the tradable and non-tradable sectors, if the productivity of a country's non-tradable sector grows faster than that of the non-tradable sector, prices of non-tradable goods will go up and result in appreciation of the local currency. And it is also valid vice versa, namely, improvement in productivity of the tradable sector and the preferences of the local goods by the citizens will also cause depreciation of the local currency. Therefore, the impact of changes in productivity on exchange rates and subsequently on the current account payments is decided by the net outcome of the balancing between the two forces mentioned here (about the mechanism, see Engel and Rogers 2006). Based on analysis of data from the United States, Europe, Japan, etc., found that under the Balassa–Samuelson effect, the major cause for the increase in the real exchange rate of dollar and worsening of external deficits is the comparative high-level development of its non-tradable sector (as compared with other countries).

In 2011, uncovered the relations between expected income and external imbalances by quantitative analysis. By establishing dynamic models and calibrating parameters, they founded that changes in productivity of labor exerted far more impact on surplus in the United States' international payment than other variables (for example, the international interest rates level often under discussion). It can be found in Chart 4.4 that if expected productivity is the only factor taken into consideration, Hoffmann's theory about the current account deficits of the

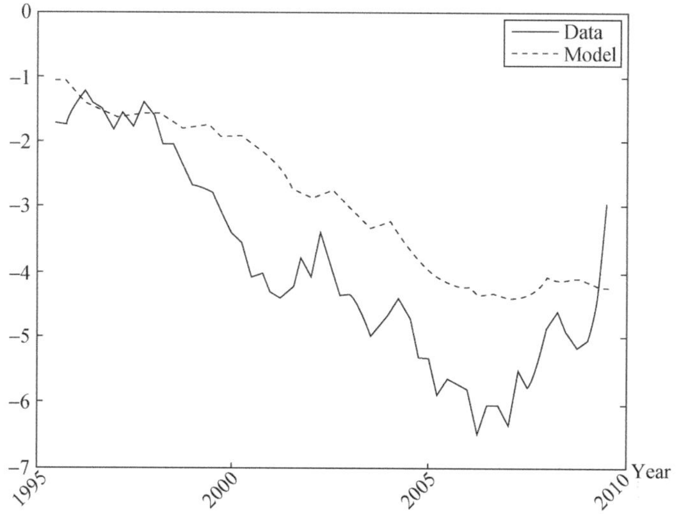

Chart 4.4 Actual United States current account surplus as percentage of GDP and estimated value after adjustment (1995–2010). The *line* is the real value; the *dash* is the estimated value

United States proved to basically fit in the actual values.[2] Besides, detailed analysis by Ruoxue Zhang and Zhigang Yuan (2010) of the Sino-US trade shows that the deficits of the United States is the result of the transferring of the lower-end production in processing and manufacturing industries to developing countries including China, since the United States is located on the top rung of the production chain thanks to its strength in technological innovation. Given this situation, although China has been in surplus, it is even more imminent for it to make readjustments of its external imbalances.

4.3 Enduring Prosperity as an "Exception"?

The above analysis seems to prove that the ability of United States to bear international payment deficits and foreign debts to a large extent depends on the future income and the prospects of technological advancement. In specific terms, so long as the economy keeps prospering and technology continues to make headway, the United States does not have to worry about external imbalances. Is this a valid assumption?

In retrospect, we can see that since its independence from the British rule, the United States rose rapidly with its brand-new political system, rich natural resources, unique geographical location, and immigrants from every corner of the

[2]Please also refer to the studies by Engel and Rogers (2006), and Bems et al. (2007).

world; and at the end of the 19th century had quickly caught up with the old colonial empires including the Great Britain and France, and eventually overtaken them to become the world's top economic power. Since the WWII, the United States was in advantageous position not only in economy, but also in a multitude of fields of politics, military, science and technology, and culture as the world's top one winner. For a time, the American Exceptionalism became the prevailing school of thought, proclaiming that the United States could rid itself of the curse of the cycle of the rise and fall of the great powers. This idea not only greatly encouraged generations of the followers of the "American Dream", but also became the evangelical that influenced all sectors of the American society. The former US president Ronald Reagan had once emotionally compared the United States to the "shinning city upon a hill"[3] in the Bible, which should stand uprightly till the eternity as was bless by the Almighty God. Nevertheless, it turned out that the exceptionalism did not hold, and the crisis eventually occurred against it.

From the perspective of the real economy, especially the transformation of the industrial structure, changes in productivity, and economic growth, it is obvious that the external imbalances were not sustainable.

In terms of industrial structure, the United States had entered the post-industrialization. In 2008, the manufacturing industry accounted for only a bit over 10% of the GDP, whereas the service industry takes up 66% of the GDP. Examining more closely, one can see that in the service sector, the share of the financial sector (i.e., finance, insurance, real estate) is surging very rapidly. Besides, that of the information industry also registered high growth rate, especially from the mid-1990s to the year 2000, when its share in GDP reached 4.7% (see Table 4.1).

In view of the development by sector, the decline of the manufacturing and expansion of the finance has been going on for some time. Statistics shows that shortly after the end of the WWII, manufacturing accounted for ¼ of the GDP, whereas finance only made up 10%. In 2008, the trend was turned diametrically around, when the percentage of the manufacturing sector decreased to 11%, whereas that of the financial sector rose to 20% (see Chart 4.5), and the financial sector contributed twice as much as the manufacturing to the GDP. In terms of employment, the manufacturing sector reached its highest point in 1979, with 206.1 million employees, and the number decreased to 131.5 million in 2008. During the same period, 1415 thousand people worked in the financial sector in 1929, and the number increased to 7.83 million in 2008. The reverse tendencies of development in the two sectors are notable (see Chart 4.6).

It is worth noting that manufacturing has contributed far more than finance to scientific and technological innovation. Although the financial sector also had its innovations, but due to the nature of being virtual economy, certain kinds of innovation (for example, sub-mortgage or other more complicated financial derivatives) sometimes, instead of ameliorating risk allocation, led to the misallocation of

[3]From the Bible, "the shining city upon a hill", referring to Jerusalem.

Table 4.1 Industrial structure of the United States (Unit: %)

Item	1950	1960	1970	1980	2000	2001	2002	2003	2004	2005	2006	2007	2008
Private sector	89.2	86.8	84.8	86.2	87.7	87.6	87.2	87.1	87.2	87.4	87.5	87.4	87.1
Agriculture, Mining, Public utilities	11.0	7.9	6.1	7.6	4.2	4.1	3.9	4.4	4.7	4.8	5.0	5.2	5.5
Construction	4.4	4.5	4.8	4.7	4.4	4.6	4.6	4.5	4.6	4.9	4.9	4.4	4.1
Manufacturing	27.0	25.3	22.7	20.0	14.5	13.2	12.9	12.4	12.2	11.9	12.0	11.7	11.5
Information	2.7	3.0	3.4	3.6	4.7	4.7	4.6	4.5	4.5	4.5	4.2	4.2	4.4
Finance	11.4	14.1	14.6	15.9	19.7	20.3	20.5	20.5	20.4	20.4	20.4	20.4	20.0
Government	10.8	13.2	15.2	13.8	12.3	12.4	12.8	12.9	12.8	12.6	12.5	12.6	12.9

Source Bureau of Economic Analysis of the United States

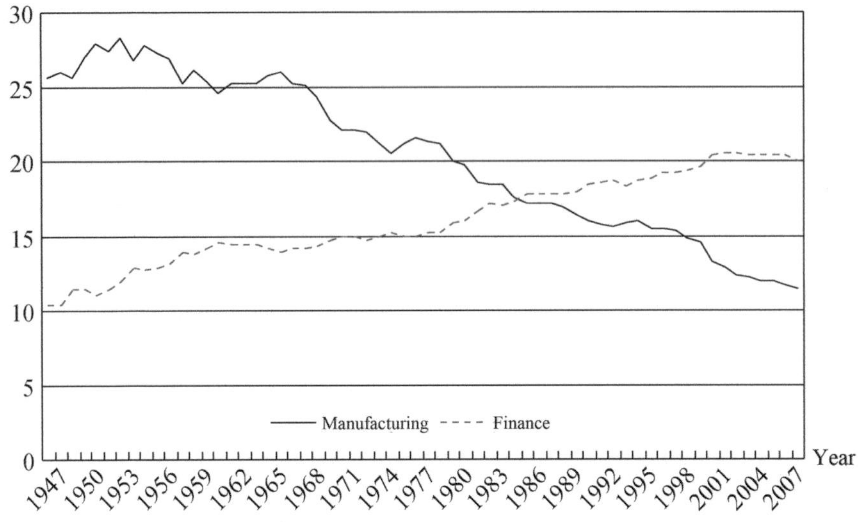

Chart 4.5 Manufacturing and financial sector in the United States (share in percentage of GDP). *Source* Bureau of Economic Analysis of the United States (BEA)

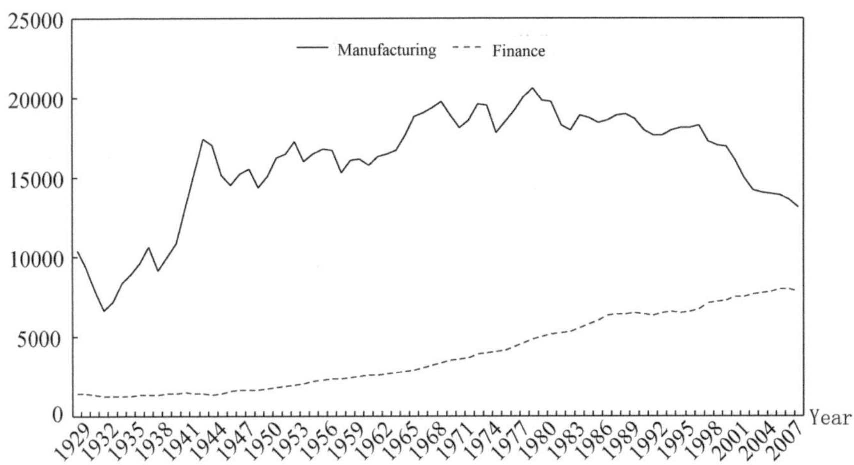

Chart 4.6 Employment in U.S. (1929–2008). *Source* Bureau of Economic Analysis of the United States (BEA)

resources and aggravate the risk. Meanwhile, the over expansion of the financial sector and shrinking of the manufacturing was also manifested that more attention was paid to the distribution of wealth while less attention was given to production. This would inevitably weaken the motivation to innovate in the real economy.

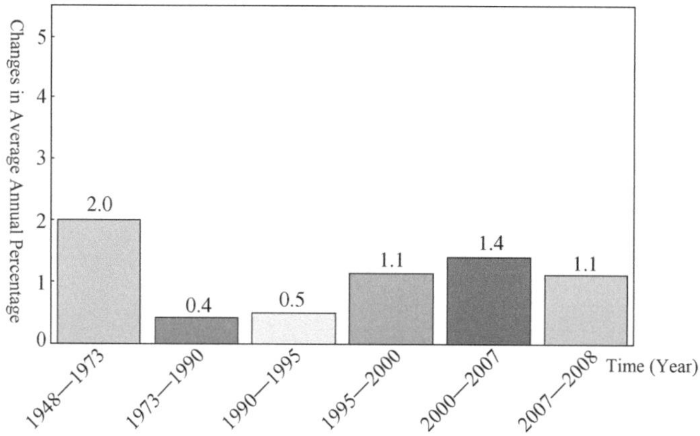

Chart 4.7 MFP of non-agricultural sector. *Source* Bureau of Economic Analysis of the United States

Now it comes to the changes in productivity. In United States' Golden Age of economic growth, between 1948 and 1973, the Multi Factor of Production (MFP) of the non-agriculture sector was 2.0, the record high in history. In the stagnation of the 1970s, and before the mid-1990s prosperity of the New Economy, the MFT had been at low level, linger between 0.4 and 0.5. Since 1995, with the rise of the New Economy and the wide spread of the information technology, MFP increased sharply and reached 1.1 during the period of 1995–2000. As the world entered the 21st century, MFP has further increased to 1.4, which provided strong support to the economic prosperity of the United States and helped to sustain the growing external imbalances (see Chart 4.7). But, this theory is not without problems after further analysis. A major difference between Diagraph 4–8 and Diagraph 4–7 is that, in the manufacturing sector, MFP started to decrease after 2000 as compared with the past, but MFP of the non-agricultural sector in Diagraph 4–7 shows MFP of the non-sector during the period of 2000–2007 is higher than that of 1995–2000. The discrepancy is caused by the fact that MFP of the financial sector was included in that of the non-agricultural sector. To put it in another way, When the manufacturing is measured in terms of MFP, then the decrease in the MFP in the 21st century (2000–2006) has proved none other than the fact that it had not been the key factor that bolstered the expansion of the financial sector and sustained the external imbalances. It is based on this judgment that this round of crisis should be viewed as the result from the sliding of the productivity.

The United States is faced with declining of the economic growth. On the one hand, indicators suggest that the economic growth is slowing down. The study by the well-known economist, Gordon shows, the annual tendency of the growth rate of GDP (or the potential growth rate) of the period of 1875–1950 was 3.42%, and the period that registered the highest average annual growth rate of 5.04% was

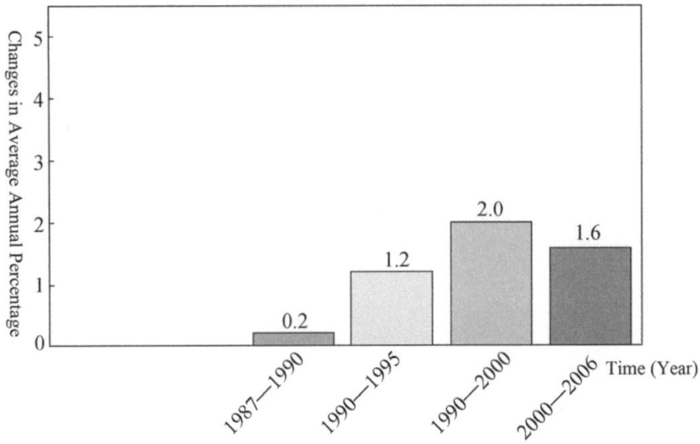

Chart 4.8 MFP of manufacturing sector. *Source* Bureau of Economic Analysis of the United States (BEA)

between 1928 and 1950, but the figure started to go down all the way after that, and reached 2.86% of the period between 1987 and 2007. Later, when the sub-mortgage crisis broke out during 2007 and 2008, the growth rate slid to as low as 2%.

Based on estimates of a variety of indices including productivity, labor hour, employment, labor participation rate, Gordon predicted that between 2008 and 2028, the United States would enter the period of the slowest growth: the average annual growth rate will slow down to 2.35% (the average per capita growth rate will be 1.45%).[4] Besides, Gordon also believed that in the upcoming twenty years, information and communications technologies will play a lesser role in uplifting the productivity when they are applied more extensively, and consequently this will also negatively impact the overall technological progress in the United States. In fact, from Chart 4.2 one can see that the latest wave of financial turmoil has already slowed down the technological progress in manufacturing in the developed economies, including the United States, Europe and Japan. Meanwhile, as is shown by Chart 4.4, as people lower their expectation for income, the imbalances of the United States had started to be rectified.

[4]Of course, economic slackness will continue in the long-run: According to the Old-age, Survivors, and Disability Insurance (OASD), the GDP of the United States is projected to increase by only 2% annually from 2015 to 2085.

4.4 Technological Revolution and Long Cycle of Economy

Between the new economic prosperity since the mid 1990s to the outbreak of the sub-mortgage crisis in March, 2007, the up-going economic cycle of the United States was marveled by the whole world. To be sure, innovation and technological progress constituted the indispensable part of the economic boom. However, as technological progress slowed down, imbalances could no longer be sustained, which caused the outbreak of the sub-mortgage crisis. This scenario testifies to the logics of the theory mentioned above. To think further following the its assumption, people have to ask the following questions: What kind of role does the United States has to play in future technological revolution? What is the prospect of global re-balancing if that happens?

Before answering those questions we'd better take a look at the dynamics of the long cycles of economy since the end of the 18th century (see Chart 4.9).

The first phase of ascendency occurred during the period from 1795 to 1825, which saw a round of economic boom resulting from innovation in essential technology represented by the steam engine the development of textile technology in Britain. The period also saw the "canal building fever" in the west and the great leap forward of the British economy.

The second phase of ascendency occurred during the period from 1795 to 1825. The prosperity was mainly attributable to innovations in steel production and construction of railways, seeing the booming of railroads and the prosperity of the Victoria Age. However, it happened mostly in Britain.

The third ascendency phase occurred during the period between 1890 and 1913. Electricity, automobile and other technological innovation not only brought about the rapid development of electricity, automobile and chemical industry, but also upgraded the industries of the industrialized countries, and eventually cultivated the automobile industry into the pillar industry of the time. Technological innovations

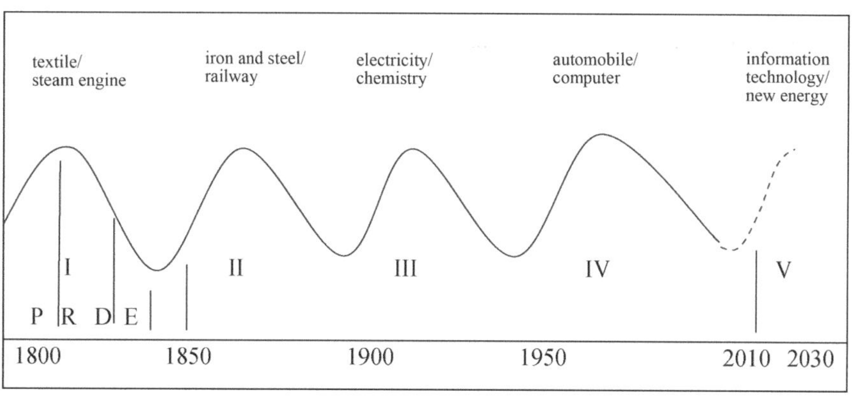

Chart 4.9 Long cycle of the world economy since the end of the 18th century. *Note* P: Prosperity; R: Recession; D: Depression; E: Economic Recovery. *Source* Made by the authors

made headway in Britain, the United States and Germany at the same time, and spilled over other areas and regions, giving birth to the Belle Epoque of Europe and the Progressive Era in the United States. It is worth mentioning that the era was followed by the WWI and WWII, and although wars with its destructive force had put an end to the rising trend, they had also "cleared up the ground", and prepared momentum for the fourth long cycle.

The rising phase of the fourth long cycle of world economy took place between 1945 and 1973. The technological innovations took place in a number of fields, including computer, biography, aerospace, and new materials, and new technologies applied to these fields facilitated the optimization of the manufacturing structure. The rising phase happened concurrently with the post WWII Golden Age of economic growth in developed economies. It was followed by the downturn, marked by the oil crisis and stagnation. To the developed economies, 1990s was recession. The bust of the Internet bubble in the United States in 2000 can be viewed as end of the Kondratiev cycle, yet, as the influence of the breakdown was not as severe as was expected, and as most of the emerging economies represented by China was comprehensively involved in the global development, the cycle was postponed. However, as is often said, what will be will, since 2007, with the outbreak of the sub-mortgage crisis, the world economy was plummeted to the bottom of the valley and has been linger there ever since.

Crisis is the end of the last cycle and the starting point of the next. In this sense, we tend to believe that the current crisis has initiated another round of the long cycle of the world economy.

The rising phase of the fifth long cycle is expected to occur in the period from 2010 to 2030, a projection that fits right into the technological deployment period termed by Perez. Innovations of this period are mainly in the period information technology, biotechnology, breakthroughs in new energy resources, new materials, etc. After the boom in the mid and late 1990s, information technology will continue to make progress at the physical level, and tap its tremendous potential at the network level. In particular, in the fields of online network, the emergence of social media like Twitter and Facebook which signifies one of the major developments and the revolution of the internet communication has become the vanguard of the present wave of innovation with its new, creative way of thinking.

While the long-term economic cycle driven by technological innovation depicts the theme of the global growth with economic imbalances and re-balancing are merely the rhythms of the melody. From the perspective, we believe that in the near future, we will experience the initiation phase of the global restructuring including restructuring of the industries and new innovations, during which the world will move towards new the new balance. In the process of the rebalancing, the emerging economies and developed economy will be in the same position on the track of growth. This gives the group of emerging economies, including China, an opportunity to take over the strategic height of developing new industries and therefore the advantageous positions in the new balanced system.

4.5 A New Round of Technological Revolution Is Taking Shape Again

Crisis is often the midwife of major technological innovation and revolution. In dealing with the crisis, the society grows a demand for technological innovation more urgent than any time before, and tends to increase the input in innovation and move along the better-delineated path of development, thus inducing the technological revolution to occur sooner. For instance, the global economic crisis of 1857 had accelerated the second technological revolution marked by the electricity revolution; the Great Depression of 1929 and later the WWII had led to the third technological revolution marked by technological breakthroughs in electronic technology, aeronautics and aerospace, as well as nuclear energy. Now, the question is, will the impact of the crisis bring forth the new technological revolution in the United States very soon?

The United States had proposed the strategic plan that gives top priority to technological innovation on the country's development agenda in the present era. Priority will be given to developing hi-tech industries, and maintain the country's leading position in global technology. In April, 2009, at the 146th annual conference of National Academy of Sciences, President Obama pointed out that the US leadership in the world economy in the 20th century was attributable to its leading role in the innovation in the world. He announced new initiatives and investments in scientific research and innovation, and said he is going to invest 3% of the gross domestic product in research and innovation. This exceeds the amount invested in 1964 at the height of the space race. With the 120 billion dollars investment in science and technology out of the 787 billion dollars economic stimulus package, the current US investment in the "New Deal for Science and Technology" that is aimed to boost the new industries has already exceeded the expense of Project Apollo and Project Manhattan. Besides, the United States intends to create an innovation friendly environment, review the manufacturing sector, and fully push forward renovation of the traditional industry by elevating them to the high-end of production. Against the backdrop of economic globalization, the United States is determined to assume of the role of global economic headquarter, and be engaged mainly in research and development (R&D), investment, education, high-end services, and put the focus of strategic competition on "innovation", "entrepreneurship", and "creation."

In fact, as early as in 2006, the American Competitiveness Initiative has stated: the strength of the US economy and its global leadership is to a large extent depends on its capability to produce and utilize the latest achievements in science and technology. The Initiative attributed the capability to strength in the three areas: scientific research, a strong education system and a social environment that encourages entrepreneurship, risk-taking, and innovation. It suggests that the national competitiveness is built on two cornerstones: science and technology; and the overall quality of the citizens. A consulting report issued by the National Academy of Sciences named "Rising above the Gathering Storm" holds the idea that in a world where advanced knowledge is widespread and low-cost labor is readily available, U.S. advantages in the marketplace and in science and technology have begun to erode. Great effort is urgently needed to bolster U.S. competitiveness to prevent the country from losing its pre-eminence in these areas. Therefore, the ultimate goal is to create brand-new, quality jobs for all US citizens by developing new industries supported by talents in scientific talents and engineers.

Porter discussed the turn in directions possibly to be made by the United States from the perspective of competition strategies, while also emphasizing the importance of technology. In his view, the federal government has overlooked the following issues of significance: (1) Decrease in investments in science and technology. (2) Inadequate attention paid to competition. Slackening the anti-trust efforts has led to quite an amount of market monopolies. (3) Supervision lags behind the rapid growth in economy and growth. (4) Educational resources are not fully utilized and logistic infrastructures are incomplete and not well-developed. (5) Inadequate support from the federal government to regionalization and specialization that will lead to economic growth. In conclusion, big changes and transformations are needed if the United States wants to regain its competitive advantages.

Among these strategies, the most significant is the new revolution in technology, the lifeline of the United States. Given the present state of affairs, the possibility of a new technological revolution in the near future is very slim. This is because: (1) Technological innovations will be made, not as fundamental changes, but only in narrower fields mostly to complement, develop and innovate the existing technologies, such as new network theories, cloud calculation, network safety and intelligent management, Human-Computer Interaction (HCI) and intelligent process of language, text and image, exploration and management of mega-data, spinning electron, molecule, quantum device, photoelectron, quantum, gene calculation, etc.… (2) In the field of biotechnology, new technology will be innovated, however, unlike technological revolutions in steam engine and electricity that would cause no harm to human body, biotechnology directly impacts the human body, and involves complicated issues like ethics and racial issues. It will go through long deliberation and complicated procedures before a single research proposal can be approved, and the related controversies will definitely slow down the innovation. (3) Low-carbon technologies. Global warming and sustainability of the mankind demands the human society to change the pattern of development that depends on the unlimited consumption of fossil fuel and natural resources, and adopt the new model that is resource-saving, highly efficient, clean and based on recycling economy. Breakthroughs have to be made to solve the basic scientific problems in the fields including development of advanced, renewable and nuclear energy, technologies in highly efficient hydrogen production and storage of hydrogen, highly-efficient utilization and clean recycling of non-renewable resources and water resources, development and utilization of bio-resources, exploration of resources in inner earth, deep ocean and outer space. In one word, it is necessary to facilitate development and innovation in low-carbon technologies. However, as this involves a variety of interest groups, it is difficult to put good ideas into laws, and there are many obstacles to overcome before increasing investment in this area. Internationally, meanwhile, many unsolved issues keep on obstructing the provision of assistance by the developed countries to their underdeveloped counterparts, a situation known as "carbon politics". Under these circumstances, it is unlikely that carbon technology will advance in large strides.

Moreover, efforts made by the US government to strengthen financial supervision and streamline the financial sector has imposed more restraints and limits on the sector, preventing it from providing the much-needed funds in substantial amount to the major innovation projects in the private sector. Although the government is intent on increasing investment in this regard, in general, the investment remains inadequate.

Our assessment is that, it is difficult to see the rise of another technological revolution in the near future in the United States. In contrast, emerging economies begins to demonstrate their strength in those areas. For instance, Huawei, the leading Chinese enterprise in switching technology has come face to face in intense competition with Ericsson, not only domestically but also in the market of developed economies in Europe and North America; Haier, the producer of white household appliances has turned out state-of-art mini refrigerator at low cost. India's Tata Motors developed the Nano car sold at 2500 dollars, setting new standards for lower-cost automobiles. Embraer of Brazil has become the world's major producer specialized in small, commercial jets. SAB Miller, the South African brewer, had succeeded in replacing the expensive imported malt with the local sorghum in producing affordable beers. As for Russia, even with an unfavorable environment for business, a number of commercial innovations come to the fore, like the Kaspersky Laboratories, the software group, has developed Own-Branding and Manufacturing (OBM), world-class security software.

To keep pace with the development, investments in R&D of the emerging economies also climb up rapidly, whereas that of the developed economy is on decline (see Chart 4.10). Take China for example, the share of expenditure in R & D increased from 0.90% in 2000 to 1.75% in 2010, and China tops other emerging economies in this regard. In terms of China's share in the global R&D, it almost doubled from 5% in 2002 to near 10%, behind only that of the United States (35% of the total world investment in 2007) and Japan (14% of the world's total in 2007). Multinationals are also promoting R&D, mostly in China and India. Twelve per cent people out of the 30 thousands R&D staff in Siemens work in Asia, higher than the percentage (7%) five years ago. Microsoft is the biggest enterprise that set up R&D center in China, among a group of nearly one hundred foreign enterprises that did the same. General Electric is one of the 50 companies that set up R&D center in India.

People had doubts about innovations in emerging economies at the beginning, who were often, not without bias, called "imitators", a situation similar to what had happened in the 1970s. At the time, when Japanese enterprises were making impression inroads into the world market, they were condescendingly called "copycat makers" of cheap and low-quality goods. It was not until later when those enterprises became recognized by the world market as respectful innovators.

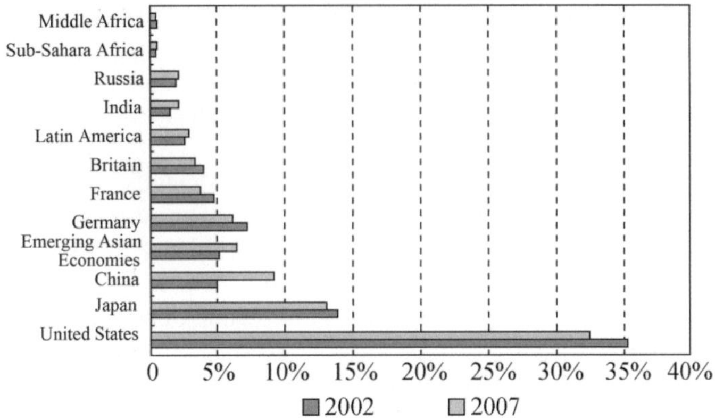

Chart 4.10 Share in the global investments in R&D by country (Region). *Source* UNESCO and Research Department, Standard Chartered Bank

In our view, the rising of the emerging economies in innovations will transform the trajectory of the future technological revolution and the landscape of global technological development. It is also our firm belief that in future, this area will no longer be dominated by the leadership of the United States alone, and the decline of the West is also projected. The shift in the rise and fall will continue to occur in the United States and the emerging economies, and it may probably take place sooner. In particular, improvements in productivity in emerging countries will advance in quicker pace, leading to the fast narrowing of the gap between the emerging economies and the United States. Since technological innovation is one important factor of external imbalances, changes in the global landscape of technological advancement will act as one of the essential forces that bring the global economy back to balance.

References

Bussiere M, Fratzscher M, Muller GJ (2005) Productivity shocks, budget deficits and the current account, European Central Bank Working Paper Series, No. 509

Engel C, Rogers J (2006) The U.S. Current Account Deficit and the Expected Share of World Output. J Monetary Econ

Glick R, Rogoff K (1995) Global versus Country-Specific Productivity Shocks and the Current Account. J Monetary Econ

Zhang R, Zhigang Y (2010) Technical Innovation Ability, Financial Market Efficiency and External Economic Inbalance. Journal of Financ Res, vol.12, 2012

Part III
From Imbalances to Financial Crisis

Introduction

The immediate manifestation of global imbalances is the imbalances of the international payments on national accounts, the root cause of which can be traced back to the imbalance between the domestic savings and investment within the countries. Such correlation is lucidly expressed by identical equations of macroeconomy. In an open economy, when domestic savings is less than domestic investment, the country needs to balance the domestic macroeconomy by taking loans from foreign savings, thus creating deficits on international payments, and vice versa. The ties between foreign and domestic economy reveal that to analyze global imbalances and look for solutions, one has to extend the scope of research to ways of development and economic structures within different countries.

This section conducts deeper analysis of the three historical periods of global imbalances from the perspectives of domestic savings, investments, and the dynamism of changes in the shortage of savings and investment. Our analyses show the following: before 1973, relations of payments in trade surplus and deficit among countries had been in conformity with the theoretical paradigms of the classic economics of development; during the period 1973–1998, with the rising of the emerging markets and relative weakening of the economic status of the United States, the world entered the period of economic restructuring. In this period, shortages in savings/investments rose alternately, with no clearly manifested orientation. Since 1998, however, world economic trend started to move in the opposite direction away from the situation prior to 1973: shortages in savings occurred in developed economies, where trade deficits started to arise and capitals flew in; in contrast, emerging countries had seen shortages in investment, and concurrently had experience trade deficits and outflow of capital. As this situation went on for a long time and the causes for the long-standing problem were not addressed by developed economies including the United States, contradictions were pent-up and eventually led to the outbreak of the 2007 global economic crisis, one of the kinds that had not been seen in a hundred years.

In this sense, the so-called rebalance, in essence, is to call on the countries to commit themselves to domestic restructuring and adjust the mode of development. This is by no means an easy job, as it is full of entangled contradictions. It is due to the many difficulties and contradictions inherently existing in this task that the recovery of the global economy needs a very long time.

Chapter 5
Internal and External Imbalances and Currency Hegemony

Some still remember that Emanuel Kant in 1795 remarked that manipulation of international credit system by a single country is "the biggest obstacle to eternal peace."

—New York Times, February 19th, 1973.[1]

The previous two chapters mainly focuses on real economy, looking for the causes of global trade and imbalances from the angle of international labor division and technological innovation, this chapter studies global imbalances and economic crisis from the perspective of currency hegemony with analyses of currency and finance.

5.1 Global Imbalances: "Old Tales Retold" Since the End of WWII

At the end of 2005, the term "global imbalances" begun to circulate widely around the world, which was officially introduced by Rodrigo de Rato, the then Chairman of the IMF in his speech entitled "Correcting Global Imbalances—Avoiding the Blame Game" on February 23rd, 2005.[2] In his remarks, de Rato pointed out that "The constellation of large deficits in one country, with counterpart surpluses being concentrated in a few others, is what we mean when we speak of global imbalances." He further observed that the present global imbalances were shown in "the large US current account and fiscal deficits, which are matched by growing surpluses in Japan, emerging Asia, and certain oil-exporting countries."

Table 5.1 recorded the current account differences between emerging East Asia (including Japan) and the U.S. from 1990 to 2000. Apparently, the so-called global

[1]Indirect quote from Hudson (2008).

[2]Remarks by Rodrigo de Rato, Chairman of the Executive Board and Managing Director of the International Monetary Fund at the meeting sponsored by Foreign Policy Association at New York on February 23, 2005.

Y. Li and X. Zhang, *Imbalance and Rebalance*,
https://doi.org/10.1007/978-981-10-6150-9_5

imbalances, to a large extent, mean the current account imbalances between the emerging East Asia and the United States.

Although global imbalances is a recent concept put forward several years ago, the economic picture it captures is merely reveals what had been going on since the birth of the Bretton Woods System after the end of the WWII.

It was mentioned previously that the Bretton Woods System is a system, in a nutshell, the system of "double pegging" which pegged the dollar to gold, and currencies of all other countries to dollar. The U.S. dollar plays a unique role under the system, being the local currency of the U.S., as well as the world currency. As the national currency, its supply has to be decided by the U.S. monetary policy goals, the country's gold reserve, as well as the running of the domestic economy; as the world currency, its supply has to meet the needs of international trade and economic development for more means of transaction and reserve assets. The two roles of the dollar are inherently contradictory. On the one hand, as a country needs incessant currency supply as its economy grows, global economic development in the same way requires more dollar as the means of payment and reserve assets; however, to keep the increasing supply of dollar, the U.S. has to run deficits on its international balance-of-payment. This explains why, since the 1960s, the U.S. has been running large deficits and accumulated huge international debts each and every year. On the other hand, the huge deficits and the subsequently big increase in dollar supply have exerted negative impacts on the stability of the domestic value of the dollar and its economy, making it difficult for the U.S. to fulfill its commitment of exchange the dollar for gold. Such is a fundamental contradiction that cannot be solved, the so-called "Triffin Dilemma" (Triffin 1960)[3] in economic theory. The "global imbalances" is merely another expression of the Triffin Dilemma. History shows that the long-existing Triffin Dilemma has become more unbearable for the U.S. and international community. As the result, since the 1970s, the dollar kept on depreciating, followed by actions taken by the international community to salvage the tendency, which failed as the Bretton Woods System eventually collapsed.

The 1974 Jamaica Agreement marked the end of the Bretton Woods System, but what had been removed was the "double peg", as the U.S. gave up its commitment to maintain the stability of the value of dollar and other countries successively unpegged their currencies to the dollar. Even by doing so, however, the world liquidity was still inadequate, because countries need to keep the supply of reserve assets, which can only be realized through the U.S. deficits, as they all acknowledge that the dollar remains the world money and major reserve assets. Chart 5.1 depicts the share of U.S. current account deficit in the GDP. It illustrates clearly that since 1977 and with only a few exceptions, the current account had been in deficit, which kept on growing. In other words, after the collapse of the Bretton Woods System, global imbalances depicted by the Triffin Dilemma still exists.

---

[3]Triffin (1997).

Table 5.1 Asian economies and the U.S: contribution of current account difference to GDP (Unit: %)

Economy	1999	2000	2001	2002	2003	2004	2005	2006	2007	2008	2009	2010
Japan	2.62	2.56	2.14	2.87	3.22	3.74	3.64	3.91	4.82	3.22	2.82	3.57
Singapore	17.07	10.86	12.88	12.89	22.70	16.97	21.11	24.82	27.34	14.58	19.04	22.21
Taiwan, China	2.67	2.73	6.45	8.75	9.82	5.80	4.82	6.99	8.94	6.87	11.37	9.43
Indonesia	3.72	4.83	4.30	4.00	3.45	0.61	0.10	2.98	2.43	0.03	2.58	0.89
South Korea	5.30	2.78	1.67	1.31	2.42	4.48	2.20	1.48	2.08	0.34	3.94	2.80
Malaysia	15.69	9.05	7.85	7.96	11.98	12.09	15.00	16.44	15.92	17.48	16.50	11.82
Philippines	−3.77	−2.93	−2.45	−0.36	0.36	1.87	2.01	4.55	4.94	2.18	5.81	4,49
Thailand	10.17	7.60	4.43	3.69	3.35	1.72	−4.33	1.12	6.35	0.79	8.29	4.64
Mainland China	1.45	1.71	1.31	2.44	2.80	3.55	7.13	9.34	10.64	9.65	5.95	5.21
Hong Kong, China	6.28	4.14	5.87	7.58	10.39	9.48	11.35	12.08	12.34	13.69	8.60	6.58
U.S.	−3.22	−4.18	−3.86	−4.30	−4.67	−5.31	−5.92	−5.99	−5.11	−4.66	−2.68	−3.21

Source Statistics by IMF and IFS

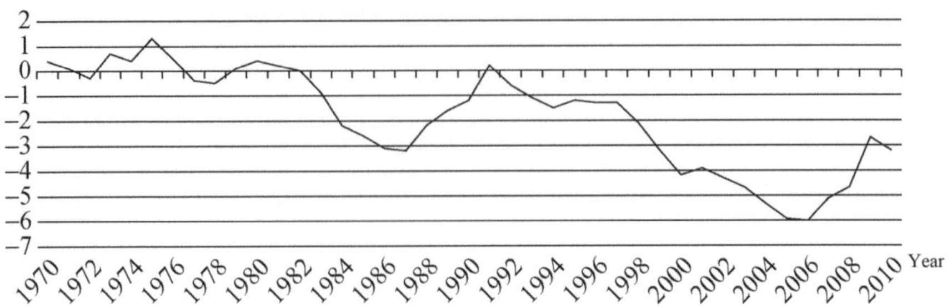

Chart 5.1 The U.S.: contribution of current account difference to GDP (Unit: %). *Source* Bureau of Economic Analysis of the U.S. (BEA)

5.2 Global Imbalances from the Perspective of Saving—Investment

The outward manifestation of global imbalances is countries' imbalanced international balance-of-payment, which has its root in the imbalance between a country's savings and investment. In theory, in an open economy, aggregate supply comes from household saving, government saving, and import; and aggregate demand is composed of household investment, government investment and export. According to the identical equation of national income, the total savings is the combination of household saving and government revenue, and aggregate national investment is the sum of household investment and government expenditure; and net export equals the difference between the aggregate savings and the aggregate investments. When a country saves less than it invests, and there is the shortage in savings, the country will run deficit to "import" other countries' saving to balance the macro economy; conversely, if a country's saving exceeds investment, there will be a shortage in investment, and the country will "export" its saving in the form of the trade surplus to balance the macro economy. Such adjustments that connects domestic and foreign economies suggests that the starting point for analyzing imbalances of international balance-of-payment is the analyses of savings, investment, and dynamics of changes in shortages of saving and investment of different countries and the world at large.

In September, 2005, the IMF analyzed the development and changes in savings and investments of the world and the major countries in World Economic Outlook. The study covers twenty-one developed economies and twenty-five emerging economies, including five OPEC member states. As the total GDP of the forty-six countries mentioned above accounted for 90% of the world's GDP, the conclusion of the study is comprehensive and valid.

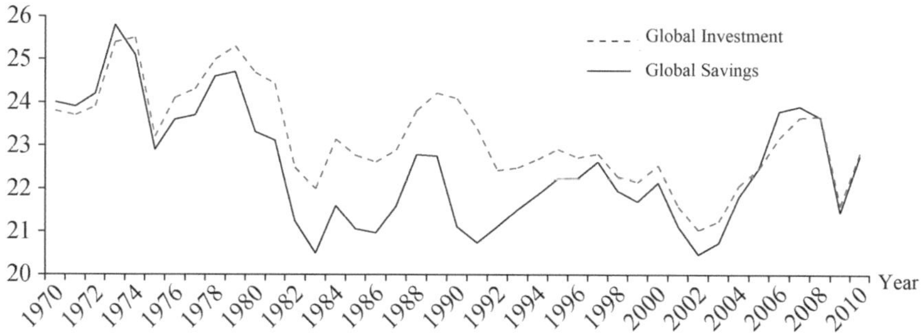

Chart 5.2 Global savings and investments (contribution to GDP) (1970–2010). *Source* IMF

The study shows that in the early 1970s, with the breakout of the first oil crisis, the proportion of the global savings and investment in GDP declined sharply, a trend that went on for more than a decade.[4] From the early 1980s to the mid-1990s, global savings and investments remained stable. Since the second half of the 1990s, though, global savings and investments begun to decrease again, and hit the all-time bottom in 2002. After 2002, as the world economy started to boom in the new century, savings and investments started to surge again.

Chart 5.2 is shows the trends of global savings and investments between 1970 and 2010.[5] It is an intriguing to analyze in comparison the dynamics of savings and investments. Between 1970 and 1974, global savings exceeded investments, corresponding to the global recession at the time. For a very long time after the period, investments had overtaken savings, reflecting the global inflation that lasted for a long period of time. After the Asian financial crisis in the 1990s, the trend changed, when the savings and investments were maintained roughly at the same level, as global prices were kept at low level during the same period. Since 2005, however, global savings again overtook the investments, which resulted in the overflow of liquidity across the world, and although prices did not seem to go up notably, asset prices surged sharply across the board. This phenomenon had been captured insightful by Bernanke, who proposed the view of surplus in global savings (Bernanke 2005).

Above is the description of how global imbalances evolved over the time. To fully analyze it, it is obviously necessary to go deeper to the country or country-group level, and look at saving, investment, and the relations between the

[4]Unless noted specifically, the term "saving" and "investment" refers to the proportion of saving and investment in GDP.

[5]In theory, combined global savings should equal investment. However, two factors contributed to the discrepancies in statistics of the indices. The first is statistic error; the second factor is the fact that this research did not cover all countries. In particular, prior to the 1990s, statistics from the countries of the former socialist bloc, including the former Soviet Union, East European countries, China, North Korea, Vietnam, etc. were incomplete and not transparent, which caused the discrepancies in the statistics.

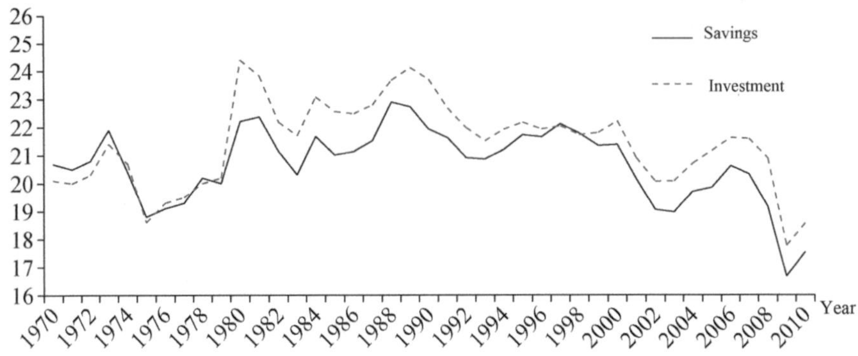

Chart 5.3 Savings and Investments in Developed Economies (1970–2010). *Note* 1970–1979: Statistics for developed economies; 1980–2010: statistics for developed countries. *Source* IMF

two by different countries and country groups. As currently the imbalances between the developed countries and emerging economies remain the focus of worldwide attention, they will be analyzed in the following part.

Statistics shows (see Chart 5.3), savings of the developed economies had been declining since the 1970s, mainly caused by the U.S., Japan, and countries of the Euro Zone. In Japan and countries at the Euro Zone, drop in savings begun first with the decrease in public saving, followed by household saving. In the U.S., in earlier times drop in household saving attributed to the decrease, and after 2000, the drop in public saving became the leading factor that for the declining trend. During the same period, investment rates of developed economies also went down, at average rates lower than savings.

On part of the emerging economies and developing countries (see Chart 5.4), since 1970, both savings rate and investment rates keep climbing, with great fluctuations, though. The first fluctuation occurred in the mid and late 1980s, when debt crisis broke out in Latin America and the economies of the Eastern bloc

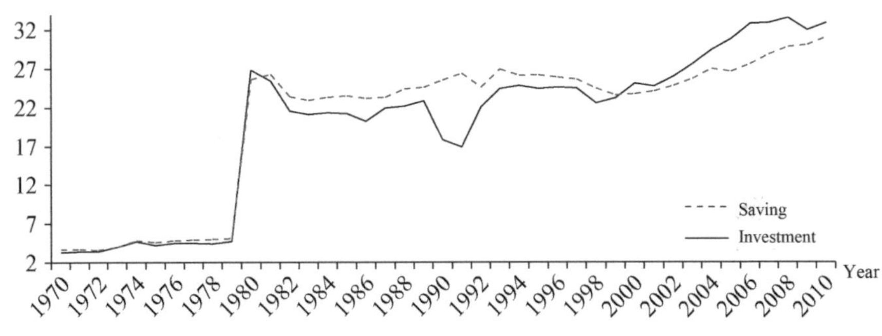

Chart 5.4 Savings and investment of emerging economies and developing countries (1970–2010). *Note* 1970–1979: statistics of emerging market and OPEC countries; 1980–2010: statistics of emerging and developing countries. *Source* IMF

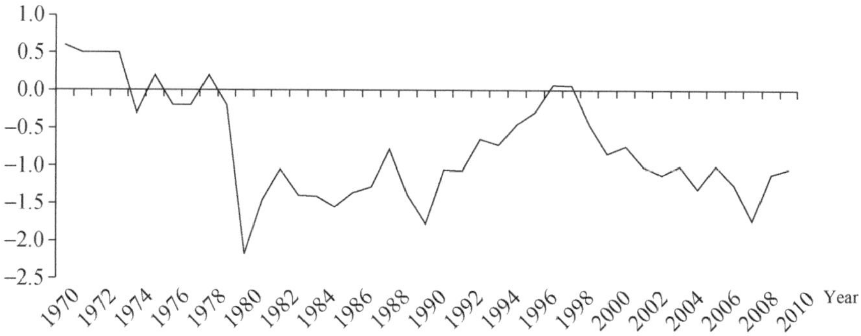

Chart 5.5 Advanced economies: shortages in saving (shares in GDP) (1970–2010). *Source* IMF

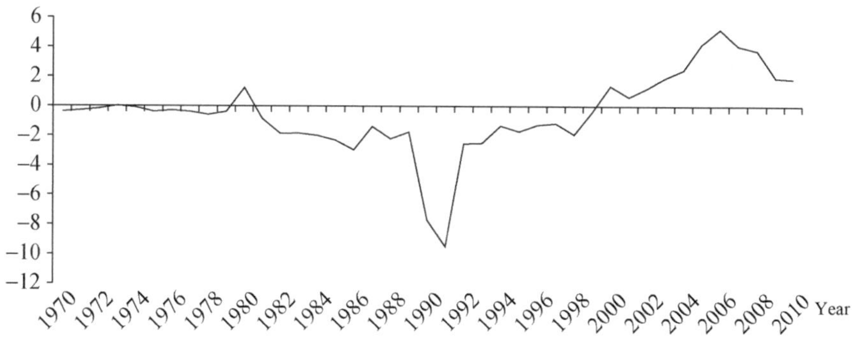

Chart 5.6 Emerging market and developing countries: shortages in saving (shares in GDP) (1970–2010). *Source* IMF

countries were in transition. The second fluctuation happened at the end of the 1990s, when economic crisis in Southeast Asian countries caused the fall.

In terms of the dynamics of shortages in saving (see Charts 5.5 and 5.6), prior to 1988, saving shortage occurred in most emerging economies and developing countries, accompanied by trade deficits and capital inflow, which means, those countries had been trying to promote economic development by persistently "importing" savings from developed economies, and had indeed made substantial achievements. What had happened in those countries provided testimonies to the classic theories of the economics of development. Nevertheless, since 1998, the trend was reversed, when shortages of investment took place in those countries, resulting in the flow of savings to the developed economies in tremendous amount.

5.3 Three Phases of Imbalances Since the 1970s

To sum up, in terms of the dynamics of and relations between saving and investment, the two most important economic factor, global economic relations has gone through three major phases of evolution since 1970.

The first phase is from 1970 to 1973. At the time, advanced economies had shortages in investment, with trade surplus and outflow of capital; as for emerging markets and OPEC countries, they had shortages in saving, with trade deficit and capital inflow. According the concept proposed recently by the IMF, this is imbalances, and the imbalances are mutually complementary, as was depicted by classic economics of development.

The dynamics of the period between 1973 seems unfathomable. In the period, no notably complementarities existed between advanced economies and the emerging market. Since the Bretton Woods System broke down officially in 1973, and the phase saw the U.S. economy mired in long-term recession and the emerging economies and developing countries, especially Asia's emerging market had made remarkable progress, we tend to define this period as the phase of global economic restructuring.

The third phase begun in 1998 and is still going on, where the dynamics has changed: advanced economies started to have shortages in savings, running trade deficit and becoming recipients of capital inflow; at the same time, the emerging market begun to have shortages in investment, which was accompanied by trade surplus and capital outflow. As for the global imbalances in greater detail, Chart 5.7 depicts the trade differences between East Asia as a whole and the United States. It shows that the absolute value of East Asia's surplus is close to that of the trade deficit of the U.S. Given this, it is basically reasonable to conclude that the so-called

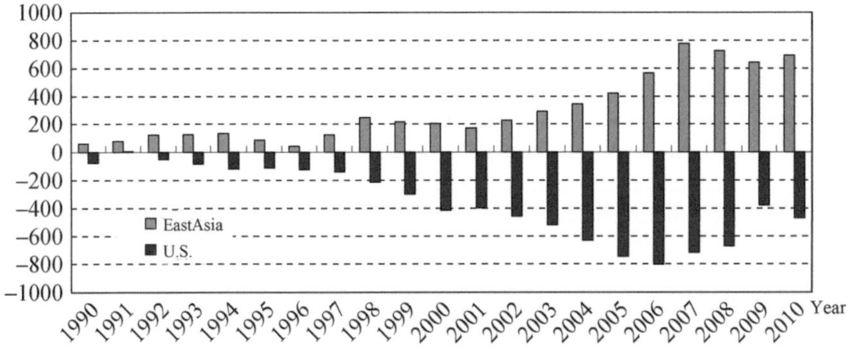

Chart 5.7 Differences in current account of East Asia and U.S. (Unit: $US billion). *Source* IMF and Bureau of Economic Analysis of the United States (BEA) (www.bea.org)

global imbalances mainly took place between East Asia and the U.S. The development economics is unable to explain imbalances of this kind, and that is why the IMF is much concerned about the situation, as was described at the beginning of the chapter.

The correlation between saving and investment has informed us more.

When global saving exceeded investment ("the surplus of global saving" in the words of Bernanke, which is one of the major causes for changes in interest rates), global interest rates would remain at the low level. And it is none other than the low interest rate that led to the asset bubble and the sub-mortgage crisis.

More importantly, worldwide imbalances of saving and investment reflected the saving-investment imbalances among different economies: on the one hand, savings in advanced economies are in shortage; on the other hand, emerging economies have surplus in savings, it further reveals the fact that generally, when emerging economies were turning savings into investment, they were confronted by institutional obstacles and non-efficiency, therefore they had to re-allocate financial resources with the help of advanced economies (especially the U.S.) that acted as "financial intermediaries." In this sense, global imbalances, seen from the view point of investment and saving, reveal that different economies have different levels of financial development. Further studies helps people to discover the deeper causes: the dominance of the international monetary system depends on the developmental level of finance, and this dominance, i.e., the hegemony of international currency, plays a fundamental role in deciding the global distribution of savings and investment.

5.4 Imbalances as the Normality, Currency Hegemony as the Root Cause

Global imbalance is nothing new. It was not until since the new century when the term imbalances started to make headlines in various media, but in fact, imbalances have always been going hand-in-hand with globalization. To further understand characteristics of the concept, we have to look back on the first period of global prosperity: 1870–1913.

The emergence of nationalism in the west in the 19th century and efforts to establish unified national government had tremendously enhanced the nation-states in the dozen of years after 1859. Major political unification and reform took place when the Germany Empire and Kingdom of Italy came into existence after the unification, the emergence of the Austria-Hungary Empire with two monarchs, and the Czar of Russia conducted reform; elsewhere in the world, the unified national government prevailed after the Civil War in the United States, the Dominion of Canada became independent and unified, and when Japan started to introduce the practice of modern politics and economy. It is these fresh transformations that enabled more frequent and easier exchange of ideas, goods and commodities and people (Palmer 2009).

The rise of unified nation-states and the second industrial revolution paved the way for the first round of globalization and prosperity. Since the time, commodities and labor moved more widely around the world, which prompted capital to flow across the world on large scale, drawing the economies closer with economic and financial ties. It is also at the time that the British Empire invested largely overseas, exported capital in large quantity, with commodity export in huge amount. Britain was the factory of the world in every sense. France and Germany were countries that also exported capital and had trade surplus. The destinations of big capital inflow and imported commodities were the "new continents", including Canada in North America, Argentina in South America and Austria, the countries where trade deficits occurred.

Looking back further, one can find imbalances at the earlier date. Actually, with loans lent and borrowed among economies, imbalances would occur inevitably. That is why cases of imbalances could be found everywhere in modern European wars and the rising of the west. These imbalances occurred only within a few countries with limited influences, and were far from being "globalized."

As interdependence has been the main feature of the globalized economy, which had its built-in logic of producing imbalances, naturally the following conclusion is reached: in the age of economic globalization, imbalances and re-balancing is the "normal state" of the global economy, and this normality is dynamic, a typical manifestation of the cycle of movement of the world. There was a time when some scholars thought that economic cycle no longer existed, and the high growth and low inflation that came with the prosperity of the new economy in the U.S. in the mid-and-late 1990s had inflated this optimism to the extreme. Some historians even went so far that they proposed that with the gradual disappearance of the periodic cycle in macro economy and marketization becoming the mainstream in the sphere of micro economy, and democratization becoming the trend in social and political sphere (especially with the collapse of the Berlin Wall and the drastic transformation in the Soviet Union and Eastern bloc), history was ended. However, the current financial crisis with its damaging power made these scholars come to realize that history is far from "being ended", and the world economy is still going through the cycle: problems keeps on cropping up, as is with imbalances, and crisis seems unavoidable.

The above analyses show that imbalances are not fearful, because they go with the operation of the economy. The problem is imbalances will lead to crisis. Imbalances or crises, both can be traced to the hegemonic role of a single currency. The entangled connections between them are noticeable in a series of events including the Great Depression, the stagnation of the 1970s, the Asian crisis in the 1990s and the financial crisis of today.

5.5 The Great Depression: Gold Being the Culprit?

If World War One was the result of imbalances in economic development of the western powers going bad, what was even unfortunate is that the end of it did not bring about new balances, but instead had deteriorated the crisis under the international monetary system based on the gold standard, and eventually led to the unprecedented (but not the last) economic disaster. Even till today, opinions are divided with regard to what caused the crisis and its proliferation, but increasing studies have shown that the major cause is the stubbornness to hold on to the gold standard when it was obsolete and no longer effective— the culprit of the economic crisis.[6]

What happened in the 1920s shows evidently that the gold standard could do nothing to solve the global imbalances, mainly because surplus country had never stood on the same ground as the deficit country when imbalances occurred. Several years before the Great Depression, what happened was that gold had flown in great amount to the U.S. and France (see Chart 5.8), and faced with the inflow of gold, neither the Federal Reserve nor the Bank of France allowed Hume's specie-flow mechanism to work by increasing money supply; instead, they used the write-off method to keep the gold stay in the country, so that to curb inflation and avoid overheated economy. What France did was even more spectacular: in the four years between 1926 and 1929, its share in the world's gold reserve had more than doubled, from 7.7 to 15.8%. Due to the market's concern about the prospect of pound sterling and the U.S. stock market, franc had for once been fervently sought after in the market as the safe haven currency, which brought about big inflows of gold to France (see Patat and Lutfalla 1986). By 1932, France held as much as 27.3% of the world's gold reserve! It was generally believed by the most of the world that France was a typical place where gold only came in but never went out.[7] Meanwhile, the fixed-rate mechanism of the gold standard had eroded the monetary foundation of the deficit countries; in order keep the foundation sound and slow down the outflow of gold, the countries could do nothing but to adopt austerity, selling assets and raise interest rates. However, it turned out that such behavior not only failed to change the imbalance, but caused deflation and unemployment "with no effort". Those actions led to Great Depression; moreover, they paved the way for the spread of the crisis around the globe—especially in countries that adopted the gold standard.[8]

---

[6]This view was shared by many world-class economists, include Friedman and Schwartz (1963), Eichengreen (1992, 2008), Krugman and Obstfeld (1998), Bernanke (2004), et al.

[7]A recent study by Irwin (2010) shows that since France dumped tremendous amount of foreign exchanges and frequently employed the "write-off" method to increase gold reserve, it should be held more responsible for the world's economic crisis of 1929–1933.

[8]Friedman and Schwartz illustrated by example and remarked that because China adopted the silver standard, basically it was not impacted by the Great Depression. And the study by Eichengreen (1992) shows more evidently that the earlier a country withdrew from the gold standard system (i.e. as Britain, Japan, and Sweden did in 1931), the less it was influenced by the

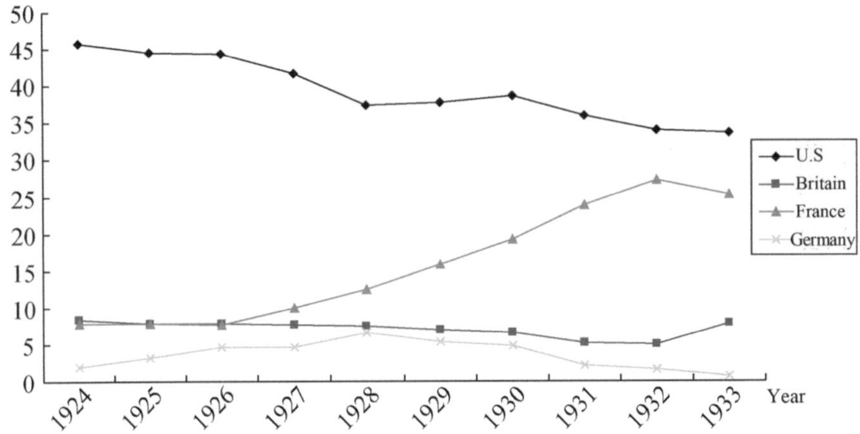

Chart 5.8 Major industrial countries: share of gold reserves in the world's total. *Source* Eichengreen (2008)

On the other hand, economic plight and debt crisis brought by the war made it difficult for countries to convert gold at the legally fixed rate, which was the foundation of the gold standard. The market started to question whether central banks were still capable of keeping their commitment to maintain the gold standard, and such doubt had soon been self-fulfilled. Britain was, perhaps the first among the western powers, to give up the gold standard. It did so because when the gold standard was restored in 1925, it insisted on fixing the exchange rates between pound sterling and gold as well as dollar at the pre-war level, but it was generally believed that the value of pound had been overestimated, about 10% higher than the real value (Officer 2008). The market was rational and merciless, and did not show its favor to pound because of its past glory. British enterprises engaged in export lost their competitiveness severely at the international market, unemployment rate climbed to over 8%, and gold started to flee the country in huge quantity.[9] In the end, in September, 1931, attacked by speculators, gold reserve of the Bank of England had been almost depleted, and the bank had to depreciate pound sterling and gloomily announced its withdrawal from the gold standard. The U.S. was the next target. In fear of the expected depreciation of dollar, people started to undersell dollar in exchange for gold. This had caused the Federal Reserve to lose its gold reserve and prompted a run on the bank, making many private banks go bankruptcy (Bernanke 2004). At last, the U.S. had to forego the gold standard in March, 1933, followed by depreciation of dollar.

(Footnote 8 continued)

economic crisis. In contrast, the members of the "Gold Group", including France, Belgium, Switzerland, stuck to the gold standard as late as 1936, had seen the most severe slide in economy.

[9]In sharp contrast to what happened in France, in 1924, Britain's gold reserve accounted for 8.3% of the world's total, and in 1931, the figure slid down to a mere 5.2%.

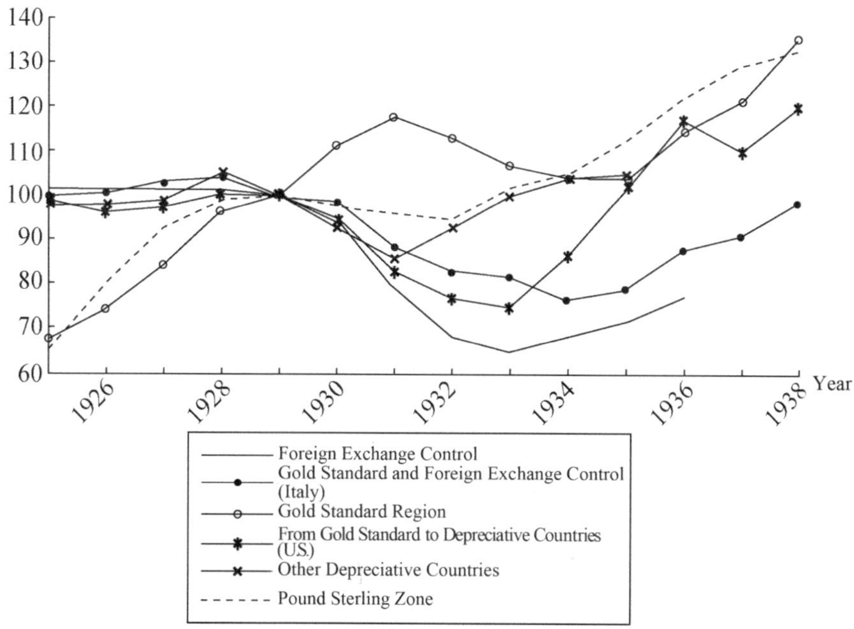

Chart 5.9 Money supply under different exchange system. *Source* Almunia, Bénétrix, Eichengreen, O'Rourke, and Rua (2009)

In order to fulfill the domestic economic goals and deal with the crisis and lift themselves out of recession, the once "respectable" countries had to risk "losing face" and depreciate their local currencies, which means they had first to let go of the gold standard. Chart 5.9 shows that whether for countries in the pound zone (after Britain rejected the gold standard in 1931, some countries begun to peg their currencies to pound sterling, thus creating the "pound zone", and when pound depreciated, other currencies followed suit), and other countries that depreciate their currencies, including the U.S., currency supplies had quickly risen up. And withdrawal from the gold standard immediately triggered the increase in money supply. In contrast, for countries that stuck to the gold standard, even during the worst period of the Great Depression, i.e., between 1931 and 1935, the supply of money had been on decline.

Relevant data shows that countries giving up gold standard did better fiscally than those stuck to gold standard and adopted foreign currency control (see Chart 5.10). Referring to this situation, Bernanke asserted that: the secret of walking out of recession is to ditch the gold standard. In his view, countries that rejected the gold standard had effectively freed themselves from the external constraints of the second-time currency inflation, and they can utilize the freedom to some extent. History also proved Bernanke's argument: Countries that gave up the gold standard at an earlier time had economically recovered sooner, quicker and stronger than those stuck to the gold standard (Bernanke 2007).

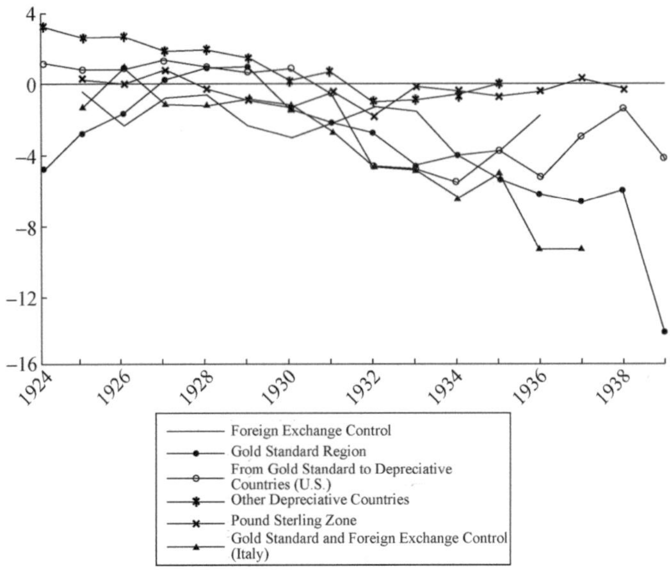

Chart 5.10 Fiscal surplus under different exchange system. *Source* Almunia, Bénétrix, Eichengreen, O' Rourke, and Rua (2009)

5.6 Another Explanation for the Great Depression: The Missing Hegemony

The analyses above shows that the traditional international monetary system, namely, the gold standard, could no longer keep pace with the changing economy. More precisely, it is proved that such a mechanism was unable to deal with the unexpected and increasingly big crisis. The reasons being, on the one hand, the gold standard prevented the imbalances from being corrected automatically, thus exacerbating and prolonging the crisis; on the other hand, in time of crisis, the gold standard became an obstacle that the monetary authority did not know how to deal with. The conclusion is, therefore, countries could not be free and able to deal with the crisis and eventually walk out of the crisis before breaking the shackle of gold standard in the first place.

To straighten out the cause-effect relations of the Great Depression is the holy grill of the field of economics. Kindleberger (1973), for one, has also tried to account for the great depression. He believed that the missing of hegemony has caused the depression to spread across the world.

Kindleberger proposed the well-known theory of "hegemonic stability" (which was discussed in Chap. 1). Hegemony, though does not sound reassuring by nature, is indispensible for the world in Kindleberger's view because of its stabilizing effect. In his study of the 1930s Great Depression, Kindleberger attributed the worldwide proliferation of the crisis to the fact that no single power was able and willing to take the responsibility to end the crisis and the "beggar-thy-neighbor policies"; no country, in particular, is willing to assume the role as the "Lender of Last Resort" to prevent the spread of the financial crisis. Kindleberger observed that the width, depth and length of the depression reflected incapability on the part of Britain and unwillingness on the part of the U.S. to fulfill the responsibility in three areas that would help stabilize the international economic system and salvage it the from the disaster. The three areas are: (1) Keep the market open for dumped products; (2) Provide reversed-cycle long-term loans; (3) Open the window for discount during the crisis.

According to Kindleberger, a global financial system with two centers, or with one center but the leadership is transferring from a country to another, cannot be stable. Citing an example, he pointed out that "a less than smart driver is better than two bright drivers grabbing for the steering wheel." He further observed that the analogy of two bright drivers contending for the steering wheel is not quite appropriate, though vivid. To be more precise, as he pointed out, instability occurred because one driver is growing weaker while the other is not interested enough in driving the vehicle.

What had happened in reality was that in the inter-war years, the international system of gold standard was in transition between the old and new hegemon, when the real powerful leadership had yet to emerge. The Federal Reserve, born in 1913, was young and strong, but under the influence of isolationism, it mainly focused on domestic affairs, and did not show much interest in and lacked experience in managing the international monetary system as the Lender of the Last Resort. As for the Bank of England with a long history and rich and profound expertise (it was created in 1694), was too debilitated by the two devastating world wars to take up the baton even though it was willing to.

5.7 Collapse of the Bretton Woods System and Stagflation of the 1970s

The stagnation happened in the 1970s in the west put an end to the golden age of growth that lasted 25 years after the WWII. In terms of the economic cycle, it was merely another cycle. People from the economics circle are no less eager to discover the reasons behind the stagnation than they wanted to unearth the causes of the Great Depression. It was found that apart from the factors like the two oil crises and relaxation of financial control, etc., the primary cause had to be the "Nixon Shock." The announcement made by Nixon on August 15, 1971 to unpeg dollar from gold led to the collapse of the Bretton Woods System, ushering in the age of floating exchange rate. The global economic also slumped to the bottom.

Table 5.2 shows that for developed economies (the G7 and the OECD), the average level of either investment increase or increase in export during the period of 1972–1984 is lower than that of the period of 1959–1971. The global economic

Table 5.2 Global investment and export (Unit: %)

	The G-7 group	OECD
Annual Growth Rate of Aggregate Investment		
1957—1971	6.1	6.0
1972—1984	2.5	2.3
Annual Growth Rate of Export		
1959—1971	7.8	8.5
1972—1984	6.2	6.3

Source OECD, Economic Outlook (various issues); IMF, International Financial Statistics (various issues)

growth rate also declined from 5% of the post-WWII golden age to 3% in the period of stagnation.

The Bretton Woods System, since the day when it was born, had carried with it unsolvable internal contradictions, i.e., the Triffin Dilemma mentioned many times before: on the one hand, countries have to obtain dollar as the currency of reserve and settlement to maintain liquidity, which caused the dollar to flow out of the U.S. incessantly and be retained in the countries, and as the result the U.S. had to keep its current account deficit. On the other hand, once the other countries' demand for liquidity were met by the huge amount of dollar retained outside the U.S., the countries started to doubt if the U.S., with the deficit, could fulfill its promise to exchange the dollar for gold at the officially designated price. Consequently, it became hard to meet the demands for "liquidity" and "confidence" at the same time.[10]

History is full of intriguing coincidences. Triffin's great work, *Gold and the Dollar Crisis* was published in 1960, when the "dollar shortage" was approaching its end and people began to worry about the prospect of the depreciation of dollar against gold (Krugman and Obstfeld 1998). It was also the time when private capital started to flow out of the U.S. on large scale, which exacerbated the overflow of dollar overseas. In 1961, to maintain the peg between dollar and gold under the Bretton Woods System, the U.S., with other seven western countries including Germany, Britain, France, founded the London Gold Pool in London, in the hope of mitigating the impact of the market on the convertibility rate of $35 for 1 ounce gold. However, with the U.S. getting more involved in the Viet Nam War and the implementation of the "Great Society" at home,[11] the country's fiscal expenditure had increased drastically,[12] with inflation surging and current account surplus

[10]Controversies naturally exist with regard to the Triffin Dilemma. For example, Aizenman (2010) pointed out that in the 1960s, when dollar indisputably became the currency for international reserve and settlement, the U.S. current account was balanced, even with a few surpluses. This suggests that the "hard choice" between liquidity and confidence proposed by Triffin is not necessarily true all the time.

[11]Refers to the Social Program initiated by President Johnson to eliminate poverty and racial discrimination in areas of education, health care and urban construction, etc.

[12]On this point, Eichengreen pointed out that in terms of figures on the surface, inflation in the U.S. was not serious compared with that of other developed economies like France and Japan. However, given its sluggish economic growth, the inflation rate was too high.

plummeting. Becoming increasingly worried about the depreciation of dollar, people begun to dump dollar and stock up gold. By 1968, the London Gold Pool was terminated, and on the international gold market, the official and market convertible rates co-existed, a sign showing that the peg between the dollar and gold had been fundamentally shaken. Meanwhile, European countries became increasingly dissatisfied with the Exorbitant Privilege[13] held by the U.S., complaining that they themselves were, in contrast, forced to keep busy, taking care of the foreign reserves. France was the one that reacted most intensely. In 1965, President De Gaulle converted most part of its dollar reserve into gold, having thus nearly "emptied" the gold reserve of the U.S. At this stage, the collapse of the Bretton Woods system was clearly inevitable.

In mid-August, 1971, words about the intention of the Britain and France to undersell the dollar for gold had become the last straw that crashed the resolve of the Federal Reserve to defend the gold standard (Eichengreen 2008). President Nixon was compelled to close the "window of gold," as the Federal Reserve would no longer automatically sell gold to foreign central banks in exchange for dollar. The administration also stipulated that a 10% VAT additional tax on all export commodities, forcing its trade partners to appreciate their currencies. In December the same year, the Smith Agreement was reached among the world's ten major industrialized countries, who agreed to adjust the official rate of $35 per ounce gold to $38 per ounce (later $42.5), and that the dollar would depreciate by 10% against major western currencies including the Deutsche mark, Japanese yen and Swiss franc, allowing the exchange rate floating range to expand from within plus and minus 1% to within 2.25%. At the same time, the U.S should terminate the additional tax on import. However, "none of these measures succeeded in bolstering the confidence in the dollar" (see Kindleberger 2006). In fact, during the whole year of 1972, the depreciation of the dollar could not be halted, and the U.S. current account deficit kept on deteriorating. In March, 1973, the exchange rate between the dollar and currencies of major industrial countries started to float freely, signifying the breakdown of the Bretton Woods system.

Up to this point, what to make of the demise of the Bretton Woods remains unsolved. In fact, the Triffin dilemma is merely the reason on the surface of the end of the dollar hegemony. The root cause was the global imbalances resulting from the capitalist development after the WWII. From Chart 5.11, one can see that period marked by the predominance of the dollar was also the time when the U.S. economy started to lose its edge, and at the same time, Germany and Japan rose rapidly in economic development, and their currencies started to compete with the dollar. As the "country at the center", the U.S. found it increasingly difficult to maintain the dollar's status as the reserve currency, and the once "periphery countries" like Germany and Japan had become the major exporter and surplus countries in the real sense. Since the future of the countries depends heavily on the international

[13]The remark was made by Giscard d'Estaing, the French Minister of Finance in the 1960s (French president between 1974 and 1981).

monetary system, those countries would not willingly be subjected to the manipulation of the dollar. The transformation of international economy would demand adjustment of the international monetary system, so that the latter will keep pace with the trend of the time. Under the Bretton Woods system such adjustment was impossible, and the only way-out is to make major and drastic changes. Looking back on the evolution of the classic gold standard, one cannot help being amazed at the similarity between the hegemony of the dollar and the pound.

The "Nixon Shock" for sure was not the only cause for the stagnation in the 1970s, but it at least triggered it. Mckinnon held that "In the late 20th century, a major conundrum of the economic history of human society is: since the 1970s, nearly all the developed economies had experienced universal, large-scale decline in real economic growth. It happened with the advent of the floating exchange rate. What is the causation between the two? Did the decline in economic growth compel the countries to adopt the floating exchange rates? Or was the universal fluctuation of the exchange rates led to the widespread slowdown of the real economic growth?" He insisted on the view that "the constant slowdown of the real economic growth across the world was originated from the fluctuations in international currency and finance, especially that of the exchange rates." He observed that "We have reasons to believe, the prolonged sluggish growth in productivity and output is the consequence of the signal errors. Inflation and stagnation came to the forth alternately, exchange rates kept deviating from the economic fundamentals and for a long time was unstable, these are the main factors that led to the derangement of the price signals. A price system in disorder will inevitably lower the efficiency of resource allocation, especially lower the efficiency in real investment."[14]

5.8 "The Original Sin" and the Asian Financial Crisis

The 1997 Asian financial crisis took place merely ten years after the sub-mortgage crisis of the United States. To put the crises into perspective, people would be surprised to see that the Asian financial crisis was just a rehearsal of the current financial crisis. Problems unveiled by the crises, such as that of the international monetary system and the dollar hegemony, are still lingering and causing serious troubles to the human society.

In the mid 1990s, Asia was the destination most favored by foreign investors. Its environment was unparalleled in the world for investors: the immensely high household saving rate made it easier for them to raise funds, and in time of financial

[14]Indirect quote from "Seven Sins" of the Dollar Standard and Floating Exchange Rate by Xiang, Songzuo, a speech made at the "Where would the eruo go?—International Seminar on Euro in Turbulence and World Economy" at the People's University on August 17, 2010, and later at the "International Seminar on Reform of the International Monetary System" co-sponsored by the Reinventing Bretton Woods System Committee and China Center for International Economic Exchanges (CCIEE) in Beijing.

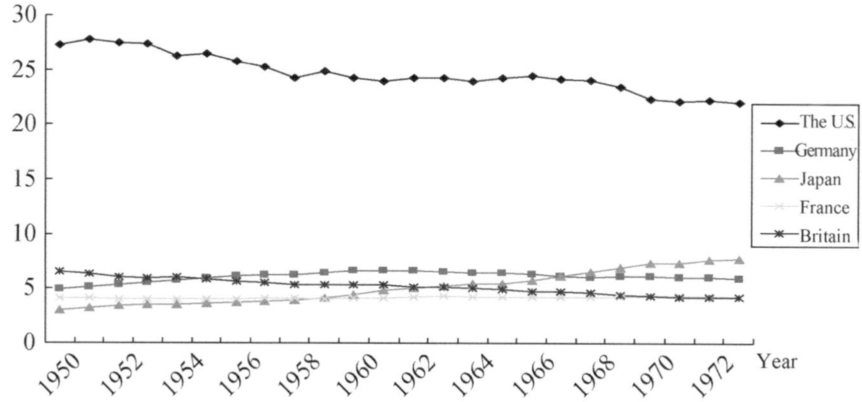

Chart 5.11 major western countries: share in the world's total GDP (1950–1973). *Source* Maddison (2006)

crisis they could go to the government for help, and would get what they need; the fiscal conditions of the governments were relatively sound, as most foreign debts occurred in the private sector; moreover, since local currencies were de facto "pegged" to the dollar, investments were safe generally; last but not least, financial crisis had never occurred in Asia (see Reinhart and Rogoff 2010).

At the end of the 1980s and in the early 1990s, with the burst of the economic bubble, Japan started to export more capital and relocate production to East Asia in an effort to fight against the deflation after the bubble, and it tried to establish the Yen Zone in East Asia. The zero interest rate gave rise to the carry trade of yen. In retrospect, the huge fluidity inflow to East Asia had created a bubble no different than the one in Japan, only on a larger scale. Decision-makers in those countries were not fully aware of the potential risk of the capital inflow. They thought at first that they could achieve both ends—by maintaining the de facto peg they could attract capital investment and at the same time obtain extensive prosperity. However, although Asia based financial system on dollar, it had no one to return to in time of crisis, because neither the Federal Reserve nor the IFM was willing to assume the role of the Lender of Last Resort (Shen 2009).

The root cause of the Asian financial crisis can be traced to the deficiency of the world monetary system and dollar hegemony. As Mckinnon has observed, the predominance of the dollar at the center had marginalized the "periphery currencies" including the yen to an unequal position.[15]

Being the world's biggest debtor, the U.S. did not fear debts. Today, seeing the sovereign debts of Europe deteriorating, one cannot help but asking: why can the U. S. be from of the crisis of sovereign debts, although share of its public debts in GDP is much larger than that of Europe? The answer lies in the dollar hegemony, which

[15]Mckinnon (2005).

enables the U.S. to pay off its debts in dollar. In extreme situations, the U.S. government can put the cash printer into full gear—as a matter of fact, such extreme situations often happened. Therefore, it is just unimaginable that the dollar will someday go under real attack like the Thai baht or Ringgit or HK dollar; in other words, even today, many would still not believe that U.S. will have currency crisis in the real sense.

Others are not as fortunate. Theoretically, except the U.S., any country will face the risk of currency mismatches.[16] Mckinnon has noted this situation in his study of Asian economies, and called it the "original sin" of Asia. In Asia, local currencies cannot be used as means of international payment, the securities markets were underdeveloped and infirm when they first emerged; as far as debts are concerned, economic entities cannot get loans in local currencies from the international market, as well as long-term loans from domestic market. As the result, economic entities cannot offset their risks of debts in dollar, and when they invest domestically, they are faced with currency mismatches (for example, investment projects for profits in Thai baht had to raise funds in dollar) and maturity mismatches (for example, to finance long-term project with short-term loans).

Moreover, before the current global financial crisis broke out, people generally thought that the "original sin" of currency mismatches described by McKinnon happened only in Asia and other underdeveloped countries. But there is the hard fact: even for economies like Europe and Japan that are able to issue securities in local currencies, in deeper crisis, those economies will be also be devastated by the crisis, like South Korea and Thailand in the Asian financial crisis. European countries came to realize painfully that their financial system could not pull through the crisis without the currency swap among central banks initiated by the Federal Reserve (see Chap. 2), they also found to their dismay that with the efforts over so many years, euro was no more than the maid of the dollar.

---

[16]Currency mismatches refers to the following situation: an economic entity (i.e. government, enterprise, bank or household), being integrated into the global economy, its asset/debt, income/expense are subject to fluctuations of exchange rate, because the movement of goods and capital are measured in terms of different currencies. According to Professor Goldstein's definition (see Goldstein, *Controlling Currency Mismatches in Emerging Markets* (Chinese translation), published by Social Sciences Academic Press in 2005), "When the net value or income (or both) become highly sensitive exchange rates fluctuation, 'currency mismatches' occurs. From the view point of storage, currency mismatches refers to the balance sheet (net value)'s sensibility to exchange rates fluctuation; in terms of flow volume, currency mismatches refers to the sensibility of the profit & loss statement (net income) to exchange rates fluctuation. The higher the sensitivity of the net value/net income is, the more serious currency mismatches becomes."

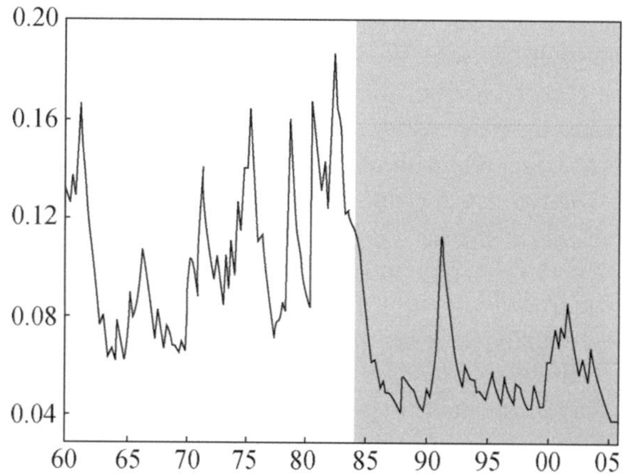

Chart 5.12 Standard deviation of U.S. GDP. *Source* From Perri and Fogli (2006)

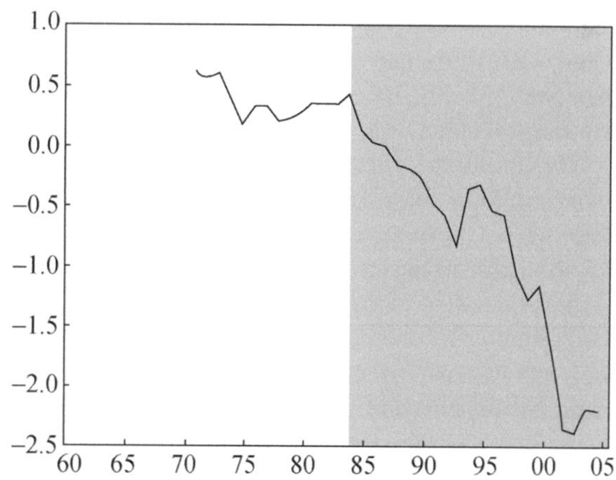

Chart 5.13 U.S. share of net foreign asset in cash in GDP. *Source* Perri and Fogli (2006)

5.9 From "Great Moderation" to Long-Term Imbalances

Different from the Latin American debt crisis of the 1980s and the Asian financial crisis of the 1990s, before the latest round of economic crisis, developed economies had undergone a period called the "Great Moderation." The Great Moderation refers to the sliding down of the cyclical fluctuation rate, which began in the early 1980s in the U.S. and in the end of the 1980s in other developed economies. It is worth noting that the Great Moderation coexisted with the long-term imbalances (external imbalances) in some developed economies, and this was a typical feature of the U.S. economy. Comparison between Charts 5.12 and 5.13 shows that from around 1984, i.e., during the Great Moderation, the standard deviation of the U.S. GDP had been declining (as is shown by the shadowed part of Chart 5.12),; meanwhile, the share of net foreign cash assets to the GDP kept on decreasing (as is shown by the shadowed part of Chart 5.13), a typical sign for long-term imbalances.

Here comes the question: Do the co-existing phenomena suggest causality? The study by Perri and Fogli (2006) shows that if an economy has lower economic fluctuation rate than other, its precautionary savings will go down, which will lead to eternal deterioration of external imbalances. Their empirical studies reveal that the fall in the U.S. economic cyclical fluctuation rate contributes to 20% of the country's external imbalances. In other words, the Great Moderation is an important explanatory factor for long-term imbalances (accounting for one fifth of it). Admittedly, there are other factors that caused external imbalances, for example, the advantages of the U.S. financial system, the dollar hegemony, international labor division and trade pattern, as well as the impact of productivity.

The Great Moderation signifies the existence of an unprecedented period of stability in developed economies. It can be attributed to the integration of a large number of emerging economies in the economic globalization led by developed economies, as well as to desirable economic structural reforms in the developed economies when they adopted the sound policy framework conducive to steady economic growth (Bean 2009). However, as the chapter is going to tell, the Great Moderation sowed the seed for the future crisis.

The longer the Great Moderation lasted, the more likely people were to forget about the risks and crisis, causing the risk premium to slide to extreme low level. Meanwhile, short-term and long-term real interest rate also became very low. This is attributable to the easy monetary policy of the U.S. and the comeback of the high savings rate after a long time when a number of surplus nations like China became increasingly globalized. Low interest rates and the seemingly low risk led to very high rate for financial leverage. Besides, as high financial leverage were often seen in the off-balance sheet transactions, due to the need to circumvent capital supervision and control over the balance sheet transactions. Emergence of a variety of financial innovations and variegated derivatives incurred potential risks and crises. With the outbreak of the sub-mortgage crisis, the Great Moderation turned into a devastating crisis "in no time".

5.10 Sustainability of Imbalances

Tremendous literature on global imbalances has emerged since the beginning of the century. The literature falls into two categories in line with the view on the sustainability of the imbalances: one group of the articles hold the view that moderate imbalances can be sustained because of the equilibrium of the world market—the sustainability group; another group believe that imbalances are not sustainable, and if not adjusted immediately, they will incur huge cost.

First let's take a look at the views for sustainability. According to Cooper, huge deficits of the U.S. can sustain at least for one or two decades, and should not be the cause of worries. Globalization is the result of carry trade, demographic changes, especially aging, which will build up saving until it reaches the highest point. In this sense, the "global imbalances" does not exist, because this balance cannot be regarded as the state of disequilibrium.

Dooley et al. pointed out that Asia had reconstructed the Bretton Woods system dominated by the dollar, with Asia's zone of fixed exchange rate as the new periphery. In this system, periphery countries pursued export-oriented strategy by undervaluing the local currency, exercising capital control and encouraging export of national capital. Exporting national capital was realized by accumulating reserve capital of the currency of the center country. The periphery countries were willing to hold reserve assets with low returns due to the low-efficiency of the domestic capital market, and the need to utilize the capital market of the center country through FDI. Reserves can be regarded as international collateral, which provided guarantee for private investment by the center country in the periphery. Its counterpart was the current account deficit of the center. The successfully implementation of this strategy would enable the economic development in periphery countries to gradually catch up with the center, and help those countries to achieve financial liberalization and eventually be integrated into floating exchange rate system at the center. The 1960s' Europe and 1980s' Japan, the Asia emerging economies had all adopted this strategy. In the foreseeable future, other countries will also embark on this path of development. So, the fundamental feature of a successful international monetary system is the U.S. current account deficits, which is healthy and sustainable.

Caballero et al. is one of the few scholars who studied global imbalances in relation to surplus in global liquidity. They proposed two key hypotheses: Different countries have different economic growth rates, and countries differ in their capabilities in supplying financial assets. Their models include: U(the U.S.), E (Europe and Japan) and R (other economies). Among the models, U and E are capable of providing "hard assets".[17] They compete with each other to attract global savings, an ability that is lacking in R; with robust economic growth, R has large amount of savings surplus, and economic growth in E is slower than U. The model shows that the slower the economic growth of E becomes, or the weaker the ability of supplying assets of R is, the larger U's current account deficit is, the bigger U's share in the global assets, and the lower the global interest level becomes. The study established connections between imbalances and liquidity surplus, and arrived at the conclusion that both are products of changes in the global economic structure. With the outbreak and spread of the international financial crisis, Caballero et al. expanded the model and focused on how liquidity surplus led to asset price bubble and violent fluctuations of the prices of bulk commodities. To certain extent, Caballero et al. shared the views of the mainstream scholars, who proposed that because the U.S. was capable of providing hard assets because it has highly

[17]Hard asset refers to assets that are reliable and can be used as collateral. For example, the US dollar securities, euro securities. Needless to say, hard assets can only be provided by developed countries, and to a large extent, by countries of the reserve currency.

developed financial market. Therefore, they concluded, imbalances and low interest rates is the product of the equilibrium.

In fact, the ideas that emphasized the advantages of the U.S. financial market and equilibrium can be dated back to the 1970s. At the time, there was a theory that tried to account for the external imbalances of the U.S.—the so-called theory of financial intermediary.

According to theory of intermediary, the US deficits on its international balance of payments are nothing but a statistical illusion. The American economy acts as a global financial intermediary: it borrows short-term savings and invests them in long-term assets, mainly mortgage loans. Like a savings bank, the U.S. borrows short-term savings from foreign dollar holders, and invests the money in long-term projects, like purchasing European companies. Foreign investors choose to lend the dollars to the overseas U.S. bank branches, instead of converting them into local currencies partially because they need to keep their assets safe against the risk of depreciation of local currencies, and partly because the European credit markets are not as mature as the U.S. market, and the stock changes markets not as open and active. In a similar vein, central banks of other countries are more willing to invest their surplus dollar in the US treasury bonds than in gold, because the latter yields no interest and is thus the "bad investment." Foreign bank subsidiaries in the U.S. would lend the dollar surplus earned in Europe to American multinationals, as a means of raising funds for overseas investments (including purchasing foreign companies). According to the theory of intermediary, by definition, "assets and debts can only be acquired out of the free will of the entity. The definition of equilibrium in other fields, according to theories of economics, is that buying and selling of moving commodities and services, or holding existing assets and securities at the current prices. The definition also applies. When increase gold reserve does not keep pace with the demand, and foreign countries have positive, net demand for floating dollar assets and gold, according to the definition of fluidity, the U.S. deficit not only is in line with the equilibrium of the foreign exchanges market, but also is the necessary condition for such equilibrium." Kindleberger et al. have also pointed out, the U.S. deficit does not represent imbalances, in fact, it the need of a sound world economy."[18]

Given this, the US government proposed that the concept of economic equilibrium in international balance of payment should change from measuring real trade supply and situation of demand to measuring if the deficit will continue with passage of time….[19] To put it in another way, irrespective of the situation of the U. S. balance of payment, whether it is surplus or deficit, short-term or long-term, it is by definition the de facto equilibrium."

The equilibrium theory is to some to some extent the polished extension of the above theory.

---

[18]Depress et al. (1966).

[19]Hudson (2008), p. 298.

Not all scholars shared its view. Some scholars believed that imbalances were unsustainable. Obstfeld and Rogoff (2000) indicated earlier that the U.S. current account deficit is unsustainable, and the consequent adjustment could have negative impacts. Later, with series of researches (Obstfeld and Rogoff 2004, 2005), they further improved the theoretical framework and strengthened the argument. They thought that now it is increasingly probable that the U.S. current account deficit will be reserved abruptly, and such adjustment will sharply depreciate the real exchange rates of the dollar, putting the world economy at big risk. Their study did not go deeper to search for the fundamental causes of imbalances, neither have they noticed the surplus of liquidity that went with the deficit. Therefore, they did not expect that the final readjustment will began with the bust of the asset bubble and the beginning of the financial crisis. Blanchard et al., attributed the US current account deficit to two major factors: the increase in U.S. demand for foreign products, and the increase in foreign countries' demand for US assets. Their model shows that changes in the factors can explain the current account of the US and fluctuation of the US exchange rates. They also discussed the impact of the drastic depreciation of the exchanges rates of dollar, holding that it does not cause much harm to the US economy, and on the contrary, it would exert great negative impact on the economies in Europe and Japan.

McKinnon (2005) thought global imbalances was caused by the dollar standard. In his view, historically as international product trade and capital movement have been measured by dollar, the U.S. have become the "only country that can afford to hold huge amount of debts in national currency, and it is not subject to risks that are encountered by other countries whose debts are measured by foreign currencies." In such situation, international loans put on soft restraints on the US, leading to the low savings rate, and the US's capability of providing hard currency is not as much important as the soft restraints exerted by the international loans due to the superiority of the dollar.

These researches are illuminating, but they did not pay enough attention to the dollar hegemony, and neither did they discuss the key role of the privileged position of the dollar in global imbalances and financial crisis. Arguably, it is the expansive fiscal and monetary policy of the U.S. that fundamentally caused the global imbalances, this round of financial crisis and its proliferation across the world. The superior position of the dollar, i.e. the dollar hegemony has played a crucial role in these events.

5.11 From Imbalances to Financial Crisis

Over the forty years since the end of the Bretton Woods system, the global imbalances are marked by fluctuations on large-scale (see Chart 5.14).

Global imbalances emerged since the mid and late 1970s, and it became more severe, and reached the peak in the mid 1980s. As the major counterparts, on the one hand, the US deficit in the two consecutive years of 1986 and 1987 exceeded

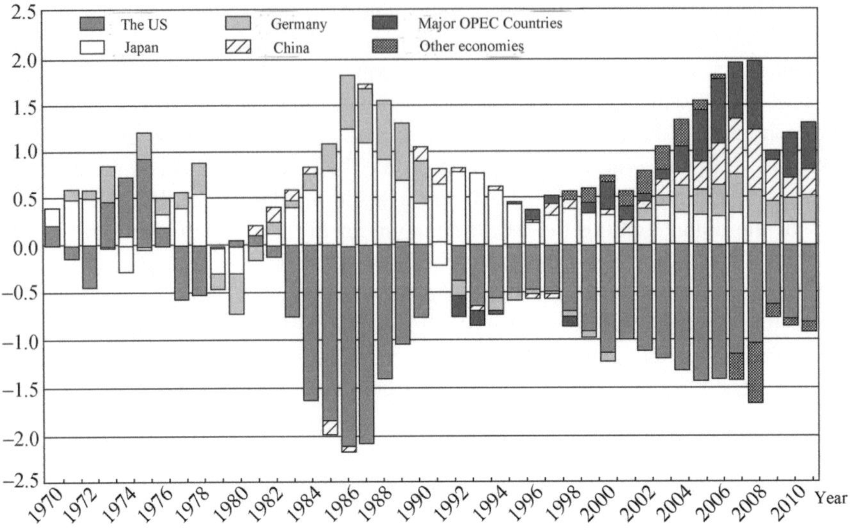

Chart 5.14 Share of global imbalances in world GDP (1970–2010). *Source* OECD, Economic Outlook 87, and statistics from the countries

2% of the world's total GDP; as for Japan and Germany, surpluses had reached unprecedented level, as high as 1.8% of the world's total GDP. The global imbalances reached its zenith in 1986, and had been gradually corrected. It fell to the lowest level during the first half of the 1990s. Corresponding to this trend was the succession of domestic crises that broke out in developed economies, including the U.S., Japan and Germany, which in turn prompted the large-scale reform guided by the maxim of new liberalism. The corrective adjustment produced different results in different countries. The U.S. attained competitive advantages again and ushered in a new cycle of growth that have benefited a lot of countries; Germany looked to the Europe for solution, and stepped up the process of European unification; Japan seemed not as lucky, since after the Plaza Agreement was reached in 1986, its economy went into recession that lasted for a long time and even today is not recovered.

What calls for the attention is that in the 1980s and 1990s, when the deterioration of imbalances had been gradually relieved, historical changes had taken place, as emerging economies and developing countries started to rise one after another, and in contrast the influence of the developed economies was faltering. This transformation begun to shape the global economic structure, and although Asian financial crisis broke out during the period, the general pattern of the strong south vs. the weak north remained unchanged. Since the Asian financial crisis, the US trade deficit kept on increasing, and its share in global GDP had sharply climbed; in the early years of the crisis, it reached as high as 1.5% in succession. On the part of its counterparts, Germany and Japan continued to have surplus, while emerging economies including China and major OPEC countries started to play increasingly significant roles in shaping the landscape of global imbalances. When the imbalances became worse, it led to the crisis, thus initiating a new cycle of rebalance, which is still going on today.

To discuss the sustainability of global imbalances, one has to answer the question: what is the threshold value for transition from sustainable to unsustainable? The two huge waves of fluctuation in Chart 5.14 shows that when imbalances have accumulated to a certain extent, it would collapse, and only a major crisis can bring it back to balance. However, if in the 1980s, the correction did not begin until the US trade deficit reached as high as 2% of the world's GDP, then the current crisis proves that though today's imbalance scale is not as big as that of the 1980s, it has gone beyond the tolerance level of the world economy.

This shows that the threshold value that will trigger the change from sustainability to in sustainability is the result of the interaction among a number of factors. One should not only take into consideration the tolerance level of the economy, but also the general situation of the global structure. For example, in the 1980s, the US imbalances accounted for as much as 2% of the global GDP, and Japan and Germany, under the pressure of a series of agreements, including the Plaza Agreement and Louvre Agreement, were compelled to make corrections. Since only a few economies were involved in the adjustment, and they are all from the same west camp, the adjustment was easier, and the world was able to bear more imbalances. Today, the number of relevant economies has increased drastically, and for some emerging economies and OPEC countries, adjustment would not be easily accepted as an alternative. Besides, or more importantly, imbalances of the 1980s occurred mostly in trade on the current account; today, imbalances occurred in all fields, of which trade-induced financial imbalances are much more complicated than any other kind of imbalances.

Over the recent years, studies on threshold value of unsustainability of the imbalances have achieved fruitful results.

Some proposed that the threshold value could be 2–4% of GDP taken up by current account surplus. In the Maekawa Report issued after the Plaza Agreement, Japan stressed that current account surplus had to be curbed within the scale that did not affect international harmony. The Report did not mention any concrete value, but pointed out that it should be around 2% of the GNP (Isamu Miyazaki 2009). At the time, Japan's current account surplus accounted for 3.7% of the GNP in 1985, 4.4% in 1986, and 2.1% in 1989, when the goal of adjustment was finally realized. In the same token, the G20 summit held in Seoul, 2010 put forward the "Referential Guideline", which demanded countries to keep the percentage of current account surplus of GDP no higher than 4% (in correspondence, the deficit countries should keep the percentage of deficit no higher than 4%). In reality, however, the percentage of the US deficit in GDP had once exceeded 6.5%, but the crisis did not take place in that particular year.

Milesi-Ferretti and Razin (1996) had made empirical analyses of the persisting external imbalances of developed economies and emerging economies to test a series of threshold indicators. They found that, although there indeed was some kind of threshold, it was difficult to draw a clear line. Freund (2000) built their

Chart 5.15 Empirical distribution of inter-crisis durations (1870–). *Source* Jordà, Shularick and Taylor (2010)

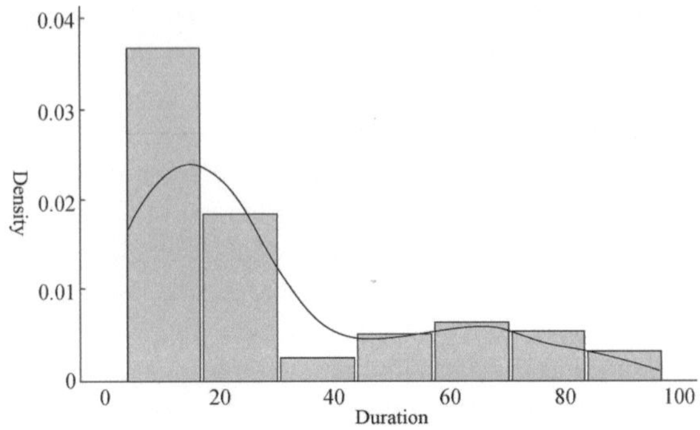

studies on Milesi-Ferretti and Razin' (1998, 2000) research, and looked at all developed economies. She believed that the threshold was 5% of GDP. Debelle and Galati (2005) discovered that in average, when current account imbalance took up 4 to 5% of the GDP, imbalances were not sustainable, and adjustments are required.

As for the threshold for the accumulation of current account imbalances, inter-temporal studies have been conducted that deeply explore the economic factors of imbalances and their role in a country's economic development. They believed that deficit was caused (or caused) by increase in investment, and investment is the driving force of economic growth. Thus they concluded that there was no reason to worry about the imbalance, and there was no need to take policy actions to adjust it. In terms of inter-temporal smoothing, current account imbalance in one country with a certain period of time should not be the concerns, because after this period, since domestic investment facilitated growth in the previous period, the country will have reverse imbalances of the previous period. The study means that from the dynamic angle, and given a time period long enough, a country will eventually achieve balance; therefore, global imbalances will not be so serious as to lead to catastrophic global crisis. If the cost of adjustment is not taken into consideration, and with the presumption that all imbalances are caused by factors that contribute to economic development, such conclusion based on inter-temporal analysis is valid. However, as some countries play decisive roles in the global economy, adjustment in those countries will inevitably exert huge impact on global economy; in other cases, for some countries that are too vulnerable to bear the cost of adjustment, under the pressure from other countries, its imbalances will entail tremendous cost of adjustment. Under these circumstances, imbalances should not be overlooked (Zhu 2007).

Although it is still difficult to give a precise threshold value, it is undeniable that long-term global imbalances will distort international division of labor and economic structure. This argument is supported by large number of empirical researches.

Jordà, Shularick and Taylor (2010) studied the economic history of 14 countries within the time span of 140 years between 1870 and 2008. They held that external imbalances were closely tied to economic crisis. Their empirical analyses revealed

Table 5.3 Summary of vulnerability indicator of crises before 2008

Leading Indicator	Total	Leading Indicator	Total
Foreign reserve	50	Real interest rate	13
Real exchange rate	48	Debt composition	10
GDP	25	Budget surplus	9
Credit	22	Trade condition	9
Current account	22	Contagion	6
Currency supply	19	Political/legal condition	6
Import & export	17	Capital flow	3
Inflation	15	Foreign debt	3
Stock dividends	13	Total	83

Source Frankel and Saravelos (2011)

that credit increase is a significant explanatory variable for crisis. And, if external imbalance is taken into account, the significance level becomes higher. Besides, since changes in external imbalances will increase credit, external imbalances can predict crisis. They further pointed out (see Chart 5.15) that, in general (the whole period sampled), imbalances would last 28 years (standard deviation is 24). Since the period between 1940 and 1973 did not see any crisis taking place, and if the period was left out, and with fewer sample periods, the imbalances would last 15 years (standard deviation is 8).

Frankel and Saravelos (2011) proposed some vulnerability indicators.[20] Based on the literature review on the vulnerability indicators since 2008 (see Chart 5.3), they found that among the 83 papers under study, the two most important indicators are foreign reserve and real interest rate. The two indicators are statistically significant in over half of the papers (foreign reserve indicator is significant in 50 papers, real exchange rate in 48; since more than one variable are significant, foreign reserve and real exchange rate are not mutually exclusive) (Table 5.3).

They went on to use a group of variables to predict the crisis between 2008 and 2009, and found out that foreign reserve of 2007 was statistically highly significant in predicting the economies that were most vulnerable to the impact of the crisis, in conformity with previous findings. Apart from that, over appreciation of recent foreign exchange rate was another important predictor, since it often led to currency depreciation, and it was also a key indicator of foreign exchange market pressure during the crisis. Since foreign reserve was an important indicator of external imbalances (sometimes, level of exchange rates also measures external imbalances, but it would lose some precision when was used to measure external imbalances), the study by Frankel and Saravelos indicated again that external imbalances is a key explanatory factor for crisis.

[20]Frankel and Saravelos (2011).

Through the general overview and analysis of the Great Depression, the Stagnation Crisis, the Asian Financial Crisis and the crisis in the new century, we were able to roughly outline the relations between currency hegemony, imbalances and crises. We hold that the most remarkable feature of currency hegemony is the inequalities in rights and obligations between the hegemon and other nations due to their different positions in the international monetary system. For example, with a small amount of international reserve, the hegemon is able to easily influence the global currency supply, interest rate and foreign change rates; the hegemon, intently or involuntarily exploit its privileged role to seek extra benefits, especially during the "golden period" of globalization; the hegemon also reap profits and transfer its crisis onto the others by influencing and controlling capital movement, etc. In one word, hegemony always brings "perks" to the dominating power. However, mainstream scholars either did not fully recognize this situation, or they choose to overlook it. As the authors of the book, we would also like to emphasize that: at certain times, currency hegemony helped to stabilize the economy, and sustained the imbalance that was kept at a certain scale. Nevertheless, due to the lack of hard constraints, the hegemony tends to abuse its prerogatives and exercise double-deficit expansion, leading to global imbalances. In the long-run, when the imbalances went beyond the threshold and could be no longer tolerated by the world economy, they would cause economic chaos and even economic crisis. On a deeper level, as long as the hegemony exists and free from "hard constraints", sooner or later it will induce crisis. This is the fate of the world economy. From this perspective, the importance to reform the current international monetary system and restrain the dollar hegemony can never be overestimated.

References

Aizenman J (2010) On the causes of global imbalances and their persistence: myths, facts and conjectures. In: Claessens S, Evenett S, Hoekman B (eds) Rebalancing the global economy: a primer for policymaking, Center for Economic Policy Research, pp 23–30

Almunia M, Bénétrix AS, Eichengreen B, O′Rourke KH, Rua G (2009) From great depression to great credit crisis: similarities, differences and lessons. IIIS Discussion Paper, No. 303

Bean C (2009) "The great moderation, the great panic and the great contraction", Schmpeter Lecture, Annual Congress of the European Economic Association, Barcelona, 25 Aug 2009

Bernanke BS (2004) "Money, gold, and the great depression", remarks at the H. Parker Willis lecture in economic policy. Washington and Lee University, Lexington

Debelle G, Galati G (2005) "Current account adjustment and capital flows", BIS Working Papers, No. 169, Monetary and Economic Department, February, 2005

Depress E, Kindleberger CP, Salant WS (1966) The dollar and world liquidity: a minority view. Economist, February 5, 1966, pp 526–529

Eichengreen B (1992) Golden fetters: the gold standard and the great depression: 1919-1939, Oxford University Press

Eichengreen B (2008) Globalizing capital: a history of the international monetary system, 2nd edn. Princeton University Press

Frankel J, Saravelos G (2011) "Can leading indicators assess country vulnerability? Evidence from the 2008–2009 global financial crisis", HKS Faculty Research Working Paper Series, RWP11-024, June, 2011

Freund C (2000) "Current account adjustments in industrial countries", International Finance Discussion Papers, No. 692

Friedman M, Schwartz AJ (1963) A monetary history of the united states: 1867-1960, Princeton University Press

Hudson M (2008) Super imperialism: the origin and fundamentals of u.s. world dominance, (Chinese Translation). Central Compilation & Translation Press, Beijing

Irwin DA (2010) Did france cause the great depression? NBER Working Paper, No. 16350

Jordà Ò, Schularick M, Taylor AM (2010) Financial crises, credit booms, and external imbalances: 140 years of lessons. NBER Working Paper, No. 16567

Kindleberger C (1973) The World in Depression: 1929–1939, University of California Press

Kindleberger CP (2006) A financial history of Western Europe, 2nd edn (Chinese translation). China Financial Publishing House, Beijing

Krugman P, Obstfeld M, Melitz M (1998) International Economics (Fourth Edition) (Chinese Translation). China Renmin University Press, Beijing

Mckinnon RI (2005) Exchange rates under the East Asian dollar standard: living with conflicted virtue (Chinese translation) (trans: Wang X, He W). China Financial Publishing House, Beijing

Milesi-Ferretti GM, Razin A (1996) "Sustainability of persistent current account deficits", NBER Working Paper, No. 5467

Milesi-Ferretti GM, Razin A (1998) Sharp reductions in current account deficits: an empirical analysis. Eur Econ Rev 42

Milesi-Ferretti GM, Razin A (2000) Current account reversals and currency crises: empirical regularities. University of Chicago Press, Chicago

Obstfeld M, Rogoff K (2000) The six major puzzles in international macroeconomics: is there a common cause? In: Bernanke BS, Roggoff K (eds) NBER macroeconomics annual, MIT Press, Cambridge, Mass

Obstfeld M, Rogoff K (2004) The unsustainable U.S. current account position revisited. NBER Working Paper, No. 10869

Obstfeld M, Rogoff K (2005) The unsustainable U.S. current account position revisited, Mimeo, University of California, Berkeley (November 30)

Officer L (2008) Gold standard, EH. net encyclopedia, In: Whaples R. http://eh.net/encyclopedia/article/officer.gold.standard

Palmer RR (2009) A history of the modern world (Chinese translation). World Publishing Corporation, Beijing

Patat J-P, Lutfalla M (1986) Histoire monétaire de la France au XXe Siècle, Economica

Perri F, Fogli A (2006) The 'great moderation' and the US external imbalance. NBER Working Paper, N. 12708

Reinhart CM, Rogoff KS (2010) This time is different: eight centuries of financial folly (Chinese translation). China Machine Press, Beijing

Triffin R (1960) Gold and the dollar crisis: the futurle of convertibility. Yale University Press, New Haven

Triffin R (1997) Gold and the dollar crisis: the future of convertibility. The Commercial Press, Beijing

Zhu J (2007) On innovation and current account imbalances, Doctoral Dissertation, Southwestern University of Finance and Economics

Part IV
The Mechanism of Rebalancing

Introduction

A truly well-developed and sound international monetary system should at least include three essential elements: choice of reserve currency foreign exchange rate determination mechanism and mechanism of adjusting international imbalances.

When, as fait accompli, diversification of reserve currency has been recognized by all, and the tendency will be further institutionalized, then the future international monetary reform will be focused on areas of foreign exchange rate determination mechanism and mechanism of adjusting international imbalances. In other words, the reform will mainly aim at coordinating the macroeconomic policies at the state level.

Chapter 6 is the theoretical discussion about coordinating macro-level policies in the international community, with the focus on the "automatic" adjustment functions of the gold standard and the floating exchange rate mechanism.

People have always hoped to find an institution or mechanism that can automatically eliminate mankind's evil doings, and, in this field, to adjust imbalances in international payment with neutrality, fairness, and in the principle of rights and duties. Gold standard and floating exchange rate have been recognized as such mechanisms. However, history tells us that the so-called automatic adjustment, if not a disillusion, is no more than a theoretical assumption.

In international economy, the so-called automatic adjustment mechanism never exists. Theoretically speaking, perhaps the systems of gold standard and floating exchange rates are good institutions; however, unfortunately, neither had been strictly observed or implemented in the real sense. In fact, the real world is much more complicated than economic models, and a chasm between the reality and theory is almost insurmountable. Scientific reasoning should follow the logical path of "deduction—induction", i.e., first to deduce the "generalized" theoretical model and fully analyze it, and then, by gradually adding elements of the real world, moving it closer to the reality. However, if a classical, theoretical model is not even close to being mirrored by some kind of reality, even though it serves as the fundamental of the research, people would have good reason to doubt there the theory is not deduced properly, as it cannot be applied to real-world practices.

It is a historical fact that during the age of the gold standard, all countries, even Britain, did not observe the "rule of the game"; as the result, the automatic adjustment mechanism designed by the gold standard became empty talk. During the time dominated by floating exchange rate system, the U.S. often compel other countries to change the rates, and other countries implemented the "peg" of different sorts out of "fear for floating". In short, under the gold standard and floating exchange rate systems, it was not the textbook automatic adjustment mechanism that kept the systems running; instead, it was the hegemony of pound and the dollar, and the international coordination mechanism that played the key roles.

Chapter 7 studied the role of exchange rate in international policy coordination. As the chapter title "Monetary Statecraft and the Gains by Dollar Hegemony" suggests, this chapter is meant to indicate that under the splendid motto of "free market", the cold reality had been dominated by rivalries driven by national interest.

Exchange rates have always been the crux of the international policy coordination at the state level. People were told that floating exchange rate conforms best to the principle of free market, as it can automatically adjust trade imbalances, cushion external impacts, and ensure the independence of domestic monetary policy. This idea was often illustrated from the opposite; under the impact of increasingly frequent cross-border capital movement at increasingly large scale, it is impossible for emerging economies, or even developed economies, to maintain any kind of fixed exchange rate.

Putting aside the many deficiencies of theories for the floating exchange rate, in reality, the role played by exchange rate and the ensuing wars in this regard make us doubt the intention behind the propaganda for floating exchange rate. What actually happened in history is that exchange rate had often been manipulated as the weapon by the "center country" to attack other countries, making them to adjust their domestic economic policies. Doing this, the center country covertly implemented its "monetary statecraft", i.e., "to influence policies of other nations by manipulating the monetary environment."

Things become complicated when the fact that exchange rate is often used as a weapon by countries at the center against other countries is disguised by finely designed theories or even maxims. Justifying their behavior with such theories, the "center countries" tried to assume dominance over the world, pointing fingers at other countries, and even coerce the latter to adjust their domestic policies. Not fully aware of what is really going on, people with good intention were often made accomplices of the evil-doers. What the US government did with the exchange rates proved to be a wonderful footnote of the story. Since 1988, once every 2 years, the US Department of the Treasury submitted the Report on International Economy and Exchange Rate Policies. Based on changes in current account and foreign currency surplus, the report will determine whether its trade partners are manipulating trade exchange rates and suggest countermeasures. Countries that were listed as manipulators earlier were Germany, Japan, and Taiwan of China, in the twenty-first century, mainland China became the target of blame. Recently, as trade surplus of Germany vis-à-vis the U.S. increased a little, the United States did not hesitate to point the fingers at Germany, could not care less for the interests and reputation of its loyal ally.

Chapter 8 analyzed international coordination of macroeconomic policies. Analysis made by the authors on the basis of their materials revealed that the so-called international coordination of macroeconomic policy is, in essence, another means employed by powerful countries to compel the less powerful to adjust their domestic policies. For a long time, some international organizations have also been used as the means by some countries to play the big power's monetary game, the IMF, World Bank, and WTO are no exception.

Notably, since the end of 2011, negotiations on the Trans-Pacific Partnership (TPP), Transatlantic Trade and Investment Partnership (TTIP), Plurilateral Services Agreement (PSA), Japan-EU Economic Partnership Agreement, and other agreements are underway, sending out a clear signal: as a whole, developed economies are no longer satisfied with the current model of globalization and its rules; to take back the dominance of global governance, a new "holly alliance" is forging, with the purpose of instituting new rules of the game. The curtain of a new round of game for a new international monetary system and global governance has been lifted.

Chapter 6
Two Myths of Rebalancing

If we only trust laisser-faire, then we will take for granted that there is an adjustment mechanism running that can spontaneously keep the balance, which is a "dogmatic illusion", as it neglects lessons of historical experience that cannot be reasonably accounted for by any theory.

—John Maynard Keynes

In A Treaties on Money which brought Keynes to world fame, there is a passage that provokes lot of thoughts for today. After citing the eloquent talks of British mainstream economists about laisser-faire, Keynes remarked, not without irony, "They did not believe what was really achieved by laisser-faire was attributable to its special status, but rather the extreme values of laisser faire. As to why the other countries did not follow the examples, it was believed was due to their bad way of governance, as their prejudice of protection of tax." He meant that the majority of British economists were not aware of the fact that it was its special status in the financial system that brought about extra benefits to Britain. History repeats itself; such comments seemed fit for some American economists. McKinnon has observed, "At the center of the world's monetary system, Americans, including most professional economists, are blissfully unaware of how the dollar standard works, whereas in peripheral countries outside of semiautonomous Europe, people are much more aware—and sometimes terrified—of it" (McKinnon 2005).[1]

Britain and the United States are the two countries in history of the world that had or have truly dominated the world as the hegemon. Apart from political, military and general economic factors and only viewed at the international financial level, similarities between the pound and dollar hegemony is very intriguing. However, mainstream economists did not fully reveal this reality and mechanism, on the contrary, the concept of automatic adjustment was idealized and popularized as facts, which were further distorted and covered up in disguise. As the hegemon also dominates in most cases theoretical researches in economics and are sponsors of mainstream theories, no wonder these theories are somewhat biased.

---

[1]McKinnon (2005).

Y. Li and X. Zhang, *Imbalance and Rebalance*,
https://doi.org/10.1007/978-981-10-6150-9_6

Two regimes under the international monetary system have often been lauded for being able to adjust the imbalances automatically, the first one is the international gold standard under the hegemon of pound, the second is the floating exchange rate mechanism. Today, these two mechanism are still extolled as the Utopia of the international monetary system, and we would like to call them the two "myths" of rebalancing the global economy.

One thing to add is that the Bretton Woods system came between the two myths. When the system was first designed and according to its rules, any adjustment under the system needs to be carried out by way of the coordination through the IMF. For individual countries, the major means to maintain balance-of-payments was capital control, whereas the means of exchange rates were rarely employed. This is because, according to the rules, changes in exchange rate parity can only made after consultation with the IMF, which might cause turbulences in the market if the information of possible depreciation is leaked. Although small adjustment of exchange parity could be made without the consultation, when there were active movements of capital, even small adjustment would be regard by the market as the signal for further government actions to adjust the parity. The lessons of the revaluation of exchange rates in Germany and the Netherlands in 1961 were cases in point. This shows that under the Bretton Woods system, the major mechanism for adjustment was capital control, and cooperation between different governments and central banks when capital control gradually lost its vigor (Block 1977).[2]

6.1 The "Golden Age" of Gold Standard (1870–1914)

As one of the major hallmarks of the splendid achievements of the Victoria, the international gold standard between 1870 and 1914 were commended by many economic historians. In one of his well-known works, Officer (Officer 1986) cited the complimentary remarks made by three famous contemporary economic historians: (1) The New York stock exchange market had reached unprecedented stability. ... any perceptible deviation from parity of the exchange rate tended to induce inflow or outflow of gold. (2) Exchange rates (pound/dollar) after 1885 had been very stable. (3) However, the performances of pound/dollar exchange rate basically conformed to the "rules of the game", and in the 35 years or so prior to 1914, they were kept with the gold points. Obviously, the working mechanism of the gold standard was somewhat sanctified.

Those remarks have, in effect, given the historians' endorsement to one of the "conventional wisdom" in the history of economics, i.e., the international gold standard between 1870 and 1914 worked. However, Officer (1986) has truthfully pointed out that the observations mentioned above are controversial. Some scholars held that in the so-called "golden period of the gold standard," governments often

[2]We are going to have deeper discussion on coordination of international monetary policies.

interfered in the market, and violations of gold points had occurred many times. Obstfeld (2000), an established scholar in international economics, gave his apropos view in this regard as he remarked, "Even in the great Victorian Age, it is an exaggeration to depict the adjustment as one with nearly no friction and to state that government intervention can be restrained by rules of the game. .... However, the classic paradigm (international gold standard) can still be viewed as a useful theoretical baseline." Unfortunately, in many cases, abstract theoretical baseline was turned into historical facts.

Hidden behind the commendation for the good performance of the international gold standard is the connotation that international gold standard is neutral and fair. In the system, countries had been positioned on an equal footing, and none of them was able to reap additional benefits when the market mechanism was able to correct the imbalances spontaneously.

In short, the international gold standard is the first myth in history of international monetary system. It is fair and efficient, and will spontaneously adjust economic imbalance, both internally and externally, facilitate economic growth and trade development, giving rise to the golden era of capitalist development.

Apart from economic historians, economists who designs mechanisms and build up models also contributed to creating the myth. The economists most frequently mentioned three mechanisms, i.e. price-specie-flow mechanism, income-specie-flow mechanism and the "rule of the game" of the gold standard mechanism. These are all key and essential concepts initiated by famous economists, and are found in any international economics textbooks (i.e. Krugman and Obstfeld 2000; Salvatore 2001).

The price-specie-flow mechanism. This famous mechanism was proposed first by Hume in debate with mercantilists. Mercantilists held that countries should maintain surplus, so that gold and silver would flow in from other countries, because they silver and gold were embodiments of national wealth, pillar of the country and key to commercial prosperity. Hume, meanwhile, pointed out that since inflow of silver and gold would change the relative prices of the two countries, surplus could not be sustained or last indefinitely. To the surplus country that received inflow of silver and gold, its domestic money supply would rise, and thus causing domestic prices to go up (as is presumed by the quantity theory of money); this would in turn lead to increase in import and decrease in export, and involuntarily bring the country's surplus back to balance. Conversely, currency supply in deficit countries would be reduced due to outflow of silver and gold, which would lead to price decrease, followed by increase in export and decrease in import, and the deficit would be corrected inadvertently and rebalancing achieved.

Income-specie-flow mechanism. This line of reasoning follows the very significant, classical quantity theory of money, so the mechanism is deemed classical. Since the linchpin of the argument is price stickiness, therefore it is a mechanism that falls into the category of New Keynesianism. The mechanism holds that as silver and gold flow to the surplus country, money supply of the country will increase. This should cause the real balance and aggregate demand to go up (price stickiness). Expansion in demand will increase import, and automatically rebalance the trade deficit. Conversely, in deficit countries where silver and gold flows out, decreasing currency supply will bring down the country's real balance and aggregate demand. As the aggregated demand shrinks, import will slide, and the deficit will consequently be balanced.

The "rule of the game" of the gold standard. While the previous two mechanism pay attention to the adjustment of price and quantity in real economy, the "rule of the game" in the gold standard pays particular attention to the mechanism of adjustment through functions of capital market. The rule stipulates that: when the deficit country is faced with outflow of gold, monetary authority will have less reserve to issue currencies and be forced to sell assets and exercise monetary stringency, and such behavior will cause the surge in interest rate, attracting inflow of funds from overseas to compensate for its external deficit. Conversely, when the country running surplus sees the inflow of gold, monetary authority will have more reserve to issue currencies, and it will buy in more assets, expand credit, which will lower interest rate and cause domestic funds to flow to other countries, thus relaxing the external surpluses. Deficit countries tended to exercise monetary stringency, whereas surplus countries will choose to practice monetary easing, and this is called the "rule of the game" under the gold standard. It is said that this term was first proposed by Keynes (Krugman and Obstfeld 2000).

Those carefully worked-out theories of mechanisms proposed by famous economists stand as strong pillars supporting the pedestal the myth of the gold standard. Either by intention or inadvertently, the theorists blurred the line between theory and reality, as economic reality was gradually reduced to the idealized situation depicted by the baseline theories.

6.2 Self-adjustment Mechanism: Myth or Fact?

As was shown above, those exquisite mechanisms, unfortunately, failed to capture the realities truthfully, and sometimes even in denial of the facts. Taking a closer look at the three classical mechanisms, one will see that for all of them, the links that is believed to first trigger the chain of reaction are the same, i.e., changes in currency supply. With the mechanism of price-specie-flow, changes in currency supply leads to price changes; as for the income-specie-flow mechanism, money supply leads to income changes; when it comes to the "rule of the game", monetary authority intends to facilitate changes in money supply in order to accelerate and complete the adjustment. Here, the crux of the issue is whether the monetary authority will condone or even facilitate changes in money supply, or adopt the sterilization policy to offset those changes. If a government adopts the sterilization policy that contravenes the "rule of the game", it actually, by severing the first link from the chain of reaction, nullifies the whole mechanism.

A large number of contemporary studies have illustrated that prior to 1914, the "rule of the game" under the gold standard was often contravened (Krugman and Obstfeld 2000; Schwartz 2008). Sterilization had been frequently employed by monetary authorities. Britain, France and Prussia had all categorically took the lead in intervening by stemming outflow of gold, and were followed by a number of small economies. We do not intend to further summarize and differentiate comments in this regard, as the literature on this is voluminous. As the researches by Krugman, Obstfeld, and Schwartz represent contemporary views on this matter, the discussion in Keynes' book—A Treaties on Money published in 1934 offers us important references on this subject. In particular, the discussion of Chapter Seven helped people to have a glimpse of the chaotic situation under the gold standard, and trace the logic through the author's way of thinking that may lead to the fundamental causes of the problem. It is surprising that, although Keynes' works are authoritative and well-known, the related views seem not dually noted by later people.

In view of modern theoretical model, the issue can be boiled down to the Trilemma, or "Impossible Trinity". Under the gold standard, fixed exchange rate plus capital movement will rid the countries of monetary policy independence. In other words, observance of the "rule of the game" of the gold standard can only be achieved at the cost of sacrificing the domestic macro-economic goals. The western countries had different mentalities of macro policy before the WWII and after the WWII. It is not until after the WWII that the governments started to make domestic goals priorities of the macro policy and pay attention to balance inflation and unemployment. Prior to the WWI, the governments did not assume much responsibility in keeping domestic balances, and could thus tolerate to some extent the adjustment mechanism of the gold standard. However, this tolerance had its limit. When domestic goals and external imbalances went into serious clashes that posed threat to the regime, the government would definitely chose to violate the "rule of the game", even rejected the gold standard once and for all.

The major obstacles to adjustment are the following two: First, inequality in obligations for surplus countries and deficit countries. For the former, complying with the rules will lead to rise of prices and decrease in interest rate, making the country less competitive and incur capital outflow. Obviously that could not be in the interest of the country. Being fully aware of this, Keynes (1986, volume 2, p. 265) made the following remarks on people's criticism of the violation of the rules by the United States and France: It would be expecting too much to hope nations to adopt credit policies suitable to some other countries by voluntarily sacrificing the interests deemed to be their own. Therefore, the deficit country should not expect the surplus country can be stimulated by flow of gold because "the flow of gold means that other countries are stimulated to meet us half-way"[3] (Keynes 1986, volume 1, p. 295). For the deficit country, things run in the opposite direction. If it complies with the rule and exercises austerity, then inflow of gold will be curbed, leading to the collapse of the domestic economy. So, deficit countries do not play by the rule in most cases. Second, impacts of imbalances caused by capital movement and trade of commodities differ. When capital is

[3]Translator's note: Maynard (1958).

moving freely, it remains highly sensitive to changes in exchange rate, any interest margin would immediately trigger capital flow, in contrast, however, trade of commodities response much more slowly to changes in exchange rate. So, to alleviate imbalances in commodities trade through capital movement is not a realistic alternative, because the quick entrance and exit of large amount of venture capital most probably will not only worsen the imbalances, but also heavily impact the domestic economy. Under such circumstances, some countries had to adopt the sterilization policy to offset the impact, even exercise capital control to limit the movement of gold.

6.3 Essence of the Gold Standard: The Hegemony of Pound

Kindleberger (2010) pertinently pinpointed the essence of the international gold standard, "Such was a governed regime, with the Bank of England as the governing center. … money order in pounds became close to substitute currencies for foreign countries in global transactions, and interest rate of pound was manipulated by London, so the gold standard is the pound standard." Schwartz shared exactly the same view, and pointed out straightforwardly that, "on this account, the so-called gold standard at the end of the 19th century was in fact a pound/credit currency standard." He further observed, "This structure of the regime determines that the gold standard cannot be economically neutral." Since the Bank of England was the one that governed the regime, then inevitably Britain would reap benefit from it either intentionally or inadvertently.

Why in essence the international gold standard is the pound standard or pound/credit standard? To answer the question one should first know the definition of currency. According to the conventional definition under the gold standard, currency is made up of gold and banknotes, and backed by gold reserve of equal value, the bank notes can be converted into gold at any time. However, it would be too naïve to think that the British monetary supply at the time was strictly made up of the two components only. Historically, credit currency much predated bank notes and became a notable component of currency supply much earlier. By the end of the 19th century, Scottish currency comprised of gold coins, bank notes, bank savings and commercial bills. Academic debates on whether the last two can be regarded as currency always exists, but no one would question the fact that in reality they have functioned as currency. The 1844 English bank law limited the issuance of bank notes, but not commercial bills and bank savings. As the result, commercial bills and bank savings increased sharply (Kindleberger 2010). Besides, global trade grew by 3.3% annually on average between 1870 and 1913, however, during the period of 1873–1892, the supply of real gold increased only by 1.3% annually on average, and although the rate went up since 1892, it reached merely 3.7% before the WWI (Schwartz 2008). When added up, these figures led to the conclusion that during the whole period of gold standard, trade volume increased five times, whereas the supply of gold had increased only four times, without taking into account the non-currency usage of gold.

Circulation of the pound credit currency had gone beyond England and extended to both sides of the Pacific where tradesmen conducted business transactions with various accommodation bills. In such context, London played a tremendous important role as the financial center of the world. Keynes (1986 volume 2, p. 266) remarked, "In the second half of the 19th century, London was in a superior position to influence the world's credit situation, so much so that the Bank of England could appoint itself the conductor of the international orchestra." At the time, Bank of England controlled money supply and discount rates of the globe, acting as the world's central bank. However, what the British banks did was driven by profits, just like any other conventional commercial banks. Schwartz (2008) also pointed out that "in fact, countries at the periphery lent money to Bank of England at low interest rate, due to the well-established credibility of the Bank of England and the short-term nature of the loans. Next, those British banks loaned the money back to the periphery countries but at high interest rate, a fact that shows the long-term nature of the loans and the poor credibility of these overseas debtors." Interest rate is the price of credibility, when one of the parties in the transaction monopolized the right to determine the price, it won't be hard to imagine the outcome. Chart 6.1 presented the discount rates of the Bank of England during the period of 1870–1850. It is interesting to note the fact that, between 1870 and 1914, the discount rate fluctuated very frequently, in big magnitude; whereas in most time since 1914, there were few fluctuations, and discount rate begun to keep steady, as is shown by the flat lines for the periods from July, 1932 to July, 1939, and from November 1939 to November 1951, twelve years in a row.

The British financial hegemony should never be taken lightly. As Karl Polanyi had stressed, "The Pax Britannica held its sway sometimes by the ominous poise of heavy ship's cannon, but more frequently it prevailed by the timely pull of a thread in the international monetary network"[4] (Polanyi 1944).

6.4 Old and New Versions of the "Myth" of Floating Exchange Rate

From close to the collapse of the Bretton Woods system to the present, mainstream views regarding the exchange regime has undergone changes. When the Bretton Woods system was first established, its designers were proponents of fixed exchange rate; at the end of the 1960s when the dollar crisis broke out, people were enthusiastic about the floating exchange rate; in the early 1980s, fixed exchange rate came into people's favor again; in the early 1990s, the middle way arrangement

[4]Polanyi (1965).

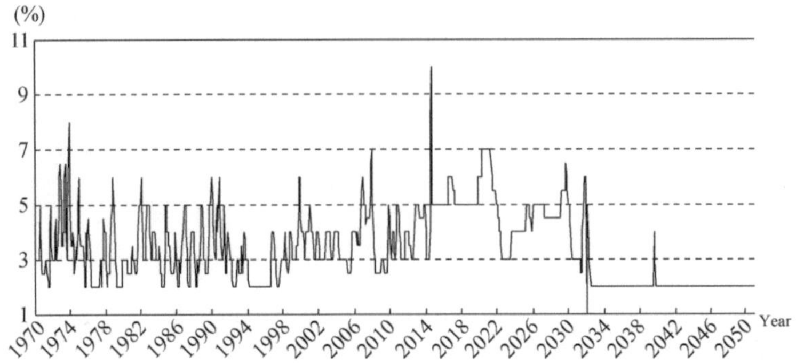

Chart 6.1 Discount rate of bank of England (1870–1950). *Source* Bank of England (www.bankofengland.co.uk/statistics/rates)

became popular; after the Asian financial crisis, the majority people adopted the so-called "bipolar view," meaning adoption of fixed exchange rate (for example, the currency board arrangement, the pegged exchange rate, or dollarization), or the real floating exchange rate regime (Carmignani et al. 2008). A close look at the transformation helps people to see that floating exchange rate arrangement was highly recognized by the mainstream view during two historical periods, which produced two versions. The old version was monetarism, designed mainly for developed economies; the new version emerged in the mid-and-late 1990s, marked by the "bipolar view" or "corner solutions", aimed to solve problems in emerging economies.

Friedman is probably the most famous proponent of floating exchange rate regime. He (Friedman) held that floating exchange rate can automatically adjust trade imbalances, cushion external impacts, and ensure monetary policy independence. Since Friedman drew analogy between floating exchange rate and the Day Light Saving Time (Summer Time), his view is often called the "Summer Time View." According to Friedman, in face of external impact, it would be better to adjust domestic prices than exchange rates, just like in summer, it would be better to set the clock than asking people to change their regular daily schedule. By the end of the 1960s, the majority of economists started to support floating exchange rate, and meanwhile, business leaders and government officials were also greatly influenced by this view (Odell 1991). Friedman's view is representative of the earlier version of the myth of floating exchange rate. It has two notable features: First, it stresses the automatic imbalance adjustment function and independence of monetary policy achieved by floating exchange rate. As another monetarist, Johnson (1973) emphasized, "The primary reason to support flexible exchange rate is that it allows countries to independently employ monetary, fiscal and other policy tools." Secondly, the earlier version is inherently associated with the economic ideology of laisser-faire. For example, a frequently cited argument is that since (domestic) price control will distort and harm the economy, why it is still necessary to (externally) fix the exchange rate?

After the naïve earlier version became a historical legacy, the myth of floating exchange rate resurrected in the mid-and-late 1990s in the guise of the "bipolar view". If the earlier version reflected the propensity of self-redemption of the developed economies (especially the United States), the new version was aimed at remedy the problems in emerging and developing countries. Obstfeld and Rogoff (1995) are the early proponents who put forward the "bipolar view". They believed that in the highly developed global capital market, to exercise fixed exchange rate among sovereign countries will incur more loss than benefits, and there is almost no "grey area" between floating exchange rate and common currency. The pound crisis and Mexican financial crisis taught people a lesson that was hard to forget, when Bank of England and the Mexican authority failed to stabilize the exchange rate even at huge expense.

Later, the financial crisis in Southeast Asia made the "bipolar" theory more appealing. Many economists published papers in support of it (i.e., Fischer 2001; Kenen 2000). IMF also conducted tremendous research, discussing the advantages of the floating exchange rate theoretically and empirically, and went so far as to discuss the concrete measures to facilitate the transition from the quasi-pegged exchange rate to floating exchange rate.

The new version critically inherited the essentials from the old version, preserving its strong points and discarding the dross. In the first place, the "bipolar view" puts the emphasis on floating exchange rate, therefore by lauding the theory they advocated the floating exchange rate regime. The fixed exchange rate under the "bipolar" theory is to be adopted in two situations: first, the common currency zone (like the euro zone), and second, dollarization, pegged exchange rate or currency board arrangement (like some Latin American countries, Hong Kong of China, and Singapore). For most emerging economies, this is not a realistic alternative. Therefore, "bipolar view" is reduced to something no other than the theory for floating exchange rate. Besides, automatic adjustment of external imbalances and independent monetary policy remain the key supportive evidence. This argument is also the essence of the old version, and serves as the major theoretical evidence in support of floating exchange rate, and the mechanism of adjustment is also classic argument of textbooks. Moreover, with the liberalization of capital account of international balance-of-payment since the 1990s, global capital movements has become increasingly frequent and on increasingly larger scale. Under the impact of the new trends, the vulnerability of pegged exchange rate in emerging economies becomes increasingly manifested. International venture capital like Quantum Fund and Tiger Global Management became globally known as major speculators, they seemed capably of ransacking the central bank of individual country, and crush the country's currency. It goes without saying that liberalization of capital account and floating exchange rate were sold as one package, accepting the former means accepting the latter. What is more, the emergence of the "bipolar view" has its roots in the real world events. Many proponents would be eager to point out that since the 1990s, many economies have gradually moved away from various pegged exchange rate to the free, floating exchange rate. Lastly, the old version drew analogies between fixed exchange rate and government intervention and administrative control, such naivety of using the dogma of free market to contend with fixed exchange rate have been abandoned. Many economists begun to realize that the debate should no longer be treated in the framework of ideological dichotomy, and interpreted as the contention of radicalism versus conservativism, government intervention versus free market, Keynesianism versus Classical Economics (Krugman 2000; McCallum 2001).

To sum up, the old version of floating exchange rate is idealistic, whereas the new version is more closely related with reality. The "myth" of the old version presented a promise of an automatic adjustment mechanism, but once the dream was shattered by the reality, the new version of "myth" reveals its ferocious true self: although floating exchange rate may not be perfect, but it is now impossible to return to fixed exchange rate regime. From this perspective, Obstfeld and Rogoff used an appropriate analogy: once the genie of floating exchange rate came out of the bottle, it would not be easy to put it back. The argument of automatic adjustment of the old myth, when mingled with the concerns for the reality of the new myth, has become the new trend of floating exchange rate that is theoretically based on new liberalism, and the trend has tremendous impact on theorists and decision-makers in different countries.

6.5 Views Opposing the Floating Exchange Rate

Viewing from the history of schools of economic thoughts, it is not until the recent years when floating exchange rate started to attract people's attention and became the mainstream school. During the periods of international gold standard and Bretton Woods system, fixed exchange rate became predominant in the discourse; between the two world wars when floating exchange rate was exercised, however, economic turbulences and financial chaos shattered the reputation of the floating exchange rate. Consequently, in the 1960s, many people became gravely suspicious of the floating exchange rate, and often equaled it to the unstable exchange rate. In fact, they believed that failure to maintain the gold parity and the damage it caused to the foundation of the fixed exchange rate symbolized the decline of the British Empire. Odell (1991) observed, "Gathering of a group of experts from the business circle and academia at Burgenstock, Switzerland, in mid 1969 could be the prompt for change in attitude. According to one participant who stood for the (exchange rate) elasticity, when the meeting started, only a banker or maybe an entrepreneur who supported the proposal, but at the end, only one participant was firmly against it. The majority of the participants voiced their intention to combine floating exchange rate at wider range with pegged floating exchange rate. Most of the advocates of this proposal are Americans, and most of them believed that the dollar remained the indisputable star of this regime." Quite often, such gradual change of the economic mentality is the precedent for drastic economic transformation in the real world.

In the real world, however, economic performances did not add splendor to the floating exchange rate regime. In the 1980s, after the regime had been in running for more than a decade, people started to attribute the poor performance of the economy partially to floating exchange rate, giving rise to the surge of fervent opposition against floating exchange rate. A research by Dornbusch in this regard is worth noting. He pointed out that after more than a decade's practice, people became less confident in maintaining independence in domestic policy under the floating exchange rate. This is because the economic policies of major countries tend to influence small, open countries, causing the letter to lose independence in policy. He concluded that any arrangement of exchange rate could only determine how the external impact was transmitted and its final outcome, and was unable to fully isolate the impact (Dornbusch 1983). Admittedly, for many countries, floating exchange rate mechanism has neither enabled country to make independent monetary policy, nor created a way to automatically correct international imbalances, on the contrary, short-term, drastic fluctuations of exchange rate had make it more difficult to maintain domestic economic stability. Schwartz (2008) also particularly pointed out that: "The theoretical expectations about floating exchange rate would be probably proved illusory, since once capital control was lifted, and exchange rates were allowed to float, monetary policy would no longer directly impact the whole economy."

The proponents of the old version of the myth were mostly monetarists. Early monetarists all believed in the "monetary veil" theory, i.e., changes in currency supply would only make all prices rise in the same proportion, and would not affect the real economy. Proponents of the new version of floating exchange rate shared the same faith in the "monetary veil" theory, only not as notable. When they tried to prove the efficiency of the adjustment mechanism, the argument was based on the hidden assumption that prices of all commodities will change in proportion to changes in exchange rate. However, this assumption did not reflect the real situation. In reality, commodities fall into three categories: non-tradable goods, manufactured goods, and resource products. The three types of products responded differently when exchange rates fluctuate. Take Japan for example, between 1985 and 1988, yen appreciated by 40%, and in the same period, export price index decreased by 31%, index of whole sale price decreased by 17%, whereas consumer price index (CPI) went up by 2%. If such situation can be compared to people's adjustment in summer time, then some had set the clock 60 min ahead of time, some 40 min, and some even set the clock 20 min behind. No doubt this would lead to chaos and distortion. Just as McKinnon and Ohno have pointed out, "Saying that exchange rate change is a veil covering the domestic price structure, is as much as to say that currency is a veil on real economy that is of no use. Neither statement is convincing. Changes in exchange rate not only plays an important role in the real work, but also is the primary root cause of micro and macro economy. Exchange rate is not subject to passive adjustment to straighten out domestic price relations, but is often a determining variable that drives domestic price level to shift from one direction into another."

An important piece of evidence used by the advocates of the “bipolar view” is that since the 1990s, many economies have shifted from pegged-exchange rate in various forms to floating exchange rate, suggesting that middle rate of exchange is not sustainable. However, after studying the exchange rate, foreign reserve and interest rate behavior in thirty nine countries, Calvo and Reinhart (2002) found that many countries claimed to adopt floating exchange rate seemed to fear to float all the time, and runs the economy through pegged-exchange rate regime in one way or another. Many researches all pointed out that, discrepancies always exist between a country’s de facto exchange regime and the de jure exchange rate as was proclaimed by its government. That is to say, those governments’ words were not matched by deeds, as far as exchange rate regime was concerned. Countries that proclaimed to adopt the pegged-exchange rate often did not live up to their words, and conversely, countries that proclaimed to adopt floating exchange rate were afraid of put the regime into practice, and tended to constrain the exchange rate fluctuation within a certain limit. In this way, just like some countries under the gold standard that contravened the “rule of the game”, in the periods of floating exchange rate, some hampered the floating of exchange rate by various policies.

As to why some countries were reluctant to tolerate fluctuation in exchange rate, researchers have offered many explanations. The study by Hausmann et al. shows that as countries adopting floating exchange rate, the G3 (U.S., Germany and Japan) have small fluctuations in reserve and interest rate, but big fluctuation in exchange rate. The opposite is true for emerging economies, where exchange rate fluctuates within small range, and fluctuations in reserve and interest rate are big. Some other industrialized countries are in-between. Hausmann et al. found two causes behind such phenomenon, namely, currency mismatch and pass-through of exchange rate. The more severe the mismatch is, and the higher level the pass-through is, the more concerned will the central bank be about the level of exchange rate and take measures to curb the fluctuation (Hausmann et al. 2001). The logic is simple, the more severe is the currency mismatch, the bigger the risk of credit and debt caused by changes in exchange rate, the higher level the exchange rate pass-through would reach, fluctuations in exchange rate will be rapidly transmitted to all sectors and fields of the domestic economy, and the country should be responsible for completing all corresponding adjustments.

In short, the nature of the “monetary veil” theory was hidden behind the idealistic explanation by the advocates of floating exchange rate. In the context of globalization, floating exchange rate hasn’t brought about independence in monetary policy, neither has it achieved the voluntary adjustment of imbalances on international payment. As for emerging economies that had high level of currency mismatch and pass-through, it might be the optimum alternative to keep exchange rate within a certain range for the purpose of avoid financial risks and distortion of the structure of the real economy.

6.6 Four Facts Contradicting Floating Exchange Rate

In fact, apart from the theoretical rebuttal against the floating exchange rate, economic realities since the 1970s also testified to the deficiencies of the argument. During the period of following the collapse of the Bretton Woods system when floating exchange rate was adopted, four major facts call for our attention, i.e. violent fluctuation of the exchange rates, exacerbation of external imbalances, high frequency of economic and financial crises, and marked increase in the net proceeds from the US external claims and debts.

Fact Number One: drastic fluctuations of exchange rates. After the Bretton Woods System collapsed in 1973, major western countries adopted floating exchange rates. The proponents of the system generally believed that it would stabilize the exchange rate. However, the fact was the opposite. The shift in the exchange rate system brought about much larger fluctuations than it was under the fixed floating exchange rate system. Apart from the enlarged magnitude, the transformation had two marked features: the strengthening of the continuity and the weakening of the correlation to the real economy. The two features usually induced perpetual deviation of the real exchange rate and widespread wrong projections of the exchange rates. Chart 6.2 shows the trends of exchange rates of dollar/pound, dollar/mark (euro) and dollar/1000 yen. It is clear that the magnitude of the fluctuation and sustainability of the exchange rates among the three countries have noticeably increased.

Fact Number Two: external imbalance has been aggravated. Talking about global imbalances, Fred Bergsten (2005) remarked, "In fact, after the WWII, similar

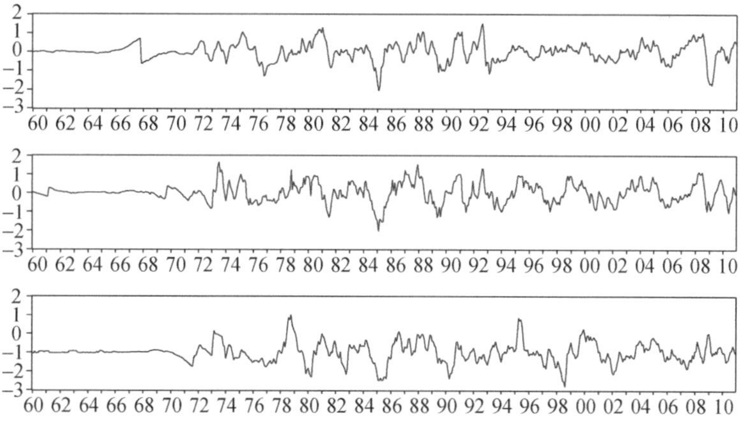

Chart 6.2 Fluctuations of nominal exchange rate in major countries (1960–2010). *Source* IMF and IFS database. From *top* to *bottom*: US dollar/pound sterling, US dollar/deutschmark, and US dollar/1000 Japanese Yen. The dollar/deutschmark exchange rate was replaced by US dollar/euro exchange rate after January, 1999. The data takes the form of logarithm and was detrended, and monthly detrend parameter is 14,400

situation has occurred at least five times: the drastic appreciation of the value of dollar caused the current account to deteriorate, followed by heightened pressure from domestic trade protectionism and deepening concerns about the slump of dollar that might soon happen, and the problem was eventually solved by more or less, sporadic readjustments of exchange rate and provisional measures of major countries." The five periods he mentioned are: the early 1970s, the end of 1970s, the mid 1980s, the mid 1990s and the beginning of the 21st century. Chart 6.3 demonstrates the share of the current account of the GDP in the United States, Germany, Japan, China and UK. Obviously, since the 1970s, the international imbalance has become grave, and apparently the much lauded self-adjustment mechanism did not work.

Fact Number Three: Economic and financial crises broke out frequently. Kindleberger has noticed that since 1973, global economic and financial crises have been notably on the rise. He pointed out in no uncertain terms that, "Between 1945 and 1975 several economic recessions occurred, all at minimal level. Recently, however, with a worldwide recession occurring between 1974 and 1975, followed by the intense financial situation in the 1980s, financial crises have increased at rapid speed." (Kindleberger and Aliber 2007). Reinhart and Rogoff (2008) had a true and panoramic description of the financial crises over the recent eight hundred years. They put financial crises into three categories: bank crises, foreign debt crises, and domestic debt crises. Their statistics shows that between 1945 and 1973, only three bank crises and fifteen foreign debt crises; whereas in 1974 and 2006, over a hundred bank crises and seventy two foreign crises broke out.

Fact Number Four: Net proceeds of the US external claims have increased remarkably. Gourinchas and Rey (2005) pointed out that exchange rate fluctuation would facilitate fast redistribution of wealth through financial channels within a short time. For example, in December, 2004, the net external debt of the US was 2.5 trillion US$, resulting from the 10 trillion US$ foreign assets minus the 12.5 trillion US$ external debt. Nearly one hundred per cent of those liabilities were valued in US dollar, and seventy percent of the asset was valued in foreign currencies. If the dollar is depreciated by 10%, ceteris paribus, an amount of wealth that equals to 5.9% of the GDP of the US will be transferred to the United States from all over the

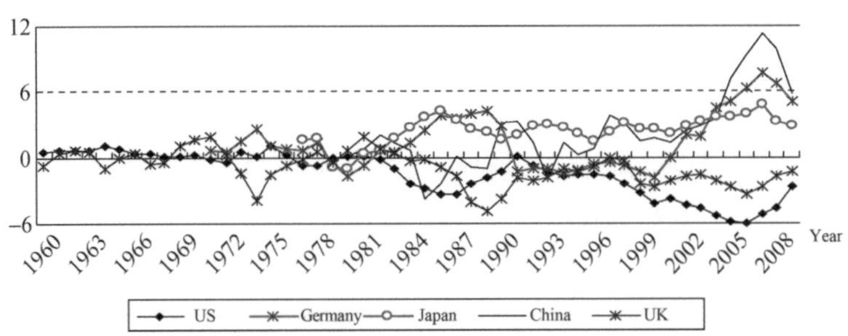

Chart 6.3 Current account balance/GDP of major countries (%). *Source* IMF world economic outlook database

world, whereas the share of the US trade deficit in its GDP is no more than 5.3%. They reevaluated the US external assets and debts since 1952 based on market price, and found that its assets had gained considerable proceeds vis-à-vis the debts. What is more, since the collapse of the Bretton Woods System, the proceeds had been noticeably increased. That gives people good reason to believe that the US has transformed from being the world's banker to the biggest capitalist for speculation.

6.7 Japan's "Financial Defeat" and the "Syndrome of Appreciation of Yen"

The four facts are tangibly and intrinsically connected, and their relations can be further revealed by case studies of individual countries. Japan, unfortunately, turned out to be an example of a disadvantaged country. Firstly, Chart 6.3 shows that Japan has been the major surplus nation, and very often the surplus counterpart of the US deficit; secondly, since the burst of the economic bubble, Japan has been lingering in the shadow of domestic economic crisis, therefore any external crisis will impact Japan heavily; lastly, when the US makes net proceeds from external assets, Japan's claim in dollar has to suffer from losses.

Table 6.1 listed a number of key indicators of the Japanese economy since 1980. In terms of economic growth, there is almost no suspense that the "Lost Decade" will be upgraded to the "Lost Two Decades". The average growth rate of the world economy between 1991 and 2009 was 3.3%, whereas Japan's growth rate in the same period was less than 0.8%. Chart 6.4 clearly shows that currently the total

Table 6.1 Major economic indicators of Japan (1980–2009)

Year	Economic growth rate (%)	Inflation rate (CPI, %)	Central bank discount rate (%)	Current account surplus/GDP (%)	Government debt/GDP (%)	Official reserve assets (%)
1980	2.80	7.81	7.25	−1.02	39.13	252
1981	4.18	4.91	5.50	0.41	40.92	284
1982	3.38	2.74	5.50	0.63	44.27	233
1983	3.06	1.88	5.00	1.76	48.14	245
1984	4.46	2.25	5.00	2.78	49.55	263
1985	6.33	2.05	5.00	3.67	50.27	265
1986	2.83	0.61	3.00	4.23	54.22	422
1987	4.11	0.12	2.50	3.45	56.07	815
1988	7.15	0.65	2.50	2.64	54.16	977
1989	5.37	2.28	4.25	2.24	50.73	849
1990	5.57	3.07	6.00	1.55	48.9	771

(continued)

Table 6.1 (continued)

Year	Economic growth rate (%)	Inflation rate (CPI, %)	Central bank discount rate (%)	Current account surplus/GDP (%)	Government debt/GDP (%)	Official reserve assets (%)
1991	3.32	3.26	4.50	2.07	47.85	690
1992	0.82	1.72	3.25	2.84	49.78	687
1993	0.17	1.26	1.75	2.99	55.38	956
1994	0.86	0.70	1.75	2.74	59.72	1228
1995	1.88	−0.13	0.50	2.16	65.90	1828
1996	2.64	0.13	0.50	1.42	68.06	2179
1997	1.56	1.78	0.50	2.27	71.49	2208
1998	−2.05	0.66	0.50	3.09	84.57	2159
1999	−0.14	−0.33	0.50	2.64	96.01	2881
2000	2.86	−0.71	0.50	2.53	103.80	3616
2001	0.18	−0.76	0.10	2.18	117.03	4020
2002	−0.26	−0.90	0.10	2.87	130.92	4697
2003	1.41	−0.25	0.10	3.21	136.68	6735
2004	2.74	−0.01	0.10	3.72	150.73	8445
2005	1.93	−0.27	0.10	3.64	162.09	8469
2006	2.04	0.24	0.40	3.93	164.03	8953
2007	2.36	0.06	0.75	4.86	162.56	9734
2008	−1.17	1.38	0.30	3.24	167.86	10,306
2009	−6.29	−1.35	0.30	2.82	185.07	10,494

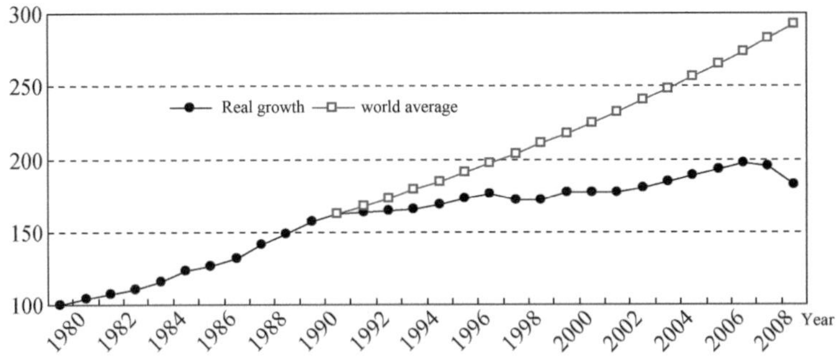

Chart 6.4 Japan's "lost two decades". *Source* Japan statistics Bureau (www.stat.go.jp/english/data). World average economic growth rate (1991–2009) was based on statistics by IMF

economic volume of Japan is merely 1.6 times of that of 1980. If Japan had been able to maintain its growth rate at the world's average since 1991, then by 2009, its aggregate economy would have reached nearly three times as much as 1980. In terms of price and interest rate, long-time negative growth in prices has caused severe deflation; and although the central bank has long maintained the discount rate at the level close to zero, the economy remains weak and is bogged down in the "liquidity trap". While fiscal stimulus plans could not jump-start the economy, issues like population aging puts the government under almost unbearable burden of heavy debt and the debt/GDP ratio is close to 200% and becomes a new tough issue. Lastly, with Japan being a surplus country for a long time, both its government and the people have accumulated tremendous amount of asset in foreign exchange.

The difficult situation of Japan had drawn extensive attention since long time ago, and researches in the regard have yielded myriad, often divided views that led to controversies. It is no exaggeration to say that it "has become the No. 1 conundrum of modern macro-economics." (McKinnon 2005). Economists have offered may explanations to this mystery, among which two are most representative. The first view was raised by mainstream economists in the west (i.e., Fischer 1998; Krugman 1998; McCallum 2003). As to the cause of the problem, those economists often equivocally attributed it to policy failure of the monetary authorities and deeply-embedded, structural problems within the financial departments. And the remedies they proposed for improving the governance, apart from methods like fiscal and monetary expansion, and currency depreciation, were further liberalization and increasing transparency. Discussing those issues they did not forget to flaunt their theories, making references extensively to literature in the field when they tried to trace the root cause of the "liquidity trap". The second view was initiated by some Japanese scholars and a few scholars from the west. They believed that the root of the problem lies in the drastic fluctuation of the yen/dollar exchange rate and the long-term appreciation of the Japanese yen, which was determined by the special position of the United States in economy and finance. For example, Yoshikawa (2000) had poignantly called Japan's setback the "financial defeat", and for McKinnon and Ohno (1999), Japan suffered from the "syndrome of appreciation of yen". Chart 6.5 is the nominal exchange rate of yen/dollar since 1960, which shows that over the forty years between the 1970s to the present, the exchange rate has risen from 360 yen/1dollar to 80 yen/dollar, and the process is not

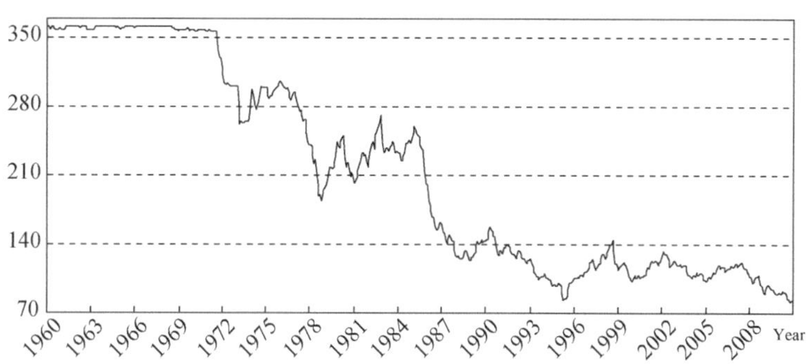

Chart 6.5 Nominal exchange rate of yen/dollar. *Source* Statistic by IMF and IFS

without drastic ups and downs (see Chart 6.2). In whatever sense, the severe fluctuation and long-term appreciation has been spectacular, and incurred severe trauma on Japanese economy.

In the first place, appreciation of yen has caused Japan to lose enormous dollar assets. Long-term surplus with the US allowed Japan to accumulate tremendous dollar assets, and the most notable direct result of the long-term appreciation of yen is the tremendous loss of such assets. Yoshikawa (2000) pointed out that, "Since the early 1980s, large amount of Japanese capital from major investors like the Nissay Group (Nippon Life Insurance Company) has flooded into the US for US treasury bonds, which constituted the majority of Japan's dollar assets… and if none of them had been sold, then by April, 1995 when the appreciation was at the apex, 70% of the assets were gone. After 1995, even when yen was relatively strong versus dollar, the loss could be as high as over 40%." In macroeconomic terms, loss like that was striking. For financial enterprises that were direct victims, such losses constituted enormous trauma, if not fatal disaster. The Nissan Life Insurance Company, for instance, used to "inject Japanese capital incessantly into the US", declared bankruptcy in spring, 1997. Though the Japanese financial sector had "deep-seated structural problem", it is undeniable that the burden of currency mismatch was the main culprit. While the US enjoyed tremendous net profits from credit and debt claims, the other side of the coin was Japan's big loss in dollar assets. Such net transfer of wealth best manifested the so-called "financial defeat".

Secondly, the exchange rate fluctuation and appreciation of yen disrupted the price signal and distorted the price structure, and eventually exerted big negative impact on the real economy. As was mentioned before, rather than being the "veil" on the price structure, exchange rate has real impact on relative prices. Besides, economy will also be influenced by the adjustments with changes in exchange rate, as the result of the transmission effect of exchange rate. For instance, if a commodity exported from Japan to the US was priced in dollar, when yen appreciates, and the price in dollar remains the same, its price in yen has been lowered, therefore the exporter in Japan has to make adjustment. In the same token, when most commodities were priced in dollar, Japanese manufacturers were the ones who shouldered the costs of adjustment when exchange rate fluctuated, while their American counterparts were much less influenced. As changes of exchange rate would impact the real economy, and when the changes were caused by factors like consumer preferences and technology of the manufacturers, floating exchange rate would be an acceptable alternative; nevertheless, if changes were induced by capital movement, political pressure or even impulsive behavior, it would not be hard to imagine how much damage the fluctuation would cause to the real economy. Miyashita, one of the Nissan Motor's board members who used to be in charge of the company's finance, once observed: "to lower the cost of each car by around one to two thousand yen would be a remarkable achievement, but this would be wiped out totally if only the exchange rate goes up 10 yen! It means, financial noise can be a hundred times as big as the real signal (McKinnon and Ohno 1999, pp. 78–79)".

Lastly, the appreciation expectation of yen and risk premium has dampened Japan's interest rate, and led the country into the "fluidity trap." Goyal and

McKinnon (2003) have pointed out that Japan's long-time low interest rate was fundamentally attributable to the expectation of yen's appreciation and the negative risk premium of assets in yen. They hypothesized the formula for extended interest premium as: $i = i^* + \Delta s^e + \varphi$. In the formula, i stands for Japan's long-term nominal interest rate, i^* stands for US long-term nominal interest rate, s for yen/dollar exchange rate, Δs^e for expected yen appreciation level, φ for risk premium of Japanese assets. Due to the expectation of yen appreciation, Δs^e had been negative for a long time (between the 1970s and mid-1990s). φ stands for the extra profit gained by investors by taking the risk of foreign exchange fluctuations. For credit countries like Japan whose debts are denominated in foreign currency, φ is negative; for debtor countries whose debts are denominated in foreign currency, φ is positive. Therefore, expectation for appreciation of yen and positive risk premium of Japanese assets decide that the interest margin between Japan and the US $i - i^*$ is negative. Table 6.1 shows that since 1995, the discount rate of Bank of Japan has been under 1%, and the interest margin between Japan and the US has been around 4%. The low interest rate led to the asset bubble of the 1980s, which prevented the monetary policy from playing its role and eventually dragged the economy into the "fluidity trap". On the other hand, low interest rate had squeezed the profit margin of financial institutions, making the later reluctant to give out loans. Those institutions on the one hand were heavily burdened by loss from exchange difference; and on the other hand their profit margin had been greatly reduced. In that case, any financial system would be filled with "deep structural problems."

6.8 Dollar Hegemony Is the Crux of Issue

The above analyses shows that the reality and myth held by the proponents of the floating exchange rate are widely different. For one thing, the self-adjustment under the floating exchange rate and the subsequent policy independence do exist, but they are only part of the picture. The crucial fact is the predominance of the US in the world's financial and economic operation and its overwhelming influence has been the causes of many problems. The US has derives special advantage from the dollar's role as the international currency, and tends to tab this advantage for its own interests.

The collapse of the Bretton Woods System in 1971 is the watershed that marked a new era of the dollar hegemony. The "Nixon Shock", the measure either of expediency or deliberation, proved to enable the US to make policy changes that would allow it to freely manipulate the value of dollar. As a matter of fact, the floating exchange rate mechanism that are highly admired by its proponents has never happened, because exchange rate is so crucial that no monetary authority would allow it to be decided solely by the force of market. Japan and China were often accused as manipulators of the exchange rate, but actually in the world, the US is the country that manipulates the exchange rate in the real sense.

Chart 6.6 Indices of dollar's real exchange rate. *Source* U.S. federal reserve (www.federalreserve.gov). *Source* Japan statistics Bureau (www.stat.go.jp/english/data), calculated by the author

In an open economy where capital and goods flow with full freedom, most transactions are done in terms of dollar, and any change of the value of dollar will start a chain of reaction. To put it simply, depreciation of dollar will cause the debts in dollar to shrink, and make the prices of commodities in dollar value to go up and force enterprise to make adjustment, and increase the return on assets of the US. Therefore, manipulation of the value of dollar will bring about enormous gains. Charts 6.2 and 6.5 depict the drastic fluctuation of the exchange rates after 1971 and changes of yen/dollar exchange rate. Chart 6.6 shows the changes of real value of dollar since 1973. To put them together, anyone would tend to sympathize with the complaints of Yoshikawa: "The US wantonly changed the value of dollar, which demonstrates its will. It turned out to be a huge disaster for Japan." Given the fact that China's current situation are in many ways similar to that of Japan, China no doubt has to give enough heed to the Yoshikawa's sagacious words.

6.9 Abstract Theory Should Never Be Equaled to Reality

We devoted much of this chapter to analyzing the actualization of gold standard and floating exchange rate, not to add one more observation to the existing vast literature, but to emphasize the following key points through the descriptive analysis:

First of all, a free market economy that adjusts itself automatically has never existed in the international economic system. In the gold standard era, almost all countries, with Britain in the lead, chose not to play by the "rule of the game", which led to the failure of the adjusting mechanism. In the era of floating exchange rate, the US often forces other countries to change the exchange rate, and out of the "fear of floating," those countries often adopted the pegged system in one form or another. It is fair to say that the gold standard and floating exchange rate might be excellent systems, but unfortunately none of them has been seriously observed or implemented. Therefore, it has been very hard to put the self-adjusting mechanisms into effect.

Secondly, realities are far more complicated than theories and models of economics. Discussion at the beginning of the chapter shows that there is a chasm between the reality and the theories, since the former is much more complicated than the latter, and the classic, textbook models too frequently have never touched up the major problems in reality.

Thirdly, as a major phenomenon of the international economy, monetary hegemony is worth serious study. In the so-called gold standard and floating exchange rate era, what had played a crucial role in the international economy were not the self-adjusting mechanisms listed on the textbook, but the hegemony of pound and dollar, with the international coordination mechanism built on the hegemony.

References

Bergsten F (ed) (2005) The United States and the world economy: foreign economic policy for the next decade (Chinese translation). Economic Science Press, Beijing

Calvo GA, Reinhart CM (2002) Fear of floating. Quart J Econ 117:379–408

Carmignani F, Colombo E, Tirelli P (2008) Exploring different views of exchange rate regime choice, J Int Money Finance 27:1177–1197

Dornbusch R (1983) Flexible exchange rates and interdependence. IMF Staff Papers 30(1):3–38

Fischer S (1998) The Asian Crisis, the IMF, and the Japanese Economy, Speech prepared for Asahi Shimbun symposium, Tokyo, 8 April

Gourinchas P-O, Rey H (2005) From World Banker to World Venture Capitalist: US External Adjustment and the Exorbitant Privilege. NBER Working Paper, No. 11563

Goyal R, McKinnon R (2003) Japan's negative risk premium in interest rates: the liquidity trap and the fall in bank lending. The World Econ 26:339-363

Hausmann R, Panizza U, Stein E (2001) Why do countries float the way they float? J Dev Econ 66(2):387–414

Johnson HG (1973) ``The case for flexible exchange rates, 1969', in his book, Further Essays in Monetary Economics, Harvard University Press, pp 198–222

Keynes JM (1986) A treaties on money (Chinese translation) (trans: Cai Q, Dingjiu F, Wang Z). Commercial Press, Beijing

Kindleberger CP (2010) A financial history of Western Europe, 2nd edn (Chinese translation) (trans: Zijian, Xu; Jianxiong, He; and Zhong, Zhu. China Financial Publishing House, Beijing

Krugman P (1998) "It's baaack: japan's slump and the return of the liquidity trap", Brookings Papers on Economic Activity (No. 2), pp 137–87

Krugman PR (2000) Exchange-rate instability (Chinese translation). Peking University Press and China Renmin University Press, Beijing

Krugman P, Obsfeld M (2000) International economics: theory and policy, 5th edn. Addison Wesley Longman Inc., Boston

McCallum BT (2003) Japanese Monetary Policy, 1991-2001. In: Federal reserve bank of richmond economic quarterly, Vol 89/1, Winter, pp 1–31

Maynard J (1958) A treaties of money. The pure theory of money, vol 1. MacMillian, London, p 351

McCallum BT (2001) International monetary economics (Chinese translation), China Financial Publishing House, Beijing

Mckinnon RI (2005) Trapped by the international dollar standard. J Policy Model 27(4):477–485

Mckinnon RI, Ohno K (1999) Dollar and Yen: resolving economic conflict between the United States and Japan (Chinese translation) (trans: Wang X, Cao L). Shanghai Far East Publishers, Shanghai

Obstfeld M (2000) International economics: beyond the mundell - fleming model. IMF Staff Papers, Vol. 47, Special Issue

Obstfeld M, Rogoff K (1995) The mirage of fixed exchange rates, J Econ Perspect 9(4):73–96

Odell JS (1991) US international monetary policy: markets, power, and ideas as sources of change (Chinese translation) (trans: Li L, Li N). China Financial Publishing House, Beijing

Polanyi K (1944) The great transformation, New York: Farrar & Rinehart, Inc. Reprinted (1957) (2001) Beacon Press, Boston

Polanyi K (1965) The great transformation: political and economic origins of our time. Beacon House Press, Boston, p 14

Reinhart CM, Rogoff KS (2008) This Time is Different: A Panoramic View of Eight Centuries of Financial Crises, NBER Working Paper, No. 13882

Salvatore D (2001) Which countries in the Americas should dollarize? J Policy Making 23(2001):347–355

Schwartz HM (2008) States versus markets: the emergence of a global economy (Chinese translation). Phoenix Publishing & Media, Inc., and Jiangsu People's Publishing House, Nanjing

Yoshikawa M (2000) A lost financial war: admonition from defeated economic powers (Chinese translation) (trans: Sun X, Yuan Y). China Youth Publishing House, Beijing

Chapter 7
Monetary Statecraft and Profits of Dollar Hegemony

Monetary statecraft, understood as efforts to influence the policies of other states by manipulating monetary conditions, has been a recurring feature of the global economy since World War II. At critical moments over the last four decades, the United States has exploited the vulnerability of countries in Europe and East Asia to changes in their currencies' exchange rates vis-à-vis the dollar in an effort to extract policy adjustments from their governments and central banks. More successful in some episodes than in others, this "exchange-rate weapon" has played a central role in international conflicts over balance-of-payments adjustment. This instrument of leverage is critical to explaining the behavior of governments and central banks and the distribution of the costs of adjustment among conflicting states.[1]

—C. Randall Henning

Imbalance is the normality of the world economy, and adjustment is an ongoing process. Among the complex multitude of adjustment mechanisms, exchange rate and institution has always been the crux of the issue. They are so important that some scholars called it the "weapon". However, the nature of the exchange rate as the weapon waged by the "central country" against other countries was often in the disguise of theories and maxims. The "central country", upholding these theories and maxims which give it the legitimacy, exercises domination over the other countries, points fingers at their domestic policies and even coerces them to adjust the policies. Therefore, to effectively correct the global imbalance and establish a relatively fair international economic and monetary system, one has to understand fully the properties and nature of the exchange rate when used as the "weapon" and "monetary statecraft" of the central state.

[1]Henning (2006).

Y. Li and X. Zhang, *Imbalance and Rebalance*,
https://doi.org/10.1007/978-981-10-6150-9_7

7.1 Foreign Exchange Rate as Weapon and Monetary Statecraft

Henning (2006) visiting researcher of the Peterson Institute for International Economics, wrote *The Exchange Rate Weapon and Macroeconomic Conflict*, which enunciated that in the era of globalization, macroeconomic conflict among states is inevitable, and the key is to coordinate the macroeconomic policies among. As to how to achieve it, Henning raised the concept of "exchange rate weapon." Though a term like this gives the international policy coordination a flavor of warfare, the pertinent observation it carries regarding the essence of the coordination is much more straightforward and powerful than the equivocal claims made by those who propagate the floating exchange rate for their own purposes.

Henning's definition of exchange weapon is as follows: one country coerces other countries to change their policy goals by means of exchange rate. When current account imbalance becomes unsustainable and inter-state economic conflict arises, a country generally has three alternatives: first, to persuade other countries to make changes in their domestic policy; second, accept changes in exchange rate; third, to change its own macroeconomic policy. In the real world of economics, the order of preferences of the government is from the first to the third, as the best alternative is to make other countries to adjust and the worst scenario is to make adjustment itself, with the second alternative in the middle. Of course, the three alternatives can also be used at the same time, forming a spectrum of different scenarios.

Under such circumstance, big powers, when waging exchange rate weapon, normally with the mechanism with three major steps: firstly, as they are fully aware of the mechanism of manipulation and its potential gains, they would deliberately induce the less powerful countries to subject to their control; secondly, major powers can manipulate exchange rate, but their tolerance for exchange rate volatility is much less than less powerful countries; thirdly, the hegemonic position of currencies of big powers enhanced their manipulative power in economy, allowing them to benefit from changes in exchange rate. As the result, when disparity exists in the scale and level of openness of the economies, influences between trade and nontradable sectors on domestic politics and under certain circumstance in the international economy, big powers are able and can often use the exchange rate weapon to achieve their own purposes.

Besides, the driving force of the US's use of the exchange rate weapon mainly was the pressure of the domestic politics, and trade policy plays similar roles as the exchange weapon.

Over the past half century, international monetary relations have noticeably undergone circles. Each cycle began with relative harmony, and gradually developed into fierce confrontation resulting from imbalance adjustment, and ended with reconciliation of some sort, thus entering a new cycle starting with relative harmony. Such a cycle repeated itself again and again. Henning held that the recent fifty years could be divided into five cycles: (1) the collapse of the Bretton Woods System since the early 1970s; (2) the solution of another round of the world's inflation conflict by the Bonne Summit in 1978; (3) the animosity in the 1980s and the Plaza Accord and the Louvre Accord; (4) the recession and recovery occurred during the early and mid-1990s; (5) the disputes of the new century. In every cycle, the US government always compelled governments and central banks of Europe and Japan to adopt the policy of monetary expansion, and voluntarily encourage the depreciation of dollar (Henning 2006). Notably, his observation is in total agreement with Bergsten's (2005) classification of the periods of the global imbalances. Surely, the overlapping of the periods of global imbalance with the US exploitation of the exchange rate weapon is no coincidence. The evolutionary logic of the different phases is: global imbalances led to economic conflicts that needed to be resolved through policy coordination, but the coordination is subject to the dollar hegemony, and exchange rate is the major weapon of the US practice the hegemonic power.

Henning's research brings about four thought-provoking conclusions: First, it is no denying the fact that the US has used the exchange rate weapon to force other countries to change macroeconomic policies. Exchange rate coercion plays a crucial role in explaining models of policy coordination and cost sharing. Secondly, successive use of the exchange rate weapon became stimulus that propels target countries actively take countermeasures to protect themselves. These measures include: initiating regional cooperation such as establishing economic and monetary union (EMU), accumulating foreign currency reserve, restructuring production with foreign direct investment (FDI). Thirdly, those countermeasures would gradually change the structure of the international monetary system, and exert certain constraints on the scope and effect of the application of the exchange rate weapon. On this point, Henning insightfully observed: "the forty-year cyclical high pressure resulting from the exchange rate suggests that in a considerably long time, the exchange rate weapon is a dissipating capital: if you keep on using it, you have to risk the possibility that you are going to lose it eventually." Fourthly, for a long time in the foreseeable future, the US will keep on benefiting from the residual rights by using the exchange rate weapon, until Europe, Japan and China forge their won monetary state policy.

Since the end of the twentieth century, the US has been pressing China to appreciate RMB yuan. It further claimed that China should "be responsible" for global imbalances. By adopting quantitative easing (QE) and withdrawing from it, the U.S. keeps on using the exchange rate weapon to exert pressure on China's macroeconomic policies, with its influences that permeated nearly everywhere. Such behaviors "smell fishy" and people would only be confused if they tried to discover the truth by studying the situation merely from the perspective of international economic order and monetary policy, and some even naively believed that this was just the one of the "international customs" of the market economy. However, if one approaches the issue from the angel of the monetary statecraft and traces the root to the "exchange rate weapon", the smoke of camouflage will be easily cleared. This is when it dawned on people that in the final analysis, the situation was caused by the exchange rate weapon of the U.S., a part of the country's monetary statecraft. Without realizing it, people were often led into similar traps.

7.2 Intervention in Foreign Exchange Market

The exchange rate weapon is often used through two means: one is to intervene in the foreign exchange market (sometimes jointly) and raise the currency value to or maintain it at an ideal level artificially through economic means; the other is to press the target country to change the value of its currency through diplomatic means in order to maintain the exchange rate of the local currency of the intervenor. The first means is the voluntary action by the intervening country, while the second is the coercive behavior inflicted upon other countries. In the sense, if the former can be called intervention in the foreign exchange market, the latter should be regarded as non-economic coercion, when the intervening country achieved its goal by blaming others for "exchange rate manipulation" and exerting pressures in various areas.

Starting from 1973, the US has achieved advantages by through exchange rate policies, especially intervention in the exchange market and even exchange rate wars. A recent, empirical research in this field by Bordo et al. (2011) reveals that between March 2, 1973 and March 19, 1997, 971 days of the US intervention had been targeted at the German mark and 243 days of the intervention at the Japanese yen, and 60% of the intervention were successful. They evaluated the intervention by constructing two criteria: Criterion 1—sell foreign reserve and the dollar appreciates, buy foreign reserve, and the dollar depreciates. Criterion 2—sell out foreign reserve and the dollar keeps on depreciating, but in smaller magnitude; buy foreign reserve and the dollar keeps on appreciating, but in smaller magnitude. If the intervention meets any of the two standards, the intervention would be counted as successful (see Table 7.1).

At the same time, the research also shows that sterilized intervention could not guarantee its effect on exchange rate independent of domestic policy, and sometimes sterilized intervention even backfired.[2] This is why Greenspan (2000) once observed that "no evidence shows, and nobody among us believes that sterilized intervention will even work."[3] After the most recent financial turmoil, governments intervened in exchange rate every now and then. The most well-known case happened several years ago when the Swiss National Bank took intervening measures to curb the appreciation of Swiss franc against the euro and dollar. The most recent example took place in Japan. When the Abe administration just came into office, it forced the central bank of Japan to cut down the exchange rate of yen against the dollar by 7%, and against the SDR basket even more sharply by 20%. As for

[2]Bordo et al. (2011).

[3]Greenspan (2000, p. 14).

Table 7.1 Success counts for U.S. intervention: March 2, 1973–March 19, 1997

	Intervention method	U.S. intervention against German marks				U.S. intervention against Japanese Yen			
		Intervention counts	Intervention successes	Expected successes	Standard deviation	Intervention counts	Intervention successes	Expected successes	Standard deviation
Success criterion 1	Foreign exchange sales/dollar appreciation	469	136	221	8	94	47	45	5
	Foreign exchange purchases/dollar depreciation	502	192	241	9	149	63	67	5
Total		971	328			243	110		
Success criterion 2	Foreign exchange sales/dollar depreciation at smaller magnitude	469	117	61	4	94	19	11	1
	Foreign exchanges purchases/dollar appreciation at smaller magnitude	502	110	65	4	149	28	20	2
Total		971	227			243	47		
General criterion	Foreign exchange sales: criterion 1 or 2	469	253	282	12	94	66	56	6
	Foreign exchange purchases: criterion 1 or 2	502	302	305	13	149	91	87	7
Total		971	555			243	157		

Source Bordo et al. (2011)

emerging economies and developing countries, intervention in exchange rate of their local currencies has been a common practice.

If sterilized intervention and monetary warfare waged through economic means haven't been as effective, to exert pressure on the target country through diplomacy and exercising the hegemonic power would be much more "effective". The conclusion of the Plaza Accord and Louvre Accord could not be simply attributable to intervention of the U.S. monetary authority, as the attempt could not be successful without the willing "cooperation" on the part of Japan.

7.3 Exchange Rate Manipulation

As a concept of international economic relations, "exchange rate manipulation" was first used by the US in its allegations against Britain during the Great Depression in the 1930s. On September 21, 1931, Britain officially announced its exit from the gold standard regime, in an effort to deal with the massive negative impacts of the economic crisis on industrial production and problems like unemployment. Meanwhile, pound sterling depreciated sharply: sliding from 1 pound in exchange for 4.86–3.75 dollars, and plummeted to 3.25 dollars in the end of the year. As industrialized countries including the U.S. and France stuck to the gold standard, British exported goods became remarkably more competitive within a short time. The U.S. blamed Britain for depreciating the pound purposefully so that the British goods could be more competitive in foreign markets, to attain advantages in the competition unfairly. More importantly, the halt to the free exchange of pound and subsequent sharp depreciation of pound had incurred heavy losses for countries like the U.S. and France that stayed in the gold standard system. On the other hand, since pound was the major currency of international reserve, its depreciation massively reduced the foreign exchange reserves of the countries who were major holders of the currency; in the months afterwards, tremendous short term capital fled the U.S., resulting in dollar panic. Under the pressure of the depreciation of pound, France, the Netherlands, Switzerland, and other countries made a run on the dollar and converted the reserve into gold.

Under the circumstances, President Roosevelt announced on April 19, 1933 that the U.S. abandoned the gold standard, which triggered a slump of the value of dollar by 15%. What was embarrassing was the fact that Ramsay MacDonald and Édouard Herriot, the Prime Ministers of Britain and France, were on their way to Washington where they would meet with President Roosevelt on issues of exchange rate stability and monetary policies. In May 1933, the dollar depreciated again, joining the pound in the devaluation trend. The gold standard group of countries headed by France was faced with grave monetary crisis, and in the franc/pound exchange market, the three-month expected valuation of franc dropped from a price 0.1% higher than spot goods price in summer 1933, to merely 67% of the spot goods price in summer, 1936.

Since President Roosevelt made domestic economic recovery the priority, the gold standard group of countries led by France and Britain made a new proposal on June 28, 1933. Emphasizing the importance of the gold standard as the instrument of international currency exchange, countries under gold standard reiterated their intention to stay in the regime, whereas as others claimed that they would reinstate the gold standard "when it is appropriate"; as for the exchange rate and the schedule of adjustment would be left to the countries to decide. However, President Roosevelt refused to cooperate with other countries to stabilize the values of currencies. He was reluctant to accept the rules as designed, let alone to renounce freedom and subject to imposed constraints. He went so far as to rejected the new proposal with the so-called "bombshell message" on July 3 and remarked, "Allowing only a few big powers to maintain temporary and artificial foreign exchange stability is a specious view that the world would not live with in the long run. To achieve the peace and stability in a nation, a sound internal economic system is the factor far more crucial than the ratio of its currency against that of the other countries. …the old day superstition of the international bankers is being replaced by the effort to make plans and arrangements for the national currency, with an aim of endowing the currency with long-lasting purchasing power. …Our goal is the permanent stability of the currency of every country."[4]

As a matter of fact, the United States, as a newly emerging trade surplus country, succeeded in maintaining the appreciation tendency for pound sterling under the lead of President Roosevelt's weak dollar policy almost throughout the 1930s.

In hindsight, nobody won the monetary war in the 1930s. Devaluing currencies and rejecting the gold standard at an earlier time seemed to help facilitate economic recovery; however, widespread trade protectionism emerged in the "race to devaluation" had caused the countries to lose their "advantage of the early-developer" in no time. In sum, the monetary war in the 1930s bore important testimony to the failure of the monetary policy coordination in the world.

After the WWII, conflicts concerning exchange rates started to diminish under the fixed change rate regime of the Bretton Woods System.

Between 1946 and 1971, the IFM took care of the supervision of the fixed parity exchange rate. Under the system, all currencies were valued in the U.S. dollar (pegged to dollar), and the U.S. dollar was pegged to gold. Without out the consent of the IMF, member states had to keep the changes of exchange within 10% of the value. According to IMF clauses, "member states should not propose to change exchange rate parity, unless in the case of addressing fundamental imbalances." In fact, this was the restraint by the Bretton Woods regime to avoid the "race to devaluation" like what had happened in the 1930s. However, this "rule" had been broken when the U.S. depreciated the dollar twice in 1971. The IMF revised the clause in 1978 as the world monetary market had experienced turmoil after some time, holding that countries could adopt any type of exchange rate mechanism—either the fixed or floating exchange rate, so long as they abided by certain rules and

[4]Tan (2009).

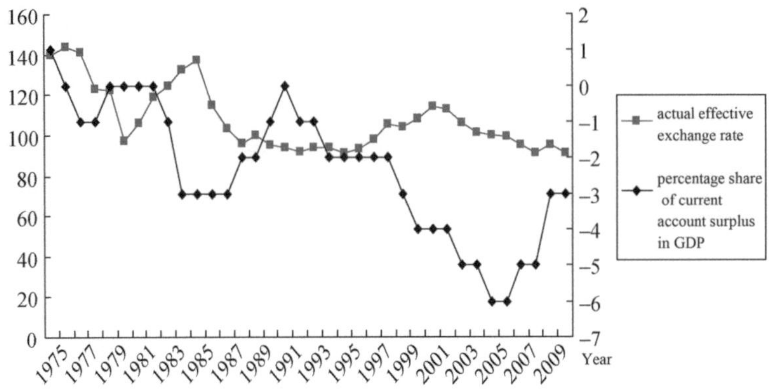

Fig. 7.1 US exchange rate and surplus on current account. *Note* (1) *left axis* exchange rate indicator, *right axis* surplus on current account; (2) actual effective exchange rate: the 2005 value is 100. *Source* World Bank: World Development Indicators, 2011

principles and did not peg to gold. They could adopt foreign exchange and monetary policies conducive to the orderly development of economy, and should avoid manipulating foreign exchange to adjust international balance of payment or obtain unfair advantages in competition in the commodity market.

IMF did not impose quantitative indicators and stringent constraints, and in fact provided more lenient conditions for the use of exchange rate weapons in the following three decades. In floating exchange regime, theoretically or intuitively, the key determining factor of exchange rate depends on ratios of actual purchasing power between countries, as in essence the value of one currency is defined in other currencies. But the reality is far more complicated, as the examples exchange manipulation, or bullying competitors were found almost everywhere. In some cases, conflicts related to exchange rates could be as atrocious as hot wars as far as the intensity and impact were concerned.

In general, in the post-Bretton Woods era (from the 1970s to present), warfare of exchange rate is manifested mostly in the wrestling between the U.S., the single most hegemon, and Japan, Germany, China and other Asian emerging economies. The conflicts are caused by a number of factors, but the root cause was the narrowing of the gap in productivity between the U.S. and those latecomers, and the U.S. current account surplus has changed from positive to negative and the situation keeps deteriorating. The U.S. was thus under urgent pressure to adjust exchange rate and improve competitiveness, so that the deficit so far accumulated could be rectified (see Chart 7.1).

7.4 A Thief Crying "Stop Thief"

The superiority of the dollar and its overall advantages gave the U.S. the capacity to manipulate the exchange rates indirectly while blaming other countries for manipulative behavior. What the U.S. did not only covered up the fact that it is the real manipulator, but also verifies Henning's statement: the hegemon is capable of choose the solution that in its own interest as possible—so that it would be able to make few or even no adjustment, while persuading or coercing other countries to change their policy objectives.

The well-known Plaza Accord and Louvre Accord reached in 1985 and 1987 were typical examples of the U.S.'s intervention in foreign exchange markets in the name of international policy coordination. As is shown by Chart 7.1, the successive interventions had effectively curbed the appreciation of the dollar and narrowing trade deficits within the short period of time (especially between the end of the 1980s and early 1990s).

If the two accords were measures of exigency, the U.S. attempted to institutionalize exchange interference mechanism. The hallmark of such transformation was the promulgation of the Omnibus Trade and Competitive Act, demanding the Treasury Department to submit to the Congress the Report on International Economy and Exchange Rate Policy twice a year, to assess if its trading partners are manipulating exchange rates based on current account and changes in foreign reserve (of other countries and the U.S.), and take countermeasures (i.e., to initiate bilateral negotiations on financial policies, impose sanctions against subsidies). Table 7.2 has helped us to briefly review the major events of the alleged manipulators on the "black list" of the U.S.

In October, 1988, the Treasury Department alleged in its first report to Congress that South Korea and Taiwan of China had acquired "inappropriate" competitive advantage by manipulation. The US had conducted "fruitful" consultation with the two economies.[5] In South Korea, in the first quarter of 1988, the exchange rate of won against dollar quickly appreciated by 5.1. As for the whole year of 1988, the accumulated appreciation reached 15.8%, overtaking the magnitude of appreciation of Japanese yen and New Taiwan Dollar. In result, although the U.S. trade deficit with South Korea kept on increasing, but only at the rate of 1%. In comparison, in 1987, the deficit had surged drastically by 39% over the previous year. In the longer term (between September 1985 and April 1989), the won had appreciated by only 34%, at lower level as compared with 53% increase of the deutsche mark and 49% of the NT dollar, fell short of the "expectation" of the U.S. Besides, since South Korea kept a reserved attitude on issues like marketization of exchange rate and opening of capital account, the U.S. did not remove South Korea from the name list of manipulators. As for China's Taiwan, the US seemed more demanding. The appreciation of NT dollar had been higher than that of won, and the trade deficit of

[5]See the Report on International Economy and Exchange Rate Policy issued by the U.S. Treasury Department on April, 1989.

China's Taiwan with the U.S. had plummeted remarkably by 21% between September 1988 and February 1989 (except the US gold export to Taiwan). At the same time, Taiwan to conduct reforms to marketize exchange rates and liberalize capital supervision. For example, in April, 1989, China Taiwan introduced the new foreign exchange pricing regime, and in particular had lessened the control on trade in large amount U.S. dollars (30 thousand dollars). In the reports, the U.S. welcomed the measures taken by Taiwan, but still listed it as a manipulator, hoping the later to "better behave itself" in the future.

In particular, when Mainland China replaced Taiwan and rose fast as a trading power, China has become the U.S. trading partner with whom the U.S. has the second biggest trade deficit, and subsequently the target of the "anti-exchange rate manipulation" policies since spring 1992. In five reports in a row, the U.S. accused of China of manipulating exchange rate based on the fact that China adopted the "double-track" system where official foreign exchange rate coexisted with a market-determined parallel exchange rate during the period (mainly between 1979 and 1994). The former was settled with non-trading foreign currency, whereas the latter with foreign currency from trade. During the period, the RMB yuan depreciated on large scale by nearly 4.5 times against the dollar. In 1991, China's trade surplus with the U.S. reached 12.7 billion US$, a huge increase by 22%. This was the major cause that prompted the U.S. to "launch an attack" on China. In fact, in faced with the disadvantageous situation, the U.S. played the trick again and pressed China to appreciate yuan and open its capital market through multilateral negotiations with China's joining the World Trade Organization (WTO) as the bargaining chip. This time, however, the U.S. met its real match, as no matter how hard it pressed China, the latter did not give into the pressure and continued to deal with issues like exchange rates, liberalization of capital items and RMB convertibility at its own pace and with measures that served its own interest.

After 1994, no economy has been identified in the end as the exchange rate manipulator. However, many were assessed as potential manipulators who were in a way threatened by the U.S. with the purpose of exerting constant pressure on those economies.

The above examples reveal that the alleged "exchange manipulators" have similar features and experiences that can be summarized into three aspects: Firstly, they are rapidly developing, newly emerging trading powers (or regions), and have accumulated enormous trade surplus with the U.S., the main cause for the conflict between them and the U.S. Secondly, the local currencies of the "manipulators" are not widely acknowledged by the internationally community (i.e., the currencies are not internationalized, and often pegged with the US dollar on their own part), and their domestic capital market were underdeveloped. Those factors led to long-term high trade surpluses, and the economies lack policies to deal with the counter-measures of the U.S. Thirdly, the "observation" period of the manipulator usually runs through two periods, obviously with "high demands" for changes and adjustments in exchange rate and trade deficit.

One thing needs to be noted is that as the only monetary power that has predominance over the world, the U.S. has crucial influence over exchange policies of

Table 7.2 Currency manipulators designated by the US

Time (as of the report)	Countries/regions as exchange rate manipulator	Major adjustment in trade surplus, exchange rate and policy		
		South Korea	Taiwan of China	Mainland of China
Autumn, 1988	South Korea Taiwan of China			
Spring, 1989	South Korea, Taiwan of China	Trade surplus with US rose by 1% in 1988; the value of won versus dollar appreciated by 15.8%; accumulated appreciation reached 34% since September, 1985	Trade surplus with US decreased by 26% (gold import excluded); accumulated appreciation of NWT dollar reached 49% since September 1985; Introduced new exchange rate regime in April, 1989	
Autumn, 1989	South Korea	Introduced "Market Average Exchange Rate" regime in March, 1990		
Spring, 1990	N/A			
Autumn, 1990	N/A			
Spring, 1991	N/A			Started to adopt regulated floating exchange rate in April, 1991
Autumn, 1991	N/A			
Spring, 1992	China Mainland China Taiwan		In 1991, China Taiwan's trade surplus with U.S. declined by 11.9%; NT dollar appreciated by 4.2% against US dollar since last report	In 1991 China Mainland's trade surplus with the U.S. increased by 22%
	China Mainland			

(continued)

Table 7.2 (continued)

Time (as of the report)	Countries/regions as exchange rate manipulator	Major adjustment in trade surplus, exchange rate and policy		
		South Korea	Taiwan of China	Mainland of China
Autumn, 1992	China Taiwan		NT dollar appreciated by 4.2% in accumulation against US dollar since the end of 1991	In October, 1992, China and the US signed the memorandum of understanding for elimination of trade barriers
Spring, 1993	China Mainland			
Autumn, 1993	China Mainland			
Spring, 1994	China Mainland			
Autumn, 1994 to present	N/A			The Chinese government decided to end the double-track exchange rate regime before January 1, 1994

other countries, especially the "manipulators." In fact, it seems that only the U.S. can effectively manipulate the exchange rate within relatively long term in today's world, therefore no other country but the U.S. is the biggest exchange rate manipulator. The accusation made by the U.S. against some other countries is merely for transferring the cost of policy adjustment to other countries with its hegemonic power.

It should also be emphasized that countries, including the U.S., are clearly aware of the detrimental effect of the exchange rate weapon as a means of trade protectionism, and have made laws to prohibit the spread of it. For example, Section 1 (iii), Article IV, of the Agreement of the International Monetary Fund amended in 1978 stipulates that members should "avoid manipulating exchange rates or the international monetary system in order to prevent effective balance of payments adjustment or to gain an unfair competitive advantage other members."[6] Apart from that, the World Trade Organization also has anti-subsidy regulations in close relations to exchange rate. However, in practice, as countries are divided as to the definition of "exchange rate manipulation" (and even "unfair competitive advantage"), they tend to interpret those rules and regulations out of their own immediate interest. For instance, why were South Korea, China Taiwan and Mainland were singled out as "manipulators"? The reason being, the U.S., on the one hand, has large trade deficit with these economies, and on the other hand, is faced with serious unemployment domestically. In other words, these economies were labeled as "manipulators" because their preponderance in trade with the U.S. and the domestic problems of the latter. Apparently such criteria made it easier for the powerful countries to intimidate the less advantaged economies in the game of exchange rate intervention. Moreover, as was mentioned previously, the effect of exchange rate in adjusting balance of payments was mostly meager and even non-existing, for a country like China whose role in bilateral trade is clearly set by the division of labor between itself and the U.S., the influence of the exchange rate on trade can be regarded as minimum. Unfortunately, some chose to be oblivious to the past. They used the exchange rate weapon again and again to achieve economic and political goals of their own. In this sense, the exchange rate weapon was not used to defend "national interests", let alone to maintain "the international order;" it was just exploited for advantages by a few countries at the cost of harming the economic development of the whole globe.

[6]However, the IMF has no right to force members to change their exchange rate policies.

7.5 Gains from the Exchange Rate Weapon: The Dollar Hegemony as an Example

Monetary hegemony lingers through international policy coordination to the use of the exchange rate weapon. In fact, any adjustment of balance of payments, especially the international "policy coordination" has never been harmonious and peaceful as they involved the conflict of interests of the parties. In this regard, the monetary hegemon enjoyed absolute advantage, and gains derived from it. The benefits reaped from the use of the exchange rate weapon accounts for a substantial amount of the gains.

Studies have been done to assess the gains from the monetary hegemony. Chinese scholars, i.e. Enfu and Wang (2008), adopted the concept of "hegemonic gain." The international academia adopted varied terms to conceptualize situations of the similar kind. Many authors used "exorbitant privilege", others, i.e., Housmann and Sturzenegger (2007) called it "dark matter". Without creating new concept, some researchers calculated the quantity of the gain obtained by the dollar hegemony through the "valuation effects" (Ghironi et al. 2009) or cost-benefit assessment (McKinsey Global Institute, MGI 2009). In addition, some also touched upon the issue of gains in discussion emphasizing the balance between privileges and responsibilities of the dollar (Gourinchas et al. 2010). In sum, western scholars have the propensity of discussing the dollar's privileges and responsibilities by way of comparing cost and benefit from a wider perspective.

It is worth noting that MGI's assessment of the cost of dollar hegemony takes into consideration both domestic and international factors. The study noticed that the changes of the value of dollar could have different kind of impact on domestic and international economy, and sometimes diametrically in opposite ways. Therefore, they tended to synthesize the domestic and international cost and benefit of the value of dollar and its changes in the calculation. This is reasonable, but when assessing the real profit gained by a country's currency when it is used as international currency from the view point of the international monetary system only, then the domestic cost-benefit analysis should not be included.

In the view of the authors of the book, the "hegemonic gain" of the dollar as international currency is composed basically of the following four elements: (1) overseas seigniorage; (2) gains from low-cost of funds, or capital cost savings; (3) excess return from external assets and liabilities; (4) return from value transfer (or transfer of loss) resulting from dollar appreciation in the rebalancing process.

(I) Overseas Seigniorage

In strict terms, seigniorage refers to the revenue from the difference between the face value and the metal value of the coins. The cost of mint is so low that can almost be neglected. Therefore, seigniorage can be valued by the face value. It should be noted here that the seigniorage is levied on overseas holders of the dollar, therefore, calculating the dollar's seigniorage, should first assess the amount of dollars held by foreigners. Although seigniorage also exists in the U.S., it is should not be included in our analysis.

According to Salvatore (2001), the annual seigniorage of the U.S. government is around 25 billion US$. Given the fact that 55–70% of the dollars are circulated outside the US territories, the external seigniorage is around 15 billion dollars a year. Based on those figures, we can estimate the seigniorage of the US in December 2010. According to statistics of the Federal Reserve, by the end of 2010, total amount of dollars in cash in circulation had reached 915.7 billion US$. Based on the assumption that 60% of the cash circulated outside the US, then on that temporal point, there were a total of 549.43 billion dollars in circulation outside the country. That is a rough estimate of the seigniorage gained from overseas by the U. S. government. Eichengreen (2011) has also observed that there were around 500 billion dollars in circulation outside the U.S. Our estimate is close to that figure.

(II) Capital Cost Savings

Since the dollar is the international reserve currency, individuals or governments of other countries have to buy the U.S. treasury bonds as fluidity reserves. Such "collective action" has greatly reduced the capital cost of the U.S. The theory of superfluity of global savings and other similar theories try to show that with large amount of funds flowing into the U.S. for the treasury bonds, return from the U.S. treasury securities is reduced, leading to lower market interest rates, and eventually lower the capital cost of the U.S. Under such circumstances, tremendous amount of capital flooded into the real estate market, which aggravated the problem of mis-match of funds. The following story of the boom and burst of bubble is widely known and further confirmed the fact that the U.S. is able to obtain capital at low cost.

Let us simply compare the interest rates of the U.S. and other countries before the outbreak of the subprime mortgage crisis in 2007. Chart 7.2 shows that the U.S. maintained a pretty low interest rate even among developed economies (Eichengreen 2011) only higher than Switzerland, Canada and Japan), not to mention in comparison with developing countries. The conclusion is, measured by the ten-year interest rate of the securities; the U.S. was able to acquire capital at the cost lower than the average cost of the international capital market.

Similar conclusions were made by other researchers. MGI's calculation shows that the capital cost of the U.S. is generally fifty to sixty base points lower than that of the international market, and their method was on the cautious side. One study found that since 2004, due to foreign purchase, the price/earnings ratio (P/E ratio) of the ten-year securities of the US in 2005 slid by 0.5% (50 base points). Another study revealed that due to foreign capital influxes, P/E ratio from 10 year treasury bonds went down by 70 base points. A research also shows that increase in U.S. Treasury bonds held by foreign investors led to a decrease of 90 base points in P/E ratio (Eichengreen 2011).[7] In fact, P/E ratio of the U.S. treasury bonds is probably 100 base points lower than that of the international market, normally at around 1%. By the end of 2010, the total debts of the U.S. government was 23.58 trillion dollars, and based on this, 1% of saved capital cost would result in a total of 235.8 billion dollars.

(III) Excess Return from External Assets and Liabilities

The so-called excess return refers to the fact that external asset of the U.S. yields higher earnings than that from its external liabilities. A large amount of analyses had been conducted in the regard, and many of them are controversial. The MGI did not include this item for two reasons: first, theoretically speaking, non-reserve country countries can copy the strategy of the U.S. (lower cost of debt and higher investment returns); Secondly, such return can be reasonably be regarded as returns after risk adjustment, and cannot be called excess return. We believe that such calculation needs a second thought.

Let us first take a look at the gap between a country's real earning from external assets and liabilities. Chart 7.3 shows, surplus in capital gains excluded, the U.S. is one of a few countries that enjoy positive excess returns. Between 1981 and 2008, annual excess return makes up 1.27% of the nation's GDP. In contrast, excess returns of emerging countries are negative, being −2.05%. Interestingly, other reserve currencies such as Japanese yen and Swiss franc enjoyed remarkably high excess return as the U.S. did. The euro did not perform well due to the crisis of the European Exchange Mechanism (ERM) in 1992, but with the creation of euro, the situation of negative P/E ratio gradually disappeared.

From Chart 7.3 alone, one may find that the US dollar seems not to enjoy too many "privileges" than other reserve currencies. However, if capital gains were included in the equation, then the situation would be widely different. It is because that among the reserve currencies, the US dollar is the only one that has the privilege to acquire capital gains, and the excess return reached 3%. It is also worth noting that except pound, other currencies had negative excess returns (see Chart 7.4).

The above analysis suggests that excess return was real, and can be regarded as the "exorbitant privilege" of the U.S. dollar, that comes with its hegemonic power.

Under this analytical scenario, we may assume that the P/E ration of the excess return is 3%. Therefore, by 2010, with external assets worth 20.73 trillion dollar, the U.S. got an excess return as high as 62.19 billion dollars.

(IV) Return from Value Transfer from Dollar Appreciation

Depreciation of the dollar is an important strategy of the U.S. to rebalance its international balance of payments along the economic cycle, as well as a major means to transfer the losses. Historically such situation had happened frequently, exemplified by the "Nixon Shock" in the 1970s and the Plaza Accord in the 1980s.

[7]Eichengreen (2011).

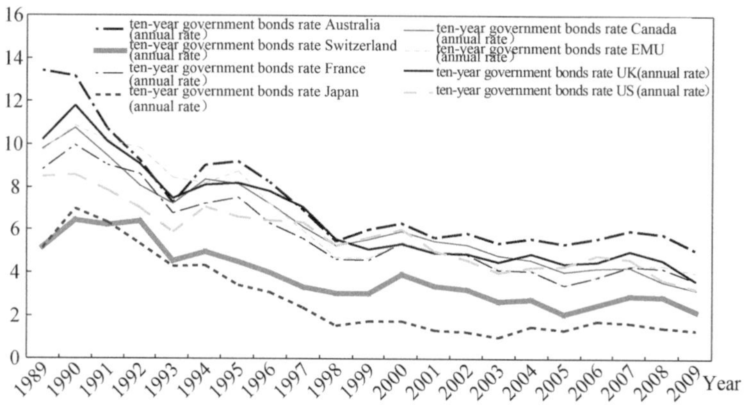

Fig. 7.2 Annual price/earnings ratio of 10 year treasury bonds. *Source* China Economy Web (m.ce.cn)

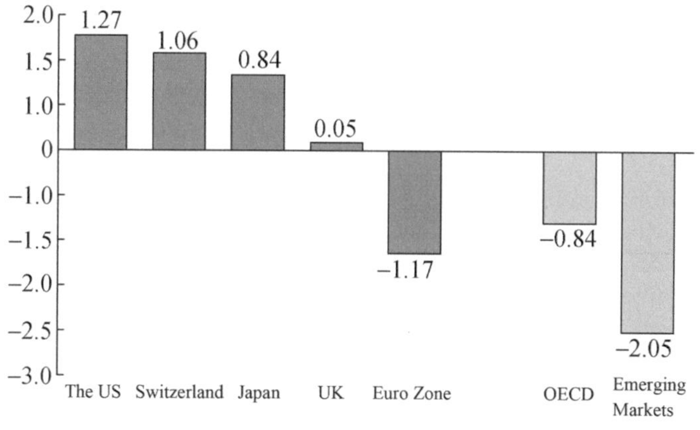

Fig. 7.3 Real P/E ration difference between external assets and liabilities (average, 1981–2008). *Source* Reorganized based on Habib (2010)

Depreciation of dollar was one major means for the U.S. government to achieve the goal of "rebalancing".

In the early 1970s, in face of the deficit on its international balance of payments, Habler used to provide the surplus countries with three remedies: inflation; appreciation or floating of currency; to increase dollar reserve. Recipient countries of dollar influx can put the inflation of dollar into effect, and the above-mentioned alternatives would produce fascinating results. In the scenario, the U.S. deficit would cause inflation in surplus economies, until the balance was achieved again. Habler explained: "Someday in the future, it will not be totally impossible for a foreigner holding dollar assets to be faced with the inflation as dollars become surplus. He will later find his dollar reserve to shrink gradually." As foreign

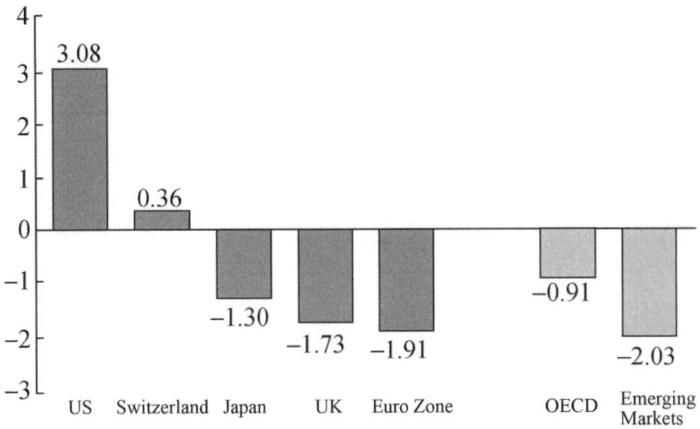

Fig. 7.4 Real difference of return between external assets and liabilities in total (capital gains included) (average, 1981–2008). *Source* Reorganized based on Habib (2010)

countries purchase commodities and assets at the inflated prices, prices of the commodities and assets across the world will go up; consequently, the U.S. government's debts will shrink as valued in terms of the current world output. If the price was to double in ten years, the real value of the debts unpaid would be reduced by half.

In essence, this is the scenario that prompted President Nixon to upgrade the "benevolent negligence." At the end of 1972, Nixon lifted the second phase's control on salary and prices, and announced the government's intention to lift the ban on capital leaving the country. As a stimulus, the Federal Reserve continued to increase money supply, which resulted in the most rapidly developing inflation since the Civil War.

As a matter of fact, the strategy of dollar appreciation is to transfer the inflation in the U.S. to other countries by consistently over-issuing the dollar, and it led to price increase all over the world, which in turn offset the value of the dollar surplus. Based on the prices and exchange rates between 1968 and 1972, the Treasury Department owed 75 billion dollar worth of debts to central banks around the world. If the debts were measured by purchasing power of the money borrowed at the time, they could be paid back with less than 40 billion dollars. According to the revaluation of the price gold, if the 75 billion dollars were paid in gold bullions, the value of the gold was less than one fifths of the original value because in 1974 one ounce of the gold was worth 200 dollars (Hudson 2008).

Since the "Nixon Shock", how much has the US dollar depreciated? In estimation of the exchange rate between dollar and gold, the magnitude of depreciation can be very large. Yet, as the price of exchange of other countries climbed sharply, it would be more appropriate if the calculation is done by comparing the depreciation of the dollar against other currencies. So, we measure the deprecation of dollar with the dollar indices of nominal major currencies. In March 1973 the index

Table 7.3 Value transfer earnings from dollar depreciation (*Unit* Trillion dollar, %)

Year	External assets	External liabilities	Changes of exchange rate of US dollar (against the previous year)	Net earnings (2005 US dollar)	Net earnings (2010 US dollar)
1976	0.46	0.29	3.94	−0.04	−0.04
1977	0.51	0.34	−0.32	0.00	0.00
1978	0.62	0.42	−8.36	0.09	0.10
1979	0.79	0.47	−1.65	0.02	0.02
1980	0.93	0.57	−0.26	0.00	0.00
1981	1.00	0.66	9.77	−0.13	−0.15
1982	1.11	0.78	10.59	−0.15	−0.17
1983	1.21	0.91	4.05	−0.06	−0.07
1984	1.20	1.04	6.90	−0.10	−0.11
1985	1.29	1.23	3.76	−0.06	−0.06
1986	1.47	1.50	−17.77	0.29	0.32
1987	1.65	1.72	−11.56	0.21	0.23
1988	1.83	2.00	−6.95	0.13	0.15
1989	2.07	2.32	4.23	−0.09	−0.10
1990	2.18	2.41	−4.64	0.10	0.11
1991	2.29	2.58	−1.51	0.03	0.04
1992	2.33	2.74	−1.69	0.04	0.04
1993	2.75	3.04	3.33	−0.08	−0.09
1994	2.99	3.29	−1.66	0.04	0.05
1995	3.49	3.92	−5.61	0.17	0.19
1996	4.03	4.50	4.53	−0.15	−0.17
1997	4.57	5.35	7.65	−0.29	−0.32
1998	5.10	5.95	4.78	−0.20	−0.22
1999	5.97	6.71	−1.43	0.07	0.08
2000	6.24	7.58	4.89	−0.24	−0.27
2001	6.31	8.18	5.99	−0.29	−0.32
2002	6.65	8.69	−1.53	0.08	0.09
2003	7.64	9.73	−12.27	0.70	0.77
2004	9.34	11.59	−8.22	0.56	0.62
2005	11.96	13.89	−1.92	0.16	0.18
2006	14.43	16.62	−1.49	0.15	0.16
2007	18.40	20.20	−5.62	0.68	0.76
2008	19.46	22.72	−4.48	0.56	0.62
2009	18.49	20.88	4.32	−0.51	−0.57
2010	20.32	22.79	−2.77	0.36	0.39

Note (1) In order to get the aggregate net earnings, we measured net earnings of each year using the 2005 dollar value, and then converted the aggregate value into the total measured by the 2010 dollar value. (2) Assuming seventy percent of the US external assets was in foreign currencies
Source Bureau of Economic Analysis

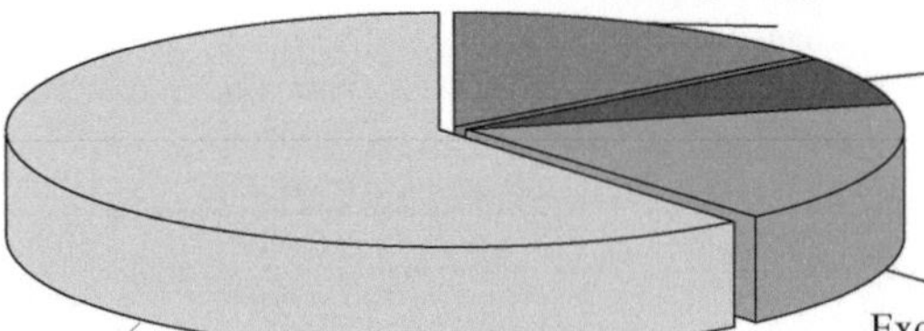

Fig. 7.5 Distribution of sources of gains from dollar hegemony. *Source* Compiled by the authors

was 100, and it decreased from 108.1883 in January, 1973 to 73.8097 in December, 2010, as the dollar has depreciated by 31.8%.

In fact, in comparison with other means, depreciation of dollar helped the hegemony to reap the biggest gains. It seems paradoxical, since depreciation, if goes beyond a certain degree, will not be able to sustain the hegemonic regime, but within a certain period of time, depreciation is sustainable. For example, a ten percent depreciation with five to ten years appears tolerable, but in the long run, the accumulated depreciation can turn out to be tremendous.

According to statistics by Gourichas and Rey, 70% of the external assets held by the U.S. were in foreign currencies, whereas the US's external debts were almost all in the dollars. Therefore, if the dollar were depreciated by 10%, it would led to 10% of appreciation of the external assets valued in dollar, without affecting other assets and liabilities valued in dollar. Along this way of thinking, we were able to estimate the net return gained externally (i.e., the improvement of the international investment cash position), among which, the exchange rate of dollar was measured by the dollar index of nominal major currencies. The outcome of our research was shown in Table 7.3. By summing up the net return of each year, we reached the conclusion that the U.S. gained a total of 2.27 trillion dollar net value transfer earnings between 1976 and 2010 through depreciation of dollar.

In generally, 549.42 billion $US seigniorage + 235.8 billion $US earnings from low capital cost + 621.9 billion $US excess return + 2270 billion $US value transfer earning = 3677.12 billion $US gain from dollar hegemony.

Gain from dollar hegemony was 3.677 trillion dollars, accounting for 23.5% of the US GDP.

Chart 7.5 shows that value transfer earnings from depreciation of dollar is the most important part of the gains from dollar hegemony, taking up 61.7% of the gain. The other parts of the gain were: 16.9% was excess returns from external liabilities; 14.9% was seigniorage from overseas, and only 6.4% was from saved capital cost.

The distribution of the sources of the gain shows that the exchange rate weapon was often used as the major means to reap profits, and it was the most important and clear manifestation of the earnings from the dollar hegemony.

References

Bergsten F (ed) (2005) The United States and the world economy: foreign economic policy for the next decade (Chinese translation). Economic Science Press, Beijing

Bordo MD, Humpage OF, Schwartz AJ (2011) The Federal Reserve as an informed foreign—exchange trader: 1973–1995. Working Paper 1118, Federal Reserve Bank of Cleveland

Eichengreen B (2011) Exorbitant privilege: the rise and fall of the international monetary system. CITIC Press, Beijing

Ghironi F, Lee J, Rebucci A (2009) "The valuation channel of external adjustment', federal reserve bank of boston. Working paper No. 09–18

Gourinchas P-O, Rey H, Govillot N (2010) Exorbitant privilege and exorbitant duty, IMES Discussion Paper Series, 2010-E-20

Greenspan A (2000) FOMC transcripts, 3 Oct 2000, p 14

Habib MM (2010) Excess returns on net foreign assets: the exorbitant privilege from a global perspective. Working Paper Series 1158, European Central Bank

Henning CR (2006) The exchange-rate weapon and macroeconomic conflict. In: Andrews (ed) International monetary power, p 117

Housmann R, Sturzenegger F (2007) The valuation of hidden assets in foreign transactions: why "dark matters' matters, Bus Econ January 2007

Hudson M (2008) Super imperialism: the origin and fundamentals of U.S. world dominance (Chinese translation) (Jingrong Diguo: Jingrong Baquan de Laiyuan He Jichu). Central Compilation & Translation Press, Beijing, p 300

Mckinsey Global Institute (MGI) An exorbitant privilege? implications of reserve currencies for competitiveness, Discussion Paper, December 2009

Salvatore D (2001) Which countries in the Americas should dollarize? J Policy Model 23(2001):347–355

Tan T (2009) From 'Monetary War' to 'Limited Cooperation': Monetary Diplomacy of the U.S., Britain and France. World Hist 6

Chapter 8
International Monetary Policy Coordination: Theories and Reality

The Pax Britannica held its sway sometimes by the ominous poise of heavy ship's cannon, but more frequently it prevailed by the timely pull of a thread in the international monetary network.[1]

—Karl Polanyi

This line is from Karl Polanyi's famous book, *The Great Transformation*. It described the Britain's power in the 19th century, which is an analogical situation of the US in the twentieth century. The monetary hegemony dominating the international coordination was pulling the threads behind the major economic events in the world.

We have mentioned previously that in the gold standard and floating exchange rate periods, it was not the textbook, self-adjusting mechanism that worked; instead, it was the hegemony of pound or other mechanisms under the hegemony of the U.S. that played key roles in the economy. There is a wide gap between theory and reality in international economies. Unfortunately, people either chose to overlook the fact, or tended to mistakenly took theories for reality. In one word, theories have been lauded as the truth that has fully worked in the real world. In this situation, talking about gold standard or floating exchange rate, one needs to clarify the concept by mentioning their key attributes: gold standard under the pound hegemony and the floating exchange rate regime under the hegemony of the US dollar.

This chapter discusses another catchword among the economists: international monetary policy coordination. Notably, we should emphasize that the coordination has always been carried through under the predominance of monetary hegemony of some country or region. It means, one can easily find many theoretical models as regards international coordination. Nevertheless, one would be too naïve to believe that international coordination was conducted as the theories posit; in reality, it has always been the predominant power that influences the policy coordination—as the gaping gap between theory and reality exists, if not insurmountable. Meanwhile, if people pay more attention to researches in international politics, they would be

[1]Translator's note: Polanyi (1965).

Y. Li and X. Zhang, *Imbalance and Rebalance*,
https://doi.org/10.1007/978-981-10-6150-9_8

surprised to see that researchers in the field of international politics have honestly captured the real situation more frankly.

The first part of the chapter is an overview of the theories concerning coordination of international monetary policy, which tries to straighten out the related literature and the phases of the theoretical evolution. The second part discusses the researches in international politics in similar vein in contrast with the studies by economists. Finally, in the conclusion, we emphasized that the discussion of the so-called international monetary policy coordination, people have the pay close attention to the role of "monetary statecraft" and "exchange rate weapon."

8.1 Theories of International Monetary Policy Coordination

Monetary policy coordination among countries has been going on for a long time, but research in the field by mainstream economists did not begin until the 1950s or 1960s, when the world had just recovered from the devastation of the WWII, and started to experience "overflow" of dollar after the "dollar shortage."

In the broader sense, monetary policy coordination takes two forms: one is "rule-based" coordination, namely, countries make and observe international rules and regimes to solve problems like international imbalances and exchange rate volatility; the other is "discretionary" coordination, whereby countries cooperate with each other at their own discretion in a more relaxed environment, so as to improve the welfare altogether. The gold standard and Bretton Woods system were the first form of coordination, and many contingent policy consultation and cooperation to deal with the crises after the collapse of the Bretton Woods system fall into the second category (Li 2006).

Theories about monetary policy coordination evolved in two phases, each generating one theoretical model. The first phase began since the 1950s and 1960s, and reached its prime in the late 1980s. In the 1970s and after two serious international oil crises, countries realized that unilateral expansion policies would be severely constrained by external environment. As the spillover effect of monetary policies of major economies including the U.S., Japan and Germany became prominent, and policy coordination in "discretionary forms" was quickly put on the agenda, with the emergence of the first-generation model of coordination. The model was founded on the Keynesian macro-economic theory, integrating game theory, measurements and analytical tools, with neo-classic elements including rational expectation and time inconsistency. The second phase of theoretical development started in the mid-1990s, and it is just unfolding. Economists began to use the New Open Economy Macroeconomics (NOEM) theories to analyze problems in this regard. By introducing the nominal rigidity and imperfect competition into the dynamic equilibrium model, The NOEM provided solid basis of micro-level analysis of alternatives.

Specifically, researches about international coordination of monetary policy are aimed at answering the following questions: Does the coordination yield gains and returns? Where will the gains come from? How big the gains will be and are they significant enough? Both models addressed these questions, with the same or different answers. However, for economists, what is important is not the answers themselves, but the ways to getting the answers.

(I) The first-generation model

The peak time of the researches on the first generation model was in the 1980s, when immense literature emerged. Mckibbin (1988) has excellently captured the situation in a comprehensive way and remarked that the first-generation model had two theoretical approaches: the first approach looks at the international transmission of economic disturbances and provides conclusion about policy conflicts; the second approach deal with coordination through game theory. Under the static framework of game theory, researchers tend to agree unanimously that the Nash equilibrium will lead to policies of over expansion or over contrition, and equilibrium reached through cooperation will bring about higher level of welfare. As the result, monetary policy coordination will have gains. But, under the dynamic, game theory framework, things become more complicated. Due to the forward-looking expectation of the player of the game, problems of time inconsistency will occur, when the policy coordination may produce worse results.

Among the researchers who studied the first-generation model, Oudiz and Sachs (1984) have done tremendous work in theory and empirical analyses, and their study was quite representative. As far as theory is concerned, they employed the framework of "targets and instruments" invented by Tinbergen, and set the target as one function of policy instrument. Under their model, foreign policy instruments were used as a function of a country's domestic policy target function, which means that external policy will impact a country's macroeconomic target. In this way, they gave the assumption that macroeconomic policy has spillover effect. Oudiz and Sachs fully explored the nature of the functions in the model, and analyzed the conditions under which policy coordination would create gains. At the same time, they conducted enlightening discussion on the sources of gains, holding that the "trading market" of policies is not safe and has externalities, but cooperation can achieve Pareto improvement. In terms of the empirical study, they conducted simulation with the then popular large-scale measurement model, and found that policy coordination did yield gains, but only accounted for 0.5% of the GNP was not significant. They further pointed out that the small amount of gain was due to the low level of economic globalization, especially the lower trade volume among big economies. Their analysis predicted that: with the deepening of economic globalization, the gains from international policy coordination would increase.

The first-generation model started to gradually lose its popularity in the 1980s after its heyday, as the under the framework subjects of research seemed to be exhausted basically. However, with the emergence of the NOEM, economists became amazed by this new tool and found that there were still many things to be explored in this area. As a new driving force and tool, NOEM reinvigorated the researches. As Obstfeld and Rogoff (2002) pointed out that "In fact, the old style, Mundell-Fleming-Dornbusch model was absolutely unable to raised the questions that we have, but it still serves as the master tool of the literature of policy coordination."

(II) The Second-generation Model

Under their own framework, Obstfeld and Rogoff (2002) researched issues of international monetary policy coordination. The research shows that although with certain special assumptions coordination has gain, but it is not empirically significant, i.e., the gain is minimal. Although this conclusion seemed no different from that of the Oudiz and Sachs (1984), actually the two researches are widely different. Apart from the differences in research methods, Obstfeld and Rogoff's research shows that after an intermediate state and with increasing integration of global commodity and capital market, the gains to policy coordination will decrease, which is contrary to the findings of Oudiz and Sachs. The spillover effect was pre-denoted, and assumed to be achieved through international movement of commodity and capital. The more globalized the economy is, the greater the spillover effect will be; the greater the spillover effect, the more gains to policy coordination. Under the model, the gains are the difference in welfare level between the Nash equilibrium and cooperative equilibrium, as the former is the result of each country trying to maximize its domestic welfare when taking the policies of other countries as given; and the latter is the outcome of maximizing the global welfare by the "global planner"; the gains came from the interactions among factors including nominal rigidities and various market distortions, and the less the other distortions is cross-influenced by monetary policy, the less the gains to policy coordination; the more integrated the global economy has become, the less the market is distorted, therefore economic integration has narrowed the space of policy coordination among countries.[2] Though Obsfeld and Rogoff's conclusion was counter intuitive, the research has greatly broadened the horizon for further exploration in the future: the NOEM framework is inclusive and allows deeper exploration from different angles; besides, since the original model is relatively simple, it leaves space for improvement later.

The question raised by Obstfeld and Rogoff (2002) is: "Are the stabilization gains from having separate currencies largely squandered in the absence of effective international monetary coordination?" Their answer was negative. As for Tchakarov, the answer was diametrically opposite, after taking into consideration incompleteness and distortions. Tchakarov looked into various forms of incompleteness and distortion, including (1) staggered nominal wage stickiness; (2) differentiated productivity disturbances in the traded and nontraded sectors (3) it is assumed that imports do not enter the domestic consumption bundle directly, but

[2]Bergin (2002) made expositions easy to understand with regard to the differences between the two generations of models.

rather participate as an input to domestic process (4) an assumed combination of producer and local currency pricing (PCP and LCP), and the incomplete transmission of exchange rate; (5) introducing a more general specification for real money balances in the utility function; (6) assuming a non-unitary elasticity of substitution between home and foreign goods. For Obstfeld and Rogoff, elements of item (1), (4), (6) plays crucial roles in obtaining gains from policy coordination. But Tchakarov's study shows that by introducing more real distortion into the model, the gains would be increased, and thus overturns Obstfeld and Rogoff's conclusion that policy coordination is insignificant.

Cazoneri et al. (2005) pointed out that Obstfeld and Rogoff's model is in fact a reiteration of the views of the Chicago school: floating exchange rate can insulate domestic economy from external impact, including that from foreign monetary policies. They reached the conclusion because of the extremely simplified theory of exchange rate determination, and the four special hypotheses that excluded terms of trade externality—all have remarkably reduced the interdependency among countries. Cazoneri et al. made distinguished productivity disturbances in the traded and nontraded sectors, finding that gains from coordination are decided by changes in productivity disturbances and their co-variances. Cazoneri et al. have contributed notably to the first-generation model, and believed that the second model had left much more space for policy coordination.

Liu and Pappa (2005) emphasized the asymmetry among the countries and captured it in their model. In their two-country, two-sector model (traded and nontraded sectors), the two countries differs in terms of the share of nontradables in consumption. This assumption is based on the general situation that references among countries, so their models have paid special attention to the difference in technological impact across various sectors. These hypotheses introduced new sources for the gains from policy coordination, suggesting that apart from terms of trade externalities, terms of trade bias also plays an role. Their study has demonstrated the necessity and importance of international monetary policy coordination.

Benigno and Benigno (2006)'s model hypothesized that with the complete integration of commodity and capital market, economies in the countries are faced with three different kinds of impact: technology, public expenditure and price markup. Their conclusion is three-fold: (1) It is uncertain which kind of exchange rate regime can enhance international monetary coordination, and it is decided by the type of disturbances. Floating exchange rate can absorb asymmetrical productivity disturbances, and therefore direct the monetary policy to domestic goals. Adjustment in price and output can absorb other disturbances, and the optimal outcome of coordination needs stabilized exchange rate regime. (2) Generally speaking, policy coordination will bring about gains. The gains come from terms of trade externality, and are influenced by the interaction among a variety of imperfections. (3) Despite of the complicated nature of the issue, it is still possible to design a simple monetary policy with the model to guarantee the optimal outcome of the cooperation.

In general, NOEM enables researchers to conduct deeper studies in greater details. For instance, the first-generation model did not differentiate policy types when it approaches international monetary coordination from broader perspective. As for how the gains are generated, the first-generation model mostly made intuitive, extensive and general discussions, whereas NOEM tends to look at a number of factors including interactions of different imperfections, the source of impacts and departmental structures. When it comes to ways of coordination, the first-generation model rarely made concrete suggestions, but some of the NOEM models helped to design monetary regimes and policy regulations. Of course, this is far from enough. So far, researches findings are still divided with regard to the gains from policy coordination. The first-generation model has been pessimistic about the gains, though findings of many recent researches have proved vice versa. Nevertheless, in the broader sense, the second-generation model creates more possibilities for policy coordination, as Tchakarov (2004) has emphasized: "…the NOEM models based on solid foundation of micro economics create ideal conditions for the factor of inefficiencies, which helps to generate nontrivial gains from cooperation."[3]

8.2 Fifty Years of Monetary Policy Coordination

Keynes remarked in 1941 that "If we trust laisser-faire alone, we will take it for granted that there is a smoothly running, self-adjusting mechanism that can maintain the equilibrium—'a disillusion of dogmatism' that overlooks lessons learnt from past experience that cannot be reasonable explained by any theory." His words seemed to have foreseen the problems of the Bretton Woods system. In fact, be it the gold standard, the Bretton Woods system or post-Bretton Woods floating exchange rate regime, none of it was able to depend solely on the self-adjusting mechanism of the market when it was necessary for countries to coordinate their policies internationally.

Prior to 1973, the Bretton Woods system made countries to peg their currencies with the dollar at the fixed exchange rate, when the IMF supervised the bilateral exchange rate coordination. After the Bretton Woods and with the introduction of the Jamaica system in 1976, coordination of economic policies, especially multilateral exchange rate policies among major western countries had been achieved through the platform of the G-7 summit or meeting of the financial ministers. In 1975, the first G-6 summit was held at Rambouillet, France, marking the beginning of international economic policy coordination in the form of meetings of major countries. However, that meeting mainly acknowledged the importance of management of domestic affairs by individual countries, rather than having discussions about economic policy coordination. It was not until meeting at the Bone when the G-7 countries proposed to take concerted actions and adopt expansionary fiscal and monetary policies to jumpstart the world economic recovery. This should be

[3]Tchakarov (2004).

regarded as the true beginning of international economic policy coordination. In 1982, at Versailles, France, the G-7 countries decided to have financial ministerial meetings on a regular basis, attended by financial ministers and central bank governors of the United States, Germany, France and Japan. In 1986, Canada and Italy joined the meeting, making it the G-7 meeting of financial ministers. The 1985 Plaza Agreement is a typical example of exchange rate policy coordination; the 1987 Louvre meeting is another example of interest rate and macroeconomic policy coordination since it introduced macroeconomic indicators including interest rate, economic growth rate, unemployment rate, etc.

Since the 1990s, the G-7 financial ministerial meeting has remained the major channel of economic policy coordination among western countries. In 1999, on the basis of the mechanism, the Group of Twenty (G-20) was established. The purpose of the G-20 is to facilitate constructive dialogues between developed economies and emerging economies on key issues of the international monetary and financial system, and further enhance the international financial structure. This turned over new leaf in international policy coordination. The G-20 did not exert real impact until the outbreak of the most recent financial crisis.

Above is an overview of the chronology of the international policy coordination. In reality, hegemony, or hegemonic powers plays predominant role in the coordination. Therefore, it is no surprise to see that if the hegemonic power needed to coordinate, the coordination might be successful; if the dominating power was not interested, there would be definitely no coordination to speak of.

8.3 The 1970s: A Few Successful Attempts at Monetary Policy Coordination

The collapse of the Bretton Woods regime shook the international monetary system dominated by the U.S. With national strength becoming greater rapidly, other currencies like yen and mark begun to take to the stage of the international monetary system. As the old regime gradually receded and the new had yet to take shape, coordination and cooperation among countries regarding economic, especially monetary policies had become increasingly significant.

The policy coordination in the 1970s aimed at the large-scale global imbalance that occurred since the end of the WWII. In 1970, the then US Treasury Secretary, David Kennedy took measures to shift the burden of the US deficits from its domestic and foreign policies to Europe and Japan, declaring that: "The inconsistency is, foreign governments urged the US to maintain surplus on payments on the one hand, but at the same time often adopted policies that hampers the realization of this goal."[4]

[4]Remarks by Kennedy (1970). Hudson (2008).

Kennedy's successor, John Connally went further by making the well-known presumptuous one liner that is still widely quoted today. When the US decided to unpeg the dollar from gold, an action that would incur losses for the Europeans but not the Americans (Europe had surplus with the US at the time), Connally told the European delegation: "American dollar is our currency, but your problem." The U.S. at the time had run huge deficit for a long time, but instead of reflecting on its policies, the US accused the Federal Republic of Germany (FRG) and Japan of intentionally underestimate their currencies and compelled them to appreciate the currencies. The FRG soon yielded to the heavy pressure, but Japan tried hard to resist with various excuses. Connally, in order to make Japan succumb, straightforwardly labeled the latter as "controlled economy".

On May, 17, 1971, the US government stepped in officially. It asked Japan in no uncertain terms to revaluate the yen, threatening to impose a specially-designed unilateral tariff on Japanese exports to the US if Japan did not go along (Hudson 2008, p. 300).

Initially Japan did not appreciate its currency but begun to lift capital control adopted since the WWII and implement the Eight-point Plan, including "liberalization of import, special favorite tariffs on developing countries, tariff cut, capital liberalization, eliminating tariff barriers, promoting economic cooperation, export standardization, and flexible fiscal and monetary policies." From July 1st onward, Japan unilaterally put a three-year limit on US textile product. Other Asian countries and regions followed suit and cut down on the sales of textile product; China's Taiwan and the ROK took the lead in announcing the decision to impose "voluntary" export quotas on domestic producers. To force other currencies to appreciate, President Nixon imposed ten percent additional charges on imported goods unlimited by trade quotas.

The 1973 Economic Report of the President of the U.S. (p. 124) stressed the importance of symmetrical nature of adjustment, i.e., either surplus or deficit countries should make adjustments; deficit countries, in particular, need to reduce demands, even though it might lead to high unemployment rate. In reality, however, the United States did not do accordingly, since it either dealt with the imbalance with "benign neglect" and did nothing, or blamed it on other surplus countries.

"The dollar ended the 1970s in the same fashion that it had started it, by falling in value. The devaluation of 1971 and 1973 had been deliberate attempts to eliminate the accumulating disequilibrium of the Bretton Woods years. The depreciation of 1977–78 also began with a deliberate attempt by Treasury Secretary Michael Blumenthal and others in the Carter administration to "talk down the dollar." In the absence of a willingness among trading partners to expand at as rapid a rate as the United States, a depreciation of the dollar was at the time viewed as the natural way of staving off the then-record U.S. trade deficits that were beginning to emerge" (American Economic Policy in the 1980s (Chinese Translation), p. 257).[5]

[5]Translator's Note: Frankel (1994).

The description above vividly revealed the nature and procedures of the so-called international coordination of macro-policy. What had happened, in essence, is that the hegemonic power always played the "non-cooperative" game to press relevant countries to change their domestic policy goals so as to resolve the imbalance in its domestic economy; consequently, the basic procedure has been the same: the hegemonic power (so far the U.S. in most cases) first designated the theme of the negotiation with predetermined expectations, and other parties had to concede, compromise, and even totally succumb.

8.4 From the Plaza Agreement to the Louvre Accord

The 1980s saw the second large-scale imbalances since the WWII. To achieve rebalance, the international community convened meetings intensively for consultations on macro-policy coordination. In doing so, the US wielded its hegemonic power again and the result is the Plaza Agreement signed in 1985.

In the early 1980s, and guided by the supply-side economics, the U.S. pushed ahead the policy of tax cut combined with a tight monetary policy. This move not only created huge fiscal deficit, but also made the dollar persistently strong against other major currencies like Japanese yen and deutsche mark due to high interest rate, resulting in constant accumulation of trade deficit. In particular, trade deficit with Japan took up nearly 40% of the total deficit of the U.S. During President Reagan's first term in office (1981–1985), since the strong dollar was regarded as the hallmark of the country's powerful political and economic fundamentals, its negative impact was not heeded enough.

Nevertheless, as the external environment for competition kept on deteriorating, trade frictions between the U.S and Japan grew more intense. In response to the request of domestic entrepreneurs, the Reagan administration began to initiated changes in economic policy after being reelected for the second term, and no longer allow the dollar exchange rate to float freely. On September 22, 1985, financial ministers and central bank governors of the US, Japan, UK, France and FRG signed an agreement at the Plaza Hotel in New York, deciding to jointly interfere the foreign exchange market so as to "orderly facilitate the appreciation of non-dollar currencies" (Eichengreen 2009), hence the widely-known Plaza Agreement.

The then US Treasury Secretary Baker in various means demanded Japan to lower interest rate and adopt expansionary monetary policy. The Nakasone administration condoned the requests under heavy pressure, and slashed the central bank discount rate five times in a row with a year. The policy coordination mostly ended with full concession on the part of other countries. Paul Volcker, the then Federal Reserve Chairman, mentioned in retrospect that "the most surprising thing at the Plaza meeting was Japan's then Treasury Minister Takeshita, who later became the prime minister, initiated a ten percent rise of yen totally unexpectedly." The former governor of Bank of Japan, Toyoo Gyohten later explained that "the

Japanese government under increasing US protectionist pressure was in panic and ready to appreciate yen substantially to relax trade tension with the United States" (Volcker and Gyohten 1996).[6]

Secretary Baker was far more ambitious in making coordinated policies among countries than interest rate policies. His efforts were resonated by Japan, the FRG (West Germany) and other trading partners. They consented to the major part of the agreement, and to expanding their domestic economy. At the Tokyo G-8 summit held in March 1986, the U.S. persuaded other countries to introduce the regime of objective indicators. The indicators included GNP growth rate, interest rate, inflation rate, unemployment rate, fiscal deficit ratios, current account and trade balances, monetary increase rates, reserves and foreign exchange rates.[7] Participants also welcomed Italy and Canada to join in the Group of Financial Ministers and Central Bankers, extending the membership from five to seven countries. They also planned to add a quantifiable indicator to review economic objectives and make forecasts, which will serve as the basis for domestic policies in future meetings. The Tokyo Declaration stated that "to make their best efforts to reach an understanding on appropriate remedial measures whenever there are significant deviations from an intended course."

One month after signing the Plaza Agreement, in order to implement the agreement and project an image of being a "responsible power", on October 31st 1985, a 17-member non-governmental consulting group for Prime Minister Nakasone named the "Advisory Group on Economic Restructuring for International Coordination" (the Meakawa Commission) was formed with the initiative of the Chief Cabinet Secretary. The commission made comprehensive proposals for Japan's economic development under the leadership of Maekawa Haruo, the former Governor of the Bank of Japan, and is known as the "Maekawa Report." The report pointed out that Japan had to expand and restructure its economy to achieve the objective of "effectively narrowing imbalances on recurrent income and expenditure." The situation at the time in Japan is highly similar to China's current domestic and international environment. Although the Meakawa Report was applauded by the international community, especially the U.S., it also triggered domestic criticism. The Report held that persistence of large-scale current account imbalances is a "state of crisis", and Japan is at the crossroad of historical transformation. Some Japanese scholars, however, believed that such judgment had the wrong point of departure. They pointed out that due to its failure to have a grip on the essential reality of Japan, the report made an unreliable abrupt turn by talking about the so-called "historical transformation." As they observed, "The crisis under discussion here is nothing but the huge surplus, which in the final analysis was caused by the huge deficit on the part of the U.S… an ongoing crisis of the US economy, and how could the situation be described as 'Japan entering a state of crisis?'" secondly, on the causes of the enormous surplus against the US, the

[6]Volcker and Gyohten (1996).

[7]The regime is regarded as the predecessor of the referential guide currently used by the G20.

Meakawa Report acknowledged that the surplus was caused by Japan's export-oriented economic structure, a de facto acknowledgement of the claim that "Japan is the one to blame." Professor Ryutaro Komiya of Tokyo University remarked, "Japan's current massive surplus in current account was caused by a number of factors in Japan and the US, particularly by the macro-economy of the latter, since the surplus was not originated from the Japanese industrial and enterprise systems…The current account balance of payments of the US was fundamentally the product of the US economy, and improvement of the situation depends on the improvement of nothing other than the US macro-economic policy. It would be the most unfair thing for Japan and even a failure of Japanese diplomacy if Japan unilaterally conceive an action program and promise economic restructuring, while the US on its part does not take corresponding initiatives to improve its policy."

The Plaza Agreement shows its effect immediately. As is shown in Chart 8.1, the U.S. dollar depreciated drastically against the yen. In September 1985, one dollar could be exchanged for about 236.9 yen, or 2.84 marks. But in October, the value of dollar fell sharply against yen and mark, when one dollar could be converted only to 214.8 yen and 2.64 deutschmark. By early 1987, the value of dollar against yen and deutschmark both dropped by nearly 35%. Despite that, the US objective of depreciation to correct trade imbalances had not been fully achieved. With two to three years since the agreement was reached, the US trade deficit kept on enlarging, only shrank for a short time between 1990 and 1991, and it continued to soar up till now.[8] The trend clearly shows that the differences in trade of the US against Japan and Germany was caused and boosted by the US, who was also responsible for the increasingly growing gap. This is mainly because that the American enterprises, in particular the production sector had become less competitive, the consumption-oriented economic structure served as the basis of the debt-based economy, the financial sector was overdeveloped, and the government took measures to protect the markets. Besides, the Plaza Agreement only addressed the issue of exchange rate, without dealing with closely related fiscal and interest rate policies. Although the subsequent Louvre Accord made it up by introducing a great deal of clauses on fiscal and interest rate policy coordination, like the Plaza Agreement, its point of departure is to blame Japan and West Germany and compel them to adjust their domestic policies. For this reason, the US played the same trick and the policy coordination barely yielded result. Notably, this major event of international coordination sowed baneful seeds for the "Lost Decade" of Japan, which was a side product should not be forgotten.[9]

[8]According to statistics of the Census Bureau, US trade deficit with Japan in 1985 was 46.1 billion dollars, and the figure rose to 55 billion dollars, and it reached 56.3 billion dollars in 1987.

[9]In fact, the role of the Plaza Agreement in dollar depreciation remained controversial in the academia. For example, pointed out that as early as March 1985, the value of dollar slumped, and its depreciation after the Plaza Agreement was merely part of the lasting trend. Therefore, the impact of the Plaza Agreement was limited.

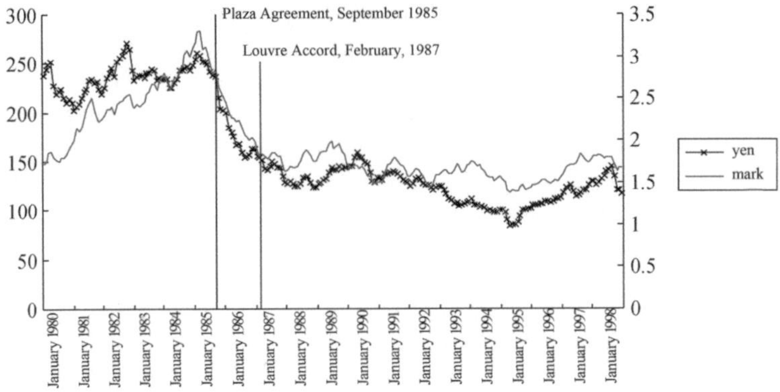

Chart 8.1 Average monthly exchange rate 1 dollar against yen/mark (1980–1998). *Note* The *left axis* is 1 dollar/yen (Tokyo market); the *right axis* is 1 dollar/mark (Frankfurt market). *Source* Bank of Japan and Deutsche Bundesbank

After the Plaza Agreement, successive interfering measures (sometimes carried out vocally) caused the dollar's value against other currencies to plummet. Very quickly the trend of depreciation of dollar had gone beyond the limit of tolerance of the other countries. Japan was most severely hit. On the one hand, appreciation of the yen greatly weakened the competitiveness of the Japanese exporters, and squeezed their profit space. On the other hand, according to the estimation by Yoshikawa (2000), Japan had lost as high as 3.5 trillion yen in net external assets due to changes in exchange rate, and the loss climbed to nearly 6 trillion yen in 1987. Depreciation of dollar was not something to look forward to for the US: it would hit the market confidence in the dollar, and undermine the US predominance, leading to volatility of financial market and decrease in investment. To prevent the situation, the financial ministers of the US, Japan, Britain, France, FGR, Canada and Italy reached the Louvre Accord at Paris in February 1987. In the agreement, the countries not only agreed to stabilize the exchange rate of the dollar at the then current level (to get it locked within a reference range), but also made extensive and coordinative arrangements in fiscal and monetary policies. For example, Japan had promised to cut down on trade surplus and lower interest rates; the US agreed to reduce fiscal deficit and maintain interest rate. Other countries went along and expressed willingness to adjust the economy by "tightening fiscal policy" and "easing monetary policy." In terms of the content, the Louvre Accord seemed to be deeper and more extensive than previous policy coordination.

Admittedly, the Accord had achieved expected result in exchange rate intervention. As is also seen in Chart 8.1, after Accord was reached, the slash of the value of dollar was contemporarily halted. Nevertheless, what happened next showed that coordination in other fields, i.e., in fiscal and monetary policy started to give way. For instance, the FGR did not lower interest rate out of the concern for the potential inflationary pressure after the reunification of Germany. As for Japan, that fulfilled the obligation of the agreement by maintaining low-interest rate for a

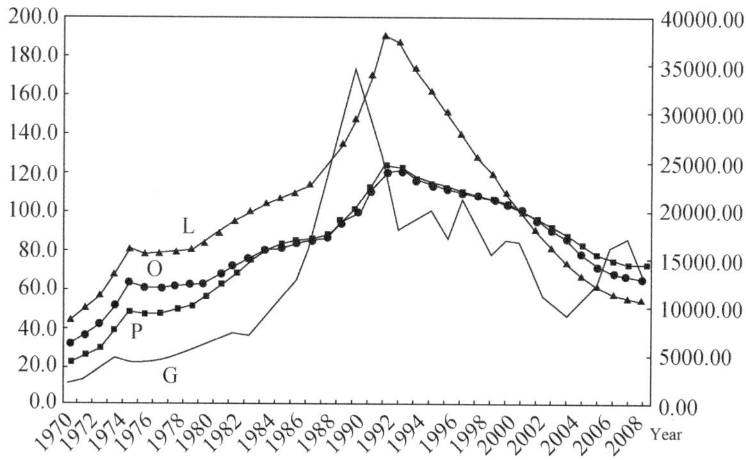

Chart 8.2 Japanese real estate and stock price indices. *Note L* commercial property price index; *P* housing property price index; *G* Nikkei index (Nikkei 225). Axis on the left: real estate price index, with the index of March 2000 as 100; Axis on the right is the Nikkei index. *Source* Real Estate Institute of Japan and Global Financial Data: from Chart 4, original text

long-time, had paid heavily: export was hurt, manufacturing industry remained sluggish, and the easing of monetary policy had rapidly boosted the stock exchange and real estate market. As is demonstrated by Chart 8.2, in the end of the 1980s and early 1990s, the prices from housing, industrial and commercial asset kept soaring up. And the stock market was in frenzy. Nikkei index (Nikkei 225) tripled between the early 1986 and the end of 1989, rising from 13,000 to 39,000 (Obstfeld 2009). Unfortunately, since the economy was still gaining strong momentum, and the price of consumer goods was generally stable, the Japanese government did not pay enough attention to the abnormal rise of the aggregate price including asset price. It is known to all that very soon the bubble burst, and Japanese economy had been mired in recession for two decades. Even now, after the Abe administration forcefully implemented unprecedented inflationary and low interest rates policy, Japan has yet to step out the shadow of stagnation and deflation.

Given all the facts, at least in the 1980s, the US hegemony in the global economy was unshakable, and with this advantage, the US dominated successive international coordination from the Plaza Agreement to Louvre Accord. As the major competitor of the US, Germany did not totally succumb to the scheme of the US thanks to its leverage as a key player in the increasingly integrated Europe Union. In contrast, with nobody to watch its back, Japan often had no choice but to follow the lead of the US, and eventually became the biggest victim of the two agreements. However, Japan is not the only victim. Another hidden victim is the concept of "international policy coordination" itself. As globalization is gaining great momentum, the importance of international policy coordination cannot be overestimated. However, since the international economic order was off balance and discrepancies between powerful and weaker countries make it more difficult to build consensus, without institutionalized mechanism coordination that should have been based on equality and mutual benefit, in most cases became means to achieving private ends of individual countries. In this case, no wonder the hegemonic power would naturally become the major beneficiary. So, such "coordination" turned out to be either diplomatic talk with empty promises, or the "donation pledge card." It is not surprising to see that the coordination had few constructive results.

8.5 G20 as the New Platform of Global Policy Coordination

At the turn of the new millennium and shortly before the outbreak of the 2007 Global Financial Crisis, not for the first time, the global imbalances became no longer sustainable. It was the third major imbalance since the end of the WWII. Like what had happened in the previous crisis of the 1970s and 1980s, this time the US again had the biggest imbalance as the hegemonic power. Prior to the crisis, the proportion of the US trade deficit in the global GDP climbed up drastically, and within several years reached as high as 1.5%. The difference though, is that this time the trading partners with the US were the emerging economies, among which China plays a major role.

The old story repeated itself again in the new century: the US government played trick again and kept on pressuring China to appreciate RMB, and threatened to label China as currency manipulator. Differently, China and other emerging economies did not act as obediently, which brought about new elements in the international coordination.

Looking back on the history of policy coordination, the trend is clear: more countries start to join in the international coordination, including emerging economies and developing countries, and the coordination platform developed from meetings of financial ministers of five countries, seven-countries, and later eight-countries (G-8), and the present 20 countries (G-20); along with the trend, the US hegemonic power has been on the decline, with its influence keeps on dwindling.

As a forum for international cooperation, the G-20 was founded on December 16, 1999 in Berlin. Being a mechanism of informal dialogue under the Bretton Woods system, it was formed by the G-7 countries (Canada, France, Germany, Italy, Japan, Britain, and the United States), plus the Eleven Major Economies (E 11, including Argentina, Brazil, China, India, Indonesia, Mexico, Russia, Saudi Arabia, South Africa, South Korea and Turkey), as well as Australia and the European Union. The summit aimed to promote open and constructive discussion on essential issues among industrialized developed economies and emerging economies, seek cooperation among them so as to facilitate international financial stability and sustained economic growth. Following former practices, the IMF and World Bank attended the meetings as non-official members. As the G20 takes up 90% of the world's total output, 80% of the world's trade 9 (including trade within the Euro Zone), and two thirds of the world's population, it is highly representative. On the other hand, as more than 170 countries are excluded from it, its representativeness, legitimacy and inclusiveness have all along been controversial.

For the ministerial meeting to the G20 summit, it took one decade for the organization to evolve into a dynamic institution, mostly driven by major crises. It is no other than the international financial crises since 2007 that called upon the leaders of the G20 members states to meet at Washington D.C. in November, 2008. It was the first G20 summit after the financial minister and central banker meetings. It is true to say that greater crises propelled the countries to coordinate at a higher level. What happened in 2007, though was similar to the situation in the early stage of the G20 (i.e. economic crisis and the rising of new powers), diverges widely from the past. Firstly, in terms of the nature of crises, the crisis occurred in the 1990s was mainly the Asian financial crisis that mainly impacted the emerging economies instead of developed countries. Secondly, as far as the emerging economies, their economic strength in the 1990s was no comparison to that of the 2007, when those countries and regions acquired strength substantial enough to cause power shift in the world economy after a new round of the boom at the turn of the century since the miraculous economic take-off and the following sustained growth over the past two decades. Statistics of the IMF shows that in 1999, emerging economies took up 37% of the world's total output compared with 63% of the developed countries. The ratios became 45% versus 55% in 2008 when the first G20 summit took place. The rapid narrowing of the output gap makes the G20 the platform of global governance and international policy coordination of unprecedented significance.

8.6 Wrestling at the G20 Summit

Between November 11, 2008 and September 2013, eight G20 summits had been held, following the meetings of financial ministers and central bankers. As the most crucial arena for macro-economic policy coordination of the 21st century, G20 addresses a wide range of economic issues including exchange rates, interest rates, modes of development, economic restructuring, etc. It is worth noting that as a participant in all those meetings, China has been playing an increasingly important role.

To find out how the G20 worked and what demands were raised by China, as well as to capture more vividly the games and maneuvers between the developed countries and emerging economies, it would be helpful to have an overview with detailed analyses of all these summits and meetings in chronological order. The following tables present the readers with China's views and standpoints (indicated by the speeches of China's head of state), issues under discussion and communiqués of the ministerial and central bankers meetings, as well as summit declarations, listed separately in columns. We italicized and highlighted the demands proposed by China, to which the concerning parties however failed to respond, hoping that would illuminate the comparison and analyses.

(I) The First G-20 Summit (Washington, November 11–15, 2008)

The G-20 financial ministerial and central bankers' meeting was held on November 8–9, 2008 at São Paulo, Brazil.

	Hu Jintao's speech	Communiqué of the São Paulo finance ministers and central bank governors' meeting	Declaration of G-20 summit at Washington
1	**Making concerted efforts to stabilize international energy and food market by curbing speculation**		Remain committed to addressing other critical challenges such as energy security and climate change, food security, the rule of law, and the fight against terrorism, poverty and disease
2	Prevent trade and investment protectionism in all its forms, push forward the Doha round negotiation for positive results as soon as possible		underscore the critical importance of rejecting protectionism and not turning inward in times of financial uncertainty; [countries] shall strive to reach agreement this year on modalities that leads to a successful conclusion to the WTO's Doha Development Agenda
3	Enhance international cooperation in financial regulation and improve supervision, formulate behavioral norms for credit ranking agencies; step up oversight over global capital flows, and strengthen regulation and supervision on various financial and intermediary institutions, increase transparency of financial markets and products	To enhance international cooperation, restore and maintain financial stability, restore normal functioning of money and credit markets in both advanced and emerging market countries [as quickly as possible], improve their regulatory and supervisory regimes and enhance transparency, we should consider ways of enhancing the identification of systemically important institutions and ensure proper oversight of these institutions, including credit rating agencies We agreed that it is important to address the issue of pro-cyclicality in financial market regulations and supervisory systems We also agreed that financial institutions should have common accounting standards. Regulators and supervisors should enhance their vigilance and cooperation with respect to cross-border flows	work together to enhance regulatory cooperation; intensify international cooperation among regulators and strengthening of international standards, where necessary, and their consistent implementation; Strengthen transparency of financial markets and products; exercise strong oversight over credit rating agencies, consistent with the agreed and strengthened international code of conduct. Promoting Integrity in Financial Markets; uphold principles of the free market, and **we must avoid over-regulation that would hamper economic growth and exacerbate the contraction of capital flows**
4	Push forward reform of international institutions, reform the selection mechanism of decision-making management, increase representativeness and voices of developing countries in international financial organizations, Set up a global early warning system of macroeconomic and financial risks, improve the internal governance of international financial institutions, establish crisis response and relief	We underscored that the Bretton Woods Institutions must be comprehensively reformed; Emerging and developing economies should have greater voice and representation in these institutions The IMF, the World Bank Group and other international financial institutions have an important role to play, consistent with their mandates, in helping to stabilize and strengthen the international financial system,	Reforming International Financial Institutions: advancing the reform of the Bretton Woods Institutions; emerging and developing economies should have greater voice and representation; supervisors should collaborate to establish supervisory colleges for all major cross-border financial institutions by March 31, 2009. The IMF and the FSF, with its focus on standard setting, should strengthen their collaboration [to]

(continued)

(continued)

	Hu Jintao's speech	Communiqué of the São Paulo finance ministers and central bank governors' meeting	Declaration of G-20 summit at Washington
	mechanism are timely and effective, enhance the ability of international institutions in fulfilling their commitment	advancing international cooperation. We urge the IMF to continue to adapt its lending instruments to adequately meet its member needs. We believe that the IMF must enhance its early warning capabilities with due regard to systemically important economies	conduct early warning exercises. Welcome the IMF's new short-term liquidity facility, We stress the International Monetary Fund's (IMF) important role in crisis response, welcome its new short-term liquidity facility
5	**Encourage regional financial cooperation and facilitate mutual-assistance in liquidities, improve regional financial infrastructures, and put regional funds relief mechanism into full use**		
6	**Improve and steadily diversify the international monetary system, work jointly to maintain the stability of the international monetary system**		

The demands made by President Hu Jintao at the Washington summit but were not fully addressed by, or different from what was conveyed in the summit Declaration and the Communiqué of the Ministerial Meeting include:

(1) Hu Jintao pointed out that efforts should be made to stabilize international energy and food market by curbing speculation, whereas the summit declaration merely addressed issues like energy safety, food safety, climate change, without mentioning the need to curb speculation.
(2) Hu Jintao proposed to enhance international cooperation in supervision over financial institutions and markets, whereas the summit declaration pointed out that while strengthening supervision, negative impact from over-regulation should be avoided.
(3) Hu Jintao emphasized the necessity of encouraging regional financial cooperation and facilitating mutual-assistance in liquidities, improving regional financial infrastructures, and putting regional funds relief mechanism into full use. This was not mentioned by either the communiqué or declaration.
(4) Hu Jintao suggested that the international monetary system needed to be diversified, which was not mentioned in both the communiqué and declaration.

(II) The Second G-20 Summit (London, April 1–2, 2009)

The G-20 financial ministerial and central bankers' meeting was held on March 14, 2009 at Horsham, the United Kingdom.

	Hu Jintao's speech	Communiqué of the Horsham ministerial meeting	London summit declaration
1	Oppose protectionism in all forms, and uphold a fair, free and open global trading and investment system		Promote global trade and investment and reject protectionism, to underpin prosperity
2	Advance the reform of the international financial system and reconstruct the international financial order; strengthen cooperation in financial regulation and formulate as soon as possible the universally accepted regulatory standards and norms; improve standards and regulation of credit-rating agencies Set up a global early warning system of macroeconomic and financial risks, particularly in major international financial centers	Strengthen financial regulation and enhance international cooperation	Repair the financial system to restore lending. Establish the much greater consistency and systematic cooperation between countries, and the framework of internationally agreed high standards, that a global financial system requires
3	International financial institutions should increase assistance to developing countries; the IMF should seek a balance between rights and obligations and combine quota-based contribution with voluntary contribution when raising resources and the new resources should be used first and foremost to meet the needs of the less developed countries A workable international financial relief system with quick response should be established	We are committed to helping emerging and developing economies to cope with the reversal in international capital flows Mobilising International Financial Institution (IFI) resources and liquidity to finance countercyclical spending, bank recapitalisation, infrastructure, trade finance, rollover risk and social support. Emerging and developing economies, including the poorest, should have greater voice and representation	Treble resources available to the IMF to $750 billion; support a new SDR allocation of $250 billion, support at least $100 billion of additional lending by the MDBs, use the additional resources from agreed IMF gold sales for concessional finance for the poorest countries. To make available an additional $850 billion of resources through the global financial institutions to support growth in emerging market and developing countries by helping to finance counter-cyclical spending, bank recapitalisation, infrastructure, provide $50 billion to support social protection, boost trade and safeguard development in low income countries. Reform mandates, scope and governance of financial institutions, The heads and senior leadership of the international financial institutions should be appointed through an open, transparent, and merit-based selection process
4	The IMF should enhance and improve its oversight on the macroeconomic policies of various economies, major reserve currency issuing economies in particular, with a special focus on their currency issuing policies		We will support, now and in the future, candid, even-handed, and independent IMF surveillance of our economies and financial sectors, of the impact of our policies on others, and of risks facing the global economy. Establish a new Financial Stability Board (FSB) with a strengthened mandate, as a successor to the Financial Stability Forum (FSF), being able to provide early warning of macroeconomic and financial risks, reshape our regulatory systems
5	**Improve the international monetary system and regulation of reserve currency issuing mechanism, stabilize exchange rates of major reserve currencies, diversify and rationalize the international monetary system**		
6	**Keep countries' macro-economic policies consistent, timely, and**		Promote global trade and investment

(continued)

(continued)

	Hu Jintao's speech	Communiqué of the Horsham ministerial meeting	London summit declaration
	forward looking. Efforts should be made to conduct substantive cooperation, in particular cooperation in areas of the real economy including trade and investment, expand cooperation in trade financing and among small and medium sized enterprises **We should energetically promote international cooperation in new industries, especially energy conservation, pollution reduction, environmental protection and new energies, and foster new growth areas in the world economy**		

The demands made by President Hu Jintao at the Washington summit but were not fully addressed by, or different from what was conveyed in the summit Declaration and the Communiqué of the Ministerial Meeting include:

(1) Hu Jintao pointed out that the IMF should seek a balance between rights and obligations and combine quota-based contribution with voluntary contribution when raising resources. Such principles were not clearly spelled out by the communiqué and declaration.
(2) Hu Jintao mentioned that it was important to improve the international monetary system and regulation of reserve currency issuing mechanism, stabilize exchange rates of major reserve currencies, diversify and rationalize the international monetary system. This was overlooked by the communiqué and declaration.
(3) Hu Jintao advocated keeping countries' macro-economic policies consistent, timely, and forward looking. He also said that efforts should be made to conduct substantive cooperation, in areas of trade, investment and investment financing. These issues were not found in the communiqué and declaration, but were indeed mentioned by the declaration of the Third G20 summit declaration.

(III) **The Third G-20 Summit (Pittsburgh, September 24–25, 2009)**

The G-20 financial ministerial and central bankers' meeting was held on September 4, 2009 at London, UK.

	Speech by president Hu Jintao	Communiqué of the London ministerial meeting	Declaration of G-20 summit at Pittsburgh
1	We should step up macroeconomic policy coordination, maintain the overall consistency of our policies and ensure that they are timely and forward-looking. **We should stay on alert against any possible adverse impact of the stimulus measures, the potential risk of inflation in particular**		The process of recovery remains incomplete. We will avoid any premature withdrawal of stimulus. We prepare our exit strategies. We need to shift from public to private sources of demand, establish a pattern of growth across countries that is more sustainable and balanced, economic policies should be collectively consistent

(continued)

(continued)

	Speech by president Hu Jintao	Communiqué of the London ministerial meeting	Declaration of G-20 summit at Pittsburgh
2	**Major reserve currency issuing countries should take into account and balance the implications of their monetary policies for both their own economies and the world economy with a view to upholding stability of international financial markets**		
3	We should energetically promote international cooperation in new industries, especially energy conservation, pollution reduction, environmental protection and new energies, and foster new growth areas in the world economy. **We should intensify international scientific and technological cooperation and make full use of the advancement in science and technology to boost the internal dynamism of world economic growth**		Phase out inefficient fossil fuel subsidies that encourages wasteful consumption, stimulate investment in clean energy, renewables, and energy sufficiency and provide financial and technical support for such projects in developing countries. Improve transparency and stability of the energy market, and avoid excessive volatility
4	We should stand firm in our commitment to advancing the reform of the international financial system. We should improve the existing decision-making process and mechanism in international financial institutions. We should move forward the reform of the international financial supervisory and regulatory regime. The reform should get to the most fundamental principles and objectives of supervision and regulation. The future financial supervisory and regulatory regime should be easy to operate and highly accountable. We should step up cooperation in financial supervision and regulation, expand its coverage, formulate as quickly as possible financial supervision and regulation standards that are widely acceptable	Enhance monitoring of systemically important financial institutions, rapid improvement in conducting prudent supervision and regulation; national authorities should implement global standards consistently; to achieve a single set of high quality global accounting standard for financial tools Discourage excessive leverage	Strengthen international financial oversight. We welcome the efforts of the FSB in financial supervision and international cooperation Discourage excessive leverage Modernize the IMF's governance, improve its effectiveness and implement the package of IMF quota and voice reforms We call on our international accounting bodies to redouble their efforts to achieve a single set of high quality, global accounting standards All major G20 financial centers omit to have adopted the Basel II Capital Framework by 2011
5	**The root cause for imbalances is the yawning development gap between the North and the South**		
6	We should build up international institutions that promote balanced development. We should encourage the World Bank to increase development resources and enhance its role in poverty reduction and development, and urge the IMF to set up a financial rescue mechanism that will provide prompt and effective assistance and give financing support to the least developed countries on a priority basis. Developed countries should implement the Monterrey Consensus in real earnest, take concrete steps to increase assistance to developing countries **Reduce man-made barriers to technology transfer, step up cooperation in green technologies.**		We are committed to a shift in quota share to dynamic emerging market and developing countries of at least five percent from over-represented to under-represented countries; generate in the nest shareholding review a significant increase of at least 3% of voting power for developing and transition countries. Developing countries should transfer part of their quota shares to developing countries, whose shares will increase from 43% to 48%. We call on the World Bank to develop a multilateral trust fund to support the new food security initiative in low-income countries

(continued)

(continued)

	Speech by president Hu Jintao	Communiqué of the London ministerial meeting	Declaration of G-20 summit at Pittsburgh
	Countries at different stages of development should be allowed to choose their own approach and pace suited to their national conditions, and the space for development that the developing countries well deserve must not be compromised		

The demands made by President Hu Jintao at the Bundesbank summit but were not reflected in the summit Declaration and the Communiqué of the Ministerial Meeting mainly include:

(1) We should stay on alert against any possible adverse impact of the stimulus measures, the potential risk of inflation in particular.
(2) Major reserve currency issuing countries should take into account and balance the implications of their monetary policies for both their own economies and the world economy.
(3) The root cause for imbalances is the yawning development gap between the North and the South.
(4) Reduce man-made barriers to technology transfer, step up cooperation in green technologies. Countries at different stages of development should be allowed to choose their own approach and pace suited to their national conditions, and the space for development that the developing countries well deserve must not be compromised.

(IV) The Fourth G-20 Summit (Toronto, June 26–27, 2010)

The G-20 financial ministerial and central bankers' meeting was held on June 5, 2010 at Pusan, South Korea.

	Speech by president Hu Jintao	Communiqué of the Busan ministerial meeting	Declaration of G-20 summit at Toronto
1	**We should shift G20's focus from concerted stimulation to coordinated growth, from emergency responses to long-term, effective governance and from passive response to proactive plan.** Strengthen macro-economic policy coordination among the G20 members, and support countries in sovereign debt crisis to tackle the difficulties. **Maintain the momentum of the world**	strong, sustainable, and balanced growth	Advanced economies will follow through and communicate "growth friendly" fiscal consolidation plans that will foster economic growth. The G20's highest priority is to safeguard and strengthen the recovery and lay the foundation for strong, sustainable and balanced growth, and strengthen our financial systems against risks. We are committed to take concerted actions to

(continued)

(continued)

	Speech by president Hu Jintao	Communiqué of the Busan ministerial meeting	Declaration of G-20 summit at Toronto
	economic recovery by making cautious and safe decision on the moment, pace, and degree of the stimulus exit		sustain recovery, create jobs and to achieve stronger, more sustainable and more balanced growth
2	Deepen the international financial regulatory reform and build financial institutions that serve the development of the real economy. Establish and implement strict standards on capital and leverage ratio, and subject shadow banking to supervision, and achieve a single set of global accounting standards. Efforts should be made to strengthen the supervision and regulation of financial institutions of systematic importance, improve precision and effectiveness of financial regulation. Enhance supervision on credit-rating agencies	Further progress on financial repair; committed to accelerate the implementation of strong measures to improve transparency, regulation and supervision of hedge funds, credit rating agencies. Urged the International Accounting Standards Board and the Financial Accounting Standards Board to redouble their efforts to achieve a single set of high quality, global accounting standards	Pursuing the G20's financial supervision reform, and ensure a stronger financial system to serve the needs of the real economy. A strong and effective regulatory framework has been set up We are committed to design and implement a system where we have the powers and tools to restructure and resolve all types of financial institutions in crisis, without taxpayers ultimately bearing the burden. We pledge to support robust and transparent peer review through the FSB. We re-emphasize the importance we place on achieving a single set of high quality improved global accounting standards. We urged the International Accounting Standards Board and the Financial Accounting Standards Boards to redouble their efforts to complete their convergence project by the end of 2011
3	Facilitate reforms of international financial institutions and speed up IMF quotas reform; give more representation and say to emerging market countries and developing countries Enable more people from emerging economies and developing countries to take up senior management positions.	Facilitate reforms of international financial institutions	We welcomed the agreement on the World Bank's voice reform to increase the voting power of developing and transition countries, and bring DTC voting power to 39.48%. We agree that a number of other critical issues will need to be addressed, including: the size of any increase in IMF quotas, which will have a bearing on the ability to

(continued)

(continued)

	Speech by president Hu Jintao	Communiqué of the Busan ministerial meeting	Declaration of G-20 summit at Toronto
	Enhance capacity—building of the IMF and deepen the reform of the international regulatory system; strengthen supervision on macro-economic policies of all economies, especially of major reserving issuing countries		facilitate change in quota shares; the size and composition of the Executive Board; ways of enhancing the Board's effectiveness; and the Fund Governors' involvement in the strategic oversight of the IMF. Staff diversity should be enhanced

The demands made by President Hu Jintao at the Toronto summit but were not reflected in the summit Declaration and the Communiqué of the Ministerial Meeting mainly include:

(1) Shift G20's focus from concerted stimulation to coordinated growth, from emergency responses to long-term, effective governance and from passive response to proactive plan.
(2) Strengthen macro-economic policy coordination among the G20 members; and maintain the momentum of the world economic recovery by making cautious and safe decision on the moment, pace, and degree of the stimulus exit.
(3) Strengthen IMF's supervision on macro-economic policies of all economies, especially of major reserving issuing countries.

(V) **The Fifth G-20 Summit (Seoul, November 11–12, 2010)**

The G-20 financial ministerial and central bankers' meeting were held on October 23, 2010 at Gyeongju, South Korea.

	Speech by president Hu Jintao	Communiqué of the Gyeongiu ministerial meeting	Declaration of G-20 summit at Seoul
1	We should stick to the country-led principle**, take into full account the different national circumstances and development of various members, and appreciate and respect each country's independent choice of development path and policies** **We need to improve the framework so that the framework can shift its focus from emergency responses to long-term governance and continue to more effective medium-to long-term global policy coordination. Enhance macro-economic policy coordination, facilitate international cooperation in emerging industries and technology;** Support the efforts of	Pursue structural reforms to boost and sustain global demand. Continue with monetary policy which is appropriate to achieve price stability and thereby contributes to the recovery. Move toward more market determined exchange rate systems	Undertake macroeconomic policies, including fiscal consolidation where necessary, to ensure ongoing recovery and sustainable growth and enhance the stability of financial markets, in particular moving toward more market-determined exchange rate systems. Implement a range of structural reforms that boost and sustain global demand, foster job creation

(continued)

(continued)

	Speech by president Hu Jintao	Communiqué of the Gyeongiu ministerial meeting	Declaration of G-20 summit at Seoul
	developing countries in economic restructuring and increasing domestic needs and exports We should encourage various economies to draw on each other's strengths for mutually beneficial growth		
2	We should continue to push for fair and merit-based selection of the management of international financial institutions, and enable more people from developing countries to take up mid-level and senior management positions. We should support the International Monetary Fund in its effort to strengthen the monitoring and early warning of capital flows and prevent the destructive impact of large capital movement, both inward and outward, on individual economies		A modernized IMF that better reflects the changes in the world economy through greater representation of dynamic emerging markets and developing countries. These comprehensive quota and governance reforms to enhance the IMF's legitimacy, credibility and effectiveness. Instruments to strengthen global financial safety nets, which help countries cope with financial volatility by providing them with practical tools to overcome sudden reversals of international capital flows
3	While tightening international financial supervision and regulation, we need to seek the right balance between financial regulation and innovation, and between government intervention and market forces, and address the systemic and fundamental problems in the international financial system so that the system will become one that relies on, serves and buttresses the development of the real economy. We should strengthen supervision and regulation over credit rating agencies, the shadow banking system and transborder capital flows. **We should improve the international monetary system and build an international reserve currency system with stable value, rule-based issuance and manageable supply. The major reserve currency issuing economies should adopt responsible policies, maintain relative stability of exchange rates**	Complete financial regulatory reforms	To enhance exchange rate flexibility to reflect underlying economic fundamentals and refrain from competitive devaluation of currencies. Advanced economies, including those with reserve currencies, will be vigilant against excess volatility in capital flows facing some emerging market economies. Work further on macro-prudential policy frameworks; better reflect the perspective of emerging market economies in financial regulatory reforms; strengthen regulation and oversight of shadow banking; further work regulation and supervision of commodity derivatives markets
4	We should advocate new ways of development and **reduce artificial barriers to technology transfer** in order to create conditions for developing countries to achieve green and sustainable development at an early date		

The demands made by President Hu Jintao at the Seoul summit but were not reflected in the summit Declaration and the Communiqué of the Ministerial Meeting mainly include:

(1) Take into full account the different national circumstances and development of various members, and appreciate and respect each country's independent choice of development path and policies.

(2) Improve the framework so that the framework can shift its focus from emergency responses to long-term governance and continue to more effective medium-to long-term global policy coordination.
(3) Promote international cooperation in emerging industries and technology; reiterate the demand to reduce artificial barriers to technology transfer in order to create conditions for developing countries to achieve green and sustainable development at an early date.
(4) Improve the international monetary system and build an international reserve currency system with stable value, rule-based issuance and manageable supply. The major reserve currency issuing economies should adopt responsible policies; maintain relative stability of exchange rates.

(VI) The Sixth G-20 Summit (Cannes, November 3–4, 2011)

The G-20 financial ministerial and central bankers' meeting were held on February, 18, 2011 at Paris, France.

	Speech by president Hu Jintao	Communiqué of the Gyeongiu ministerial meeting	Declaration of G-20 summit at Seoul
1	Strong growth is the primary goal in pursuing strong, sustainable and balanced growth. We should introduce new and strong measures to ensure the fiscal and monetary policies are fully implemented and that funding is channeled into the real economy to boost production and employment. **We should make major efforts to support the development of small-and medium-sized enterprises and help them speedily overcome the current difficulties by provide financing and fiscal support and tax incentives**, thus laying a solid foundation for promoting economic recovery. **We should fully tap into the potential of science and technology, nurture growth drivers and build up the internal dynamism of economic recovery**. At the same time, we should speed up the adjustment of our respective economic structures and endeavor to achieve fairly balanced growth of the global economy	Taking into account different national circumstances, will achieve medium-term fiscal consolidation	
2	We should strengthen consultation and coordination, introduce mutually supporting and complementing policy measures, and tackle sovereign debt risks, massive unregulated cross-border flow of capital and other financial risks, maintain the stability of commodity prices at a reasonable level. We should keep the fluctuation of commodity prices under control, mitigate global	International monetary system has deficiencies. Avoid persistent exchange rates misalignments. We reiterate that excess volatility and disorderly movements in exchange rates have implications for economic and financial stability. Increase long-term investment in agriculture of developing countries	We welcome the euro area's determination to bring its full resources and entire institutional capacity to bear in restoring confidence and financial stability, and in ensuring the proper functioning of money and financial markets. We endorse the recommendation by the International Organization for Securities Commission (IOSCO) on the regulation and supervision of

(continued)

(continued)

	Speech by president Hu Jintao	Communiqué of the Gyeongiu ministerial meeting	Declaration of G-20 summit at Seoul
	inflationary pressure and make sure that the economic policies pursued by various countries do not offset each other		commodity derivatives markets. Market regulators should be granted effective intervention powers to prevent market abuses. In particular, market regulators should have, and use formal position management powers, including the power to set ex-ante position limits
3	We should advance the reform of the international monetary system in a steady manner, expand the use of the SDR of the IMF, reform the SDR currency basket, and build an international reserve currency system with stable value, rule-based issuance and manageable supply. **We should work to make the commodity pricing and regulating mechanism more equitable and transparent**. We should ensure global energy security and food security, and in particular, meet the energy and food needs of developing countries	To reform the financial sector	Deepening financial sector reforms and take comprehensive measures to strengthen the regulation and oversight of the shadow banking system We agreed that the SDR basket composition should continue to reflect the role of currencies in the global trading and financial system. The SDR composition assessment should be based on existing criteria, and we ask the IMF to further clarify them. We call on the IMF to make further progress toward a more integrated, even-handed and effective IMF surveillance; better identify and solve the spillover effects We will keep progress on the implementation of the Action Plan on Food Price Volatility and Agriculture of June, 2011

The demands made by President Hu Jintao at the Paris summit but were not reflected in the summit Declaration and the Communiqué of the Ministerial Meeting include:

(1) Make major efforts to support the development of small-and medium-sized enterprises and help them speedily overcome the current difficulties by provide financing and fiscal support and tax incentives.
(2) Tap into the potential of science and technology, nurture growth drivers and build up the internal dynamism of economic recovery.
(3) Make the commodity pricing and regulating mechanism more equitable and transparent.

(VII) The Seventh G-20 Summit (Los Cabos, June 18–19, 2012)

The G-20 financial ministerial and central bankers' meeting was held on February, 26, 2012 at the capital of Mexico, Mexico City.

	Speech by president Hu Jintao	Communiqué of the Mexico City ministerial meeting	Declaration of G-20 summit at Los Cabos
1	The international community should, in a spirit of helping each other and seeking win-win cooperation, address seriously the systemic risks in the world economy and seek proper solutions, consolidate and strengthen the hard-won recover; the international	Fully implement the commitments of the Cannes Action Plan, enhance monitoring and accountability to ensure the commitments on fiscal, financial, monetary and exchange policies	Strong, sustainable and balanced growth remains the top priority of the G20. We are committed to adopting all necessary measures to strengthen demand, support global growth and restore confidence, enhance creation of high quality jobs, as reflected in the

(continued)

(continued)

	Speech by president Hu Jintao	Communiqué of the Mexico City ministerial meeting	Declaration of G-20 summit at Los Cabos
	community should continue to support some European countries to solve the debt problems in a constructive and cooperative manner and strives to get these economies back onto the track of stable growth at an early date; the international community should strengthen macroeconomic policy coordination and take full account of national circumstances and reasonable concerns of each country; the international community should promote technological progress and innovation, foster emerging industries, and provide driving force for the continuous growth of world economy. The international community should pay high attention to the negative impact of excess commodity price volatility on world economic growth		Los Cabos Growth and Jobs Action Plan Euro Area members of the G20 will take all necessary measures to safeguard the integrity and stability of the area, improve the functioning of financial markets and break the feedback loop between sovereign and banks. We look forward to the Euro Area working in partnership with the next Greek government to ensure they remain on the path to reform and sustainability within the Euro Area Enhancing food security and addressing commodity price volatility
2	The international community should unswervingly deepen the reform of the international financial system. The priority is to implement the 2010 IMF quota and governance reform packages to provide long-term and stable resources for the IMF. and increase the representation and voice of developing countries. The international community should strengthen international financial regulation, making it serve better and promote the development of the real economy **We should improve the international monetary system, expand the use of the SDR of the IMF, reform the SDR currency basket, and establish an international reserve currency system with stable value, rule-based issuance and manageable supply** The international community should stand firm to promote trade liberalization and facilitation, implement commitments of the previous summits	Continue working towards the reform of the quota of the IMF and ensure sufficient resources of the IMF	We recognize the importance of effective global and regional safety nets. We welcome the firm commitments to increase the resources available to the IMF. This is the result of a broad international cooperative effort that includes a significant number of countries. The commitments exceed $450 billion. These resources will be available for the whole membership of the IMF, and not earmarked for any particular region. This effort shows the G20 and the international community's commitment to take the steps needed to safeguard global financial stability and enhance the IMF's role in crisis prevention and resolution Reaffirm the commitment to reform the financial sector and foster financial inclusion and resist protectionism in all its forms
3	Oppose all forms of protectionism; continue to authorize international institutions including the World Trade Organization and the United Nations Conference on Trade and Development in their efforts to strengthen oversight on trade and investment restrictive measures. The international community should maintain the openness and inclusiveness of various bilateral and regional free trade arrangements, making them important driving force for global free trade		
4			

(continued)

(continued)

	Speech by president Hu Jintao	Communiqué of the Mexico City ministerial meeting	Declaration of G-20 summit at Los Cabos
	Strengthen cooperation with the United Nations, and support the UN and its specialized agencies to continue play a key role in development; enhance the capacities of international financial institutions in promoting development and poverty alleviation. Make greater efforts to encourage foreign trade of developing countries, address the concerns of the least developed countries in trade with effective resolutions, and implement tariff and quota exemptions for those countries. Increase input in addressing issues of development, including food safety and infrastructure; and prevent the imbalances between the South and North from exacerbating by tackling bottleneck issues		Eradicate poverty and achieve strong, sustainable and balanced economic growth Enhancing food security and addressing commodity price volatility
5	**The international community should actively develop green industries such as energy-saving and environmental-friendly industries,... and build a resource-saving, environment-friendly society; the international community should adhere to the principle of common but differentiated responsibilities and support the parties to choose the road of sustainable development in line with their national conditions, including endowment in natural resources, phase of development, and capabilities; the international community should enhance international technological cooperation avoid new green trade barriers**		

The demands made by President Hu Jintao at the Paris summit but were not reflected in the summit Declaration and the Communiqué of the Ministerial Meeting include:

(1) The international community should tap into the potential of science and technology, and promote technological progress and innovation, and provide driving force for the continuous growth of world economy.
(2) The international community should make the selection process of the leaders of international financial institutions more transparent and reasonable.
(3) The international community should improve the international monetary system, expand the use of the SDR of the IMF, reform the SDR currency basket, and establish an international reserve currency system with stable value, rule-based issuance and manageable supply.
(4) The international community should develop green industries such as energy-saving and environment-friendly industries; encourage countries to choose voluntarily the path of development in accordance with their national situation.

(VIII) The Eighth G-20 Summit (St. Petersburg, September 5–6, 2013)

The G-20 financial ministerial and central bankers' meeting was held on February, 15–16, 2013 at the capital of Russia, Moscow.

	Speech by president Xi Jinping	Communiqué of the Moscow ministerial meeting	Declaration of G-20 summit at St. Petersburg
1	Development and innovation are required by the sustainable growth of the world economy. All countries should **improve the quality and efficiency of economic growth**, avoiding measuring progress solely in terms of GDP growth. Enhance economic competitiveness through active structure reform	We will continue to implement our previous commitments, including on the financial reform agenda to build a more resilient financial system and on ambitious structural reforms to lift growth	Members have committed to a wide range of reforms to strengthen the foundations for strong, sustainable and balanced growth over the long term by boosting investment, addressing fundamental weaknesses, enhancing productivity and competitiveness, increasing labor force participation, improving financial stability and credit access, and addressing international and external imbalances. These reforms are key to achieving a lasting improvement in potential growth, job creation and rebalancing demand
2	All countries should build the awareness of a community of common destiny, cooperating in competition, and achieving win-win results in cooperation. Give consideration to the interests of other countries, when pursuing the national interests of our own, and taking care of the development of other countries when seeking our own development. Integration of interests is required by the balanced growth of the world economy. We should form a linkage between the development of one country and that of other countries, and bring positive spillover effects for each other	Advanced economies will develop credible medium-term fiscal strategies; monetary policy should be directed toward domestic price stability and continuing to support economic recovery. We commit to minimize the negative spillovers on other countries	Strengthening growth and creating job is our top priority, and we are fully committed to taking decisive actions to return to a job-rich, strong, sustainable and balanced growth path, and avoid policies that could cause the recovery to falter or promote growth at other country's expense. We commit to cooperate to ensure that policies implemented to support domestic growth also support global growth and financial stability and to manage their spillovers on other countries
3	Adopting responsible macroeconomic policies. The major economies should take care of their own matters, ensuring no big mess in their own economy. All countries should strengthen macroeconomic policy coordination and communication. Macroeconomic, microeconomic and social policies should be integrated, and countries should make social policies solid foundation for economic policies and create favorable conditions for macroeconomic and microeconomic policies		Coordinated and integrated public policies are crucial to achieving strong, sustainable and balanced growth, and restoring confidence in the global economy. We will mobilize, coordinate and integrate our national policies (macroeconomic, financial, fiscal, education, skills development, innovation, employment and social protection) to promote creation of quality jobs while increasing productivity
4	Tap into comparative advantages of countries and optimize allocation of global resources, improve global industrial layout, build a global value chain that shares interest, and foster a big global market that benefits all parties, achieving win-win results. Safeguarding and developing an open world economy. We should oppose all forms of protectionism, maintain a free, open and non-discriminatory multilateral trading system, and avoid	Move more rapidly toward more market-determined exchange rate systems. We will refrain from competitive devaluation	Achieving the open, rule-based, transparent and non-discriminatory and WTO-based trading system. We stress the crucial importance of strong multilateral trading system, and oppose trade protectionism in all its form. We are committed to open market, and extend our commitment to refrain from protectionist measures and aims at enhancing transparency in trade, including in regional trade agreements

(continued)

(continued)

	Speech by president Xi Jinping	Communiqué of the Moscow ministerial meeting	Declaration of G-20 summit at St. Petersburg
	fragmentation of the world market and division of the trading system. **Improve the global investment rules, guiding the rational flow of capital in global development, and allocate resources for development more efficiently.** Recognize the division of labor of countries in the global value chain, as well as the value added and gains acquired by individual country, strengthen trade policy coordination, and **help trade capacity-building of the developing countries**		We value monitoring of trade and investment restrictive/opening measures by the WTO, the OECD and the UNCTAD. We call on them to continue and reinforce this work consistent with their respective mandates so as to better resist protectionism and promote liberalization of global trade and investment Identifying the opportunities and challenges of participation in GVCs and making valuable value-added trade statistics may help countries in due course to decide upon appropriate policymaking options to benefit from GVCs
5	Improving global economic governance, make it fairer and more just. Making the G20 an important force of stabilizing the world economy, establishing the international financial safety net and improving global economic governance. The relevant countries should further push forward the implementation of the quota and governance reform on International Monetary Fund (IMF). Make share formula that reflects the weight of economic aggregate of various countries in the world economy. Continue to strengthen the international financial market supervision, build a stable and anti-risk international monetary system, conduct reform on the basket of currencies for Special Drawing Rights, strengthen the connections among international and regional financial cooperation mechanisms, and build a financial risk firewall	We remain committed to the full, timely and consistent implementation of the internationally agreed financial sector reforms. We urge all jurisdictions to adopt the agreed Basel III reforms as expeditiously as possible. We reaffirm our previous commitment that the distribution of quotas based on the formula should better reflect the relative weights of IMF members in the world economy, which have changed substantially in view of strong GDP growth in dynamic emerging market and developing countries	We have agreed and are implementing a broad range of financial reforms to address the major fault lines that caused the crisis. We are building more resilient financial institutions. Recognizing the importance of effective global safety nets. Ensure that all financial institutions, markets and participants are regulated and subject to oversight appropriate to their circumstances in an internationally consistent and non-discriminatory way. We are promoting regulatory reforms targeted at reducing moral hazard and systemic risk and fostering a stable financial system that supports sustainable and balanced economic growth. We are resolved to see the financial reform agenda through to its completion in a manner that avoids fragmenting the global financial system. We will continue to cooperate on all financial regulation issues. Continue to support the decision by the IMF Executive Board to integrate the final consensus on the new formula with the fifteenth general quota review. The formula-based quota distribution should better represent the weight of the IMF members in the world economy

The demands made by President Xi Jinping at the Moscow summit but were not reflected in the summit Declaration and the Communiqué of the Ministerial Meeting mainly include:

(1) All countries should improve the quality and efficiency of economic growth, avoiding measuring progress solely in terms of GDP growth;
(2) Improve the global investment rules, guiding the rational flow of capital in global development, and allocate resources for development more efficiently;
(3) Strengthen trade policy coordination, and help trade capacity-building of the developing countries.

(4) Build a stable and anti-risk international monetary system, conduct reform on the basket of currencies for Special Drawing Rights.

8.7 The "Mutual Assessment Process" (MAP)

The G20 voiced its opinion on a variety of international issues in its declarations and communiqués. For an institution of international coordination at the highest level, those statements need to be implemented, as no one wants to see the G20 be reduced to a forum of empty talk. In this respect, apart from giving the emerging economy more voting power in the World Bank and IMF, progress in "mutual assessment" and the "reference guide" can be regarded as substantial improvement.

The leaders of the G20 committed at the 2009 Pittsburgh summit to make concerted efforts to ensure medium-term sustained recovery and strong and sustainable growth. To achieve the objective, they launched the Framework for Strong, Sustainable and Balanced Growth. At the center of the framework is a multilateral process by which the member states would be able to identify global economic and policy targets that serve the objective. Besides, the leaders have also made commitments to mutually assess each other over the progress towards the common goal through the mechanism of the "Mutual Assessment Process". The G20 asked the IMF to provide necessary technical analysis to facilitate member states to coordinate their policies and assess if they have achieved the designated target.

The first phase of MAP: From Pittsburgh to Toronto. At the Pittsburgh summit, the leaders enunciated that the first phase of assessment depends on two key steps: to assess the collective implications of their national policy frameworks; assess whether their policies are consistent with the G20 objective, and assess potential policy alternatives.

The second phase of MAP: from Toronto to Seoul. The key result of the first phase assessment is: that well-designed action program of the G20 could facilitate growth, create jobs and alleviate global poverty. On this basis, the leaders of the G20 reiterated their commitment to the Mutual Assessment Process, and designated policies that would enable the economies of individual countries to keep up-going. The presumption of "up-going economy" highlighted the risk that global current account imbalances would widen again absent further policy action, thus impairing the target of growth set by the leaders. MAP entered the second stage at the Seoul summit in November 2010, when the leaders committed to make greater effort to solve imbalances that might risk the economic growth. Also at the summit, they proposed the indicative guidelines to identify and assess imbalances.

The third phase of MAP: from Seoul to Paris. At the meeting held in Paris, February 2011, the G20 decided on a number of key indices after consultation (including public debt, fiscal deficits, income movement including trade differences and net investment gains), laying foundations for assessing external and internal imbalances that would potentially risk the shared growth. The member states agreed to, with technical support of the IMF, construct the Indicative Guidelines, which set the benchmarks for qualitative and quantitative assess major imbalances, in order to solve the problems by making corrections based on analysis of the causes and impacts.

In April, 2011, the ministerial meeting was held at Washington, D.C., and marked a new phase of the MAP, when the countries reached consensus on the guiding principles that indicate major imbalances. It built solid grounds for authorizing qualified economies to assess the domestic policies of each other, and made proposals on policy relief measures that will help removing potential, destabilizing imbalances and boost the economic growth in the member states. It outlined the priority of MAP at the next stage, i.e. by properly taking into consideration individual domestic situations, review and assess the progress in meeting the target of improving external sustainability set in the Seoul Communiqué. Specifically, the MAP will further analyze the nature, causes of the imbalances in countries with major potentials, as well as obstacles to adjustments. The IMF will provide independent analysis, which will be added to the G20 data with the consent of the latter's.

8.8 "The Indicative Guidelines"

The "Indicative Guidelines" refers to a series of indices, covering internal and external imbalances in developed and emerging economies. The Communiqué of the financial ministers and central bank governors meeting in Paris in February, 2011, designated six major indices of the "Indicative Guidelines" to measure internal and external imbalances: government debt-to-GDP ratios, fiscal surplus-to-GDP ratios, private saving-to GDP-ratios, private debt-to-GDP ratios, trade surplus-to-GDP ratios, net investment gains and transfer payments-to-GDP ratios. In April 14 the same year, at the meeting of financial ministers and central bank governors, plan for quantifying the Indicative Guideline indices was passed, and following final instrumental documents provided by FWG, China, the US, Japan, Germany, France, Britain and India had entered the second phase. The countries need to implement the MAP, analyze policies of sustainable development of the imbalances and make adjustment proposals. Based on the analyses and proposals, the Working Group of the Framework of Growth drafted the Cannes Action Plan to present at the Cannes summit. The Plan illuminated short-term and long-term policy proposals (fiscal policies in particular) for major member states, especially those were systematically imbalanced.

Serving the goal of achieving strong, sustainable and balanced growth, the MAP focuses on imbalances and the correction, but did not touch upon issues regarding constraining the monetary policy of the country that issues international reserve currency and correcting its imbalances. Besides, although the MAP and Indicative Guidelines had expected to exercise constraining power over the member states, but how much the action program can be executed is doubtful. The 1985 Plaza

Agreement and 1987 Louvre Accord keep on remind us of the difficulty in this regard. In those agreements, the US had promised to cut down on fiscal budget deficit, but the promise was unfulfilled; whereas its counterpart Japan had implemented the items on the list. Such situation makes the future of the current coordination doubtful, as the past might be repeated under similar circumstances. At the 2010 Toronto summit, the members committed to reduce fiscal deficit by half by 2013, and achieve stabilization or reduction of government debt-to-GDP ratios by 2016. These are the target for debt and deficit in developed countries; however, in view of the debt crises in Europe and the US, it is barely possible to reach the target. Meanwhile, the developed economies pressed extremely hard on emerging countries over issues like trade surplus, current account surplus and elasticity of exchange rates (though some of the issues are not under the G20 framework). Evidently, inequality and hegemony of some country are still lingering in the current international economic system.

8.9 Epitome of Hegemony and Anti-hegemony Movement

Frankly, from the Washington summit to Pittsburgh summit between 2008 and 2013, international macro-economic policy coordination had yielded some results. For example, with the establishment of the Global Financial Stability Board (FSB) financial supervision has been greatly enhanced; reforms of the IMF and World Bank in terms of global governance had given the emerging economies bigger say in the matters; macro-economic policy coordination among G20 members had made considerable progress, especially with the consensus reached on some indicative guidelines. In general, however, the G20 agenda still centers on the developed economies. To improve their status (mainly marked by the voice or voting power), emerging economies had increased their contributions to the funds or made more contributions to solving the crisis.

First of all, the purpose of the G20, to a large extent, is to salvage the world, particularly the developed economies from the crisis. The reforms in the international monetary system have made progress, but still have a long way to go. Up to now the self-restraining mechanism for international reserve currency issuing countries has yet to be built. Other alternatives including enhancing the role of SDR, expanding the varieties of the SDR currencies and internationalizing the RMB were under discussion, but with little progress. Moreover, as Chapter Two has pointed out that, on October 31st, 2013, central banks of six developed economies, including the US, Europe, Canada, UK, Japan and Switzerland announced that they would extend the established currency swap agreement and make it unlimited and multilateral, pointing out the new direction for future evolution of the international monetary system. This time, the emerging economies were again excluded from the system.

Secondly, the G20 is biased on the issue of rebalancing. The MAP and Indicative Guidelines aim at solving major imbalances, but they are biased in two main aspects: firstly, they focus on surplus and deficit, and touches little on imbalances between the south and north. Although they included assistance programs for some poor countries or regions, they were equivocal measures of expediency, with few real benefits for those underdeveloped economies. Secondly, during the rebalancing process, the surplus and deficit countries do not have equal responsibilities. The truth is, the primary agenda is to press the surplus countries to reduce surplus, and little attention has been paid to prompt the deficit countries to make adjustment, not even in empty talks. Even in the "fairest" cases whereby some developed deficit countries were able to remove the deficit just as the result of the adjustment achieved by some surplus countries.

Thirdly, in the fields of investment and trade liberalization, the major purpose was to force developing countries to open their market, but there are a lot of restrictions on opening the markets of developed countries to the former, and it is still hard for emerging economies to enter the market of developed economies in the fields of intellectual property rights protection, energy and environmental conservation, social security and the so-called "sensitive industries". Besides, developed economies have imposed restrictions of exporting high technologies.

Fourthly, although strengthening financial regulation and supervision has been the theme of the G20, the supervision on cross-border capital movement has never made to the G20 agenda. If, say, enhancing financial supervision is to solve problems of the developed economies (specifically to avoid financial crisis caused by lack or relaxation of regulation and supervision), to a certain extent, capital regulation was designed to reduce the risk of attack of hot money on developed economies. Study by the IMF shows that countries with capital regulation were the least impacted by global financial crisis. Since 2009, it has been acknowledged by most people that financial regulation is helpful in solving the large-scale rush of hot money into the emerging markets. Therefore, the IMF, G20, and the Financial Stability Board (FSB) need to remove the stigma attached to capital regulation and protect the capabilities of the countries in capital regulation. In fact, the IMF, G20 and the FSB should work together to conduct global dialogues among the countries on conducting cooperation in capital account regulation. Unfortunately, this proper demand had been "benignly overlooked" by the G20, especially the developed economies.

Fifth, despite the global governance structure have somewhat been improved with the facilitation of the G20, there is still a major problem, namely, the veto power of the U.S (in the IMF) remained unchallenged. As long as the US still has the single veto power, its hegemony will remain in place.

8.10 A Game Without an End

The above analysis shows that as the world's most important policy coordination mechanism, the G20 is still subject to the dominance of the hegemonic power, manifested by the powerful intervention of the government of the hegemon and the unfair competition in the international market, contravening the principle of competitive neutrality raised by the hegemon itself.

Since the 1990s, developed economies headed by the US first raised the framework of "competitive neutrality", which means to maintain a level playing field for state-owned enterprises, private businesses and non-profit organizations by removing government protection and privileges for state-owned enterprises (SOEs), in order to fundamentally change the low-efficiency of the SOEs supported by the government. Reforms under the framework of "competitive neutrality" has taken effect in domestic policy adjustments and SOE reforms, and with the gradually removing of the constraints on SOEs in OECD countries, the markets have regained dynamism.

Nevertheless, in this global game whose rules were mainly made by developed economies, the behaviors against the principle of neutrality remained a salient feature of the system. Powerful interventions by developed economies can be seen in variegated, phenomena of unfairness including the regulations of investment and trade liberalization in the aforementioned developed economies, the uneven responsibilities assigned to surplus countries and deficit countries, and the veto power of the U.S. It suggests that although emerging economies have had a bigger voice than the past, to a large extent, they have to succumb to various non-neutrality principles imposed by the hegemonic powers, as money can buy a bigger say, but not the decisive power to change the existing global rules. In sharp contrast, big powers are not bound by any restraints.

It should also be noted that, in contrast to some official international organization or institutions, the G20 has provided the emerging economies with better opportunities. So far, international institution or global mechanism that would allow the large number of developing countries and emerging markets to play key roles have yet to be created. What we need to do, is to consolidate the mechanism of the G20, making the G20 the stage where China and other emerging markets to play important roles. In line with this principle, we support France's proposition to establish the G20 Secretariat (of course, we also hold that the proposal should be implemented in a progressive manner); we should also make efforts to incorporate the G20 in the existing global institutions along the path of developing a mechanism of global governance; we need also play a more proactive role in setting the agenda for the G20 summit.

The new model of global governance can only be shaped by crises. The G20 was born from the Asian financial crisis; and it was not heeded and did not start to play a key role after the 2007 global financial crisis. As it will still take time for the developed economy to fully recover from the crisis, they still need the G20 to serve as the platform of coordination with the mechanism of consultation and problem-solving. We need to pay great attention to and fully utilize such a platform.

Prior to the current crisis, if it is true that international policy coordination featured countries giving way to domestic policy target of the hegemon, then with the declining of the hegemonic power and rise of the emerging economies, perhaps coordination in the real sense would be possible in the power shift. However, in the era of hegemonic predominance, although coordination was achieved asymmetrically with most countries shouldering the cost transferred from the hegemonic power, since the coordination can be implemented, and is often effective, adjustment becomes possible. Without the hegemon and its leadership, as Kindleberger held, coordination would turn out to be ineffective since states would be made enemies in the state of anarchy. This is perhaps the "dilemma" that is bothering all of us. Given this situation, improvement of the G20 platform of governance and international policy coordination requires more efforts to strengthen the mechanism of the G20, making it more representative, legitimacy and efficiently in policy implementation. Meanwhile, emerging economies should play a more active and guiding role in shaping the new framework of global governance.

References

Benigno G, Benigno P (2006) "Designing Targeting Rules for International Monetary Policy Cooperation", Journal of Monetary Economics, vol 53, pp 473–506

Canzoneri MB, Cumby RE, Diba BT (2005) "The Need for International Policy Coordination: What's Old, What's New, What's Yet to Come?" Journal of International Economics, vol 66, pp 363–384

Frankel JA (1994) In "5.1. exchange rate policy". In: Feldstein M (ed) American Economic Policy *in the 1980s*—a National Bureau of Economic Research Conference Report. The University of Chicago Press, Chicago, p 295. Accessed online at http://www.nber.org/chapters/c7756

Hudson M (2008) Super Imperialism: The Origin and Fundamentals of U.S. World Dominance. (Chinese Translation), (Jingrong Diguo: Jingrong Baquan de Laiyuan He Jichu) Beijing: Central Compilation & Translation Press, p 300

Kennedy (1970) Foreign trade barriers pushes the US patience: Kenney says congress better limit imports. New York Times, May 21st, 1970

Liu Z, Pappa E (2005) "Gains from International Monetary Policy Coordination: Does It Pay to Be Different?" European Central Bank, Working Paper Series No. 514, August

Mckibbin WJ (1988) "The Economics of International Policy Coordination", The Economic Record 64(187):241–253

Obsfeld M, Rogoff K (2002) "Global Implications of Self-Oriented National Monetary Rules", Q J Econ 117(2):503–535

Oudis G, Sachs F (1984) "Macroeconomic Policy Coordination among the Industrial Economies", Brookings Papers on Economic Activity, vol 1, pp 1–75

Polanyi K (1965) The great transformation: political and economic origins of our time. Beacon House Press, Boston, p 14

Tchakarov I (2004) The gains from international monetary cooperation revisited. IMF Working Paper, p 4

Part V
Conclusion

Chapter 9
Moving Towards a New Balance

> *Bismarck used to describe how our world evolved in history: transformation has never been "in uniform motion of the locomotive," once it started, it became unstoppable. If the West could not come to grips with the real problem, i.e., how to deal with the rise of the emerging economies in Asia by renovating itself, the prospect will be a sad decline, only to be interrupted by short and temporary recoveries before the next financial crises.*
>
> —Gordon Brown[1]

Today, the most difficult problem is global economic imbalances, and with no question the primary task is to correct it. The current global financial crisis that broke out in 2007 was triggered by global imbalances.

Crisis by definition refers to "deviation from the normal state", and therefore can be remedied in two ways: firstly, going back to the old track; and secondly, exploring a new path. Small crisis that did not cut deep into the system often can be redeemed once corrections were made after the turbulence, when the economy was able to return on the right track and move forward; if the crisis was caused by deep-seated problems in the system and structure, and with powerful interference, the economy often had to blaze a new path to achieve recovery.

Clearly, the current crisis took the second trajectory, due to the serious deficiencies in development pattern, economic, fiscal and financial structure of the developed economies at the eye of the storm. At the same time, the traditional pattern of globalization led by the developed economies has past its prime. The rising of the emerging markets and economies, especially the growing strength of their economic muscle vis-à-vis the developed economies has caused seismic changes in the global economic system, with numerous new ramifications for the prospects of global economy. It is foreseeable that a large number of developing nations and emerging markets will play an increasing important role in the future.

[1]Translator's Note: Translated from Chinese text. No citation.

Y. Li and X. Zhang, *Imbalance and Rebalance*,
https://doi.org/10.1007/978-981-10-6150-9_9

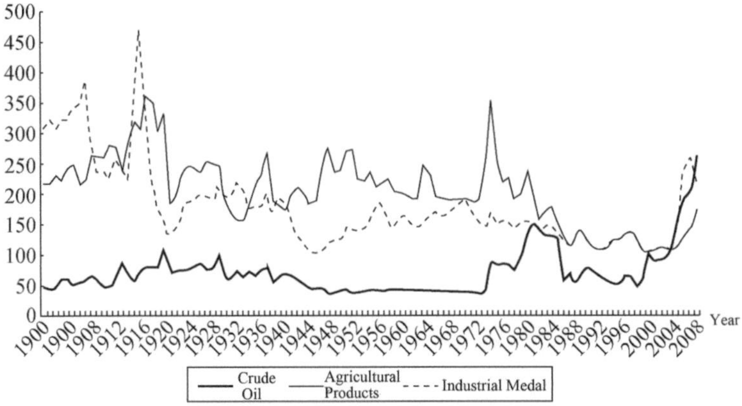

Fig. 9.1 Ups and downs of bulk commodity prices (1900–2008). *Note* Industrial metal refers to aluminum, cooper, and zinc. The index of bulk commodity is relative to the manufacturing unit value (MUV) deflator. *Source* Based on Pfaffenzeller et al. (2007)

9.1 A Millennium of Vicissitudes

Human history over the past thousand years has seen successive power shift with the rise and fall of the East and West. At the turn of the last millennium, "the Chinese civilization was at its zenith in the Song Dynasty" (remarks by Chen, Yinke).[2] It was the time when the East was far ahead in development than the West. As Fig. 9.1 shows, China's output accounted for ¼ of the world's total, and Asia was ¾ of the world's total, whereas Europe, in the shadow of Medieval rule by religious authority and feudal lords, had only 14% of the global GDP.

However, as the world entered the 14th century, the shining lights of Renaissance started to dawn on the religious bastion on the Italian Peninsula, from where enlightenment spread to the rest of Europe. Afterwards, driven by a series of major historical events like the Enlightenment, Great Geographical Discovery, the Enlightenment, the Industrial and Capitalist Revolution, and the colonial expansion, Europe was reinvigorated with unprecedented vitality so much so that it rose quickly in the fields of economy, politics, military, science, culture and arts, emerging as the winner from competition with other civilizations, particularly the civilizations in the east widely influenced by China and became the new center of the world system, the one we inherited and are still living in today.

In 1820, the output of the west accounted for as much as one fourth of the world's total, whereas that of the Asia slipped to sixty percent. At the time, though China was at its zenith, taking up as high as one thirds of the global output, and it was also when the nation begun to go downward, as its share in the world output kept on declining, as Asia's share was declining concurrently. Between 1870 and

[2]Chen, Yinke (1890–1969) Chinese historian and scholar.

1913, the world experienced prosperity brought about by the first wave of globalization, whereas the East flagged and waned, being marginalized gradually. In 1913, Asia's share in the global output was lower than twenty percent, and China's share plummeted to less than five percent. In contrast, the share of the western world had climbed up to 45.3%, and has been leading the world over the past two hundred years, with the eastern nations becoming followers at the periphery of the world system, who sometimes were even reduced to tributaries.

After two world wars in the first half of the twentieth century, and the Great Depression in-between, the west-dominated world order had been greatly shaken. In the west, the perspicacious Marxist criticism on capitalism, the rise of Keynesianism, and state interventionism and liberalism gaining predominance alternately have greatly changed the classical capitalism and gave it new forms. A large number of developing countries have shaken the shackles of colonialism and embarked on the path of independent development and equality, enriching the world with tremendous diversity.

It is particularly worth noting that since the end of the 1950s, East Asia had blazed a trail of trade-oriented development that has led the countries out of poverty, first headed by the "four small dragons" which were followed by the "four small tigers". As the later comers are catching up with the advanced economies, the global labor division and patterns of production and trade has undergone major changes, posing challenges to world economic and financial system dominated by the West. Over the past two decades, emerging economies represented by China, India, Russia and Brazil has become more integrated into the global industrial division system, with sustained and rapid economic growth and social development, transforming the world deeply and extensive on an unprecedented scale: a new pattern of global labor division and industrial value chain was established with the West taking the lead in technological innovation and financial services and the emerging economies focusing on production. The new "center vs. periphery" structure emerged, which has, in the past two decades, ensured a win-win situation for most stakeholders of the system.

9.2 The Old Global Economic Pattern

Since the second half of the 1980s, as emerging economies like the former Soviet Union, the Eastern European countries and China become increasingly integrated into the global economic system, the global pattern of division of labor has seen great transformation and meanwhile, the industrial chain has also been restructured. The fast ascendency of the emerging economies (China, India and Eastern Europe) and their integration into the world economy in the first decade of the 21st century has doubled the world's working force to three billion, which aggravated the global economic imbalances.

First, changes in global work force. Prior to the 1990s, when the former Soviet Union, East Europe, China and India had yet to be integrated into the global economy, the global work force had 1.5 billion. When those countries joined in, the number rose the 3 billion. The Great Doubling fundamentally transformed the economic layout. The drastic increase in labor supply had lowered labor costs, and with global marketization and technological progress, prices of manufactured goods remained at the low level. The Growth Report (Spence, 2008) discussed the decline of manufacturing prices. This tendency made the manufacturing sector more competitive, enabling export countries to accumulate substantial surpluses, especially in the cases of China and other Asian economies.

Secondly, relative to manufacturing prices, prices of bulk commodities have climbed up rapidly since the mid-and-late 1990s, particularly after the turn of the century, resulting from the world's economy entering the long period of prosperity. Against this backdrop, crude oil prices, which had been sliding since the 1980s, had taken an upward turn abruptly since the turn of the century (see Fig. 9.1). This is attributable to the prosperity of the new century, and is also the result of rising demand for bulk commodities by the emerging economies as global economy growth accelerated. The windfall for resource export countries helped the petroleum exporting countries accumulated tremendous trade surplus.

In short, either the manufacturer exporter or oil importer has profited from this round of prosperity brought about by globalization. And the so-called "surplus savings" have flowed back to the U.S. in various forms and accumulated to provide the U.S. with ample capital supply, causing the interest rate to go down, which led to the mismatch of financial resources across the globe and triggered financial crisis.

Hence the current world economy is structured as the follows: most developed countries are service-oriented, whereas the emerging markets are centered on manufacturing; and resource-rich countries mainly depend on export of bulk commodities. Such a structure partially decides the global division of labor, which,

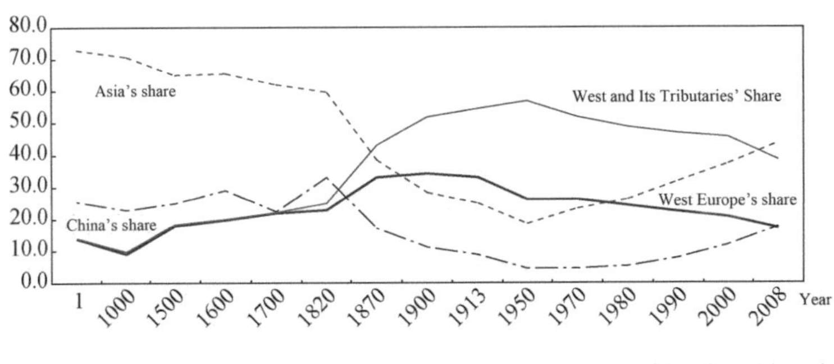

Fig. 9.2 Change of world pattern in east and west over the past two millennium (share in global output). *Source* Maddison (2009)

in the final analysis, is translated fully into the right to speak of different nations, as was defined as the center theme of Wallerstein's world system theory. The current division of labor, in our opinion, is not necessarily the result of the marketization of the global economy, but rather is shaped by the hierarchical, "center vs. periphery" structure as part of the current world order.

In such world system, developed economies, on the one hand, focus on developing high valued-added service industry, the financial sector in particular, while working on "making" various "rules", "standards" as well as "order" and exporting them to other nations. On the other hand, as the "periphery" of the global economic system, a great number of emerging economies has become the recipients of the industries transferred from the developed countries, whose cheap labor makes them engaged in conventional manufacturing, at the expense of their natural resources and environment. The commodities they produced are exchanged with service products of the developed countries, at irrational price difference. Meanwhile, they had been submitted to the rules, standards and order, termed as "international common practice" and "the best practice", which were created in the practices and on the basis of value system of the developed economies.

Obviously, such pattern of trade and division of labor is unreasonable. It had led to global imbalances, which, since it was not very serious, could still be amended through policy coordination among countries before the Asian financial crisis broke out. After the crisis, as the rise of the emerging economies led by China, international balances of the developed economies, especially the U.S. became worse, which was caused by current account imbalances with the emerging Asia, as well as with petroleum exporting countries. As the imbalances grew bigger and more concentrated in a few countries, they became a lingering problem that is hard to tackle. Two decades ago, twenty two percent of the global deficits were distributed among the world's five major countries; now, the world's five major countries take up seventy six percent of the total trade deficits.

To fill up the gap on the balance sheet, countries at the center have increasingly relied on using financial serves and even international reserve currencies in exchange for manufacturing goods produced by periphery countries. As the result, developed countries became creditors and the emerging countries debtors. This irrational situation makes it hard to maintain the old international economic order, as turbulences and frictions caused by imbalances aggravated into a total crisis.

Nowadays, as the emerging economies rising to become the main locomotive of the global economic growth, the old mode of development led solely by the developed economies is losing its vigor. In face of the situation, developed countries had to propose new tasks of economic restructuring. On the one hand, they need to straighten out the service industry, especially the financial sector by curbing their excessive growth; and on the other hand, they are committed to developing new industries and sectors. Most recently, the developed economies also enunciated the strategies to reinvigorate the manufacturing industry.

The world is developing unevenly, and countries at different stage of development differ vastly from each other as far as the development phase and position in the production chains are concerned. The efforts in correcting imbalances, improving complementarities, and seeking new mechanism to drive growth are for the purpose of raise the global productivity and achieving better balance, coordination and sustainability.

9.3 Things Are Changing

After a number of crises, the current world system has undergone major changes. Maddison's statistics (2009), by 2008, the share of the East in the global output reached 43.7%, with that of China making up close to 18%, and the share of the West was below 40%, less than that of China (Fig. 9.2).

So far, we have used the concepts of "East" and "West" in analysis of the global economic and political power shift. With historical and political implications, those concepts are often associated with the Cold War, but they are still used today since they mirror the vicissitudes of the traditional world structure over the thousands of years. Today, the mostly used generic terms in international economy and politics are the dichotomy of the developed economy and emerging economy. By this standard, in 1013 and calculated in PPP, the emerging economies exceeded the developed economies for the first time in history (see Fig. 9.3). Calculated in market dollar, by 2015, the emerging economy will take up 40% of the global GDP. According to statistics issued by Standard Chartered Bank (2010), by 2030, two thirds of the world's growth will come from the emerging economies. The sea change is truly amazing.

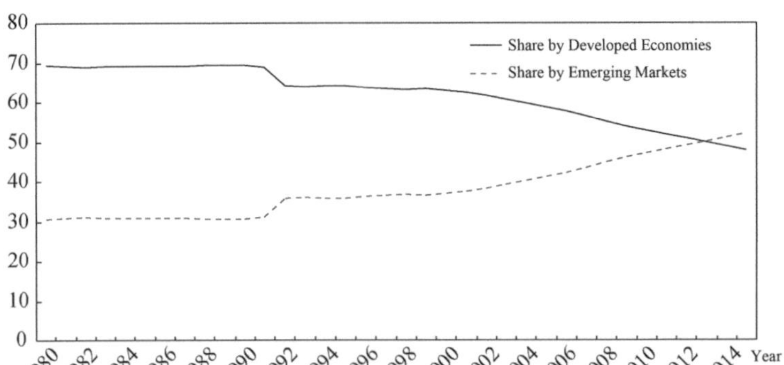

Fig. 9.3 Share by developed economies and emerging markets in global output (PPP, %) share of developed economies. *Source* IMF

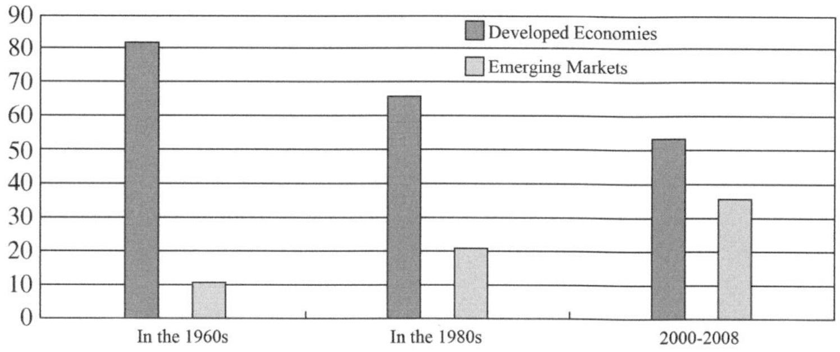

Fig. 9.4 Trade among emerging economies (%). *Source* Based on Kose and Prasad (2010)

Moreover, now there is the trend that emerging economies are spinning off from the developed economies, and therefore the global economy is undergoing "double speeds" and the "delinking" process. "Double speeds" refers to the fact that emerging and developed economies are developing at their own growth rates, and the "delinking" process means that each group of countries are moving along their parallel paths, with little impact on each other. The strong growth of the emerging markets has ensured exporters' economy to be robust, especially during the periods when the economy of the developed world was sluggish. Statistics shows that inner-group trade of the emerging economies has grown from ten percent in the 1960s to twenty percent in the 1980s, and reached thirty five percent before the crisis. It is the rapid growth of trade among those economies that helped them to remain substantially "detached" from the developed economies, another hallmark of the ascendency of the emerging economies (Fig. 9.4).

Besides, the traditional roles of the developed economies and emerging economies in terms of international investment position have somewhat shifted. Table 9.1 shows that the major creditors are Japan, China and Germany and other OPEC countries. In terms of debtors, the US and Eurozone countries are major creditors, plus countries that were former members of the G-7, such as the UK, Italy, France, Canada, etc. It means that China and some OPEC countries has net capital outflow, whereas some developed economies became recipients of overseas capital. As is illustrated by Fig. 9.5, traditional European and US powers became net debtors, whereas China and Japan became net creditors.

In view of such changes, former British Prime Minister Brown (2010)[3] remarked that the once west-dominated world economy with only ten percent of the world's population carrying out the majority of the export and investment has gone forever. After monopolizing global economies for over two centuries, the western countries have been overtaken by other regions in manufacturing and production, trade, investment, etc.

[3]Translator's Note: with only (2010) in the text, no detailed citation.

Table 9.1 International investment position of major creditors and debtors

	International investment position (100 million $US dollar, current value)	International investment position Percentage of GDP (%)
Creditor		
Japan	28,918.4	56.1
China	18,219.5	36.5
Germany	12,769.7	36.8
Saudi Arabia[a]	3845.2	100.7
United Arab Emirates	3738.8	207.5
Kuwait[a]	2866.5	256.5
Libya[a]	1787.1	255.8
Russia	1183.9	9.1
Iran[a]	1056.5	36.9
Venezuela[a]	721.1	31.7
Argentina	593.4	18.5
Debtor		
US	−27,378.4	−19.4
Eurozone	−21,869.0	−16.1
Brasil	−5266.2	−33.5
Australia[b]	−4991.4	−58.1
UK	−4613.5	−21.8
Italy	−4194.2	−19.8
Mexico	−3529.3	−38.8
France	−3159.3	−11.5
Turkey	−2685.8	−43.7
Indonesia	−1974.1	−36.6
Republic of Korea	−1480.3	−11.3
Canada	−1140.2	−7.8
India	−1088.5	−8.8
South Africa	−356.2	−12.4

Note IMF: Principal Global Indicators (2009) data unless otherwise specified
[a]From Lane and Milesi-Ferretti (2007) and online source at http://www.philiplane.org/EWN.html.
[b]IMF data (2008)

9.4 China Is Rising

It goes without saying that China is rising. In terms total GDP, it has replaced Japan as the world's second largest economy. Maddison has estimated that by 2012, China has taken up 18% of the global GDP, which means that the US

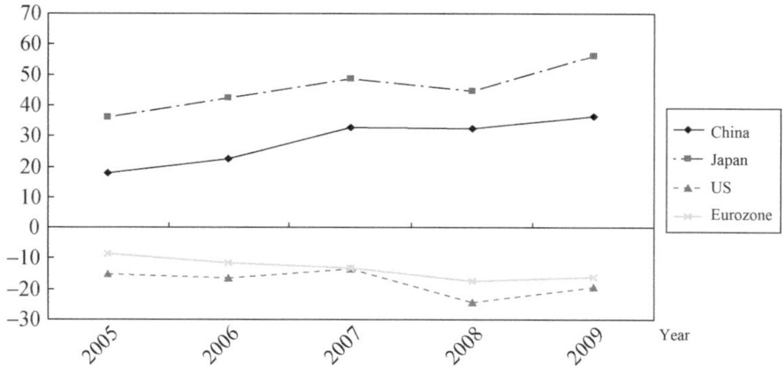

Fig. 9.5 Share of international investment position in GDP (China, Japan, US, Europe). *Source* Based on Freeman (2006)

manufacturing sector has ceded its leading position that had been maintained for nearly a decade.

In terms of trade, China has become the world's biggest exporter and the second largest importer.

Since 1978, China's total trade volume of commodities has reached an annual increase rate of 16.3%, and between 2000 and the present, the annual increase rate is 19.9%, an increase of 3.6% than the past. In other words, compared with other historical periods, twenty-first century has seen the fastest expansion of foreign trade in China. In comparison with other major trading countries, since 2000, China's export and import registered the fastest growth, pushing its ranking quickly to the top. As Fig. 9.1 has illustrated, in 1999, China ranked ninth in export with trade volume of 194.9 billion US$, and tenth in import with trade volume of 165.7 billion US$. In 2009, China became the world's biggest exporter, and the seconded to none but the US in export.

Meanwhile, Table 9.2 also shows that when China is rising fast to the top of the list, the rankings of other major commodity trading countries has not changed much. Countries of Europe and North America, and Japan and South Korea remain the mainstay of commodity trading. As for other BRIC countries, they are still way back behind China either in terms of absolute volume or ranking.

With its rising status in the world economy, China's influence keeps increasing across the world. Three decades ago, people were mainly concerned about how China had been affected by the world, but recently and even in the upcoming three decades; most people are and will focus on how China influences the world. Such influence is found in three major fields:

First, China's market. Soon after China adopted the reform and opening up policy, China's market has played a crucial role in attracting foreign investment and introducing advanced technology and ways of management. The so-called "market for technology" and "market for management" has testified to the appeal of China's market. With China's rapid economic growth, rapid GDP per capita increase,

Table 9.2 The world's top 12 importers and exporters (country and region)

Rank of 12 exporters (country and region)						Rank of 12 importers (country and region)					
1999			2009			1999			2009		
Rank	Country (region)	Volume	Rank	Country (region)	Volume	Rank	Country (region)	Volume	Rank	Country (region)	Volume
1	US	6958	1	China	12,015	1	US	10,594	1	US	16,038
2	Germany	5435	2	Germany	11,209	2	Germany	4740	2	China	10,057
3	Japan	4176	3	US	10,569	3	UK	3249	3	Germany	9314
4	France	3255	4	Japan	5808	4	France	3157	4	France	5511
5	UK	2722	5	Netherlands	4986	5	Japan	3100	5	Japan	5507
6	Canada	2384	6	France	4750	6	Italy	2206	6	UK	4799
7	Italy	2356	7	Italy	4047	7	Canada	2202	7	Netherlands	4458
8	Netherlands	2186	8	Belgium	3698	8	Netherlands	2062	8	Italy	4104
9	China	1949	9	South Korea	3635	9	Hong Kong of China	1807	9	Hong Kong of China	3527
10	Belgium	1792	10	UK	3507	10	China	1657	10	Belgium	3510
11	Hong Kong of China	1744	11	Hong Kong of China	3297	11	Belgium	1648	11	Canada	3303
12	South Korea	1437	12	Canada	3156	12	South Korea	1198	12	Canada	3231

Unit: 100 million US$
Source World Trade Organization

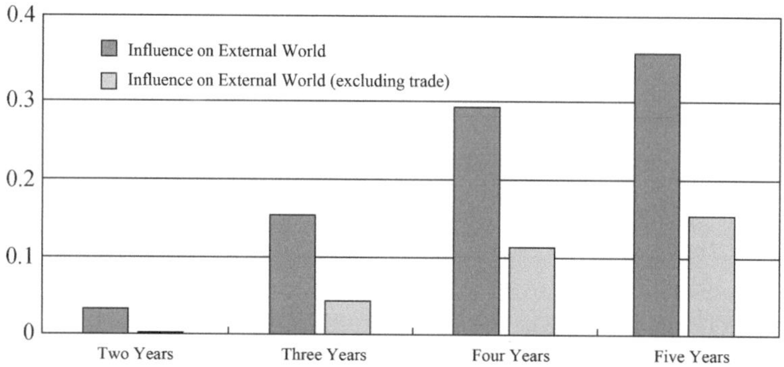

Chart 9.1 China's external influence (%). *Source* Based on Arora and Vamvakidis (2010)

deeper urbanization, and rise of the middle class, China will become one of the world's largest commodity market, and the locomotive of the world economic growth.

Second, China's price. As the manufacturer of tremendous products, China, to a large extent, decides the up and downs of manufactured goods; prices of a large number of products and bulk commodities depends on China's huge market demand; with its economy open to the world market, China's capital goes global, with the continuous increase in overseas financial and green field investment, China has been exerting greater influence on global asset values.

Third, China's participation in global governance. Crises have made people more aware of the necessity of re-writing many rules of globalization. China is obliged to play a more active role in restructuring the mechanism of global governance.

An empirical study by IMF (Arora and Vamvakidis 2010) shows that one percent change of China's GDP will increase its influence on other countries by 0.4% five years later, sixty percent of which is trade-induced and forty percent is attributable to non-trade factors (see Chart 9.1).

9.5 Crisis Ushered in a New Era

The outbreak of the latest economic crisis entailed two major trends of transition, ushering the new pattern of international system.

Firstly, the transformation occurred in real economy. Since the end of the 1980s, contribution by emerging economies to global output has been higher than the developed economies. After this round of economic turmoil, it has become a seemingly irreversible trend that the developed economies have been in recession whereas the emerging economies have seen continuous high growth. Such historical shift in relative economic strength has push the emerging economies to the center stage where they are going to play a bigger role in leading the world economy; in this sense, the old patter of globalization dominated by the developed economies will be changed.

Secondly, the transformation occurred in the area of finance. Capitalist global economic crisis is always accompanied by financial crisis, and over the years, global financial crises mostly are featured with debt crises of the developing countries or emerging markets. So recovery from the crisis should always be preceded by global debts restructuring, and each time after the restricting, the supremacy of the developed economies had been consolidated and enhanced. This time things are totally different. The developed countries, issuers of international reserve currencies and rule-makers of international system, are now bogged down in the debt crisis, being tied up by the genie that they themselves called out of the bottle. To shrug off the crisis, they earnestly seek the help from the emerging economies; hence international mechanisms like the G20 were set up. Thus, to achieve recovery, emerging economies has acquired more right to speak and greater influences in the international financial system, which will facilitate the reserve currency system to moving towards diversification; and at the same time, the developed countries' decision-making power in the rule-making of the financial system will be weakened gradually. In other words, a new global pattern is gradually taking shape.

Such trends of transformation have provided new opportunities for establishing a new equilibrium and moreover, for China to develop. This is because, firstly, as the world economy enters the period of restructuring and industrial transition, China can take the opportunity to "explore new advantages" and "occupy the strategic highland for future development". Secondly, in an overall perspective, the world is in the period of the "ascendency of the emerging markets" and "global governance reform", where China can make efforts to make itself stronger and play a bigger role in global governance.

If, looking back on history, one can say that global industrial transition, economic restructuring and reform of the governance mechanism always take place every several decades, as part of the world economic cycle and are in no way extraordinary, then the catching up with or even taking over the developed countries by emerging economies in terms of total economy is the new changes since the Industrial Revolution and presents new opportunities. For China, this could be the opportunity that appears once in a millennium. Whether China will be able to seize it to find itself a new position in the equilibrium that is taking shape, depends on whether it can successfully transform its pattern of development.

9.6 From "Made in China" to "Invented in China"

Hundreds and thousands years of human practices in economy development and classical theory of growth, either illustrates a simple but profound truth: "innovation" is the only source of long-term economic growth. Nevertheless, experiences of China and other East Asian emerging economies have shown that expanding investment of the essential factors alone can help maintain high growth rate for a considerable long time. Such a phenomenon has to some extent blinded the view of people, even leading them to throw the above-mentioned belief out of the window. In this case, will China still be able keep to the existing path of development and its role in international division of labor, and still sustain the miraculous high growth as "the exception"?

In light of China's domestic economic and social structure, over the past three decades, the economic growth model based on high savings, investment, labor migration and natural resources depletion has been imbedded, along with the building of the industrial structure centered on manufacturing and demand-supply structure highly dependent on investment and export. Numbers of serious problems like low economic efficiency, lack of scientific and technological innovation, huge destruction of natural environment and resources are often covered by the "glamorous" numbers of high growth. This was possible mainly because, at the lower stage of development, input of essential production factors often implies great potential of growth with high marginal return, and will prolong the economic growth period substantially. The dependence on processing industry and manufacturing and efforts in introducing technologies are both necessary and reasonable given the country's weak industrial foundation, insufficiency in science and technology, and lack of human capital. But, as China enters into a higher stage of development, investment and labor supply tends to slow down, margin return declines and pressure from environmental and natural resource preservation become intensified. The extensive, "non-normal" mode of economic growth driven by expansion of essential economic factors is unsustainable, and therefore, it is imperative to put the economy back on the track of long-term growth driven by innovations in science and technology, as well as organization and management. China has just joined in the rank of the middle-income countries, and therefore is at the critical moment of transforming the mode of growth and industry restructuring. The transition may, inevitably, incur the "growing pains" caused by slowing down of the growth rate, closing down certain industries that used to be competitive, and breaking down the old pattern of interest distribution.

In broader context of the system of international labor division and the emerging new global equilibrium, the competitiveness of one country highly depends on its innovation capability and the corresponding production force. In fact, the current chain of production and value has not changed much: developed countries in the west still tightly clings to the two ends of the value chain—design, R&D and service and marketing, that yield high added-value and interest rate, and low environment cost; whereas the emerging economies including China are positioned between the two ends of the chain, mostly involved in manufacturing that yield low added-value and interest rate. Since China adopted the policy of reform and opening up, its economy had long been the beneficiary of such pattern of division of labor, receiving the "dividends of globalization"; nevertheless, as China entered into higher stage of development, its comparative advantages in the world—in particular, the abundant supply of cheap labor and relaxed constraints regarding environmental and resource protection—are also undergoing changes. It is no longer an alternative for China to following the old pattern of international labor division and live with the role as a "periphery" country. Meanwhile, if its efforts to upgrade into the "center" fail, then most possibly China will fall into the "middle-income trap" as the "old center" and "new periphery" will force it out of the international production and value chain.

In emphasis, history shows that major economic and financial crises often gave birth to major innovations in science and technology and sometimes, even industrial revolutions. As a matter of fact, under the impact of this economic crisis, and suffering from the "excessive growth" of the financial sector, developed countries have come to realize the importance of the entity industry and innovation, and subsequently stepped up their support in those fields through policies and public expenditure. At the same time, the recent "Third Industrial Revolution" featuring new energy and information and web technology has brought about more opportunities in development for the developed countries. Notably, even at the peak of the crisis, the Obama administration put forward a number of plans such as the "new policy for technology" and the plan to revamping the high-end industries. Deep in debt, the Europeans seem to have higher expectation for the "Third Industrial Revolution": as early as 2010, the European Commission initiated the 50 billion euro Program of "Connecting Europe", aimed at building an integrated network of transportation, communications, and energy supply, providing logistic support for industrial upgrading and enhancing competitiveness of the European economy.

Against such domestic and international background, China needs to fundamentally change its mode of development by means of domestic reform and opening up to the outside world, so that to facilitate the transformation from "Made in China" to "Invented in China". At the same time, efforts should be made to encourage and promote good practices and eliminate deficiencies, meet the challenges of the "growing pains" and restructuring of the international system of labor division, so that China will be able to seize the opportunity and make to the commanding heights in the new round of scientific and technological revolution and industrial restructuring.

9.7 Internationalization of RMB: "Strength of China" in International Monetary System Transition

As the supportive pillar for the real economy, development of the financial sector is a crucial part of China's economic transition and enables China to participate as an active player in adjusting the global imbalances. The most eye-catching move in this regard is the internationalization of REM. In fact, since this financial crisis broke out, China has earnestly encouraged the use of RMB in foreign reserve, cross-border trade, and foreign investment, and internationalizing RMB in various means and at different levels, which started to demonstrate the "strength of China" in pushing ahead the changes of the international monetary system.

First, China has signed currency swap agreement with nearly thirty countries (please see chapter two), covering most neighboring emerging economies and a number of developed countries. Such arrangements not only reduced risk caused by volatility of exchange rate, but also paved way for internationalizing RMB. Over the recent years, countries like Malaysia, South Korea, Russia, and the Philippines have made RMB their reserve currency. In March, 2012, Japan was also approved to purchase China's treasury bonds (with a cap of 65 billion yuan RMB).

Secondly, since 2009, China started its pilot project in cross-border trade of RMB, and quickly spread the practices, achieving tremendous progress. By September 2013, cross-trade settled in RMB had reached 8.6 trillion yuan, realized through cross-border barter, trade in service and settlement of current account; all provinces and autonomous regions in China have been authorized to conduct the trade, as well as extending the trade outside China. At the same time, RMB financing and investment are also put into practice in foreign countries. Obviously, these measures have reduced the vulnerability of RMB to exchanges volatility against US dollar and other currencies in foreign trade and investment.

Thirdly, RMB offshore transactions, including bonds and securities, settlement, bank savings and loans have expanded rapidly, providing richer and more reliable financial instruments and services for the RMB asset management, preserving and increasing value of RMB. According to statistics issued by the Bank of International Settlement (BIS) shows that by April 2013, RMB is among the nine currencies of foreign exchange, marking a key step in internationalization of RMB. In terms of the venue of trade, China Hong Kong has become the biggest RMB offshore center, with London, New York and Singapore actively exploring related business. Recently, the Shanghai Pilot Free Trade Zone has also put the plan of establishing a RMB offshore center on the agenda.

It needs to be noted that either in terms of practice or policy, RMB internationalization is in the first place one of the key measures to promote China's financial reform and opening up. As is known to all, for a long time China's financial sector has been mostly monopolized by state-owned bankers, with structural deficiencies including lack of competition, weak elasticity in exchange rate, inertia in financial innovation, retardation in non-credit business, and the isolation of the financial system. Those problems made the financial system hard to adapt to the upgrading of the real economy, let alone to give it much support. To internationalize RMB, China has to make breakthroughs in the areas of opening capital account, marketizing interest rate, opening its financial market, etc. One major purpose of those steps is to "compel" from within the financial sector to accelerate reform and restructuring. Take capital account opening as one example, being one of the key elements of the internationalization, it has to allow international capital to freely flow into China's financial market, which requires a relatively developed, elastic, and deep domestic market. In other words, the prerequisite for capital account liberalization is to speed up building a developed domestic financial market and make it a favorable area of investment for foreign investors.

Internationalizing RMB is the exploration conducive to reforming international monetary system—especially to building a multipolar monetary to address the global imbalances: the ascendency of RMB and deepening reform of China's financial sector is conducive to providing more safe, quality assets with higher return and better fluidity, as well as valuable means of investment, and helpful in solving the over-dependency of global trade and finance on US dollar in the fields of trade, investment, and reserve, and eventually address, though partially, the "Triffin Dilemma".

Lastly, as far as RMB internationalization is concerned and from the policy-making perspective, although the issue of risk gains needs to be further scrutinized, and it remains controversial as to whether capital account opening should precede the reform of China's financial sector or vice versa, one thing is certain that the process is in keeping with the "general trend of the history", as deficiencies of the US dominated, unipolar system has become increasingly salient and China begun to take to the center stage with growing national strength. At the technical level, internationalization should proceed in solid steps, and not be implemented in haste, because everything will fall into places when the condition is ripe, just as the channel will form when water flows. However, this does not mean that the policy-makers should stand aloof, instead, they need to take initiatives and "go with the current" by eliminating the obstacles in the system, while taking precaution against the risks so that eventually avoid them.

9.8 Make the Best of the Shanghai Free Trade Zone (SHFTZ)

On September 27, 2013, the State Council of China released the Program of the China (Shanghai) Pilot Free Trade Zone, signifying the opening-up entering a new phase.

Reform and Opening up are the two pillars of China's modernization drive with socialist characteristics which has made the spectacular achievement that catches the attention of the world. To facilitate reform by opening up has always been the clearly delineated roadmap. The blueprint of the Pilot Free Trade Zone followed the path, further allowing reform and opening up, the mutually complementary factors to work together and achieve better effect.

The reform and opening up over the past thirty three years has gone through three notable progressive stages:

In 1980, the "four special economic zones" including Shenzhen were established, which were expanded to China's coastal belt, until Pudong development zone in Shanghai was established. This was the period during which China embarked on the path of reform with firm determination. After that, the reform was pushed forward with implementing policies focused on further opening to the outside world, with China's joining the World Trade Organization as the fruition.

This second stage was characterized by China's selecting specific fields, regions and industrials to attract foreign capital, technology, management and market by voluntarily offering preferential treatment with the purpose of gradually establishing an export-oriented economic system.

Persistent efforts during the thirteen years had enabled China to become an official member of the WTO in 2001, ushering in the era of "opening" based on institutional reforms. This period was marked by the fact that China had been integrated into the globalized world economic system, by adopting rules, systems, methods and "best practices" set by the developed countries, and after implementing the strategy for a long time of "adopting global practices", Chinese enterprises took the steps to "go global".

The Launch of the Shanghai Pilot Free Trade Zone marked China's opening up entering a new stage. After a decade of comprehensive institutional construction in opening up, this time a more ambitious goal of "building an open economy in all fields" has been set, so that China will steadily grow into a major nation with more contributions to the international community as well as the welfare of the mankind as a whole.

The SHFTZ is China's strategic move in face of the major changes of the "situation of world", which is, so to speak, the transformation of the system of global governance.

Since the founding of the WTO in 1995, more than twenty countries have joined the organization. As emerging economies became its members one after another, this global economic pattern sponsored by the developed countries has been consolidated, but on the other hand, with the increasing influence of those new members, the organization is steered into the direction more in line with the interest of the emerging economies. Such change made the developed nations realize that the organization is no longer able to function as it used to be in helping them to achieve their global strategic objective as had been expected.

As the result, the developed countries turned to the G-20, a platform that serves as the forum for setting the agenda in their interest and can, at the same time, as the nucleus of governance that enables to excise their power by circumventing the 157 WTO members who do always get along. As the result, the G20 has become the arena where the developed countries attributed the global imbalances to China's domestic issues like RMB exchange rates, trade surplus, low consumption level and high savings, in an attempt to defend the established international division of labor system by suppressing China. Such attempts, however, is due to fail since with waning power, those countries were no longer able to achieve their purpose.

In the current situation, developed countries became increasing intent on directing the trajectory of global governance transformation. This intention is manifested clearly a number of agreements including the Trans-Pacific Partnership (TPP), Trans-Atlantic Trade and Investment Partnership (TTIP), Plurilateral Services Agreement (PSA), Japan-Europe Partnership and the most recent Comprehensive Economic and Trade Agreement (CETA). Nothing can better illustrate than those agreements that as a group, developed economies, no longer content with the current pattern or rules of globalization, are going into a new "Holly Alliance" and trying to set new rules.

Those rules, with clear strategic implications for China and aimed at excluding China from the club, exerting severe pressure externally on China's future development.

The initiating of the Shanghai Free Trade Pilot Zone is China's quick response to such situation and part of the Chinese government's proactive strategy in face of the new pattern of the international economy: while participating actively in various rule-making negotiations; on the other hand, China started to adopt some of the reasonable rules of the TPP on a most important region on its territory, and "by opening up to the outside world to further promote development, deepen reform, facilitate innovation and accumulate experiences that can be copied and popularized, so that to serve the greater cause of overall development in the country."

In this sense, we may say that launching the SHFTZ is the strategic response to changes in China's domestic situation. It is hoped that after two to three years' trial, it will further open up in financial service, shipping service, trade and commercial service, professional service, cultural service and social service, greatly promote opening up of the service sector and reforms in the managerial system of foreign investment, further explore ways to all-round liberalization of convertibility on capital items and the financial service sector, making the SHFTZ a pilot free trade zone where traders will enjoy conveniences in investment and trade, freedom in currency convertibility, highly efficient supervision that is also fast and convenient, as well as a sound legal environment, all matching up to the international standard. In one word, the SHFTZ is created as a market that grants equal accessibility to all kinds of investors, and by letting Shanghai take the lead in establishing a set of rules for cross-border investment and trade that meets the international standard in law and practice, it will serve as the vehicle that helps the country to be further integrated into the global economy and an important platform for comprehensive reform in government supervision and regulation, so as to carry forward China's domestic economic reform.

References

Arora V, Vamvakidis A (2010) IMF Working Paper: China's Economic Growth: International Spillovers, Washington, D.C.: 2010, p 7 (https://www.imf.org/external/pubs/ft/wp/2010/wp10165.pdf, accessed Sep 15, 2017) (translator's note)

Kose MA, Prasad ES (2017) "Emerging Markets Come of Age" Finance & Development, December 2010, Vol.47, No.4, p 9 (http://imf.org/external/pubs/ft/fandd/2010/12/kose.htm, accessed on Sep 15, 2017) (translator's note)

Maddison A (2009) Historical Statistics of the World Economy: 1–2008 AD, OECD

Pfaffenzeller S, Newbold P, Rayner A (2007) A short note on updating the Grilli and Yang commodity price index. *World Bank Econ Rev* 21(1):151–163

References

Amin S (2000) Imperialism & unequal development (Chinese translation). Commercial Press, Beijing

Bergsten F (ed) (2005) The United States and the world economy: foreign economic policy for the next decade (Chinese translation). Economic Science Press, Beijing

Bernanke BS (2000) Essays on the great depression. Princeton University Press, Princeton

Bernanke BS (2007) Essays on the great depression (Chinese translation). Dongbei University (of) Finance & Economics Press, Dalian

Chen J, Liu W (2008) Distribution of Interest in U.S.-China trade imbalance from the perspective of inner labor division of goods. Res Financ Econ Issues (11). ("*changpinnei fengong shijiaoxia meizhongmaoyishiheng zhong de liyi fenpei*" in *Caijing Weiti Yanjiu*, Issue 11, 2008)

Cheng E, Wang Z (2008) The dollar hegemony: an important means of exploiting wealth of other nations by the US. World Econ (4). ("*meiyuan baquan: meiguo lueduo taguo caifu de zhongyao shouduan*" in *Shijie Jingji Daokan*, Issue 4, 2008)

Clapham JH (2009) An economic history of modern Britain (1750–1939) (Chinese translation). Commercial Press, Beijing

Commission on Growth and Development, The World Bank (2008) The growth report: strategies for sustained growth and inclusive development (Chinese translation). China Financial Publishing House, Beijing

CourtWHB (2009) A Brief History of British Economy: 1750–1939 (Chinese Translation). Translated by Fang, Tingyu. Beijing: The Commercial Press, 2009

Eichengreen B (2009) Globalizing of capital: a history of the international monetary system (Chinese translation). Shanghai People's Publishing House, Shanghai

Frank AG (2008) ReOrient: global economy in the Asian age (Chinese translation). Central Compilation & Translation Press, Beijing

Friedman M (2008) Money mischief: episodes in monetary history (Chinese translation). The Commercial Press, Beijing

Fukuyama F (1998) The end of history and the last man (Chinese translation). Yuanfang Press, Hohhot

Hudson M (2008) Super imperialism: the origin and fundamentals of U.S. world dominance (Chinese translation) (*Jingrong Diguo: Jingrong Baquan de Laiyuan He Jichu*). Central Compilation & Translation Press, Beijing, p 300

Isamu M, Syougen SNK (simplified Chinese edition). China CITIC Press, Beijing. Chinese title: Riben Jingji Zhengce Qinlizhe Shilu (Japanese Economy as Experienced: the Story)

Kawai M, Park YC, Wyplosz C (eds) (2009) International monetary system, monetary and financial cooperation in East Asia (Chinese translation). Jilin University Press, Changchu

Kennedy P (1990) The rise and fall of the great powers. World Affairs Publishing House, Beijing

Kennedy P (2006) The rise and fall of the great powers: economic change and military conflict from 1500 to 2000 (Chinese translation). International Culture Publishing House, Beijing

Y. Li and X. Zhang, *Imbalance and Rebalance*,
https://doi.org/10.1007/978-981-10-6150-9

Keynes JM (1986) A treaties on money (Chinese translation) (trans: Cai Q, Dingjiu F, Wang Z). Commercial Press, Beijing
Keynes JM (2008) The economic consequences of the peace (Chinese translation). Huaxia Publishing House, Beijing
Kindleberger CP (1986) The world in depression, 1929–1939 (Chinese translation). Shanghai Translation Publishing House, Shanghai
Kindleberger CP (1996) World economic primacy: 1500–1990 (Chinese translation). The Commercial Press, Beijing
Kindleberger CP (2003) World economic primacy: 1500–1990 (Chinese translation). The Commercial Press, Beijing
Kindleberger CP (2006) A financial history of Western Europe, 2nd edn (Chinese translation). China Financial Publishing House, Beijing
Kindleberger CP (2010) A financial history of Western Europe, 2nd edn (Chinese translation) (trans: Zijian, Xu; Jianxiong, He; and Zhong, Zhu. China Financial Publishing House, Beijing
Kindleberger CP, Robert A (2007) Manias, panics and crashes: a history of financial crises, 4th edn (Chinese translation) (trans: Zhu J, Ye X). China Financial Publishing House, Beijing
Krugman PR (2000) Exchange-rate instability (Chinese translation). Peking University Press and China Renmin University Press, Beijing
Krugman P, Obstfeld M, Melitz M (1998) International economics, 4th edn (Chinese translation). China Renmin University Press, Beijing
Li R (2006) International money and finance (Guoji Huobi yu Jinrong), 3rd edn. China Renmin University Press, Beijing
Lu F (2004) Intra product specialization. China Econ Q ("Chanping Neifengong", Jingjixue Jikan), 4(1)
Maddison A (2003) The world economy: a millennial perspective (Chinese translation). Peking University Press, Beijing
Maddison A (2009) The world economy: historical statistics (Chinese translation). Peking University Press, Beijing
McCallum BT (2001) International monetary economics (Chinese translation), China Financial Publishing House, Beijing
Mckinnon RI (2005) Exchange rates under the East Asian dollar standard: living with conflicted virtue (Chinese translation) (trans: Wang X, He W). China Financial Publishing House, Beijing
Mckinnon RI, Kenichi O (1999) Dollar and Yen: resolving economic conflict between the United States and Japan (Chinese translation) (trans: Wang X, Cao L). Shanghai Far East Publishers, Shanghai
Odell JS (1991) US international monetary policy: markets, power, and ideas as sources of change (Chinese translation) (trans: Li L, Li N). China Financial Publishing House, Beijing
Olson M (1996) The logic of collective action (Chinese translation). Shanghai SDX Joint Publishing Company & Shanghai People's Publishing House, Shanghai
Palmer RR (2009) A history of the modern world (Chinese translation). World Publishing Corporation, Beijing
Polanyi K (2007) The great transformation: the political and economic origins of our time (Chinese translation). Zhejiang People's Publishing House, Hangzhou
Pomeranz K (2010) The great divergence: China, Europe, and the making of the modern world economy (Chinese translation). Jiangsu People's Publishing, Ltd. and Phoenix Publishing & Media, Inc., Nanjing
Reinhart CM, Rogoff KS (2010) This time is different: eight centuries of financial folly (Chinese translation). China Machine Press, Beijing
Schwartz HM (2008) States versus markets: the emergence of a global economy (Chinese translation). Phoenix Publishing & Media, Inc., and Jiangsu People's Publishing House, Nanjing
Sheng A (2009) From Asian to global crisis: an Asian regulator's view of unfettered finance in the 1990s and 2000s (Chinese translation). Shanghai Far East Publishers, Shanghai

Smith A (1974) An inquiry into the nature and causes of the wealth of nations (vols 1 & 2) (Chinese translation). The Commercial Press, Beijing

Stavrianos LS (1971) Man's past and present: a global history of world since 1500 (Chinese translation). Shanghai Academy of Social Sciences Press, Shanghai

Triffin R (1997) Gold and the dollar crisis—the future of convertibility (Chinese translation). The Commercial Press, Beijing

Volcker P, Gyohten T (1996) Changing fortunes (Chinese translation). China Financial Publishing House, Beijing

Wallerstein I (1998) The modern world system (vols 1 & 2) (Chinese translation). Higher Education Press

Wallerstein I (2000) The modern world system (vol 3) (Chinese translation). Higher Education Press

Yoshikawa M (2000) A lost financial war: admonition from defeated economic powers (Chinese translation) (trans: Sun X, Yuan Y). China Youth Publishing House, Beijing

Zhang H (2006) Dynamism for global value china and strategies for industrial development. China Ind Econ (1) ("*Quanqiu Jiazhilian Donlijizhi yu Chanye Fazhan Zhanlue*" in "*Zhongguo Gongye Jingji*")

FSC
www.fsc.org

MIX
Papier aus verantwortungsvollen Quellen
Paper from responsible sources
FSC® C105338

If you have any concerns about our products,
you can contact us on
ProductSafety@springernature.com

In case Publisher is established outside the EU,
the EU authorized representative is:
Springer Nature Customer Service Center GmbH
Europaplatz 3, 69115 Heidelberg, Germany

Printed by Libri Plureos GmbH
in Hamburg, Germany